VOYAGES TO THE EAST INDIES

VIEW OF BANTAM
(*From W. Schouten's "Ost Indische Reyse,"* 1670)

VIEW OF BANTAM

(*From W. Schouten's "Ost Indische Reyse,"* 1670)

VOYAGES TO THE EAST INDIES

CHRISTOPHER FRYKE
CHRISTOPHER SCHWEITZER

With Introduction and Notes by

C. ERNEST FAYLE

MANOHAR
2020

First published 1700
Reprinted 1929, 1997, 2020

ISBN 978-93-90035-12-0

Published by
Ajay Kumar Jain *for*
Manohar Publishers & Distributors
4753/23 Ansari Road, Daryaganj
New Delhi 110 002

Printed at
Replika Press Pvt. Ltd.

THE SEAFARERS' LIBRARY
General Editor: G. E. MANWARING, F.R.Hist.S.

VOYAGES TO THE EAST INDIES

CHRISTOPHER FRYKE
AND
CHRISTOPHER SCHWEITZER

With Introduction and Notes by
C. ERNEST FAYLE

WITH 8 HALF-TONE PLATES

CASSELL AND COMPANY LTD.
LONDON, TORONTO, MELBOURNE & SYDNEY

CONTENTS

LIST OF ILLUSTRATIONS

INTRODUCTION

OLD books of voyages and travels do not necessarily depend for their interest on the historical importance of the voyage, or the celebrity of the traveller. A humble trader or seaman, going about his daily business, will often preserve for us a hundred details of the life aboard ship and in the ports he visited, that would have been passed over silently by the envoy intent on great affairs, or the man of letters straining after the picturesque. It is through the impressions made on the mind of the ordinary man—provided he had the wit to observe accurately and record clearly—that we can best recapture a picture of the seven seas and the lands surrounding them, as they appeared to our hard-living, hard-fighting, hard-trading ancestors.

Let it not, then, be counted against Mr. Christopher Frick and Mr. Christopher Schweitzer, here introduced to readers of the "Seafarers' Library," that neither of them was a man of mark, nor took any prominent part in great events. They were both minor employees of the Dutch East India Company; the one a surgeon, the other a volunteer who went out as a ship's steward, and filled various subordinate posts, ashore and afloat, in the East Indies. They were engaged, for the most part, in the humdrum routine of trade, administration, and police in Eastern Seas and islands. For this very reason, they present us with a livelier picture of everyday life in the great overseas Empire of the seventeenth century Netherlands, than if they had borne heavier responsibilities and been concerned with wider issues.

Modest as was their station, Frick and Schweitzer were shrewd, observant men, keenly interested in everything new and strange, and their accounts of life on board a Dutch East Indiaman, of battles and shipwrecks, of seaports from Colombo to Nagasaki, of Cape Hottentots, Chinese traders, Cingalese pearl fishers, and Javanese villagers, are vivid, detailed and trustworthy. Their good fortune took them to seas and countries of which we have not, at their date, too many accounts, and took them there at a time of great historical interest.

We are so accustomed to think of Great Britain as the Mistress of the Seas and of the Honourable the East India Company as one of the chief factors in building up her maritime and commercial supremacy that it is something of a shock to be taken back to days when Dutch trade and shipping excited the despairing envy of English merchants, and the East India Company was everywhere hemmed in and overshadowed by its wealthier and more solidly constituted rival at Amsterdam. We are apt to forget that the Spice Islands, not the Indian Peninsula, were regarded originally as the richest prize offered by the Eastern trade and that it was only after crushing and humiliating defeat in the struggle for the commerce of the Malay Archipelago, that the English Company turned, as an afterthought, to lay the foundations of an Indian Empire.[1]

At the time when Frick and Schweitzer went out, the influence of the Dutch East India Company was felt throughout the Far and Middle East. Settlements at the Cape of Good Hope, Mauritius, and Malacca, secured their lines of communication. From their capital at Batavia, already a fortress, a great seaport, and a great *entrepôt*, they dominated the Malay Archipelago and wielded an ever-extending suzerainty over the native rulers of Java and the Spice Islands. A ring of ports and settlements round the coast of Ceylon gave them a monopoly of the pearl fishery and the trade in cinnamon and areca nuts. On the mainland of India, in Persia, and in Siam, their factories stood alongside those of the English, in continuous and unfriendly competition. In Japan they enjoyed exclusive rights of intercourse.

It is the special interest of Frick and Schweitzer that they covered, between them, practically the whole field of Dutch activities in the East during the period when the Dutch East India Company was at the height of its prosperity and vigour. A very brief summary of their careers in the Company's service will show how well they were qualified to give a picture of its ships and its settlements ; of its wars and its commerce ; of the peoples with whom it traded and over whom it ruled. Frick's narrative, as the longer and more valuable, takes priority in printing, but Schweitzer, as slightly the earlier in date, demands our first attention.

Of the life and fortunes of Mr. Christopher Schweitzer, of Würtenberg, we know nothing prior to November, 1675, when he volunteered for the Dutch East India Company's service, or later than September, 1682, when he gave up his accounts to the Company on his return. He sailed on January 14, 1676, as steward of the *Asia*, the flagship of five vessels bound to the East Indies. Holland being then at war with France, they proceeded down channel under strong escort, as part of a big outward-bound convoy. After the dispersal of the convoy, the *Asia* had a brush with a " Turkish " pirate off the Canaries, but beat her off successfully, and after calling at the Cape, where Schweitzer

[1] Factories in India had, of course, been established at an earlier date, but the trade of the Spice Islands was the chief object of the Company.

made good use of his eyes and ears during their nine days' stay, arrived safely at Batavia on June 26, 1676.

In Java, Schweitzer saw some active service as a soldier, but on October 3, 1676, he sailed for Ceylon, where he was stationed during the remainder of his five years in the East. Having the wits to master Sinhalese and Portuguese as a stepping stone to advancement, he obtained promotion, and a wide variety of employment. In 1677, he was Master of the Stores and Paymaster to the troops at a frontier fort. In 1678 we find him acting as a sort of unofficial secretary to the commander of the garrison at Colombo. Later in the same year he was in the fort of Malvane when threatened by the Sinhalese, and witnessed the desertion to the Dutch of the great Sinhalese general Tennekon Appuhami. In December he went on a punitive expedition to the Coromandel Coast. Next year he was selected to serve, with the acting rank of Captain, on a mission to the King of Kandi, and in 1680 he was again afloat, as " Commodore " of a light squadron sent to stop the native trade in pepper along the Malabar coast, which the Dutch regarded as an infringement of their monopoly. After a successful cruise up the coast as far as Goa, he returned to Colombo and was made Secretary, or Overseer of the Clerks, at the East India House. Here he remained till the expiration of his contract, pestered by the matrimonial advances of a half-caste widow with whom he lodged.

Christopher Frick had a more varied and adventurous career, including a much larger proportion of sea service. He belonged to a medical family of Ulm,[1] and was himself bred a surgeon, but in his own words :

" Ever since I came to years, that I could tell my inclinations, I found the chiefest of my desires was to travel and see strange countries."

After about three years spent in travel on the Continent, he made his way to Amsterdam, in search of " a fair opportunity of undertaking some voyage to the East Indies." This he obtained by engaging to serve the East India Company for five years as a surgeon, and on May 31, 1680, he sailed in the *Ternate*. His outward voyage was disastrous, for the *Ternate* ran into a thick snowstorm off the Cape of Good Hope and piled up on the False Cape.[2] Frick himself was one of the few who escaped to land and, after making their way overland to the Dutch settlement at Table Bay, were eventually taken off by the *Ternate's* consort, the *Europa*.

Soon after his arrival at Batavia, Frick found his hands full professionally through the outbreak of the Bantam War of 1682, which gave the Dutch control of the one important native state in Java that

[1] Melchior F. Frick (Friccius) of Ulm, published " *Tractatus medicus de virtute venerorum medica*," 1693, and other medical works. (Hirscty, " *Biographisches Lexicon*," 1885.

[2] Cape Hangklip on False Bay.

had remained wholly independent, and led to the final expulsion of the English from the island.[1] In this war, of which more anon, Frick saw much active service, including a naval battle (in which he was Captain of a ship),[2] two stoutly opposed landings, and a good deal of mixed fighting ashore.

After the war, Frick returned to Batavia, where he was placed in charge of the hospital, and enjoyed lucrative private practice, but true to his earnest desire " to travel and see strange countries," he used every scrap of influence he could procure by merit, by importunity, or by bribery (" I had now and then greased the Chief Surgeon's fist "), to obtain as much employment afloat as possible. In this way he contrived to visit almost every centre of Dutch trade in Asia, with the exception of the Persian Gulf.[3] Setting aside short coasting passages when transferred from one station to another, he was employed in the following voyages and cruises :

(1) Voyage to the Moluccas. In the *Phœnix* from Batavia to Banda, where he fell ill and remained for three weeks ; thence in the *America* to Amboina, and back to Batavia (Chap. VIII).

(2) Voyage to Ceylon. In the *Europa* : Batavia—Colombo—Batavia.

(3) Voyage to Japan. In the *Asia* to Formosa (after being forced by a heavy storm into the Gulf of Manilla to refit) ; thence *viâ* Kowchow to Nagasaki ; returning *viâ* Formosa to Batavia (Chaps. VIII–IX).

(4) Cruise in the Indian Ocean. In one of a squadron of eleven ships sent to intercept an expected Anglo-French expedition to take reprisals for the affair of Bantam (Chap. IX).

(5) Voyage to Bali. In the *Hollandia* : Batavia to Bali and back along the northern coast of Java (Chap. X).

(6) Voyage to Surat. In the *Gelderland* : Batavia—Surat—Galle—Batavia (Chap. X).

(7) Voyage to Burma and India. In the *Gelderland* : Batavia—Pegu—Arakan—Bengal—Masulipatam—Straits of Malacca—Batavia (Chaps. X–XI).

(8) and (9) Two short coasting voyages in the *Bali* (Chap. XI).

(10) Voyage to Celebes. In the *Tyger* : Batavia—Japara—Macassar—Batavia (Chap. XI).

(11) Voyage to Siam : in the *Bergen in Norvegen* with two other ships : Batavia—Bankok—Batavia (Chap. XII).

[1] Frick's narrative suggests that the war broke out about five months after his arrival. He was probably writing from memory and confused the dates.

[2] So the translation. The German of Frick's original edition may mean only that he was Master-surgeon, or chief surgeon on board.

[3] On page 78, he refers, in passing, to being off the Persian coast in the *Gelderland*, but this voyage is nowhere described in his narrative. Possibly he went out a second time to the East.

(12) Expedition against Pirates in the Sunda Straits. In the *Ceylon* (48) with another ship and eight small craft; capture of five pirate craft (Chap. XIII).

The expedition against the "pickaroons" was his last bit of service in the East, and his next voyage was the homeward passage, which gave him the opportunity to amplify his observations at the Cape.

Both men, it will be seen, had much to tell, and both made good use of their opportunities. It is our good fortune that Frick, who saw the most, was also the more intelligent observer. He was a man of some taste (as shown by his enthusiasm for Japanese craftwork) and of a scientific spirit. He confines himself mainly to reporting what he had seen with his own eyes, and when it is necessary for him to throw in a little history as background, as in his account of the origins of the Bantam War, he has evidently taken some care to inform himself of the facts. The scorn of the educated professional man for mere travellers' tales comes out well in his reference to the "simple and credulous people" who believed that elephants had no joints in their legs and were caught by sawing through the tree against which they leaned to rest. Although he fully appreciated a well-paid post or one that was "very genteel," he never lost sight of his real object in going to the East Indies. Neither his shipwreck in the *Ternate*, nor the heavy storm encountered on his voyage to Japan, nor his sufferings when the *Gelderland* lay becalmed for three weeks in the Bay of Bengal and he was glad to give two dozen silver buttons off his waistcoat for one draught of water, could abate his eagerness to embark in any ship bound to a place he had not yet seen. When ashore, he lost no opportunity of acquainting himself with native life and customs. He gives no favourable description of the Javanese of his day, but his strictures are not unsupported, and he shows considerable freedom from racial prejudice in his account of the "Chineses," whom he "found by much the most generous sort of People and best to deal with," and the "right Moors" of the Great Mogul's country, who were "very civil, handsome and well shaped, courteous and genteel in their Behaviour . . . great Merchants and very sincere in their Dealings . . . very generous and grateful."

Frick is more concerned with relating facts than with reflecting upon them, but his occasional comments on the Dutch East India Company's monopolistic policy are just and shrewd. He has, too, an occasional touch of humour that serves to enliven his narrative, as when he describes the eloquent address of the General to his troops, and how, "to make his speech more truly Rhetorical and persuading, he gave to every Man a month's pay *gratis*." He can even laugh at himself, as in his description of the first rough weather he met at sea—"a very fresh gale of Wind (I call it now, tho' then I reckoned it a hard Storm)"—or his delightful account of his forced sentry-go—"there was no manner of relation between the Musquet and me."

Schweitzer was a man of less information and coarser fibre. He shared the crude superstitions of his time; he believed, or half believed that his fighting cock was invincible because it had been dedicated to the devil; he believed in witchcraft and love philtres. In matters outside his own observation he was an easy prey to travellers' tales, and remarks quite gravely that the most dangerous of the "Green Serpents," who try to put out men's eyes with their sharp tongues, are "the two headed ones, which have a Head at each end." He shows no sympathy with the natives: he could not, like Robert Knox, appreciate the grave courtesy and gentleness of the Sinhalese, and his account of their religion is a caricature, comparing very unfavourably with Frick's description of the Javanese hermits. With all this, Schweitzer was a man who kept his eyes open, and he gives, in the main, a lively and reasonably accurate account of what he saw—the catching of elephants, the pearl fishery, and the like. His early history of the Dutch in Ceylon is not too accurate, but his account of events that happened during his own service is confirmed by independent authorities. His attempts to reproduce Sinhalese and Tamil phrases show an imperfect ear, but no bad faith.[1] His account of the life and discipline aboard a Dutch East Indiaman is valuable, adding several important details to those contained in Frick's narrative.

Both Frick and Schweitzer touch so frequently on the commercial and administrative policy of the Dutch East India Company, and its relations with European rivals—especially the English—that some account of that company seems to be required as a background to their narratives. It must inevitably be very brief, but it will serve at least to bring out the significance of the wars, punitive expeditions, and missions in which they were employed.

It must be remembered, in reading both narratives, that Holland, in the seventeenth century, stood far above all other countries in shipping and commerce. Petty, in his "Political Arithmetick," estimated the Dutch shipping at 900,000 tons, as against 500,000 tons for England, and 600,000 tons for all other European countries put together; the Dutch were the "Factors and Carriers for the whole World of Trade."[2] This great mercantile fleet, coupled with the geographical position of Holland at the mouth of great rivers, flowing

[1] I am told that his transliterations clearly represent an honest, though not very successful, attempt to put down what he had heard.

[2] "Economic Writings of Sir W. Petty," ed. C. H. Hall, Cambridge, 1899, pp. 251, 258.

through some of the richest countries in Europe, made the Dutch ports emporiums and entrepôts for the products of all lands. A fully developed banking system, a low rate of interest, and wise commercial laws rendered the Hollanders irresistible in commercial competition. Sir Josiah Child, one of the great names in the history of the English East India Company, summed up the impression made on the merchants of other countries in the bitter cry: "The prodigious increase of the Netherlands in their Domestick and Foreign Trade, Riches, and multitude of shipping, is the envy of the present, and may be the wonder of all future Generations."[1] The envy to which he refers was felt with peculiar keenness as regards the East India trade, in which, ever since the beginning of the seventeenth century, England had been toiling painfully behind her great rival in the race for the reversion of the Portuguese monopoly.

For nearly a century after Vasco da Gama fulfilled the dreams of Henry the Navigator by opening up the direct sea route to India, the Portuguese monopoly, claimed in right of discovery, and confirmed by Papal Bulls, remained unshaken. The arrival of Drake at Ternate in 1579, on his voyage of circumnavigation, and his treaty or projected treaty with the Rajah,[2] gave the first hint of the storm that was gathering in the North, and the union of the Spanish and Portuguese crowns in 1581 exposed Portuguese possessions throughout the world to the depredations of the Dutch and English seamen. It was not to be expected that the Protestant Sea Powers should long refrain from an attempt to wrest from their enemies a share in the fabulous riches of the East, especially after their appetites had been whetted by Drake's capture of the great carrack *San Felipe* in 1587, with her rich cargo of spices and precious gums, silks and velvets, porcelain and gems. Her papers, disclosing, in part, at least, the long kept secrets of the East India trade, were a prize as valuable as her cargo and in 1591–94 Captain James Lancaster wrote his name in history as the first Englishman to sail round the Cape of Good Hope to the Malay Peninsula and Ceylon. Nevertheless it was the travels of John Huyghen van Linschoten of Haarlem that gave the final impetus to the Dutch and English merchants. From 1583 to 1589 he had lived at Goa in the train of the Portuguese Archbishop, and the publication, in 1595, of his account of the routes to India, was followed in the same year by the despatch of Cornelius Houtman, with a squadron of four vessels, "to the countries lying on the other side of the Cape of Good Hope," with Linschoten's sailing directions as their guide. The appearance of an English translation of Linschoten's "Itinerario," in

[1] "A New Discourse of Trade," 1698, p. 1.

[2] It is doubtful whether any formal treaty was concluded. See Corbett, "Drake and the Tudor Navy," I, 299–300.

1598, led directly to the establishment of the English East India Company.[1]

Between 1595 and 1601, fifteen Dutch expeditions, comprising altogether 69 vessels, sailed for the East by the Cape of Good Hope, or the Straits of Magellan, and associations for trade with the Indies were formed throughout the United Provinces. In 1602 a tremendous step forward was taken by the amalgamation of all these associations in the United East India Company.

This was a very different affair from the rival Company already formed in London. The English East India Company was, in its inception, a regulated Company on the mediæval model. The Company itself was a permanent body, ensuring continuity of management, but the capital for each voyage, or group of voyages, was raised by successive groups of subscribers, and the affairs of each group were wound up at the conclusion of the voyage or period covered by the subscription. It was not until Cromwell's charter of 1657 that the Company finally " grew into one united, continuous, and permanent Joint Stock Corporation in the full sense of the words." [2]

The Company itself was formed for trade, not for conquest, and it was only very gradually that, as its commercial importance and the number of its factories increased, it became assured of diplomatic support in its struggles with foreign rivals, and its prosperity became a definite object of national policy. Even its monopoly against other English traders was far from watertight. Down to the end of the eighteenth century, it had to fight hard for the suppression of " interlopers," and it was not until the fusion of the " Old " and " New " East India Companies in 1708, that it entered on its career of unchallenged supremacy in the India trade.

The Dutch Company was, from the first, a national institution, conceived on the largest scale. The fusion of the local chambers was brought about by the States General themselves, in order to provide common defence against the power of Spain, as well as to prevent the cut-throat competition which had previously forced up the price at which pepper and spices were bought in the East, and depressed the selling price in Europe.[3] The Company was empowered by the States General to make war or peace, to seize foreign ships, to establish colonies, construct forts, and coin money ; and although the Council of Seventeen, who administered its affairs were required to present reports to the States General, it speedily became almost an independent Power, exercising throughout its far-flung Eastern possessions all the

[1] For Linschoten's influence on the formation of the East India Companies, see Sir William Hunter, " A History of British India," I, 230–35.

[2] Hunter, *op. cit.*, II, 135.

[3] Hunter, *op. cit.*, I, 238 ; Clive Day, " The Dutch in Java," 40.

attributes of sovereignty, but assured, in any crisis, of support by the whole diplomatic and military resources of the Republic. Its capital was the (for that day) enormous sum of 6,500,000 gulden, or from £540,000 to £650,000.[1]

Before the combined attack of Holland and England the Portuguese Empire in the East went down like a house of cards. From the first it had contained within itself the seeds of decay. The Portuguese came to the East as crusaders rather than as traders. They regarded their activities in Asia as an extension of the age-long struggle between Christendom and Islam, and had no compunction in seizing Mohammedan territory, or attacking Mohammedan trade wherever they found it. Unbelievers of other faiths fared little better at their hands, and even their commercial treaties were mostly extorted at the point of the sword. Forced to hold down, with very insufficient numbers, a sphere of influence extending from the Persian Gulf to the Moluccas, they were driven to rely on the terror of their name, and their splendid record as fighters and explorers was stained by horrible atrocities. Disdainful of trade and industry, they relied for their subsistence mainly on slave labour, and when their brief period of brilliant but artificial expansion was succeeded by the inevitable exhaustion, accentuated by the union with Spain, the Portuguese settlements degenerated more and more into nests of pirates. Everywhere, in the Malay Archipelago, in Ceylon, and on the Indian coast, the Dutch and English found ready allies, filled with a consuming hatred of the Portuguese name.

By 1615 the Dutch had finally driven the Portuguese from the Moluccas, and the English, in two hard-fought battles, had destroyed the naval supremacy of Portugal on the Indian coast. In 1623 the English, in concert with the Persians, captured the great fortress of Ormuz, founded by Albuquerque in 1515 to dominate the Persian Gulf. In 1641, the Dutch secured the western entrance to the Malay Archipelago by the capture of Malacca. In two strenuous campaigns, 1638–45 and 1652–58 they drove the Portuguese from Ceylon, and

[1] According to whether the gulden is taken at *1s. 8d.* or *2s.* (See note, p. 5.) The capital employed in the English Company's nine separate voyages, 1600–12, averaged a little over £50,000 for each voyage. The subscriptions to the various joint stocks (1613–57) were sometimes very large. The aggregate subscription to the First Joint Stock (1613–16) was £429,000, for four years' trading; about one-quarter being called up for each year's voyage. That for the Second Joint Stock (1617–20—three voyages) reached the unprecedented sum of £1,629,040. These subscriptions, however, did not represent permanent capital available for the general development of the Company's business. Each syndicate wound up its accounts separately at the conclusion of its trading period. The permanent Joint Stock under Cromwell's Charter of 1657 (more than half a century after the formation of the Dutch Company) was £739,782 subscribed; £369,891 called up. (Hunter, *op. cit.*, I, 306–7, 364; II, 135, 177 n 2.)

seized the valuable Tuticorin pearl fishery. In 1662, Bombay was ceded to England as part of the Infanta Catherine's dowry, in the vain hope of preserving the scanty remnant of the Portuguese possessions in the East.

To the greater part of those possessions the Dutch East India Company had now fallen heir; but its position had not been achieved without much friction and some hard fighting with the rival adventurers under the English flag. From the first the chief object of the Company's ambitions was the exclusive control of the Spice Islands, for the cloves of Amboina and Ternate and the nutmegs and mace of Banda were the most profitable of all the products of the East. When Pieter Both went out, in 1609, as the first Governor-General of the Dutch East Indies, he carried with him instructions that, "The commerce of the Moluccas, Amboyna and Banda should belong to the Company, and that no other nation in the world should have the least part,[1] To achieve this end he built up, during his six years of office, a network of treaties with the native princes, which gave the Dutch exclusive privileges of trade, and practically converted the richest islands into Dutch protectorates.

This policy of exclusion was bitterly resented in England. The English denied that the Dutch exercised any such effective occupation of the Spice Islands as could justify their claims to monopoly; they put forward, rather inconsistently, a claim based on Drake's priority of discovery, and they complained of Dutch ingratitude for the assistance rendered them in their war of independence. This last plea found little response in Holland. The Dutch regarded King James's peace with Spain as a shameful betrayal, and had no mind to admit their disloyal allies to any share of the lucrative commerce their own arms and diplomacy had opened up.

There is no need to go into the details of the diplomatic struggle, sometimes breaking out into open hostilities, for the trade of the Spice Islands in which the English were steadily overmatched by the larger resources and stronger backing of their rivals. Two outstanding events only need be mentioned; the founding of Batavia, and the tragedy of Amboina.

To secure their passage to the Moluccas, the Dutch needed a good fortified harbour, on or near the Sunda Strait, and in 1618, they obtained leave to erect a fort at Jacatra, on the northern coast of Java and not far from the Strait. While this fortress was in process of erection, the native chiefs became jealous of the growing power of the Dutch, and applied to the English to assist in its reduction. On February 1, 1619, the Dutch garrison surrendered, but before it could be shipped to India in accordance with the terms of the capitulation,

[1] Hunter, *op. cit.*, I, 341.

the Dutch Governor, Jan Pieterszoon Coen appeared off Jacatra with a strong force, drove away the English, and utterly destroyed the native town of Jacatra. In its place he erected, on the estuary of the river, the city and fortress of Batavia, as the commercial and administrative centre of the Dutch East Indies. There seems to be no foundation for the discreditable story, repeated by Schweitzer, as to the stratagem by which the Dutch obtained possession, which has a suspicious resemblance to Uring's account of the seizure of Elmina in another volume of the "Seafarers' Library."[1]

For the moment matters were patched up by a treaty, according to which the English were to have a one-third share of the trade in the Spice Islands, and one-half of the Java pepper trade; the expense of the garrisons was to be shared in a corresponding ratio; each Company was to furnish ten ships of war for common defence in the East; and a joint Council of Defence was to direct the protection of Dutch and English trade. This treaty, however, proved only a new source of strife. The Dutch accused the English Company of failing to provide its quota of ships and money. The English replied that the Dutch were using the ships for aggressive purposes and not for defence, and were erecting unnecessary fortifications. The English Company, in fact, had no territorial ambitions, it sought only for open ports; the Dutch Company had already committed itself to a policy of territorial aggrandisement as the foundation of its commercial monopoly; and the opposition of policy made effective co-operation impossible.

In 1623 matters came to a head. Herman van Speult, the Governor of Amboina, accused the eighteen Englishmen in Amboina and Ceram of conspiring with some Japanese soldiers against the Dutch authorities. Not one shred of evidence was ever produced except confessions wrung by the extremity of torture from the Japanese and the English themselves; but these confessions were enough to justify van Speult in his own eyes. The English factory was closed; ten of the Englishmen were executed.[2]

The news of these proceedings aroused a storm of indignation in England. Torture was then part of the public law of Europe. Under James I the rack was still used in England; the boot in Scotland. But Englishmen had never taken kindly to the refinements of the fire and water torture, and the fact that men, universally believed to be innocent, had been filled with water till their bodies were swollen to twice or thrice the natural size; tormented by lighted candles held under the armpits, the palms of the hands, and the soles of the feet —these things roused the nation to fury. Even by the Dutch law

[1] "The Voyages and Travels of Captain Nathaniel Uring," Ed. Capt. A. C. Dewar, pp. 104–105.

[2] For a full account of the affair of Amboina, see Hunter, *op. cit.*, I, 383–429.

the torture had been illegally used. There was no such reasonable presumption of guilt as would warrant its employment to extort confession ; the confessions were not, as they should have been, acknowledged and signed twenty-four hours after the torture ; the pleadings at the trial were scandalously imperfect.

The Governor-General at Batavia, the States-General, and the Stadtholder all expressed their disgust at van Speult's proceedings, but the Company were loth to disavow the action of their Governor, and still more loth to allow another Englishman to set foot in the Spice Islands. Redress could have been obtained only by war or the threat of war. James, as usual, blustered, threatened, and gave way. Charles succeeded James with the question still unsettled. Charles negotiated and, it is said, was bribed. Then came Cromwell, and the English Company, who had never ceased to urge their claims, found a ruler able and willing to back them. By the Treaty of Westminster (1654), which put an end to the First Dutch War, the States-General agreed :

"That justice be done upon those who were partakers or accomplices in the massacre of the English at Amboyna, as the Republic of England is pleased to term that fact, provided any of them be living."

In August, 1654, damages of £85,000 were awarded to the English Company in satisfaction of this and other wrongs, and an additional £3,615 was paid to the heirs of the murdered men.

The reparation came too late to wipe out the memory of the tragedy which, for forty-one years, had worked like a gangrene in the relations between Great Britain and Holland. A set tradition of bitter hostility embittered the commercial rivalry between the two countries, and in 1673 Dryden could still hound on his countrymen to the Third Dutch War by placing on the stage his *Tragedy of Amboyna.*

It is unnecessary to trace in detail the progress of the rival companies after the final expulsion of the English from the Spice Islands—the captures and recaptures that marked the course of the three Dutch Wars, or the succession of aggressions and reprisals, claims and counter-claims, that marked the intervals of peace. Throughout the whole period between the tragedy at Amboina and Schweitzer's outward voyage, the Dutch were bringing Java and the Spice Islands more and more completely under their control, partly by their victories over the Portuguese, partly by treaties with native kings—often obtained as the price of armed assistance against a rival or pretender—which ensured to the Company a trade monopoly, and usually converted the native ruler into a tributary puppet. Only in the Kingdom of Bantam, and in one or two small settlements on the Sumatra Coast, could the English retain a foothold in the Malay Archipelago. In Persia and in Siam the English had to struggle hard against Dutch intrigues. In Ceylon they never obtained a footing. Only on the mainland of India did fortune gradually incline towards the English Company. The Dutch, accustomed as they were to domineer irresponsibly over petty island chiefs and feeble Javanese potentates, found themselves hopelessly at sea in dealing with the haughty and powerful Moghul and Mahratta rulers. The centralisation of all authority at Batavia was another serious handicap. Outmatched in diplomacy, and fettered by the necessity for continued reference, both in political and commercial affairs, to the Governor-General and his Council, the Dutch factors in India reported, in bitterness of spirit, that they were being rapidly outstripped by their English rivals.

During the years that Frick and Schweitzer were in the East, the struggle between the two Companies was carried a long stage forward. The Bantam War, in which Frick himself took an active part, was the last act in the drama that opened at Jacatra in 1619. Ever since the expulsion of the English from the Spice Islands, they had clung to their factory at Bantam as the chief staple of their trade in the Far East. In 1630, it had been made subordinate to Surat—a significant indication of the trend of the English Company's activities—but it still counted as one of their main trading stations. Bantam, when Frick and Schweitzer went out, was still an independent kingdom—the only important native state in Java that was wholly free from vassalage to the Dutch. Englishmen, Frenchmen, and Danes were all made welcome.[1] The town of Bantam stood on a good harbour in an important strategical position, flanking the approach to Batavia through the Sunda Strait; it was the port for the richest pepper-growing district of Java; a convenient *entrepôt* for spices and Chinese products, and a convenient centre for the distribution of English goods.[2] It was the Naboth's vineyard that disturbed the rest of Governor-General after Governor-General.

Bantam, however, was a hard nut to crack. The kingdom was large; the people warlike; and the monarch, from about 1662 onwards, took every opportunity to strengthen himself by the importation of guns and gunpowder from England. Busy as they were elsewhere, the Dutch had not, before 1682, found strength to spare for more than an occasional blockade of the port.

[1] The French East India Company was not formed until 1664, and from the first was chiefly concerned in the trade with India proper. The Danish Company was formed in 1614, and had a factory at Tranquebar on the Coromandal coast, but owing to lack of capital, never became a serious competitor in the Eastern trade.

[2] In 1664 the Court of Committees of the East India Company allocated the outward trade for the year as follows: To Surat, 800 tons of shipping and £50,000 of stock; to the Coast and Bay, 1,000 tons and £60,000; to Bantam, 1,000 tons and £18,000 (*Court Minutes*, 1664–67, p. 85).

Frick's account of the causes leading up to the war is substantially correct.[1] In or about 1671 the reigning Sultan, Abul Fath, decided to associate one of his sons with him in the government, and from 1678 the young Sultan, Abdul Kahhar Abul Nasr, became an equal or predominant partner in the Crown. Deeply apprehensive of the Dutch, he decided, in 1681, to send a mission to London, with the main object, apparently, of procuring heavy guns from Charles II. In April 1682 the Ambassadors arrived, and were very graciously received. Evelyn, in his diary (June 19, 1682), describes them, unsympathetically but graphically, as follows:

"They were both very hard-favour'd, and much resembling in countenance some sort of monkeys. . . . Their garments were rich Indian silks, flower'd with gold, *viz.* a close waist-coate to their knees, drawers, naked legs, and on their heads capps made like fruit-baskets. They wore poison'd daggers at their bosoms, the haft's carv'd with some ugly serpents or devils heads, exceeding keene and of Damasco metal. . . . They sate cross-legg'd like Turks, and sometimes in the posture of apes and monkeys; their nailes and teeth black as jet and shining, which being the effect, as to their teeth, of perpetually chewing betel to preserve them from the toothache, much raging in their country, is esteemed beautifull. . . . They seem'd of a dull and heavy constitution, not wondering at anything they saw, but exceeding astonished how our Law gave us property in our estates, and so thinking we were all Kings, for they could not be made to comprehend how subjects could possess anything but at the pleasure of their Prince, they being all slaves; they were pleas'd with the notion, and admir'd our happinesse."

Still, he admits "they were very sober, and I believe subtle in their way," and though they did not succeed in procuring cannon, they took away with them, on their return, a present of 500 barrels of gunpowder from the King, and a promise to maintain "a good correspondence" with the Sultan.

This present was never delivered. Early in 1682, the young Sultan quarrelled with his father; the majority of the chiefs and people took the old man's side, and the young Sultan found himself, with about 500 adherents, besieged in his fort. In his despair, he appealed to the Dutch for assistance, offering them a monopoly of the pepper trade in return. The Dutch Company, of course, jumped at the opportunity, and sent a strong force under Major St. Martin to the relief of the fort. In the fighting that followed, of which Frick gives an animated account,

[1] For what follows see Sir William Foster, "John Company," pp. 97–120; "A Justification of the Directors of the Netherlands East India Company . . . translated out of Dutch," London, 1688; "An Impartial Vindication of the English East India Company," London, 1688.

they drove the old Sultan's forces into the hinterland, and established Abdul Kahhar Abul Nasr as sole Sultan—though now little more than a puppet of the Company.

Abdul Kahhar lost no time in fulfilling his side of the bargain. He accused the English of having aided his father both with supplies and with men. In vain they pleaded (perhaps disingenuously) that the Englishmen who fought for the old Sultan were deserters, and that supplies had only been furnished under compulsion. Abdul Kahhar would listen to no excuse, and gave orders for their immediate expulsion. On April 12, 1682: "The English with their trumpet sounding left Bantam to embarque upon their ships, leaving the Comp^as Flagg flying upon their factory as usuall, and all ye shoar filled wth the sorrowfull Inhabitants, shewing the greatest signs of grief at their departure, and thus ended the English trade and Possession of the English Apartment at Bantam, built at ye sole charge of the Comp^a and being their freehold, w^h they had uninterruptedly enjoyed for above 70 years, and to which place they traded many years before that, since the Charter granted to y^em in Queen Eliz^a." [1]

Transport was provided by the Dutch, who allowed the Englishmen temporary quarters in Batavia. The French and Danes were expelled from Bantam at the same time.

Thus, when the English Company's *Kempthorne* arrived, with the returned Ambassadors, the English factory at Bantam was already in Dutch hands. The Sultan, under Dutch tutelage, refused the present of gunpowder, and the *Kempthorne* sailed disconsolately for Surat. In the following year the Dutch discovered that the English at Batavia had been secretly buying cloves, and in August, 1683, they were finally expelled from Java.[2]

It could hardly have been expected that the English would sit down quietly under the injuries received at Bantam, and Frick's narrative shows clearly that the Dutch were deeply apprehensive as to the possible consequences of their high-handed action. They had reason for their fears, for in 1683 a fleet of twenty-three ships was prepared for the purpose of recovering the port; but, to quote Davenant: "By delays and artifices, they [the Dutch] got the taking of Bantam passed over in silence." [3] At first, the Dutch professed themselves ready to meet the English demands, with the result that the fleet never sailed, and the squadron with which Frick cruised in the Bay of Bengal found no

[1] Document quoted in Anderson, "English Intercourse with Siam," 171.

[2] Individual English merchants continued to reside at the port, and English ships traded there in non-prohibited goods. See references in Frick, and the voyage of the *Mary Galley* in "The Papers of Thomas Bowrey" (Hakluyt Society).

[3] Charles Davenant, "Political and Commercial Works," 1771, V, 450.

they drove the old Sultan's forces into the hinterland, and established Abdul Kahhar Abul Nasr as sole Sultan—though now little more than a puppet of the Company.

Abdul Kahhar lost no time in fulfilling his side of the bargain. He accused the English of having aided his father both with supplies and with men. In vain they pleaded (perhaps disingenuously) that the Englishmen who fought for the old Sultan were deserters, and that supplies had only been furnished under compulsion. Abdul Kahhar would listen to no excuse, and gave orders for their immediate expulsion. On April 12, 1682: "The English with their trumpet sounding left Bantam to embarque upon their ships, leaving the Comp^as^ Flagg flying upon their factory as usuall, and all ye shoar filled wth the sorrowfull Inhabitants, shewing the greatest signs of grief at their departure, and thus ended the English trade and Possession of the English Apartment at Bantam, built at ye sole charge of the Comp^a^ and being their freehold, w^h^ they had uninterruptedly enjoyed for above 70 years, and to which place they traded many years before that, since the Charter granted to y^em^ in Queen Eliz^a^." [1]

Transport was provided by the Dutch, who allowed the Englishmen temporary quarters in Batavia. The French and Danes were expelled from Bantam at the same time.

Thus, when the English Company's *Kempthorne* arrived, with the returned Ambassadors, the English factory at Bantam was already in Dutch hands. The Sultan, under Dutch tutelage, refused the present of gunpowder, and the *Kempthorne* sailed disconsolately for Surat. In the following year the Dutch discovered that the English at Batavia had been secretly buying cloves, and in August, 1683, they were finally expelled from Java.[2]

It could hardly have been expected that the English would sit down quietly under the injuries received at Bantam, and Frick's narrative shows clearly that the Dutch were deeply apprehensive as to the possible consequences of their high-handed action. They had reason for their fears, for in 1683 a fleet of twenty-three ships was prepared for the purpose of recovering the port; but, to quote Davenant: "By delays and artifices, they [the Dutch] got the taking of Bantam passed over in silence." [3] At first, the Dutch professed themselves ready to meet the English demands, with the result that the fleet never sailed, and the squadron with which Frick cruised in the Bay of Bengal found no

[1] Document quoted in Anderson, "English Intercourse with Siam," 171.

[2] Individual English merchants continued to reside at the port, and English ships traded there in non-prohibited goods. See references in Frick, and the voyage of the *Mary Galley* in "The Papers of Thomas Bowrey" (Hakluyt Society).

[3] Charles Davenant, "Political and Commercial Works," 1771, V, 450.

and even debiting him with the expense of the garrisons so maintained in defiance of the treaty.

In January, 1645, the peace between Portugal and Holland, signed in 1641, at last became operative in Ceylon; but in 1652 war broke out again, and within six years the Portuguese had been finally driven from the island. Colombo was captured by the Dutch in 1656, after a desperate resistance of eight months. Jaffna, the last Portuguese post in Ceylon, once the capital of an independent Tamil kingdom, fell in 1658, and during the next few years, Admiral Rykloff van Goens, who commanded the fleet throughout these operations, completed the good work by reducing the Portuguese settlements on the neighbouring Malabar coast.

By this time, the alliance with Raja Sinha was at an end. The King's forces had co-operated in the siege of Colombo, and a summons to surrender, sent by Geraard Hulst, the Dutch Director-General of India, was issued " in the name of his Imperial Majesty Raja Sinha and that of the Most Noble Dutch East India Company." [1] Had Hulst lived, a breach might possibly have been averted—he was the one Dutchman whom the King really trusted—but Hulst was killed during the siege, and neither his successor, van der Meyden nor van Goens, who became Governor of Ceylon in 1662, had the slightest intention of abandoning Colombo to the Sinhalese. There is no foundation for Schweitzer's story of a treacherous attack on the King's forces, but the breach of faith involved in the retention of Colombo—the prize to the recovery of which Raja Sinha had dedicated his life—was quite sufficient to turn him from an ally into an enemy.

" You state in your letter," he replied to van der Meyden's remonstrances on his change of front, "that the Governor-General of Batavia will be displeased. If the Governor-General and the Company are persons who keep their word they will have reason to be displeased; and if things go on after this manner, there will follow more and more sorrows." [2]

Even now, the King could not quite forget the services rendered by the Dutch in the expulsion of the hated Portuguese, and after the fall of Jaffna he actually wrote a letter of warm appreciation to van Goens, but with every year that went by, his resentment at the trick played on him became deeper, and it was continually quickened by Dutch encroachments on his territory. His forces could not stand up to the Dutch in the open field; but from time to time small columns were cut off in the forests, and minor garrisons captured. Sinhalese armies, hovering on the borders of the Dutch territory, interfered with the collection of cinnamon and the carrying on of the pearl

[1] Pieris, " Ceylon and the Portuguese," 271. [2] *Id.*, 288.

fishery. In the intervals between these intermittent hostilities trade embargoes were resorted to by both sides, with results mutually injurious. In 1672 the King found a new method of annoyance. On the outbreak of the Third Dutch War, a French fleet was sent out to India under Admiral De la Haye, to whom Raja Sinha joyfully granted the Bay of Trincomalee. De la Haye, however, went off to the Coromandel coast, narrowly escaping destruction by van Goens, who was in considerable strength, and attempted, in the following year, to surprise Bombay from the English. A French garrison left in Kottiar was speedily forced to surrender.

This was the position when Schweitzer arrived in 1676. It was an uneasy position for the Dutch; uneasier than would be realized from his narrative. The restriction of trade due to their unfriendly relations with the King, and the military expenditure forced upon them, were alike unwelcome to a trading company. Both Rykloff van Goens the younger, who succeeded his father in 1675,[1] and his successor, Laurens Pyl (1679–92), made frequent overtures of peace, and Pyl went so far as to write a private letter to Raja Sinha, acknowledging that the Dutch had done wrong in retaining Colombo; declaring that the whole island belonged to the King, and describing himself as his "faithful and humble Governor."[2] Schweitzer himself took part in one of the many missions despatched in the hope of placating the injured monarch, but so long as Raja Sinha lived there was little peace in the island.

One other incident of Schweitzer's narrative has a special interest—the story of the "Two grey Old Men" who came to the fort at Sitawaka, and declared themselves English refugees from the tyranny of the King of Kandy. A gallant and chivalrous warrior in his earlier days, Raja Sinha had degenerated, though long brooding over his wrongs, and his powerlessness to avenge them, into the gloomy and suspicious tyrant whom Schweitzer describes; but he had never lost his old liking for Europeans, and it became one of the hobbies of his later years to collect a sort of menagerie of the Western races—Dutch and Portuguese deserters, ambassadors of all races, and sailors who had landed to water or refit. As a rule, these men were not badly treated; many of them rose to high rank in his service; but hardly one European who fell into his hands was suffered to leave his dominions. Among these prisoners was Robert Knox, son of the master of an English ship, who was taken near Kottiar in 1660, and endured nineteen years captivity before, in 1679, he succeeded in making his escape. Knox, a shrewd and observant man, afterwards published an account of

[1] The elder van Goens went to Java in that year, and was Governor-General at Batavia from 1678 to 1681.

[2] Pieris, "Ceylon and the Hollanders," 30.

Ceylon which is one of the most important authorities for Sinhalese life at this period,[1] and it is with interest that Schweitzer's "Two grey Old Men" can be identified as Knox and the companion of his flight. It is pleasant to add that Knox's own account of the kindness he received from the Governor at Colombo, and afterwards from the elder van Goens at Batavia and on the voyage home, fully bears out Schweitzer's account of his reception.

In addition to illustrating the Dutch East India Company's relations with native states and European rivals, the narratives of Frick and Schweitzer throw valuable light on its administrative and commercial policy, its forces, and its shipping. Its policy was based throughout on the narrowest and most rigid conception of monopoly. Instructions issued in 1650 stated in the bluntest terms that "the whole welfare of the East India Company of this country consists in this, that she may enjoy solely, to the exclusion of all others, the fruits of the trade granted to her."[2] Within the limits of the Company's jurisdiction, whether exercised directly or through native tributaries, no one but the Company's agents was allowed to buy spices, cinnamon, pepper, gold, pearls, opium, sapanwood, or the other more valuable products of the East Indies. Even at the Cape, all trade in ivory, sealskins, or any other goods than trifling curios was "wholly engrossed by the Company."[3] The private trade permitted to the Company's own servants was limited to less jealously guarded products, and those who were permitted to reside in the East after quitting its service were restricted both as to the articles of their trade and the places where it might be carried on.

In enforcing their monopoly, the Company stuck at nothing. We have already seen what lengths they were ready to go to, in preventing European rivals from poaching on their preserves, and their treatment of native traders was equally drastic. "The natives were forbidden to sail beyond certain limits from their respective coasts, under pain of piracy; they were prohibited from trading with Indian or other Asiatic ports; and they were compelled to root up their spice trees in islands which competed with the produce of the Dutch settlements."[4] Schweitzer's cruise for the purpose of breaking up the native pepper traffic on the Malabar coast was a typical illustration of a policy steadfastly and relentlessly pursued.

So far as rival Dutch traders were concerned, the monopoly was complete. The Dutch Company was too powerful, and too well backed by the State, to suffer from "interlopers," such as caused so much

[1] "An Historical Relation of the Island of Ceylon," 1681.

[2] Day, "The Dutch in Java," 52 n 3.

[3] See Day, *op. cit.*, and list of prohibited commodities in Hunter, *op. cit.*, I, 343.

[4] Hunter, *op. cit.*, I, 343–44.

trouble to the English Company. On the other hand the complete suppression of illicit trade by the Company's own servants proved as impossible as with the English and Portuguese. The plain fact was that the Company's servants could not live on their legal salaries and allowances, and were inevitably driven to enrich themselves by underhand means. There were continual complaints of officials buying large quantities of goods on their own account and sending them home as private ventures in the Company's own vessels. In 1676, the year of Schweitzer's arrival in Java, Governor-General van Goens wrote home that the Company's business was being ruined by the private trade, and that the bulk was carried in the Company's ships.[1] At the same time, illicit trade in the prohibited goods was a risky businesss unless the offender held high position or had great influence. Frick makes several references to the severity with which the restrictions were enforced, and the one occasion on which he was tempted to engage in an illicit venture so nearly cost him his neck, that he never again strayed from the path of virtue. The china-ware, tea, and linen, which he brought home as his private venture, were openly purchased from the Company. Both he and Schweitzer refer to the rigorous search of chests and bedding, on their arrival in Holland, for prohibited or excess goods.

As against foreign competitors, the Company's monopoly was complete in the Spice Islands and Ceylon, giving them control of the more valuable spices, and cinnamon. After the fall of Bantam it was practically complete in Java; but the English settlements in Sumatra and India proper enabled them to retain a share of the pepper trade. Charles Davenant estimated that between the fall of Bantam and 1688, the average total import of pepper into Europe was 5,000 tons, of which 500 tons was imported by the French and Danes, 900 tons by the English, and 3,600 tons—nearly three-quarters of the whole—by the Dutch.[2]

In addition to enforcing a monopoly the Company had other ways of pursuing its main object—to buy as cheap and sell as dear as possible. Towards the end of the seventeenth century, the Dutch began to enforce a system of "contingents," and "forced deliveries," by which the native governments were compelled to supply pepper and other products, either gratuitously, as tribute, or at a fixed price—fixed by the Company.[3] The "contributions" of the Chinese, to which Schweitzer refers, were probably forced deliveries collected by them from the natives; for the Chinese were the middlemen and tax-collectors of Java.

[1] Day, *op. cit.*, 102.
[2] "Political and Commercial Works," ed. 1771, I, 120.
[3] Day, *op. cit.*, 63 ff.

While these forced deliveries, which in the eighteenth century became more and more important in relation to the ordinary trade, enabled the Company to buy cheap, it secured its other object of selling dear by limiting the quantity of products thrown on the market. It was the desire to keep up prices that led them, in some instances, to prefer the uprooting of clove trees outside their own settlements to an extension of their borders, and in any year when a heavy pepper crop threatened a fall of prices in Europe, they found a simple remedy in burning, or throwing into the sea, the surplus above the normal demand. Frick refers to this practice, though he does not pause to explain its significance.

Cheap labour was secured by the importation of slaves from Africa and elsewhere, by the enslavement of conquered islanders, by slave-raiding on the Chinese coast, and by the enforcement of tribute, payable in slaves on feudatory native states.

In the end, this policy of ruthless exploitation defeated its own aims. The extreme centralization of authority through which the monopoly was enforced, hampered enterprise and led to inefficient trading. The Company's native policy, and the severity of its restrictions on the enterprise even of " free " burghers, led to constant friction, and the authority of the Company came to rest on a system of terrorism following only too closely the Portuguese model. Frick tells us that the gibbet, the wheel, and the whipping post in the great square at Batavia were in frequent use, and his pages preserve the record of tortures exceeding in barbarity those used at Amboina half a century earlier. To guard against native risings, and to prosecute the almost incessant wars, strong garrisons were required, and the expenditure on fortifications and troops constituted a heavy drain on the Company's resources.

In the efforts to cut down this expenditure the Company treated its troops abominably. Sent to serve in a most unhealthy climate, they were ill-paid, ill-clothed, and ill-fed. The pay of a private, Schweitzer tells us, was £1 a month, with 40 lb. of rice and 8*s*. subsistence allowance; a Captain received no more than £8 to £10 a month, with a subsistence allowance of £2 10*s*. monthly, together with seven cans of wine, and two of oil.[1] For one half of this scanty pay, the soldier had to wait until he had completed his service; the other half was paid, as Frick relates, partly in cash and partly in clothes, " which are rekon'd to him at a sufficiently high rate." After describing a company " very prettily accoutred with silk-stockings on their legs, and shoos made of sail-cloath," Frick goes on to warn intending recruits that this treatment is only for a few, who " have a great many Friends and great Recommendations," and are selected to make a show at the principal factories, " whereas many a brave soldier is forced

[1] Converting the guilder at the highest rate, 2*s*.

to spend his time in Bantam, Amboina, Banda, and other unhealthy Islands, where they must trudge it without either shoos or stockings, and it may be perish miserably."

Only ignorant or desperate men could be recruited for such a service, and the Company's troops were the scum of all nations, with few genuine Dutchmen among them. Frick's "Comical fellow who had beaten one to death in a quarrel at Tyrol" was probably quite typical. Schweitzer gives a graphic account of the crimps who enticed strangers to their lodging-houses, and filled them with stories of easily acquired riches in the East; they were "not ashamed to go so far as to put a Hammer into their Hands, to knock the Diamonds out of the Rocks they shall meet with."

The Dutch "Soul-Buyers" were no worse than the keepers of sailors' boarding-houses in London, New York, or 'Frisco, in the nineteenth century, and the English East India Company recruited its forces much in the same way—Macaulay describes the recruits sent to Clive as "the worst and lowest wretches that the Company's crimps could pick up in the flash-houses of London"—but the conditions in the Dutch service seem to have been peculiarly bad. The majority of the troops were Germans, and were doubtless good fighting material, but their treatment was not such as to get the best out of them.

Civil officials fared little better. A list of salaries so late as 1720 shows that a book-keeper received only £3 a month—taking the guilder at 2*s*. and a clerk might receive as little as £1. Merchants received £6; Upper merchants—men in a very responsible position received only £13 a month. To these salaries must be added various subsistence allowances, amounting to about one-fourth of the salary in the case of the higher officials. Like the soldiers, the officials had to wait till the expiration of their service for one half of their pay, and it is probable that the other half was paid partly in truck.[1] Of our two authors, Schweitzer received £2 a month—a sergeant's pay—and Frick, as a surgeon, £2 16*s*. a month, with a subsistence allowance of about 15*s*. when ashore.

These terms compare unfavourably with those in the service of the English Company. The establishment at Surat in 1658 shows the yearly salaries as follows: Accountant, £150; General Purser, £100; Warehousekeeper, £70; Chaplain and Surgeon, £50 each; Secretary, £40; Factors, £30; Writers, £10 to £20; but to this must be added full board and lodging, provided by the Company. Moreover, the English Company's servants received greater facilities for legitimate private trade, together with some interest in the Company's adventures.[2]

For soldiers and civilians alike, the conditions of service were oner-

[1] Day, "The Dutch in Java," 96.
[2] Hunter, "British India," II, 160–1.

ous. They must bind themselves for a term of five years at least, to serve ashore or afloat wherever required; should they elect to remain in the East they were under severe restrictions as to residence and trade. Permission to buy land at the Cape was the reward of ten or twelve years service, and should the settler ultimately desire to return thence to Europe, he might not sell his estate, which was forfeited to the Company.

It is not surprising that these conditions failed to attract men of education or commercial standing; for there was little to be made except by illicit trade, and that was dangerous in default of influence. Schweitzer's description of affairs at Colombo was perfectly typical. The President of the Council had been a cabin-boy; "the best part of them could neither read nor write," including the Commandant of the garrison.

For the soldier there was always the hope of plunder. Such a haul as was made by the lucky drummer to whom Frick refers in Chapter XI, must have been very rare; but one such incident would whet the expectation of the troops for a long time. For the minor official, without influence in high places, there was not much to hope, although a few men rose from the ranks to the top, like Camphuis, who was Governor-General when Frick was in Java. Beginning as a junior clerk, he attracted the attention of Joan Maetsuyker, "who is said to have arranged a telescope so that he could observe how business was being carried on in the counting-room," and pushed the young fellow along, "because he could work, in contrast with the mass of the young employees, the nephews and favourites of the directors."[1] This, however, was exceptional, and Frick was probably justified in recommending those who wished to try their fortunes in the Indies, "to go among the English, who with more honour and generosity give a man the liberty to advance himself." So early as 1631, the Dutch factors in India were contrasting the initiative and freedom of action allowed to the English agents with the Dutch method of "having to wait for orders from the Governor-General in Java."[2] Where more discretion was allowed, it was easier for an able man to prove himself, and so to secure advancement.

Over-centralization, and terms of service which kept good men out and put a premium on dishonesty, did not make for efficient trading. Even so, enormous profits were made. Davenant states that pepper bought at *2d.* per lb. would sell in Holland for *1s.*, and that about one-half the Company's imports were re-exported at 750 per cent. profit; but against these commercial profits there were very heavy overhead charges to be set. The Company's accounts were kept, apparently of set purpose, in such a way as to make an accurate esti-

[1] Day, *op. cit.*, 99. [2] Hunter, *op. cit.*, II, 176.

mate of its financial position impossible; and the dividends, often paid out of borrowings, afford no clue to the real profits. It seems clear, however, that Frick's and Schweitzer's service fell within the Company's most prosperous years; indeed one authority considers the period from about 1639 to 1693, as the only really prosperous period in its history. Even then, however, the heavy military and establishment charges at Batavia outweighed the commercial profits of the Java trade; the best results were obtained in the traffic with Coromandel, Surat, Japan, and the Persian Gulf, where the Dutch were traders rather than rulers.[1]

The profit derived from the Japan trade was bought at the cost of humiliations which Frick describes with his customary candour. Dutch trade with Japan dated back to Pieter van den Broeck's mission in 1609. At first it was carried on in rivalry with the English and Portuguese; but the English factory was badly managed, and abandoned, as unprofitable in 1623, and the methods of proselytism adopted by the Portuguese led to their expulsion in 1638. The Dutch, who forbore to mix missionary with commercial enterprise, retained their trade; but only by accepting the most humiliating restrictions. Their factory was removed from Firando to the islet of Desima in Nagasaki Bay, and they were forbidden to set foot ashore without special permission, to hold services, or to carry religious books; the rudders, guns, and ammunition of their ships were removed, while in harbour, as security for their good behaviour. The trade, however, was lucrative; the imports of silk, etc., from Japan were valued at about £600,000 a year, those of silver at £500,000, and the Dutch were ready to stomach all affronts. Frick, a pious Lutheran, appears to have chafed.

To protect the trade route, the Dutch established, in 1624, at Tainan, on the west coast of Formosa, a fortified factory, which served also as the entrepôt for Chinese products: silk, porcelain, and ginger. In 1661 they were expelled by the great pirate Coxinga, who overran the island, and whose son, in 1670, granted the English East India Company permission to take over the old Dutch factory. The English, however, failing to develop a profitable trade, withdrew from the island in 1682, and in the following year, the island became part of the Chinese Empire. It is not clear who was in the possession of Fort Zelandia when Frick's ship called there; but his voyage would seem to have been later than 1683.

There is another point in which this voyage of his has historical importance. It is usually said that, from the expulsion of the Portuguese until comparatively modern times, the Dutch were the only Europeans who had any intercourse with Japan, and it is certain that when, in 1672, the English East India Company applied for permission to re-settle, their request was refused on the ground of King Charles's

[1] Day, *op. cit.*, 70–79.

Portuguese marriage. It would seem, however, that the prohibition was not always strictly enforced against private traders; for Frick found three or four English and French vessels in the harbour at Nagasaki, and while these might, possibly, have put in merely to refit, he speaks of meeting an English "flyboat" at the Cape "bound for Jappan," obviously in expectation of trade.

This is only one of many references to "flyboats" in Frick and Schweitzer, and the term requires a few words of explanation. It is derived by the *New English Dictionary* from *Vlie-boot*, one of the small boats used on the Vlie, a channel from the Zuyder Zee; but in the seventeenth and eighteenth centuries it was used as equivalent to the Dutch *fluit*.[1] Falconer defines, "Flyboat or Flight," as "a large flat-bottomed Dutch vessel whose burthen is usually from four to six hundred tons. It is distinguished by a stern remarkably high, resembling a Gothic turret, and by very broad buttocks below."[2] It was the rounded stern, "a survival of the round stern of 15th-century Low Country Vessels," with a high, pinched poop above, that was the real distinguishing feature of the *fluit*, and the term "flyboat" seems to have been used in England for any vessel of similar construction, employed as a cargo carrier in peace, or as a transport or storeship in war. In Holland, the type was very popular, and was used in the East Indies, as well as in the Baltic and Mediterranean trades.[3]

The East Indiaman proper, in the Dutch, as in the English service, was usually a strongly constructed, well-armed vessel, of very similar type to the battleship of the period. The *Prins Willem*, shown in Mr. Morton Nance's book of ship-models, "differed from contemporary ships of war chiefly in lacking a forecastle," and the model shows her as carrying about 30 guns, and provided with a waist board pierced for musketry. She had, in fact, taken part in the action off the Kentish Knock in 1652, and both sides frequently used East Indiamen in this way, to augment the regular fighting fleets.[4] When going about their own business they had to be ready to defend themselves against pirates, privateers, or enemy cruisers, on the long voyage out and home, and to fight pitched battles with rival fleets in the East Indies. The Dutch Company, indeed, seems to have kept a number of heavily armed ships in the East Indies exclusively, or mainly, for convoy or other warlike duties.

[1] "Fluit, Fluischip, a flyboat": Sewel's "Dutch-English Dictionary," 1766.

[2] "Dict. Marine." Buttocks—"The convexity of the ship behind, under the stern."

[3] Morton Nance, "Sailing Ship Models," 51, 68; Plates 20, 40, 50. Jal, "Glossaire Nautique," 1848, derives from fluit, the French term *flute* ("Nom d'un navire de charge, à fond plat, large, gros et lourd dont la poupe était rond"); hence *armée en flûte* for a man-of-war employed. as a storeship.

[4] "Sailing Ship Models," Plate XXI; note on pp. 68–69.

Neither of our authors mentions the tonnage of the ships in which he sailed, but in a document put in by the Dutch during the Bantam negotiations, the *Europa* is stated at 1,200 tons.[1] As this was in a claim for freight, we can be certain that the figure is not under-estimated, but if Frick is not exaggerating when he says that 800 men were crammed into her for the attack on Bantam, she must have been a large ship. English East Indiamen of the period mostly ranged from about 200 to 700 tons, and most of the ships in which Frick and Schweitzer served would probably fall within these limits. The *Ternate* and *Asia*, from the number of people they carried on the long outward voyage, were evidently of the larger class.

In appearance, all these ships would be bluff-bowed; high-sterned, with elaborate carvings (including the monogram of the United East India Company); carrying courses, topsails, and top-gallant sails on the fore and main masts, with a lateen mizzen (in place of the later spanker), and a square topsail above. Under the bowsprit they would carry the old square spritsail; the larger ships might have a small sprit topsail on a miniature mast mounted at the outer end of the bowsprit itself; but they would have no fore-and-aft headsails, which did not come in until the early eighteenth century.

Two other classes of vessel mentioned by Frick and Schweitzer—the yacht and sloop—need some brief definition, owing to changes in naval vocabulary. A yacht, in the seventeenth century, did not necessarily mean a pleasure craft. The term *jacht* originally implied, like the French *chasse marée*, a vessel used for chasing. In the opening years of the century it was applied to small, three-masted trading vessels. By the second half of the century, when its use spread to England, it had acquired something more like its present meaning. The first English royal yacht was presented by the Dutch East India Company to Charles II in 1660, and the patronage of the King and the Duke of York made yachting, in its modern sense, a fashionable pastime. Nevertheless, the yacht remained something more than a plaything. The term was loosely used to cover any small craft, usually fore-and-aft, but occasionally ship-rigged, used either for pleasure and state ceremonial, or, in the Navy, as a despatch vessel or light cruiser. Between 1660 and 1686, twenty-six yachts appear on the English Navy List, varying from 25 to 166 tons burden, and armed with from four to eight 3-pounders.[2] Both uses of the word are illustrated in Schweitzer's narrative. The owners of the *Asia* came off for a farewell visit to the ship in their own private yacht; but Schweitzer himself had

[1] "An Impartial Vindication," p. 87.

[2] Morton Nance, *op. cit.*, 67, 70; Plates 12, 13, 31, 33. Tanner, "Catalogue of the Pepysian MSS.," (Navy Records Society), I, 225–26, 237 and lists of ships.

the yacht *Trinconomala*, with a crew of sixteen, and twenty soldiers, as the flagship of his mosquito squadron for operations on the Malabar coast.

He had also two sloops, each manned by seven seamen and twelve soldiers, and of these no very clear account can be given. In the eighteenth century, a " sloop " was a small fore-and-aft rigged vessel, distinguished from a cutter by a fixed bowsprit and some small differences of rigging ; a " sloop of war " was simply a small cruiser, ship or brigantine rigged. In the seventeenth century, however, the term was very loosely used, and in the East Indies, was applied to various types of native small craft. It is idle to guess at the rig of Schweitzer's " sloops," and we are left in equal doubt as to the one-masted English ship " laden with Tobacco from Brazil " that he met on the homeward voyage. She merely reminds us that, in the seventeenth century, men were accustomed to make long voyages in cockleshells.

The crews of the Company's ships were, beyond doubt, of better quality than its land forces ; for the Dutch themselves took kindly to the sea and were first-class sailors and sea-fighters. There seems, however, to have been a foreign element among the crews, and it is somewhat surprising to learn that the mate of the *Asia* was an Italian. Still more surprising is the age of some of the principal officers. The Master of the *Ternate* was " upwards of four-score Years of Age " ; the Provost (responsible for the discipline on board) was an old man ; and the Master of the *Exchange*, in which Frick came home, was " a good old Man of near 90 Years of Age."

Frick gives in detail the complement of the *Exchange*, and Schweitzer that of the *Asia*, though the figures of neither inspire great confidence in their arithmetic. Under the Master, the chief officers were the Provost, the two Quartermasters (" to Order the Watches "), the Steersmen or Helmsmen (of whom three or four were carried), the Boatswain, and the Gunner, or Gunners. The Mates, in the *Exchange* at least, were only reliefs to the Helmsmen. Both ships were well provided with Surgeons, but only the *Asia*, the larger vessel, carried a Chaplain. In the *Exchange*, prayers were read by the Book-keeper who, with a Merchant or Factor, looked after the business side of the voyage.

Both Frick and Schweitzer give interesting details of the discipline aboard a Dutch East Indiaman. From the former, we learn that the soldiers who were being carried out, as well as the crew of the ship were divided into two Watches, called by names that had come down from the war of independence—" the Prince's Quarter " and " Count Maurice's Quarter." The periods of duty which, at this time, varied in the ships of different nations, were four hours, as in the English service, and Frick tells us that the second watch, from 4 p.m. to 8 p.m., was known as the dog-watch (*Hunde-wacht*). This statement is of great interest, as it is the first-known use of a term afterwards so familiar. The dog-watch, however, was not yet divided—at any rate in the Dutch service—into two short watches of two hours each; a procedure adopted "to change the period of the night watch every twenty-four hours; so that the party watching from eight to twelve in one night, shall watch from midnight till four in the morning on the succeeding one."[1] Lists of the men in each watch, with their times of duty on deck, were fixed up on the main mast at the beginning of the voyage.

Prayers were said morning and evening; absence being punished by forfeiture of the daily tot. Cards, dice, and gambling in general were strictly prohibited among the soldiers. Even "Tables" (i.e. backgammon) and draughts might be played only for love. Smoking had necessarily to be regulated for the prevention of fire; but the Dutchman's attachment to his pipe made it impossible to confine it too stringently. It was forbidden below decks at night, but allowed everywhere else, and a length of slow match (such as was used for the old match-lock) was kept continually burning, at which any man might light his pipe.[2]

The punishments for serious offences partook of the savage nature of the times. The rope's end was used as freely as in the English Navy, though the lashes were inflicted on the breech, not on the back. Ducking from the mainyard, and keel-hauling—of which Frick gives an excellent description—were both in vogue. Use of the knife in a quarrel was punished in the cruel mediæval way; the offender was fastened to the mast by a knife struck through his hand, and left there in agony until he could summon up the courage to wrench himself free. Any man who struck the Provost aboard ship was punished by keel-hauling; if the offence took place ashore, the offender lost his hand. Those guilty of certain odious offences were simply tied back to back and thrown overboard.

In Frick's voyage to Japan, there is an interesting reference to the "Sea Articles," though whether they were laid down by the Company or common to all Dutch ships does not appear. By these articles the Master was obliged, at whatever risk, to lower a boat on the cry of "man overboard," provided the man remained in sight; if he were carried out of sight, the Master could use his own discretion as to lowering a boat to search for him.

The outward-bound ships sailed in squadrons, of which three were usually despatched every year, "about June, September, and December." The squadrons were quite small—two ships in Frick's voyage, five in Schweitzer's—for the East India trade, consisting chiefly of

[1] Falconer, "Dict. Marine," 1769.

[2] The instructions for the English Cadiz Expedition of 1625 prohibit smoking at any time, except on the forecastle or upper deck (Corbett, "Fighting Instructions," Navy Records Society, 54).

specie and piece goods outwards, and spices, silks, and fine Eastern wares homewards, did not require a large body of shipping. Frick, sailing in a period of peace, makes no mention of any escort down Channel, but in 1676 Holland was at war with France, Jean Bart was establishing his great reputation as a corsair, and Schweitzer's squadron formed part of a big outward bound convoy, comprising the East and West Indies, Mediterranean and Portugal trades. In his first chapter he gives a set of orders drawn up for its guidance, the most interesting of which is the second : " That as soon as the Enemy came in sight of us, we should draw into the Form of a Half Moon."

There is very little doubt that this means the formation adopted by Tromp off Portland in 1653, " with his fleet in a crescent or obtuse-angle formation and his convoy in its arms."[1]

After the dispersal of the convoy, in the Bay of Biscay, the ships for the East Indies went on their way together, but no great importance seems to have been attached to their keeping company, and in actual fact, they proceeded more or less independently. On the homeward voyage, with the rich cargoes of Eastern products aboard, greater precautions were necessary. The majority of the homeward bound ships sailed in one body, " the return fleet,"[2] and we learn from Frick that all ships were under strict orders to keep in company, the faster sailers being obliged to take in canvas, when necessary, to allow the laggards to close. They were escorted by heavily armed vessels through the Sunda Strait, as a protection against pirates, but afterwards relied on their own armaments until they reached European waters. Vessels from Ceylon joined those from Batavia at the Cape; and it is a striking illustration of the leisurely way trade was then conducted, that when Schweitzer arrived at the Cape, the Java ships had been waiting seven weeks at Table Bay for their consorts from Galle.

The combined fleet (six large vessels and two smaller in Schweitzer's voyage) usually called at St. Helena to replenish their stores, or, at least, spoke the English fort, in order to obtain the latest European news. This was an anxious moment, for much might have happened since the last intelligence was received, and it is with a great sigh of relief that Schweitzer records the St. Helena news that " it was a general Peace every where at sea." It is highly characteristic of the times that " we very joyfully fired all our Cannon " to celebrate it. The seventeenth century was prodigal in gunpowder on all occasions of rejoicing or ceremony.

[1] Corbett, " Fighting Instructions," 94 and note. In these orders " the Admiral " clearly refers to the commander of the whole convoy, not to the " Admiral " of the East India ships.

[2] Day, " The Dutch in Java," 61.

On reaching European waters, the ships were invariably brought in north about, to avoid the risks of piracy, or a sudden outbreak of war, in the Channel. The usual route was between the Orkneys and Shetlands, but in Frick's voyage, the Admiral issued instructions, on crossing the Line, to adopt the more northerly passage between the Shetlands and the Faroes. Off the Shetlands the fleet met an escort of men-of-war (four vessels in Frick's voyage), together with a tender, loaded with provisions to supplement their remaining stores.

On the cross-voyages in the East Indies, the ships often sailed singly; but when two or three sailed together, the senior Master was duly appointed "Commodore" or "Admiral," and given general direction of the voyage. These cross voyages, by which the spices of the Malay Archipelago were exchanged for bullion and specie; Indian sugar, saltpetre, and opium; Siamese dyewoods, skins, and spelter; Japanese copper and lacquer, and Chinese silks, porcelain, and ginger, were a very important and lucrative branch of the Company's trade, and employed, as Frick's narrative shows, a large number of vessels.

The length of the passages made by both Frick and Schweitzer brings out very clearly the contrast between seventeenth-century and twentieth, or even nineteenth-century navigation. Frick's outward voyage was interrupted by the wreck of the *Ternate*, but he went on from the Cape in the *Europa* which had sailed in company with the *Ternate* on May 31, and arrived at Batavia on November 30. The *Europa's* passage, therefore, was 184 days, including a stay of some few days at the Cape. Schweitzer's voyage in the *Asia* can be given in more detail:

Jan. 14. Sailed from the Texel.
Feb. 25. Sighted the Canaries: 42 days out.
Mar. 27. Crossed the Equator: 72 days out.
Apr. 22. Arrived at the Cape: 98 days out.
May 1. Sailed from the Cape.
June 25. Arrived Batavia: 55 days out from the Cape; 162 days from the Texel.

These were by no means exceptionally slow passages. Schweitzer mentions the arrival of "a new ship" from Holland after a voyage of nine months, followed by another vessel which had taken eighteen months to reach Batavia, having been blown almost on to the Antarctic continent. Even in those days, a passage of eighteen months was beyond all expectation, and it is not surprising that this particular vessel had been given up for lost.

It would be unfair to compare with these voyages the passages of such a flier as *Cutty Sark* which, in 1870–71, passed the meridian of the Cape 41 days out, and arrived at Ombay Passage in the Malay

Archipelago, 75 days out; but there is a striking contrast between these early voyages and the performances of an iron clipper like *Patriarch*, which never approached record, yet could average under 87 days for fourteen consecutive passages to Australia.[1]

For the homeward voyage Frick gives us no data, but Schweitzer arrived at Amsterdam 116 days out from the Cape and 231 days from Galle in Ceylon, and this was not a specially bad passage, for the average homeward voyage from Batavia appears to have taken six or seven months.[2] Here the comparison with performances by more modern sailing vessels is even more difficult; for the faster sailers in the East India fleets were seriously hampered by having to keep company with their slower consorts, and much time was lost by calling at the Cape. Nevertheless, it is just worth while to note that in 1865, *Black Prince*, known as "the whipper in" of the tea fleet, from her slow passages, ran home from Anjer on the Sunda Strait in 94 days, and that a crack like *Thermopylae* could reach the equator in 16 days from the meridian of Cape Agulhas, as against Schweitzer's 73 days from Table Bay.[3] The present writer, nearly thirty years ago, came home from Adelaide. in the *Torrens*, then long past her prime, in 125 days, including a fortnight in port at Durban and ten days' quarantine at St. Helena.

Frick's coast to coast passages in the East are mostly given with an irritating absence of detail. Whereas Schweitzer stated definitely that his voyage from Batavia to Ceylon took 49 days (a bad passage), Frick is content to describe his own similar voyage as made in "five weeks' time," and the return to Batavia as "a kind voyage of three weeks." The round voyage between Batavia and Japan occupied five months, including time spent in port, and that to Surat "three months' sailing." To Banda, by way of the Sunda and Bali Straits was a three weeks' affair; from Bali to Batavia, along the north coast of Java, was eighteen days. The best run recorded is nine days, from Batavia to Pegu.

The scale of victualling aboard a Dutch East Indiaman in 1676 is given by Schweitzer as follows:

Weekly: Biscuit, 3 lb., salad oil ¼ pint, vinegar ½ pint.

Sun., Tues., Thurs: "Pork, or other Flesh" for dinner.

"On some days," stock fish (dried haddock or hake) and pease; on the morning after a fish-day, a dish of boiled barley.

Daily: 1 gill brandy.

By the time Frick set sail, in 1680, the weekly ration of biscuit had been increased to 5 lb.; and an allowance of ½ lb. butter was also issued every week. (Possibly Schweitzer forgot to mention this.)

[1] Basil Lubbock, "The China Clippers," 327–8; "The Colonial Clippers," *passim*.

[2] Day, "The Dutch in Java," 61.

[3] Lubbock, "China Clippers," 263, 280.

The meat-days, in 1680, were Tuesdays, Saturdays, and Sundays, and Frick gives the ration for each day as ¾ lb. beef or pork. Curiously enough, he makes no mention, in his account of the victualling, of either fish, pease, or barley, but a few pages later he has a passing reference to pease and "grout," and there can hardly be any doubt that fish continued to be issued, probably on the four days that were not flesh days. Frick tells us also that each man was presented, at the start of the voyage, with five Dutch cheeses, and that beer was in common, "as long as it lasts, which is not very long." When the beer gave out, they drank water; a state of things that would certainly have driven an English crew to mutiny.

It is interesting to compare this scale with that fixed for the English Royal Navy by the victualling contract of December 31, 1677.[1] This contact provided that each man should receive:

Daily: 1 lb. wheaten biscuit, 1 gallon beer.
Sun., Mon., Tues., Thurs.: 2 lb. salt beef, or as an alternative (on two days only) 1 lb. bacon or salt pork, and 1 pint pease.
Wed., Fri., Sat.: ⅛ of a North Sea Cod 24 inches long, or its equivalent in haberdine (salt or dried cod); or 1 lb. Poor John (dried hake).
Wed., Fri., Sat.: 2 oz. butter and 4 oz. Suffolk cheese, or two-thirds that quantity of Cheshire cheese.

This would make the normal weekly allowance compare as follows:

	English Scale	Dutch Scale
Biscuit	7 lb.	5 lb.
Salt Beef	4 lb.	2¼ lb.
Salt Pork or Bacon	2 lb.	
Salt Fish	3 lb.	? amount
Pease	2 lb.	? amount
Butter	6 oz.	8 oz.
Cheese	12 oz.	none after first few weeks.
Beer	7 gallons	none after first few weeks.
Barley	—	? amount
Salad oil	—	¼ pint
Vinegar	—	½ pint
Brandy	—	1¾ pints

It will be observed that the English seaman had a larger allowance of biscuit, and nearly three times as much meat as the Dutch; the

[1] "Catalogue of the Pepysian MSS.," Vol. I, ed. J. R. Tanner, Navy Records Society, 1903, pp. 165–67.

deficiency in the Dutch scale being presumably made good by a larger allowance of fish and pease, and the issue of boiled barley.

Neither scale provided a healthy dietary for tropical waters, and the English scale, with its lavish issues of salt beef and salt pork, simply invited the ravages of scurvy. The Admiralty were quite aware of this, and the victualling contract contained a separate scale of permitted alternatives for ships employed south of 39° N. This scale allowed the substitution of rusk for biscuit, and of stockfish for North Sea Cod ; but its most important alternatives were as follows :

For any meat ration : 3 lb. flour and 1 lb. raisins, or ½ lb. currants, or ½ lb. pickled suet.
For " a sized fish " : 4 lb. rice.
For 1 lb. butter or 2 lb. Suffolk cheese : 1 pint olive oil.
For 1 gallon beer : a quart of wine or ½ pint brandy.

The free use of these alternatives would enable a commander to give his men a diet comparing very well not only with the Dutch East Indiaman's outward bound rations, but with the allowances on board the local trader in which Schweitzer sailed from Batavia to Ceylon, viz :

Weekly : 2 lb. biscuit, ½ pint vinegar, 1 gill Lisbon oil.
Daily : ½ lb. boiled rice, ½ pint arack, 1½ pints water.
Sun. and Thurs. : ¾ lb. meat.
Tuesday : " a quartern and a half " of bacon.
Mon., Wed., Fri., Sat. : " Gray-Pease," eaten with oil and vinegar.

It is doubtful, however, how far the alternative scale in the English Navy was actually applied, for the English sailor insisted on his beef and beer with a fine disregard for the requirements of a scientific dietary. In Captain Boteler's " Six Dialogues about Sea Services " (published in 1685, but written some fifty years earlier), the Captain, one of the interlocutors, remarks, very sensibly :

" Our much, and indeed excessive feeding upon these salt meats at sea cannot but procure much unhealthiness and infection, and is questionless one main cause that our English are so subject to calentures, scarbots, and the like contagious diseases above all other nations ; so that it were to be wished that we did more conform ourselves, if not to the Spanish and Italian nations, who live most upon rice-meal, oatmeal, biscake, figs, olives, oil, and the like, yet at the least to our neighbours the Dutch, who content themselves with a far less proportion of flesh and fish than we do, and instead thereof do make it up with pease, beans, wheat, flour, butter, cheese, and those white meats (as they are called.")

To which the Admiral replies:

"The difficulty consisteth in that the common seamen with us are so besotted on their beef and pork as they had rather adventure on all the calentures and scarbots in the world than to be weaned from their customary diet, or so much as to lose the least bit of it."

According to Pepys, the victualling in the merchant service was little or no better than in the Navy—"only the East India Company victuals well"[1]—but he was probably referring to the quality rather than the variety of the food. It is likely enough, however, that wise merchants, engaged in the eastern trades, provided a somewhat more varied diet. The list of stores on board the *Mary Galley*, which sailed for the East Indies in 1704, shows that (apart from delicacies like "Neat's Tongues," obviously provided for cabin use), flour, oatmeal, and probably small quantities of sugar and "fruite" were regularly issued to the men.[2]

The main question for the sailor, as every student of naval history knows, was not the quantity of biscuit, beef, and beer allotted to him, but whether he actually received it, and whether he could eat or drink it when he got it. It is some consolation to find that the evils which were rampant under the bankrupt naval administration of Charles II, were not unknown in the ships of the wealthy Dutch East India Company. Long before Frick reached the Cape, not only the unrationed cheese and beer, but the brandy had almost given out, and the "Bacon salt as Brine, Gray-Pease half boyl'd, Grout and stinking Water," were also, apparently, running short. Schweitzer's ship—although the beer lasted better—had to be put on short allowance of food and drink between the Cape and Java, "which did not please most of us very well"; and in the voyage from Batavia to Ceylon, the ship's company suffered severely from hunger and thirst.

Slow passages, bad and often insufficient food, overcrowding, and lack of sanitation, made a voyage to the East Indies in the seventeenth century a very terrible experience. Before the *Ternate* had sighted the St. Paul's Rocks, "the Dropsie, the Bloody-Flux and Scurvey" had reduced her to "a meer Hospital," and Frick tells us that between St. Paul's and the Cape, scurvy and small-pox "carried off almost all the oldest of our Men." Schweitzer's tale is even more tragic. On nine days in the doldrums the *Asia* threw overboard 62 dead.

The losses would have been still heavier but for the Company's possession of a half-way house at the Cape. The settlement at Table Bay, founded in 1652, was valuable as a base for the protection of the long trade route to the East; but it was even more valuable as a place

[1] "Samuel Pepys' Naval Minutes," ed. Tanner, Navy Records Society, 135.
[2] "The Papers of Thomas Bowrey," Hakluyt Society, 194–95.

where ships could call to refit and replenish their stores, and where, above all, they could obtain " Sallads, Cabages, Turnips, Cowcumbers, and all sorts of Kitchen Herbs," for the relief of their scurvy-stricken men. Prior to their colonisation of the Cape, the Dutch had made use of St. Helena (seized in 1645) for a similar purpose, but on their occupation of the Cape they abandoned the island, and it became the " Sea Inn " of the English Company.

Even apart from the ravages of disease, the passages were not only far longer but far more dangerous than in the later days of sail, and the narratives of Frick and Schweitzer illustrate most of the " Adventures and Perils " set out with such terrifying detail by the policy of marine insurance: perils " of the Seas, Men-of-War, Fire, Enemies, Pirates, Rovers, Thieves, Jettison, Letters of Mart and Countermart. . . ." Frick, it is true, sailed during one of the brief intervals of European peace, and the fleet in which Schweitzer sailed was too strongly escorted to tempt even the daring Dunkirk privateers to attack, but European enemies were not the only foes to be dreaded. The fleets of Javanese praus might not look very formidable, but the Bantam War was no mere naval demonstration, and Frick relates that the battle in which he took part cost the Dutch two ships, as well as many small craft. Trade itself was almost as dangerous as war. Schweitzer's experience reminds us that Algerine and Moorish corsairs still infested the Atlantic tracks, and in the Malay Archipelago piracy was endemic—as indeed it long remained. Towards the end of Frick's period of service, the Sunda Straits were almost impassable, except to strongly armed vessels, though the Company, characteristically, " never concerned themselves about it " until one of their own ships, the *Bali* (in which Frick had made two voyages), was captured and burnt.

Fires and explosions were so frequent as to cast some reflection on the discipline of the service. The *Europa* caught fire and blew up immediately after Frick had returned in her from Ceylon to Batavia. He witnessed the destruction of the *Elephant* at Batavia, and shuddered to see " so many human Bodies toss'd at such a vast distance into the Air, for some of them went over our ship." Schweitzer saw the *Utrecht* burnt at Batavia, in 1676, with her rich cargo of 400 lasts of pepper, and three boats blown up while landing powder at Colombo in 1680. This last accident, at least, was due to the grossest carelessness.

Above all, there were the " perils of the seas." No doubt the Dutch East Indiamen were built and navigated in accordance with the best scientific knowledge of their time; but the seventeenth-century sailing vessel at her best was top-heavy and unhandy, and the science of navigation, in the absence of any sure method of obtaining latitude and longitude, or any adequate provision of charts and sailing directions, was still largely empirical.[1] Exposed as the East Indiamen were both to the Atlantic gales and the typhoons of the Eastern Seas, trading often in little-known, reef-studded waters, the perils of the Company's sea service were enough to daunt any traveller less avid than Frick of new sensations.

Frick's own ship, the *Ternate*, was wrecked on the outward voyage, with the loss of 300 lives ; two out of eleven ships in the squadron with which he cruised in the Indian Ocean, went down in a great storm off Atchin ; one of the three ships in his voyage to Siam ran aground and was only got off with great difficulty ; the *Lion* was lost on the Nicobars shortly before he passed them. Of minor casualties, he saw plenty. In the great storm off Mauritius, of which he gives a remarkably vivid description, the *Europa* sprang so many leaks that they were forced to heel the ship, by transferring all the heavy cannon to one side, in order to stop the flow of water from gaining on the pumps. In the storm off Atchin, his ship had to be " swaddled " with " a four double Cable Rope, lest it should have split by the violence of the Waves " ; the *Asia*, going to Japan, carried away her bowsprit and, apparently, other spars, and had to put into Manila to refit. The impression his sea service left upon him is summed up in his matter-of-fact comment on the stranding of the *Eckersloo* : " It is almost impossible for two or three ships to make so considerable a Voyage, without some lett or misfortune."

Schweitzer spent much less time at sea, but he too had his unpleasant experiences. He was in a serious collision going down Channel ; his ship had to cut away her mainmast on the voyage between Batavia and Ceylon ; he was shipwrecked on his coasting voyage down from Colombo to Galle. On his homeward voyage, the Vice-Admiral had to jettison nearly 400 lasts of costly spices to save herself from sinking. He records, too, the loss of two ships blown ashore at Colombo in 1680.

This is a striking list of casualties by fire and water to have fallen within our two authors' limited experience, and while many of them were due to those unavoidable risks before which the stoutest ship and the most skilful seamanship are helpless, there is reason to suppose that the Company's own parsimony was sometimes a contributing cause. Its directors seem to have been none too ready to expend money in replacing worn-out vessels. The *Europa*, and the ship in which Schweitzer made the voyage home, are both described as " very old," and the latter was also " mighty slow in sailing." A consort of

[1] Latitude was still obtained by use of the cross-staff and astrolabe ; the sextant was not invented until 1730. Longitude was largely a matter of guesswork ; the art of lunar observation was still in its infancy ; the first successful chronometer was completed in 1735, and its use did not become general until the end of the eighteenth century.

Schweitzer's ship from Batavia to Colombo had pumps that were "good for nothing." Moreover, the retention in the service of masters 80 and 90 years of age can hardly have made for safe navigation.

Day, in "The Dutch in Java," attributes the heavy losses of homeward bound vessels during the first half of the eighteenth century to the fact that they were "overladen with goods representing the private ventures of the Company's officials."[1] The voyage home seems, at any rate, to have been universally dreaded. Nothing brings out more clearly the perils of the seventeenth century seafarer than Frick's statement (which there is no reason to doubt) that:

"There are many hundreds, who when their time is expired, bind themselves afresh rather than venture the danger of going home again . . The frequent news of ships being cast away, and losing one half of the Fleets, and sometimes the whole ones, increases their fears daily."

It is fortunate for us that Frick was of sterner stuff.

Both Frick and Schweitzer originally published their travels in German. They appeared as: "Christoph. Schweitzers Wurttemb. Journal-und-Tage-Buch Seiner Sechs Jahrigen Ost Indienischen Reise," Tubingen, 1688; and "Christoff Frikens Ost Indienische Räysen und Kriegs-Dienste," Ulm, 1692.

In 1694, a Dutch translation of both books, by S. de Vries, was published at Amsterdam, in a volume which includes also the travels of Elias Hesse in the East Indies, and was entitled: "Drie Seer Aenmercklijcke Reysen nae en door veelerley Gewesten in Oost-Indien."

S. L.'s translation of 1700, here reproduced, was made from the Dutch version. It has not been possible, for the purpose of this edition, to collate his version with the original German. As the translation of a translation, it would be surprising if it exhibited close verbal fidelity, but a cursory examination leaves little doubt that it reproduces with reasonable accuracy the matter of the original.

The illustrations have been selected from contemporary prints with a view to covering as many aspects as possible of the life ashore and afloat described by our authors. A "Cora-cora" of which an example is given as typical of the native fleets against which Frick fought, is described in Smyth's "Sailor's Word Book," as: "Koracora. A broad-beamed Molucca vessel, with high stem and stern, and an outrigger. It is common among the Malay islands."

I regret that it proved impossible to find a contemporary map, covering Frick's many voyages, which would bear the necessary reduction in size, without losing all clearness; but nearly all the principal places

[1] p. 78.

mentioned by Frick and Schweitzer can be identified and found in any good atlas.

In selecting the illustrations, and in tracking down material for the introduction and notes, I have been greatly assisted by Mr. G. E. Manwaring, the General Editor of the Series. To him and to the authorities of the London Library I am deeply indebted.

C. Ernest Fayle.

A RELATION OF A VOYAGE MADE TO THE EAST INDIES

By CHRISTOPHER FRYKE, one of the Surgeons to the E. India Company, from the Year 1680 to the Year 1686

CHAPTER I

The Author gives an account of his mighty desire to travel. Of his Country and Profession. He sets out on his Travels, and passing first thro' several Countries of Europe, he comes at length to Amsterdam: Where he makes his application to the East-India Company to be admitted into their service, and is accordingly chosen one of the Surgeons. The manner of his setting out on his Voyage. The Orders, Laws, Customs, etc. that are constantly observed on board the East-India Fleet. Reflections on the Voyage, and those that undertake it

EVER since I came to years that I could tell my own inclinations, I found the chiefest of my desires was to travel and to see strange Countries. And whilst, by reason of my youth, and my more absolute dependance and subjection to my Parents, I could not think of moving in person; yet, in my thoughts, I was often transported from one Country to another. And by the help of Books, I did in some measure enjoy that satisfaction in imagination which I hoped one day to enjoy in reality; and that too as soon as might be; for the more I read Voyages, Journals, and other such Books, which gave me an account of strange Adventures, places, things, etc., which Men had met with in those more distant parts of the World, the more my desires encreased to see those things they gave so pleasant a description of. Nor did the greatest of dangers which those accounts represented to me, so much affright me from the like undertakings, as the joyful deliverances out of them encouraged me to trust so much the more firmly in Divine Providence, And I proposed to myself so much the greater a degree of satisfaction, in as much as I might be induced so much more effectually thereby to admire the great power and wisdom of God ; which, tho' visible enough every where, yet are more conspicuous in those wonderful works of Nature which being less common and less familiar to us, are more apt to raise our admiration and love of him, who is the Creatour of them all.

As soon then as my years and affairs did fairly permit me, I prepared my self to be gone, and to spend the best part of my time in Travels.

In order therefore to put my resolution into practise, I set out from home in the year 1677, on the 28th of *February*, and took my shortest way to *Vienna*, the chief City of the Empire ; from whence I went and took a view of most part of *Hungary*. After that I went into *Bohemia*, *Moravia*, *Silesia*, *Saxony*, and other Countries adjacent ; thence I went into *Swisserland*, where I spent about six months at *Zurich*.

But my earnest desire to be a travelling something farther would not permit me to stay and afford my self much ease at any of those neighbouring Countries ; but I went away for *Baden* ; taking a Boat that carried me all up the River *Limat*, which is a little River that flows from the *Zurich-Zee*, and passes thro' the Country of *Zurichgow*, and below *Baden* runs into the River *Aar*. Above *Waldshut* I took a Boat on the *Rhine*, which carried me all down that River to *Nimeguen*, whence I went by Land to *Utrecht*, and from thence by Water to *Amsterdam*, where I arrived about *Christmas*, A.D. 1679.

The vastness and beauty of that famous City, and my being a stranger there, made me not a little to stand amazed, and look about me ; as well to admire the rarities that offer'd themselves to my view every where, as to consider whither I should go first, and where it was most likely I should meet with what I sought after, which was a fair opportunity of undertaking some Voyage to the *East-Indies*.

While I stood in this doubtful manner considering what I should do next, a good Woman (in all appearance) observing me to be a stranger, and full of thoughts, askt me whom I wanted, or whither I would go. I told her that the first thing I was to see after, was a Lodging ; for I was but just come, and the night was drawing on apace ; but withal I told her, what sort of one I wanted, for I had not much money left. Upon which she very compassionately told me I should be very welcome to her poor Apartment (as she call'd it) if I pleased, I did not stand long to consider the matter, but took hold of the opportunity, and went straightway with her to her house : Being come in there, she bid me stay a while till her husband came home. It was pretty late at night ere he came ; being abroad at work, a Bricklayer by Trade ; when he came, he shewed himself very courteous ; and being all sate down, we fell a-talking, and he asking me several questions, as it is natural to do to a stranger, and amongst others, to what intent I was come thither. I told him the truth of the matter, and the only thing I proposed to my self was to find an occasion to go to the *East-Indies* ; and begg'd his assistance and advice the better to go about my design and to compass it.

The honest man did not seem a little surprized at my design, and endeavoured by all means he could to dissuade me from it, by setting before me all the dangers I was to run, *viz.* of hardships, excesses of heat, hunger and thirst, and oftentimes of losing life itself. But the more lively he presented all these and other kind of dangers to me, the more eager it made me to go thro' 'em, and the more it established me in my resolutions, as if the dangers had been the only charm that drew me. Which my honest Landlord observing, he found it was in vain to attempt to turn me from my design ; and upon that turn'd all his persuasions into a friendly promise that he would assist me to the utmost of his power and he accordingly recommended me to some of the Chief Men of the *East-India* Company, and did me very considerable service.

Having in this friendly manner broke the Ice for me, and prepared some of the Gentlemen to receive my applications, I went chearfully to wait upon them my self, and told them that it was my desire to be employed by those honourable Members in any service suitable to my profession, which was Physick. They carefully examined the reasons that induced me to go the Voyage, and advised me to weigh well what I was about, before I fixt my resolution ; that I might not have cause to repent my rashness when it was too late ; and withal they told me that I must expect to engage myself for five years. I told them that I had not wanted leisure to consider it, and that I was fully satisfied of the reality of my intention, and that there was no danger of my repenting, or of performing with any regret a thing I had resolved upon with so much deliberation. At which they were very well satisfied, yet they could not chuse but wonder to find me, who was but a Youth, so undaunted, notwithstanding dangers, which they themselves represented to me. I was then appointed to appear before the Chief Physicians, and to undergo an examination; which I accordingly did, with twelve more with me, who were, like me, Candidates to serve in several parts, out of all which there were but six to be chosen, three being designed to each Ship, of which there were but two to go this Voyage.

Having been all examined, we retired to the Hall belonging to the Hospital, where we were order'd to wait for our answer. The expectation and hope which every one of us were in, of being one of those that were chosen; and on the other side, the fear of ill success, and of disappointment, made us all very uneasie. We were not put out of our suspense that day, but we were bid to come again and make our personal appearance before the Commissioners the next day following; which we did, and I was one of them that were chosen, and my Post was assigned me aboard the Ship called the *Ternate* which was the only one that went the Voyage in company with the *Europa.* I was not so very uneasie as the rest were during the time of our suspense, because I was prepared against all disappointments in relation to my particular Profession; for I was resolv'd to go upon any account rather than not to go at all; and a Man so resolved may easily find admittance into some Post or other. And indeed I utterly despaired of success as to my being chosen for a Physician, being I was so very young, and the number of Candidates so very great; but beyond all expectation I was one of the six Persons that were called in to give in their Names, tho' indeed I was but the last of them. And being all order'd to stand by the Secretary, we were every one askt sevrally the second time whether we would promise faithfully to execute our Office, and strictly to observe all and every the Articles enjoyned by the Company. There were enter'd with the other Physicians, and myself a Surgeon for each Ship, and to each of them a Mate, who serves as a Barber. So that we were six in number, who answering all in the affirmative, were sworn, and a Declaration was made to us of the several Offices we were all accepted into, and what Salary each of us was to expect: *viz.* Each Physician was to have 42 *Gilders*[1] per month, and his Table, and ashoar instead of it 6 Ricksdollers. The Surgeons 28 Gilders, and Diet, and on Shoar 3 Ricksdollers. The Barbers 14 Gilders a month, and their Diet, and on Shoar an allowance proportionable to the others instead of it. Then we all subscribed to their Articles, and the Cash-keeper paid us two months Salary before-hand; and three Dutch Skillings every day while we stayed on Shoar; which was eighteen days.

After which, a review being first made of all the Ships Crew, we were all put on board three long flat Boats (which are for that purpose, and tho' small, yet so close Deckt that in a rough Sea they will go quite under the waves and retain no water. They carried us from *Amsterdam* to *Texel*, where the two ships, bound for the *East-Indies* lay. *Texel* is a Sea-Port lying on the open Sea, about 16 miles from *Amsterdam*; we had a very fresh gale of Wind (I call it so now, tho' then I reckoned it hard Storm) but it was not fair for us; so that we made something more than four days, before we could reach Texel. Whither being come, and having nothing to do but to Sail, I will in the meanwhile give my Reader an account of the preparations that those Ships generally make for this great Voyage.

Before they go off from *Holland*, they take a general view of every person that belongs to the Ship, and each man hath two months pay advanced to him: But the full and regular pay begins only after they are passed the *Tonnen*, which is a place so called, about a League out at Sea; from that time the full pay is to continue whether the Fleet go forward, or is forced back again by contrary Winds, as they frequently are; and sometimes kept there a great while, insomuch that in the Winter they are laid up for several weeks, the Water being frozen all about them, so that they cannot stir; and when that happens, they do sometimes discharge their Ships Crew to lessen the charges which would otherwise be very great.

[1] The *Gulden* (Guilder), *Rijksdaalder* (Rixdoller), and *Schilling* (Skilling), were silver coins of 20, 50, and 6 *Stuivers* (Stivers) respectively. The par of the stiver is usually given at 1*d.*, but Thomas Scott (1672) and Thomas Bowrey (1698) reckon 10 stivers to the 1*s.* ("The Papers of Thomas Bowrey," Hakluyt Society, 23 n. 1, 43 n. 3). The guilder was thus worth from 1*s.* 8*d.* to 2*s.*; the rixdoller from 4*s.* 2*d.* to 5*s.*, and the skilling from 6*d.* to a little over 7*d.*

But when the Wind is fair, and the Fleet hath been two or three days under Sail, then there is distributed to each person, little and great, 5 Dutch Cheeses as a Present from the Company. Then must all and every Officer, Soldier and Mariner, make his appearance upon Deck, to be divided into their several Quarters, which are two. The one of them is called the *Prince's Quarter*, the other *Count Maurice's*.

Each person is assigned into one of these Quarters, in which he is always to be found on any occasion; and there he is to keep the Watch by turns. And that all may know to what part every Man belongs, the names of them all as they are divided is affixed to the Main Mast, on two distinct Tables; where also is set the order and time that every Man is to watch in. The *Prince's Quarter* hath the first turn, and is therefore called the first Watch. There is a Provost, whose Office it is to call them together, and to set the Watch; each Quarter watches four hours, and then is relieved by the other. *Count Maurice's* Quarter hath the second Watch, and is also called the *Dogwatch*.[1] There is a Bell in the Ship, by which notice is given them of the time. It is rung at the setting of the Watch, and with a loud voice charge is given by the Provost to every one to take care not to be drunk upon pain of punishment. There are four Hour-glasses put up conveniently for him that stands Centinel, and the Helmsman to see; and as soon as the first Glass, which is but of half an hour, is out, they strike one stroke on the Bell; when the second is out, they give two, and so on, adding one for each half hour, until the Bell is rung again. Then another Officer comes and calls his Men together out of his Quarter, and releases the other.

There is likewise one Man or two always to stand on the Main Top-Mast head; but the Soldiers that go to the *East-Indies* are always free from that service, tho' in their return from thence Home, that duty lies upon them equally with the Sea-men. Yet (if they can afford it) they may buy it off with a matter of 25 Ricksdollers, tho' the Voyage should be a year in compleating.

When there are a great many sick in the Ship, then those that are in health are again divided, that they may have the duty as equally shared between them as may be. And when a Storm threatens them so as to be forced to hand

[1] In the original German "*Hunde-wacht.*" *See* Introduction, pp. xxxiii–iv.

their Sails, all hands must be at work to help; and so likewise when the Ship is forc'd to clap upon a Wind,[1] so that she must tack every two hours.

When any one neglects his turn, or is negligent in his duty his punishment is to have a 100 or 200 (or sometimes more) blows on the breech with a Rope's end. Every one that doth not come every morning and night to the Prayers that are constantly made twice every day, loseth for the day his portion of Wine and Brandy: There is a Psalm also sung every night, and for that purpose a Psalm-book is presented by the Company to every person in the Ship.

Smoaking of Tobacco is strictly forbidden at night below Decks, to prevent any mischief that might be caused by it, the Beds being all stuft with very good Cotton; but every where else it is allowed. And there is a great square Chest with a Pin in the middle, about which there is 10 or 12 fathom of Match, where any one may light his Pipe.

At the third Watch it's the business of one of them to take care to call up the Cook, who, as soon as Prayers are over, goes about the Dinner. Three Meals a day are allowed to all, and immediately after Prayers they ring the Bell, then every one comes for his *Quantum* of Brandy, which is about a *quartern* of our measure.

Every Saturday each Man receives five pound of Biscuit, about a quartern of Oil, and no doubt that quantity of Vinegar, and half a pound of Butter, which a man must husband as he thinks best; it is to serve for the whole week. Three times a week are Flesh-days, *viz. Tuesdays, Saturdays* and *Sundays*, on which days each Man hath three quarters of a pound of Beef or Pork, but most of it is so salt, having lain in the Salt it may be five or six years, that when it is drest it hardly weighs half a pound.

As for the Drink. At the setting out the Beer is in common as long as it lasts; when it is out, then every one is reduced to his measure of Water, which is about a large quart to a Man, and very well too. But when they come into the *Indies*, if they chance to be commanded away to any other parts, they are often forced to be satisfied with half that quantity, and then you may imagine what a value a Man sets upon his Liquor; and a Man may as well steal all ones money, as a drop of Water from any one.

There is a very great severity exercised over the Male-

[1] "To clap on (or by) a wind: to bring the ship's head closer to windward, sail nearer to the wind."—*N. E. D.*

factors, of which we shall have occasion to speak more particularly hereafter. In the mean while to inform the Reader of the general Customs, they are as follow.

If any one wounds another with a Knife, or other Weapon, he is forced to hold up his hand against the Mast; and the Barber takes a Knife, and strikes it thro' his hand a little below the fingers; and sometimes as the fault is greater or less, thro' the middle of his hand, and there he leaves it sticking in the Mast; so that the Offender must pull his hand thro' if he designs to have it to himself again. He that strikes an Officer, or Master of the Ship, is without hopes of pardon to be thrown into the Sea fasten'd by a Rope with which he is thrown in on one side of the Ship, and drawn up again on the other, and so three times together he is drawn round the Keel of the Ship, in the doing of which if they should chance not to allow the Rope enough to let him sink below the Keel, the Malefactor might have his brains knockt out. This Punishment is call'd *Keel-halen,* which may be call'd in English *Keel-drawing.* But the Provost hath this Priviledge more than the other, that if any one strikes him on Shoar, he forfeits his hand, if on Board, then he is certainly *Keel-draw'd.* Part of the Provost's Office is diligently to observe the behaviour of the Soldiers, &c. and to see that they be exercised every day by some disciplined Soldiers that have been the Voyage already. Punishment also is inflicted by his orders on the Soldiers that are catch'd at Cards or Dice, which are strictly forbid; but Tables and Draughts are allowed, yet must they not play at them for Money.

And I shall add concerning the manner of going about this Voyage, is by way of directions to those who have a mind to undertake it. There are occasions enough for any Man among the Dutch, French, English, and Portugueze, and every Man must take his choice which he will go with, according to the Nation he is of. But for the Dutch (if not for the others too) the best way is to go to *Amsterdam,* whence a Fleet is dispatched three times every year, which for management of their affairs at Sea yields to no Sea-men whatever, and therefore is most safe and convenient; they go off about *June, September* and *December.* But they will hardly receive any Passenger, as such; and therefore for his admittance, he must enter the service into some Post convenient to him, at least for the Voyage.

Indeed when one comes to Great *Java,* which is by way

of *Batavia*, one may quit their service, but the Rules which their Articles bind a Man to observe, makes it a freedom not much different from the service, by reason of the great restraint the Company will lay upon a Man. For first, he must oblige himself not to stir out of the Country in less than ten years time : Nor must he Traffick in several goods, as he would desire ; nor with such Countries as would please him best : For he is only permitted to deal with some small part of the Country, at the Islands of *Molucco* : And if a Man transgresses these Injunctions, he doth not only forfeit all he is worth, but also his honour and reputation.

Those that design, then, to give themselves up wholly to the service of the Dutch *East-India* Company, must bind themselves to them for five years, besides the Voyage forwards and backwards ; and take his chance for what part of the Country he is to live in : For it doth not lie in his power to chuse this or that part, as a Man might wish ; some parts being so much more healthy than others are, and some much more advantageous than the rest ; for that he must take his Lot as it falls. It seldom happens, too, that any one is removed from the place into which he is ordered at the first : but it falls hardest of all upon those that are order'd to stay all the while at Sea on board ; tho' indeed it is more profitable for him.

Any one that goes thither cannot have any prospect of advancing himself much, unless he understands Trade very well, and the Dutch Tongue ; and hath Friends there, that are able and willing to help him. For when the Company take men into their service, they take 3 or 4 times as many Men as they have Employments for, and out of them they employ those only that have good recommendations. Some men indeed by their Industry and good Fortune, or rather I should say, good Providence, have advanced themselves considerably from nothing, or very mean beginnings ; but there are abundance who want neither parts, nor industry, who notwithstanding do not move a step towards Preferment all the while they stay there. Which hath made several of them to despai , and betake themselves to very ill courses. The condition of life wherein a Man meets with least disappointments under them, is that of a Soldier ; where he hath four Ricksdollers a month and his meat ; the latter is very mean and sparingly allowed, both in the Ships and in the Garrisons, insomuch that it is a very hard and uncomfortable employ for any one that hath any thing of Education.

The Soldiers receive their Pay as follows; one half of it is paid at two payments in one year; and that not in full, but one part in Cloths, which are reckon'd to him at a sufficient high rate, and the other half is paid him when he is come home again. He receives for his Subsistence (beside his pay) 40 pounds of Rice (instead of Ammunition-bread) per month, and ¾ of a Ricksdoller.

Besides, all the Countries where the Company hath any footing are very unhealthful, except *Cormandel*, *Batavia*, and some few others, and most very ill provided with necessaries, much less with conveniences, for life.

The Soldiers that remain on Ship-board, are yet worse used than those that are at Land, and by reason of the Foggs they are often in, are more subject to sickness; and besides, both there and on Shore, there is more severe Justice exercised on Offenders than in Europe, and a small matter brings a Man to open and shameful punishment.

All this being well considered, I presume no Man can be very fond of going to the *East-Indies* on those terms, unless he is reduc'd to Poverty, or driven to it by some other necessitous occasion. But my advice would be to any one that hath a mind to see the Indies, to try his Fortune with freedom, to go among the English, who with more honour and generosity give a Man the liberty to advance himself, or to pass his days there as he thinks most convenient, and in as much satisfaction as his circumstances will permit him, which are left to a Man to improve as he is best able, and may then comfortably enjoy the fruits of his Labours and Industry.

CHAPTER II

Their setting out on their Voyage out of Texel. Come to the Canary Islands. Excessive Heat there. The way of Burying at Sea. Sharks very dangerous. Many fall sick in their Ship. They pass by the Island of St. Paul. They are shipwreckt by the false Cape de Bonn' Esperance. How far distant that is from the right Cape, so called. Their arrival there, and description thereof, of the Lewenbergh. A fight between a Lion and a wild Boar. An account of the Inhabitants both Natives and Foreigners, &c.

A REVIEW of all our Ships Crew being made, which was three hundred and fifty persons, on the last of *May*, 1680, we weighed Anchor, and set out with a good Wind, and the other Ship with us. And the next day about Sun-rising we passed between *Dover* and *Calice*, which are seven Leagues distant from each other. The same day five Fly-boats from the *Maes* joyned us; they were bound for *Portugal*, by which we were to pass.

The third and fourth day we still had France on the left of us, and kept *England* in sight on the right, and sailed successfully, save that one of the Master's Boys going to ease Nature at the Ships Stern (whereas the Bow is the usual place) dropt into the Sea; and tho' we hall'd out our long Boat immediately, yet the Ship sailing so very fast, they could not come to him; so the Boat was hoysted in again. The Wind continued good for us till we came within sight of the Island *Salvagues*, where we lost our Companion the Ship *Europa*, which had steered another course. In the mean time the common Articles which are to be observed at Sea, were read; to inform every one of his duty upon all accidents and occasions; and also what allowances every Man was to have.

We passed by the said Islands, tho' with a contrary Wind, which obliged us to tack three or four times a day, till we at last at three weeks end got in sight of the Canary Islands, and with a side Wind at N.N.E. sailed thro' between the two Islands. There we saw that vast high Hill call'd *Pico de Canaria*, or the *Peak of Teneriff*, which is of such an incredible height that none in the World is to compare to it. 'Tis admirable to see how far it stretches itself above the Clouds. It was at that time so excessive hot about us in our Ship, that we were forced to have a sail stretched, and that continually kept wetting, to keep us a little cool; and defend us from the Sun's piercing Beams: And yet you might see through the Clouds, the top of that mountain covered with Snow.

Here our Master died, being upwards of fourscore Years of Age, and having made three Voyages to the *East-Indies*: Upon which, a Council being called, one *Peter Peters* was chosen in his Place. This old Gentleman was the first I saw buried after the Sea-fashion, which is in this manner. They take the dead Body and tye it on a Board, and fasten two Cannon-Balls to their Feet, and so throw them overboard, just as Morning Prayers are over. In this manner they served the Master. But my Comrade had not all this pother made about him; for without a Salute or a Cannon-Ball he was barely ty'd to a Board, and thrown over; so that he floated a great while. This Solemnity gave occasion to a Dispute among some of our Seamen, concerning the dead Bodies that were thus thrown overboard; some affirming that when they were loose, floating upon the Water, you might turn them how you would, and they would still turn again, with their Face or Head towards the East: Upon which, one of those who could not give Credit to that Opinion, went down (the Water being pretty still) and with a Pole turned the Corps about, which immediately turn'd again, by what Cause I know not, but it convinced him that the other's Assertion had somewhat of Truth in it.

Such dead Bodies float till some Shark, or such like great Fish, devours them: But I do suppose they spit out the Plank again. These *Sharks* we as often call *Men-Eaters* in Dutch, because they are very greedy of Men's Flesh. They have a large Mouth, which they open very wide, and Teeth of great length, and exceeding sharp, which shut into one another; so that whatever they get between them, they bite clear through. They are about 20 or 24 Foot in length; and they keep about the Ships in hopes of Prey; but are much more frequent in the *Indies*, than in the Way;

where they do abundance of Mischief among the Seamen when they go to swim, as we afterwards found, when we came in the Road near *Batavia*, where one swimming at a distance from the Ship a Shark came up to him, and drew him under Water, and we never could hear of him more, or much as see any remnant of him; which made the old Seamen wonder, who said, They never knew a Shark take any more of a Man, than a Leg, or, it may be, a good Part of the Thigh with it: But for this Man, we did not perceive so much as the Water bloody. Near *Japara* we had a Man, who had lost a Limb by this means, under our hands to cure; and he lived seven Days after it; but at the end of that time he died, being mightily tortured with a vehement Cramp. Another time, at the Isle of *Onrust*, about eight Leagues from *Batavia*, our Ship being layed up to mend something of the side of it, the Carpenter going to do something to it, about a Knee deep under Water, had his Arm and Shoulder snap'd off. I took him and bound him up, but to no purpose; for in less than three Hours time, he was dead.

But now to return to my Purpose; which is, To give you an Account of our Voyage.

We had now been above eight weeks at Sea, and had had very favourable Winds; in which time most of our Provisions of Brandy, Cheese and Tobacco being consumed, and the Heat daily increasing, to which we must add, That many were not used to such sort of Sea-Diet (and that at last we could hardly get neither) viz. Bacon as salt as Brine, Gray-Pease half boyl'd, Grout and stinking Water: Our Ship became a meer Hospital, so many fell sick. The chief distempers were, the Dropsie, the Bloody-Flux and Scurvey. Upon this the sick were divided from the rest, and had the Larboard side allotted them, which is the side on the left hand. The Starboard was for the others. Thus we continued our Course till we reached the Island call'd *The Island of St. Paul*, which we left about 30 Miles off on the left-hand, and steered our Course for the *Cape of Good Hope*.

After about seven days sail from the said *Island of St. Paul* with very little Wind, the number of our sick increased daily, and the distempers that now reigned most, were the Scurvy, and the Small-Pox; which carried off almost all the oldest of our Men, but the younger sort quickly recover'd. Many were light headed, and ailed nothing more; which was occasioned, as I presume, only from the excessive heat we suffer'd, as we passed under the Line, and came to the other side of the Globe. In this dismal condition we went on; our only hope being that we should not be long ere we should reach the *Cape Bonne Esperance*, or the *Cape of Good Hope*.

But our hopes were strangely frustrated; for we quite lost our course; For the Snow fell so mighty thick (as it is usual about *Africa*) that our Men could not see one another the length of the Ship. Then our Master gave Orders that one should go up the Main Top-Mast head, and keep strict watch; because we were continually in expectation of coming to Land. Early the next morning I got me above Deck, and went to take my allowance of Brandy at the usual place: After which my Comrade, and I, who had been old acquaintance before we went to Sea, and between whom an inviolable friendship was contracted, we agreed to go and smoak our Pipes, and fell into a chearful conference about our approaching Joy of setting our feet on dry ground.

While we were thus talking, we heard of a sudden cry of "Land, Land," which mightily increased our Joy; little knowing after what manner we were drawing nigh to the Shore. But we quickly saw our mistake, when the Master upon this outcry, comes out, and with death in his looks crys out, "Oh my poor Ship! we are all undone!". At which we stood in amaze, not knowing what to say, or to take in hand to help our selves.

All this while the Ship was running violently to shore, the Wind being very high, and having no time to hand our Sails, we were forced to cut the Gears, upon which the Wind carried off our Sails over-board, with such a violent noise, that one would have thought Heaven and Earth were coming together. While we were all running hither and thither, in a miserable confusion, the Ship begun to crack; which made us all cry out with a loud voice, to Almighty God, to receive our poor Souls. It is easie to imagine what a dismal condition we were in, with the noise the Ship made, and the crying and sighing that so many of us made, for we were still 343 persons on Board, and the Ship kept still cracking more and more, till at last the After-part broke, and the Sea beating in violently, sunk our Stern in an instant.

None now expected to escape, and we saw nothing but death round about us, by reason of the depth of the Sea on one side, and on the other the Shore so high that it was inaccessible. Yet every body was willing to try what they could do; and to prolong their lives as long as they possibly could. We resolved therefore to leap into the Sea; and, if possible, to make to Shore, which was near enough to us, if haply we might reach it: But we foresaw it almost impossible to come to it, by reason of its steepness, and the violent beating of the Waves.

Thus recommending my self to Almighty God, and having implored his pardon and assistance, I committed my self to the Sea, and strove with the utmost of my power to get to the Rocks. I toucht them twice or thrice, but the Waves carried me off again; by this time some of our Company were got out safe, and they could not help us any otherwise, than by calling to us, and advising us what was best to do; which was no small help to those that swam; for the directions they gave from the Shore, was a great guide to those poor people who were still in the Sea, and whom fear made so insensible, and so hasty, that they could not of themselves think to take the advantages they might have done, had they been less terrified.

After I had been carried off again from the Rock, so far, that I had little or no hopes of ever recovering it again, it pleased God that I was thrown on again, and I luckily struck my hand into a clayey part of it, and thus got safe to shore.

Seven more got out after me, and 35 before, so that 43 of us only escaped, viz. the Master, the Steers-man, two Surgeons besides me, three Carpenters, the Cook's-men, the Swabber, the Gunner, 22 Sea-men, and eight Soldiers.

The rest, 300 in number, miserably lost their lives.

Here we all fell on our knees, and returned our hearty praise to the merciful God who had so bountifully deliver'd us from so great a danger; after which we went to look a little about us; but none of us knew where we were; which added much to our sorrow; besides that three of our men were almost dead with the cold caused by the Sea-water.

The Ship sunk down-right, so that we could not see the least part of her, nor had we saved the least thing about us. Her Cargo was worth above 328,000 *Ricksdollers* in ready Cash, and many thousand Gilders in goods besides, which were all lost.

Finding out at last that it was the false [1] *Cape of Good Hope* we were got upon, and that we were at 40 Miles distance from the right one, where the Dutch Garrison lay, we were forced to go further into the Country, which was the more tedious, by reason of the sick men we had with us. We knew that the Country had good store of admirable fruits, which we wished to come at; and at last we got some excellent good Water-Melons, which served us for Meat and Drink.

In this poor condition we saw some Hottentots at a distance, whom we could not come to speak to; for they run away from us. But it was to fetch some of them that could speak Dutch; and when we had made our case known to them, they immediately went and acquainted the Governour with it, who streight sent another parcel of these Hottentots (who are the wild Inhabitants of that Country) together with several Files of Soldiers to fetch us. They took up our sick men, and carried them on their shoulders upon Beds made of Reeds; and we were comfortably entertained with good Canary, good Rice, Bisket, and all sorts of excellent fruits, all of which were extreamly welcome to us.

When we came to the Cape, our Master and the Steersman went immediately before the Governour, to clear themselves from whatever might be laid to their charge, for the loss of the Ship, and of so many mens lives; and there alledg'd, that it could not be imputed to their negligence, or want of due care; but that it was the good pleasure of Providence to afflict them in that manner. After which we were all lodged within the Castle, and furnished with the usual allowance, and there waited for the *Europa's* coming; which was no less than three weeks: So that we gave that over for lost too, fearing it had undergone like fate with ours. What observations I made in this Country, during that time of our stay, I will now give you an account of.

In the year 1650 a Fort was built by the Dutch in this Cape, and ever since all the shipping that comes thither, whether French, English, or any other Nation, must pay Tribute at their first Landing. This Land, for its situation and fruitfulness, is very commodious for all that go from any part of Europe to the *East-Indies*, for refreshing of themselves, and recruiting of Provisions, and taking in of

[1] Cape Hangklip, on False Bay.

DUTCH EAST INDIAMEN
(*From F. Valentijn's "Oud en niew Oost-Indien,"* 1726)

fresh Water, which comes out of the Rocks and Mountains of the Country. Within the Land, it is richly adorn'd with abundance of Fruit-trees; but near the Shore, there are few, or none, by reason of the terrible Winds and Hurricanes, that beat upon it in a fearful manner, which come generally down from the Mountain called by the Dutch *Tafel-bergh.* And by reason of these stormy Winds, this Cape goes frequently with us by the name of the *Storm Cape.*

The Dutch that are there in Garrison have planted good Orchards and Gardens, which afford all sorts of Sallads, Cabages, Turnips, Cowcumbers, and all sorts of Kitchen Herbs: All which are great refreshments to those that come from Sea. And likewise the free inhabitants, of which there were already some hundreds when I was there, have Land which produces good Corn, Wheat, and Oats, &c. and Vineyards: So that one finds there plenty of good Beer, Wine, excellent Bread, and such sort of things as well as in Europe.

I dieted at one of these Free-men's houses, and I had a very good Dinner of Meat, roast and boil'd, and Fish, with excellent Sallad, and Butter, all for one *Skelling* (which is but six pence English) but Wine I was forced to pay for, after the rate of half a Ricksdoller the quart.

Besides the great store of Fruits which are common in Europe. There is great plenty of admirable Lemon and Orange Trees, which afford a very beautiful prospect.

The Haven is called *Tafel-Baey,* which is to say, Table Bay, so called from a vast Mountain just by the Shore which is called *Tafel-bergh,* in English *Table-hill,* from its figure, which is seemingly square and flat at top. It is seen a vast way off at Sea; and it lies about five Miles from the utmost point of the Cape, between which, lieth the Hill *Lewen-bergh,* or *Lion's-hill,* so call'd by reason of its resembling a Lion in shape; the head comes quite up to the Table-hill, and the tail comes down in the Sea.

I had a great desire to go up to the top of that Hill ere I went from the Cape; So having got some other who desired it too, we got leave, and set out the next morning early. It is about a Mile distance from the Castle; we went up it a good pace for a matter of four hours, and yet we were not near to the top: We were pretty well tired, and more afraid of being too long about it, and of being belated: for in the evening it is extraordinary dangerous being there, by reason of the wild Beasts that then come abroad; so we e'en resolved to go back again to get in by day-light: For we thought if we had fallen under their clutches, we should not have been much the better for our experience: And besides, a Cloud came over us which wetted us to the Skin, whereupon we returned back streight, and came into the Castle about half an hour before night; so that we could not compass our desire, nor could ever yet hear of any one that had been up to the top of it.

Provision is here so plenty that the Dutch have it mighty cheap, for a little Copper wire, for Bracelets, for Tobacco, and for any such trifle; so that a large Beast doth not stand a man in more than a couple of Shillings.

There are a great many Lions and wild Boars. In the Governours Hall are two Lions Skins. The one was of a Lion, that one of the Hottentots shot with his Arrow: The other was kill'd by a Boar. This last creature, I mean the Boar, hath on its back a sharp sort of Prickle; near a span long, and so hard, that they serve many trades-men for Bodkins. And the Lion falling furiously upon this Boar, the Boar struck him with his prickly Bristles into the belly, and made him bleed to death, tho' the Boar perished likewise in the fight; and they were found dead by one another, and both their Skins were hung up for a *memorandum*.

Besides these, there are many Elephants in that Country, and a sort of Beast they call *Bavians*, the same we call Baboons; which very much resemble aged Men. Some of our Men had orders once to go into the Wood to cut down part of it. Amongst them was one Comical fellow, who had beaten one to death in a quarrel at *Tirol*; and being forc'd to fly, had listed himself a Soldier in the *East-India* Company, and so made his escape. He staid a little after the rest to ease Nature; and laid his Satchel down at some distance from him; we saw one of those Baboons coming towards him, which made us stand still to see what he would do; and laying hold on his Satchel, away he went with it, and robb'd the fellow of all his provision of Bread and Cheese and Tobacco; which made very good sport for the rest. Ostridges are here also very common; the Eggs whereof are very good to eat. And among many other sorts of Birds, which they have, that are uncommon with us, there are a sort called *Sea-Ravens*; but of these there hath been account enough given by several Writers.

In the Sea, all round this place, one may see abundance of

great Fish called *North-Capers*,[1] but none of them are catched about the Cape, they have a snout like that of an Hog, thro' which they throw up Water as high as an house, and in such a quantity, as to fill almost a small Vessel, and it comes down like a violent shower of Rain: They are always to be seen about the Cape, but they do no manner of harm.

There is a prodigious quantity of other sorts of Fish, both in the Sea, and in the Rivers too. We went one night with a Net to have some sport, and at two pulls we had so many, we could not carry the tenth part of 'em. The Fish we caught were made very much like our Carps; and here are also abundance of Tortoises.

The natural Inhabitants of this place, are called *Hottentots*, meer Heathens; of no extraordinary size, for the most part very lean, and meagre; their Language very unpleasant, rattling like Turkies when they speak. They go stark naked, only having a Sheeps Skin about them, the Tail whereof comes before their Privities.

When a Ship is new come in, as soon as the Boat lands any of the Men, they get in as it comes back, to beg Bisket of the Sea-men, which they love exceedingly; when they ask for it, they cry "*Broqua*," which signifies Bread.

It is their custom to cut out one of their Testicles when they are young. Their chief Ornaments (if such may be so called) is on their Legs; they take an Ox, or Sheep's guts, and thrusting out the excrements a little, just to let them lye close and flat, and while they are moist, they wrap them about their Legs and there let them stick. These very guts is part of their food too; for just in this same pickle, they broil them a little over the fire, and eat them. So that it may properly be said, that they are meat and cloth to 'em: But to see them use it either way, might very probably give any man besides them a vomit. They use to besmear their body with all manner of dirt and nastiness, which makes them stink worse than a Goat.

Upon their heads they stick all sorts of little Sea-shells, and small Copper Rings, that come from *Neurenbergh*, which the Sea-men bring with them, to give them: And for one of them they will shew you some of their Tricks; among which one is, to throw a Dart or long Stick, with which

[1] A term applied to a species of whale, variously identified with *Baloena mysticatus*, the Greenland right whale, and *B. biscayensis*, the black whale, or southern right whale.

they'll hit within the compass of a farthing a mighty distance off.

As for their Religion, little can be said of it, their Language, it not being understood by any that ever I heard of. They use commonly to get together near to the Sea-shore in the morning by Sun-rising, and there they get in a Ring, holding each other fast by their hands, and dance about upon the Sand; looking up towards Heaven, saying something in their Language; and then write some strange unintelligible characters and figures in the Sand, and so depart; all which undoubtedly is intended in honour to some Deity. I have asked some of them that could speak a little broken Dutch, what thoughts they had of a God, and whom they believed in; they answered, that they thought that there was one above, that had made the Hills, and that Sea which we saw, and all that was in them; and that Homage was due to him; but I could not learn any thing further.

They are very good Footmen, and run very swiftly, which make the Dutch keep always a Troop of Horse there, to catch them in case of any Insurrection: For they dare not trust them in the least. In mischief they are cunning enough, tho' wonderfully stupid in any thing else. If they are not hungry, they'll not work, tho' you would beat them to death; but when their belly incites them to it, they'll work like Horses. It is not safe to break ones word with them; and if one should not give them what was promised, when their work is done, a man would go in danger of his life.

Their Habitations are most on green Meadows, and grounds that bear sweet Herbs for Pasture for their Cattle. Their Houses are made of Sea-Reeds joyn'd together, and fastned at top; just like our Hop-poles, when they are laid up for the Winter; and when their Cattle hath eaten up the Pasture all about them, then they remove their Houses, to some fresh place, and settle there again for some time.

As to what belongs to those we call Free-men, of which I made some mention before, they are such of our Men, as have served the Company in the station of a Soldier, or any other way during the space of ten or twelve years, and then desired to settle there, to trade or plant, which they may then do, paying a certain sum of Money, and all Imposts and Customs to the Company. These have dwelling-houses built after a manner like as in *Holland*, but not so high nor so fine.

The chief Commodities which the Company trades in, to quit the Costs of their Garrison there, is Sea-Dogs [seals], which are catched here in vast quantities They boil the fat out of them, and the Skins are hung up to dry, which they send afterwards to Holland.

When any Ship comes there, an Order is read to all the People that are on Board, forbidding them all to buy any thing of the Hottentots, except Ostridges Eggs and other like trifles. All Commodities of any use or value, as Rhinoceros Horns, Elephants Teeth, and Sea-Dog Skins, are wholly ingrossed by the Company.

Justice here is very severe, in respect to any of these Heathens especially; one instance whereof I was an eye-witness of, while I was there; Three of them having ravish'd a Christian Maid-servant, were hung up by the heels on a Gibbet, and so ended their lives, after they had hang'd there about thirteen or fourteen hours.

There are four Seasons of the year here, tho' in a quite different time from ours: For our Summer is their Winter; and in *September*, which was the time I was there, it was their Spring season.

Their Winters are cold, and always foggy and misty, but there is never any Frost or Snow. Thus far will suffice to inform the Reader of the nature and customs of the *Cape de Bona Speranza*. I proceed now with the continuation of our Voyage.

CHAPTER III

The Author's departure from the Cape, in the Ship called the Europa. *They met with a most violent Storm, which held them four whole days about St. Maurice's Island. Their arrival to the Streights of Sunda, then to Batavia. Description of the City, and Castle ; and of the Government of them both. Customs of the several Inhabitants there ; especially the Chineses. Many Crocodiles in that River, they are called Caimans by the Inhabitants. The Author present at the catching of several of them. The manner of it. Tygers, Apes, Coco-trees, Mangoes, Bislang Figgs*

AFTER we had spent a pretty while here, and were very well recovered from our late Affliction, we prepared our selves to be gone in the *Europa*, which by this time was come, and ready to sail off again for *Batavia* ; and with the first fair Wind we set Sail, and in the name of God we ran out of *Tafel-Bay*, leaving only one English Fly Boat behind us at the Cape, which was come thither, since we.

All that day, and the next the same fair Gale continued, which blew us along so briskly, that on the next day we were got out of sight of *Africa*, and came into the Main. We had this brisk and fair Gale for eight days together, which carried us merrily along beyond the Island called *St. Maurice* [Mauritius], about which place men seldom fail of a storm and bad Weather ; so that it was no small joy to us, to have so fairly escaped it : But alas ! our joy was soon palled ; and our security proved very deceitful, while we foolishly took the measures for our safety, more from the Climes and Latitudes we were in, than from *His* Providence, to whom the Winds, and Seas are every where subject ; for when we least thought on't, the Sky darkned all of a sudden, and such a Hurrican rose upon us, as made us all tremble. No sooner had it given us the first toss, but our Ship outdid almost the noise of it, with the dreadful cracks it gave, insomuch that we expected nothing but to sink in the instant. All the while the Clouds grew darker and darker, and the Wind increased to that degree, that we could not hear one another speak. The Sea gaped so hideously, that it could not be thought we should ever escape being swallowed up; our Ship sometimes mounted on the top of a Wave, plunged down with such a terrible force, as it had been down a Precipice, that we expected every moment to be overwhelmed with it. And no sooner had we escaped one Gulph, but we were raised up again to fall into another. All this while, what with the Sea dashing in upon us, and what with the great Gaps that were in the Ship, we were so full of Water, that we were all forced to pump like Slaves, for three days together; all which yet was little enough. I for my part, who little thought to have been in any such employment, yet was forced to fall to, and stick to it for four hours together, which would have been intolerable to me at any other time: But on such occasions a Man does not much stand upon Niceties: And I do not remember that I was so much as tired with it, for the hopes we had that God would still cast an Eye of pity upon us, and relieve us out of our misery, was now all the comfort we had left. But the Weather still continued, or, rather indeed, grew worse, so that mounting our Ship up on end, one of our Carpenters was toss'd out of his Cabin, and had tumbled directly into the Sea, had not one of the Sea-men luckily caught hold of him. I tryed several places to get a little rest in, and, amongst others, I got in by some Sheep that we had brought from the Cape with us, which I found almost dead, never a one of them being able to stand on its Leggs. Not finding my self safe there, without holding fast by the Boards, which was very tiresome work, I went to the Gunner's Room, where the Surgeons Chests always lye, to try to get into a Hammock: But all the Chests there were turned topsie turvy, and in such a confusion, that I could not get to the place I designed for 'em; so I sate me down: But I had not been there three minutes, but I heard a low broken voice just breathing out the Name of God; at which, being mightily surprised, I looked and found our Provost, an old Man, lying under those Chests that were jumbled together, and crusht to pieces with the vast weight of 'em. I ran up to acquaint our Master, who in the hurry took little notice of it, only order'd some of the Men to throw him over-board, which was immediately done, without any formalities, or so much as a Plank; for we had no time to tye him to one, as it is usual; but over they threw him, cloaths and all on.

It was now the fourth night that we had been in this condition; and that we gave our selves for gone every moment of that time: So we were all called to Prayers, and every one got out upon Deck with much ado, and held fast, some by one thing, some by another, to hear our Minister, who very earnestly sent up most devout Prayers to Heaven, that God would in his mercy deliver us; or, if it were his good pleasure, to receive our poor Souls unto himself.

To those who are altogether strangers to the Sea, the Affliction we went in is altogether unconceivable; and for my own part, tho' I have been oftentimes in great dangers by Sea and by Land, and upon many occasions, with Courage enough, stood before the Enemy; yet did none of these dangers ever terrifie me comparably to this, where death doth not only seem sure and inevitable, but comes attended with all the Horrour imaginable, and drest in its most hideous and terrifying shapes.

But by how much the greater our danger was, so much the more admirable was the power and goodness of God towards us: For on the fourth day in the morning the Winds fell, the Air became serene, and the Sea calm, which restored us all, as it were, to life again. We then, as in duty bound, first fell to praising of God, whence our help came; and with Hymns and Psalms to rejoyce in him for his goodness, and our miraculous deliverance.

After which we went to set things to rights about us, and to mend our tattered Ship. To this purpose we put all the heavy Cannon on one side of the Ship, to raise up the other, that the Carpenters might get at it to work; which they went about immediately: But the Calm did not last long enough for them to do half what we wanted. We had a brisk Gale, which was very fair for us, it's true; but having so many Leaks unstopt, we were forced to keep our Pumps going continually. This Wind held us six days, during which we passed the Latitude of *St. Maurice*, and got in sight of *St. Paul de Amsterdam* [1]; which we left about

[1] St. Paul and New Amsterdam Islands in the Indian Ocean, on which provision depôts for shipwrecked mariners were established in the 19th century.

sixteen Miles on the right off us, and steer'd right upon Great *Java*, whereof *Batavia* is the chief Town. In all this time we had a great many of our Men sick, and seven of them died, and were cast overboard.

The Wind being so fair for us, the allowance was large, and there was no stint of any thing almost : Yet we wish'd heartily to be ashore, and the more, for the sake of our Sick : But we wanted more than a hundred Miles sail to the place we were to go to. But by God's assistance we reach'd it, beyond our expectation ; for, by Sun-setting, a Sailor cryed out, Land ; which caused a sudden joy amongst us all ; and the Master straight presented him a Ducat, or two Ricksdollers, two Cheeses, and a Bottle of Canary, according to custom.

Upon this we fell to tricking up our selves, painting our Long-Boat and Shallop,[1] and making our Ship very fine : We fastned our Anchors, and made all preparations to go to Shore, which was not now above forty Miles from us. By the next morning we got within two hours sail of it ; but we over-shot it by above thirty Miles on the Westward of it ; so that we were forced to tack about to the East ; and after some days sail we came up to some small Islands that lye within five Miles of Great *Java* ; there we cast Anchor immediately, hawl'd out our Boat, and went on Shore, to fetch some Coco's, which we divided among the rest on Ship-board. Three days after this, we came into the Road of *Sunda*, wherein a great many little Vessels came to us (which they call *Prawen*,[2] which sail prodigious swiftly) and brought with them several sorts of fruits, as Coco's, Pisang Figgs, which are a long kind of Figg, Eggs, and such like. Lastly, On the last day of *November* we arrived safely at *Batavia*, where we cast Anchor before the Castle, having lost thirteen of our Men, and about 20 sick still aboard. Here we return'd God thanks for our

[1] Longboat was "The largest and strongest boat belonging to any ship. It is principally employed to carry great burthens, as anchors, cables, ballast, &c." Generally furnished with a mast and sails (Falconer, *Dict. Marine*, 1769). The Shallop was "A large heavy undecked boat, with one mast, fore-and-aft mainsail, and jib-foresail. . . . Also a small boat rowed by one or two men" (Smyth, *Sailor's Word Book*, 1867).

[2] Proa or Prau is a Malay boat propelled by sails and oars ; double-ended, with an outrigged canoe attached, to add to its stability and stiffness under sail.

safe arrival; embraced each other heartily, and discharged our Cannon very briskly. After which the Master taking some company along with him, went immediately to Shore, to wait on the General, who was the *Heer John Speelman*,[1] at that time Governour of all the East-Indies.

In the mean time the *Fiscal* came to our Ship, to take a view of all the Men, and to demand all their Letters: After which the Men were landed, and the Ship unladen: The sick were put into the Hospital, and those that were in health marched in good order into the Castle of *Batavia*; where being drawn up before the General's Apartment, he came out to them, and kindly bad them welcome; and ordered the Major to divide them amongst the Militia; but first they had three days freedom given them to rest and take their ease: After which they were obliged to gather together every day without fail on a place appointed for them to exercise, until they were well vers'd in it, and made thorow-pac'd Soldiers of, and fit to be sent on any Expedition to any part of the Indies.

For my part, I went to Shore several times, and diverted my self very well, until I received an Order from the Surgeon general to take my Post in a small Fort, about a Mile or somewhat less, from *Batavia*; where I found an Ensign, two Serjeants, two Gunners to eight Pieces of Cannon, and sixty private Soldiers. I was mightly well pleased with my Station here; the Place being very finely and advantageously situated, with the Sea on the one side, and a very pleasant River on the other, which came down from *Batavia*, upon which there were continually a great number of *Prawen* sailing to and fro with Chineses, going to a certain place, about half a Mile from thence, where their *Mosque* is, wherein they sacrifice at several times in the year to their Idol, called by them *Jasgin*, and by the Dutch *Josie*; and there they perform all their Religious Ceremonies, which are very diverting to a stranger to see.

As for *Batavia*, the City and Castle are as well worth a description, as they are a Man's sight: And truly mine was ravisht with it; for I must confess, that I think them yet finer even than *Amsterdam* itself. It is five or six Miles in compass. The River *Jacatra* runs thro' most Streets of the Town, and almost encompasses it. Upon these Canals the Inhabitants have the conveniency of going in

[1] Apparently a mistake for Cornelis Spielman, Governor-General 1681–84.

Boats to their Gardens and Pleasure-houses : The sides of them is wall'd up with good square Stone, and all along each side of it, there goes a Row or two of fine Cedar, Coco, or Figg-trees, where the Free-men use to walk at night under a most pleasant Shade.

The Castle stands toward the Sea. It hath four Bastions; two of them to the Sea, called the *Ruby* and the *Pearl*, the other two to the City, which go by the name of the *Saphir* and the *Diamon*.

It is in the whole exact square, and from top to bottom built up with excellent good square Stone. On each of these Bastions are sixteen half-Culverins [1] planted : Besides this, they are full of fine Trees, such as Lemons, and Mango's, which makes them look most sweetly. While I was there, there was a third Gate built to the Castle, which before had but two. One of the Gates looks toward the Sea, thro' which the Goods come in from the Ships into the Warehouses, and it's call'd the Water-Gate. The other goeth into the City, which therefore they call the City-Gate.

In the middle of the Castle is the Generals Apartment, and over against it are the Houses of two of the Council-men. The rest, (which are four more) live in the City.

The Government of the *Indies* lies upon these six Men. The General's Retinue is not very sumptuous : He had but twelve Halbardiers, drest much after the manner of our Yeoman of the Guard, but in Red and Yellow. One of these is always to stand Centinel an hour before his Chamber. When he rid out, he was attended by a Troop of Cuirassiers, and a company of Foot-men, and six Halbardiers. But all this is nothing to his Revenue, which exceeds that of several Princes of Europe.

There are in the Castle many other Inhabitants, some of the chief Merchants ; some Assistants, and Book-keepers ; also several Handycraftsmen, as Gun-Smiths, Lock-Smiths, Joyners, and such like, that are to be employed in any Military business. The Soldiers have their standings under the Gates, and on the Bastions : Sometimes more, sometimes less, as they have occasion to send them abroad, or call them home again. Every day about four in the afternoon, they must come to the Parade, and pass by the General's house three times ; sometimes he comes out, and takes a view of them, to observe their carriage, and behaviour, and to see whether their Arms are kept in good order.

[1] The demi-culverin was a long nine-pounder.

When any one neglects the Parade, he must expect to be severely punished; for the Military Discipline is most strictly kept up there. If any one should chance to sleep upon Centry; for the first time, his punishment is to be loaden with heavy Arms, for some days; the second time he is whipt; and the third time it is death, without remission.

The Castle is encompassed with very wide Grafts or Canals; over one of which there is a fine Stone-Bridge of one and twenty Arches, that goes into a large Field, which is called the *Galgveld*, that is, the *Gibbet-field*; where Malefactors are executed. There is a Gibbet, a Wheel, and a Whipping Post; all of which are frequently made use of. Cross this Field is another smaller Bridge, (where a Centry always stands) which leads to the chief Street of the City, which is called the *Heere-straet.*

Within the City are Shops for all Kinds of Merchandize, and very good and reasonable Victualling-houses: The Inhabitants are of all Nations, as Amboineses, Malabarians, Mardigarians, &c. but the Chineses, being the chief and greater part, I shall pass by the others, and give you some account of them only.

They exceed all the others by far, in cunning and policy; and are very good Mechanicks; and there are of them of all Trades, excepting Clock-work, or Watch-work, and they dive into all manner of Commerce whatever.

They wear most commonly White or Blew. Their Coats are very large, and the Sleeves so long, and wide that they fall over their hands. Their Breeches likewise of the same colour, are very wide, and come down to their feet. They wear a sort of broad Slippers, like Hungarian Shoes: But they are only made of Past-board; so that when they are to go thro' any wet or dirt, they take their Slippers in their hands; then wash their feet at the next Canal, and wipe 'em; so put their Slippers on again: But in bad Weather, if they are to go thro' a great deal of dirt, they wear woodden Shoes, such as the Country People do in *France.*

They are very neat in their Hair, which they have trimm'd, and comb'd every week by their Barbers; they do 'em up with a Bodkin, and stick a small Tortoiseshell Comb in it behind, and so put a Coif over it, made of Horse-Hair, like a Net; so that at the first, a stranger would take their Men for Women.

Their Hair they value at the highest rate, since it is the last thing they will stake at play. They are the greatest

Gamesters that ever were known; insomuch that they'll play away their Wives and Children, when they have lost all their Wealth: And when their Houses and Family are gone, then goes the very Hair off of their heads: But if one loses that, he loses with it all his Credit and Reputation, and is lookt upon as a Slave, and is forced all his life long to work and sell for other People. Their Beards are very extraordinary, both for their length, and thinness. I have seen them with only five or six Hairs on their chin, and those hang down to their feet.

Their Women are most of them Slaves, bought out of the Island *Baly* and *Macassar*; not very black, but of a deep tawny; short and very well sett. They may have as many of them as they are able to keep. When a Chinese dies, his Heir sells all his Wives away again; except that one that he loved best, who is by his Will made free. This makes them Gentlewomen, and their Heirs are esteemed as the right Chineses; and they are but rare in the Country; for while I was there, there was not above twenty of them. They have none but Sons, almost; it is rare to see a Daughter in a Family. I was very curious to know whence that might proceed: But in vain did I imagine many things, to be the natural causes of it. But Being intimate with one of them, the cruel and barbarous method they take was made plain to me, which is, that they destroy their Females; and to this purpose, as soon as their Big Bellies begin to be perceived, they keep within doors, so that none knows of their being delivered, unless they bring forth a Male. At the same time this discovery was made to me, I was entrusted with the life of the discoverer, and therefore I was made to promise all the secrecy imaginable. Every morning their custom is, to wash their Children in the River.

Their Weddings are kept openly. The Men and Women go in Procession, and the Relations among them carry all their Presents to the Young Couple, and all their Riches openly before them. Before the doors, where they are to have their Entertainment, is a fine Scaffold made up, where their Musick stands, which consists of several Instruments peculiar to the Country; as the *Gungumma*, which is a kind of Drum, and a sort of Musick they make with little Bells, which is agreeable enough. All the way they go, as also the house they are to come into, are strowed with all sorts of Greens and Flowers: Or sometimes they go by Water in their *Prawen,* on the Canals that run thro' the City, with their Hair down about their Ears, or hanging down in the Water. When they are come home, the first thing they do, is to sacrifice to their Idol; which is done after this manner. In a corner of the Room they have an Altar set out with abundance of pretty little Trinkets, upon which is an Image made of Clay, about a span long. The face of it is very broad, with a large pair of Eyes; it is black, and painted with some round streeks of Red; a vast large Nose, and a long white Beard: On the head stand two Horns painted with all sorts of Colours. This Image they call Josgin; to this they bow, and make many salutations; clapping their hands altogether, begging it to keep them from all harms, and to take care that no evil may happen to them.

They own that there is a powerful God, that hath made the Heavens and the Earth: But they say, that he is of a good nature and disposition, and that there is no fear of harm from him: But that all their fear is from the Devil, whom they appease by their Offerings and Prayers under the shape of that Image: Therefore they are very careful to please him, and will not fail at night to light Candles made of red or yellow Wax, which they set before it: And there they bring Meat and Drink, and all sorts of Fruit, which is all taken away the next day, and then it is eaten by the People of the house, and other fresh Meat is set in the room of it.

But to return to their Feasts; the Men and the Women eat always apart. They take up their Meat with an Instrument made of two pieces of Wood, which go cross one another, something like that which the Gold-beaters use with us to take up their Leaves of Gold or Silver, which they use very dextrously to take up their Meat with: This serves them instead of Forks, and they keep them very neat and clean. They sit on the ground cross-legg'd: And if at any time they do sit on a Chair or Stool, they still sit down with their Leggs cross-wise under them, and by that means they have them so pliant, that they can lay them on their Polls, with as great nimbleness and ease as we can our hands.

But now to make an end of the Description of the City of *Batavia.* That is likewise encompass'd with a strong Wall, above forty paces broad, and Earth thrown up against it.

The Bastions are like those of the *Sluys,* built with large cut Stone, and all square and well provided with Guard-houses on all sides of it, where the Soldiers have their Quarters, and none of them dares to be absent one night from them, without especial leave, and that is but very seldom granted. Besides this, there are Canals on each side the Wall all round. The Cannon is always ready to turn, as well upon the City it self, as upon an Enemy without, in case of any Insurrection or Disturbance amongst the Inhabitants, which are of all Nations. So that to be the better prepared, if such a thing should happen, every Street hath a Bastion that commands it, from whence they could immediately cut off any Party that should be made in any part of the Town against the Castle.

The same care hath been taken, and the like provision made in all places in the *Indies* that are in possession of the Dutch, and they are always well provided with Europeans, Christians, in the Service of the Company; and there is of course a considerable number of such as are settled there, and are married, some to European, and some to Indian Women. And of what Nations soever they be, they are permitted to keep the same Religion, Manners and Customs, as they have in their own Country.

The Magistrate consists of persons that are in the Service of the Company, and of Burghers, which are Free-men; made such after they have spent that time in the Company's Service, as was agreed upon betwixt them. The President is one of the Council, but cannot direct in any thing of moment without the consent of the General.

Each of the other Nations have also a head and chief of their own: But when there is any thing in hand that concerns the Publick; or if they cannot agree among themselves, they are forced to appear before the Magistrate of the City. And in all things their Government is very well and prudently established.

The four chief Gates of the City are called by the names of the *Utrecht*, the *Delft*, the *Rotterdam*, and the *New-Gate*, so called, on the out-sides of which, are the Suburbs, which are large and spacious, and very fine, and inhabited most by Chineses: A vast number of which have been forced by the Wars they had with the Tartars to retire, and seek a Refuge in the *Indies*, over which they have spread themselves: And especially in all Maritime Towns, where they are fallen into Trades and Commerce with admirable industry and success.

The River *Jacatra* is no small Ornament as well as Advantage to *Batavia*; besides which, it is beautified with abundance of very fine Orchards, Fruit-gardens, and Pleasure houses, which are very neatly contrived and kept. There is but very little Rice all about it; tho' it is their staff of life. And, as in all the other parts of the *Indies*, the only thing that serves instead of Bread; but yet there is never any want of it, it being always brought in great quantities, and the City sufficiently furnished with it from *Bantam, Japara* &c.

The Rivers thereabouts are much pestered with Crocodiles. While I was there, as we used to go a walking in the Evenings, we observed one of them for several nights that used to run out of the hedge into the River, as soon as it spied or heard us coming towards him: Upon which a desire took us to try to catch him if we could; which we did in this manner.

We took a long Rope, to which we fastened a strong double Hook, full of beards: And instead of arming it with Wires, we did it with Pack-thread; which being loose about it, gets in between its Teeth, and hinders him from snapping the Hook off: This done, we tyed a Dog to this, with the Hook under his belly: And setting him upon a Board, thrust him out into the River, and fasten'd the Cord to a Tree: Quickly after, the Dog fell a barking and howling, and the Crocodile did not fail to come to him, and very greedily swallowed him in: Upon which the Hook struck into his Throat, and had him fast. We had so good success with this, that we afterwards caught a great many of them. The biggest we caught was twenty-seven foot long; and when we opened it, we found two *Steen-Bockiens*,[1] and a head of a black Boy in his belly. We were forced to knock him him on the head with great Iron Bars, after we had fired several Muskets upon him to little purpose. When the Soldiers kill one of these Creatures, they get some Blacks to carry it for 'em to the General: who immediately gives them six Ducatoons, for their pains. The only advantage I sought for, was to have some of their Fat, it being very good for several operations in Physick and Surgery.

The Inhabitants use to catch them with Nets; which is very dangerous, as I my self have seen; at *Bantam*, on such an occasion, a Crocodile bit off both leggs of a Javan; yet do they continue that way still, and go often to catch them in that manner.

[1] The Steenbok is a wild goat.

A MERCHANT OF JAVA
(*From J. Nieuhof's "Voyage to the East Indies"*)

Besides these Crocodiles, there are abundance of other sorts of Wild Beasts in the said Island of *Japatra*.

The Fort where I was order'd to be at my first coming, was very near to the Forest, and just in the way to it, from *Batavia* ; so that the Huntsmen coming by us, I often went out with them and saw them catch most sorts of those Wild Creatures that the Country affords. It will not be amiss to give the Reader an account of some of 'em ; and first of a sad accident that befell the Hunts-men one day.

We had two Hunts-men that were made free by the General, and had the liberty to go abroad for that purpose, to catch what they could. These being gone one day to get some game for the General ; which was commonly Wild Pigeons, and other sorts of Wild Fowl, and Wild Boars, and a sort of Creature they call *Steen-Bockiens*, which is made much like a Hare, and differs only in that it hath small Horns, and the Meat of 'em is far more delicate ; while they were only prepared for the pursuit of things of this kind, and sat down to rest under a Tree, a Tyger fell in a most furious manner upon them. They were pretty much used to be followed by them ; but they used to be in such readiness to receive them, that they were the death of them whenever they did but offer to come near them.

But being now surprized by this more than ordinary fierce Creature, coming of a sudden upon them : It was as much as the one could do to lay hold of his Fowling-piece, while the other had nothing to defend himself with, but his lighted Match in his hand ; which he shook about, but to no purpose. The other had no sooner got his Gun, but in a hurry he fires upon him ; but not taking good aim, did not do any execution, but what served to enrage him the more ; him the Tyger throws down under him ; and seizing the other by the hand, bit off three of his Fingers ; notwithstanding which, he luckily seizing his Gun, fired it, and by good providence laid the Tyger flat on the ground. Upon this he bethought himself of what he might do for his best security, for the night coming upon him, the danger increased ; besides that he was now alone, for his Companion was by this time expired, being miserably torn. He took up the Corps, lest it should become a prey to the rest of them ; and climbing into a Tree, drew him up with him : There he remained in great fear and excessive pain caused by his wound. When he had been there a while, there came a couple of Wild Boars, which he could not see : But he heard them scratch and tear at the bottom of the Tree, which they did the more furiously, because the blood of his dead Companion was spilt about the place ; so he shot upon them at random, and hit one of them, so that he fell dead some few paces from thence.

The day being come, and the Coast clear, he gets down, and leaving his dead Companion upon the Tree, the Tyger and the Wild Boar on the ground, comes forthwith to our Fort to me, to have his hand drest : Which being done, he gave us the account of this Adventure. Our Ensign went to acquaint the Major General with it, upon which Orders were given immediately to a Serjeant, to go with six Soldiers, and six *Negro* Slaves, with a Bier to the place where this Slaughter was, and the wounded Hunts-man went with 'em, to shew them the place. There they found all according to the Information he had given. The Man was brought to *Batavia*, and decently buried in the *Malaish* Church-Yard ; and he that was come off, had for a Reward twelve Gilders given him, and a settled Table for his life, besides his former Pay, and withal a Corporal's place.

On the other side of the Fort, is almost all Woods, which are cut down every other Year by the Soldiers. These Woods harbour vast numbers of Monkeys, which make there such a strange noise, that one would be amazed to hear it. We made it almost our daily diversion to go a Hunting after them ; and we used to catch such abundance of them, that a Man might have one of them for a Pipe of Tobacco. They are a very docile sort of Monkeys, and not in the least inferiour to those that are brought out of Africa and America for playing of Tricks ; but they come but seldom over hither, being very tender, and not able to bear the change of Climates, nor the hard-ship of so long a Voyage : For at my return I took a couple of them with me, but as soon as ever we came on this side of the Tropick, where we begun to feel a change of Air, they were seized with the Bloody-Flux, fell lame, and died.

One way to catch them was, by taking of Coco-Nuts, which are very plentiful there ; and making a small hole in 'em, just big enough for 'em to force their Paws into ; we hung them up all about the Trees where they came. As soon as they espyed the hole, they wanting to get at the Kernel, would strive hard but they would get their Paws in : And when they go to take them out again, they have not the sense to squeeze their Claws together to slip their Paws out, as they had to get them in : Besides that, the surprize which the person causes, who watches them, makes them less able to rid themselves of their Manacles; and as they went to run down, they fall with the very weight of the Nut, which is or may be five or six pound weight. But this way there was no hopes of catching any more than one at one time; for when the others see one of their company thus caught by the Legg, they won't come near the Coco-Nuts all that day.

I went out once for a fancy after them with a Fowling-piece, but I found it impracticable; for after I had spied one of them, and got my Shoes and Stockings off, because the place was a kind of Moorish ground; but he had his Eye upon me too, and led me such a dance, that I had almost stuck in the Slouth, for want of minding my way: And since that time, I never went after them again for they are so shy, that it is almost always labour lost. And if one doth happen to shoot one of them, if he doth not kill him dead upon the spot, they'll run and stop up their wounds with grass, and so get far enough from you, tho' they drop in the long run, and go and die in some hole where you cannot get at 'em.

My chief Recreation was to take a walk to the City, which was a most delicious walk indeed, all along shaded with fine large Coco-trees. Sometimes I took a Boat, and went to the Fort *Jacatra*; where lay a whole Company of Soldiers, of the number of which our Men was a sort of Detachment: It lies about two Miles more to the South, and is the chief Pass into the whole Country of *Java*, in the direct way to *Japara* and *Kartiri*. Near this Fort flows the famous River *Jacatra* (from which the Fort had its name) which thence running thro' *Batavia*, empties it self in to the Sea about half a Mile below it. There are by the Fort three Powder Mills upon that River, which I used to walk to frequently, being very well worth ones sight for their largeness and ingenious contrivance.

The outward parts of this Country, and that for a considerable way within too, are very well cultivated, and richly set out with abundance of fine noble Gardens, which produce all manner of fruits, for refreshment and for sustenance. There are of all sorts of Figg-Trees; some of which are the most delicious fruit that ever was tasted: So that with its lofty Cedars, which over-top the fruit-bearing Trees, and look so sweet and green, and what with their more useful Coco-Trees, and other fruit-trees, which are always verdant, and afford a cool retreat, and pleasant shade; besides that their fruits are all of them most delicious, I think truly, it may be called an Earthly Paradice, and that no Country in the World can outdo it for gratifying the Eye and taste.

But of all the fruits that the *East-Indies* produce (now I am about 'em) I think it will not be amiss to give you a description of three of the chiefest of them.

That which deserves the first place amongst them, is the fruit which they call the *Manges Tanges*; of the bigness of a common Apple; the shell is of a dark brown colour, in which are contained four Kernels, of a flesh colour, sticking to each other, which melt like butter upon the tongue, and of so fine and refreshing a taste, that I never met with any fruit comparable to it, in any other part of the World. It is generally served up at the greatest Tables, as the most delicious Dish that can be made; drest with Sugar, Spice and put into fine China Dishes. It is also a most pleasant and infallible Remedy against the Bloody-Flux, when boiled in Water. The Tree that bears this, is about the bigness of a Mulberry-Tree, and very slow of propagation: For when you have planted it, you must never expect to see it bear; and if it doth chance to bear any fruit within the life of him that planted it, it comes to nothing; but withers away: But then there shoots out a little shoot, which you take and plant very carefully, and that becomes your Stock.

The next to this is the Coco-Nut. The Tree is all smooth and even from the bottom to the very top; where the Leaves spread themselves all in a fuff,[1] and the Nutts under them, twenty or thirty on a Tree. The Country people have a pretty Art of Tapping these Trees, with long *Bamboe* Canes, that will hold two or three quarts, or more which they very artfully stick into the Tree, and let them fill themselves with the Juice: When they are fill'd, they put it into the Vessels to keep, or else they go away with it to *Batavia*, and sell it fresh there, as it comes from the Tree. Thus they call *Suri* which is to be sold at the *Suri*-houses, and is a very pretty refreshing Liquor, and extream pleasant; especially when the Weather is hot: With this Liquor they make the best Vinegar, and *Arack* or Brandy, which goes far beyond our best Rhenish Wine for strength, taste and colour: And mixing it with Water and Wine, with Sugar and Lemon-

[1] Fuff means a puff of wind. The *N.E.D.* gives also, " ? a soft feathery mass, cf. fluff," citing this passage in support; but Frick may mean that the leaves look as if blown out by a puff of wind.

juice, it makes an excellent sort of Lemonade, which they call Massack and Burabols, but sufficiently known in England by the name of Punch.

The Leaves of this Tree serve the Inhabitants for a common covering for their Houses, and keep them as dry as our Tiles. The stalks of them they bind together, to make Brooms ; and they use hardly any thing else throughout all *India*. The outward Coat of the Nutt is good to make Match, which burns better than that we use in Europe. The Sap serves for Oyl to burn. The Kernel being prest, yields a Milk, of which they make a very pretty kind of Cheeses ; and it is good for several other uses, as our Milk is. The Shell is good to make Cups, Spoons, &c. It would be too tedious to relate the many uses every part of this Tree is good for : Besides that, it hath in a great measure been done already by other hand.

The third fruit I was to mention, is the Bissang-Figgs, which is mighty common amongst them ; and so cheap, that when a Ship comes out of Europe, it is the first fruit that it brought to 'em, and you buy it for a trifle ; notwithstanding it is excellent ; it is in shape pretty much like our Pine-Apples. The Tree is somewhat like our Elder-Tree ; and bears all the year in abundance. The Leaves are so large, that one of them will shelter a Man from the Sun and Rain, being about two Cubits in length, and one or more in breadth : Which makes some people apt to believe they were the Leaves which *Adam* and *Eve* made their Aprons of, after the Fall. They are likewise made use of instead of Paper to pack up goods.

These I have only taken notice of, as being the most considerable fruits of the *Indies*, and must pass by several others, which might be worth a description, both for their excellency and variety, that I may not be too tedious.

CHAPTER IV

The Author is removed from the Fort to the Hospital of Batavia. The Hollanders War with Bantam. An account of that Country, which hath been very mischievous to the East-India Company, occasioned by the English and Danes, who made it their business to incense the King of that Country against the Dutch. Bantam heretofore under the Government of the King of Japara. The Dutch spoil Jacatra and Japara, and wanted an opportunity to do the like to Bantam, which offered itself by a falling out between the old King and the young one, which broke out into a bloody War. The Son sends to the Dutch for help. An exact account of that Expedition from the beginning of it to the end of it, which proves very advantageous to the Dutch.

HAVING been now four months in this little Fort, an Order came to me to remove from this place, to take the care of the Men that lay sick in the City, and the Hospital, which was very welcome to me; not but that the Post I was in was profitable enough, and very genteel, and the place extraordinary pleasantly situated: But it being a token of the respect the East-India Company had for me, and withal more advantageous, I accepted of the invitation with much satisfaction.

About a fortnight after there came a general Order for all that were in the Company's Service, to make their *Rendezvous* in the Execution-field; so that you might see there all their Forces drawn up together; excepting those only, that were absolutely necessary to stand Centinels at the Gates and Redoubts. And indeed a finer sight of that kind could no where be seen; for there were some thousands of Europeans, which were all very lusty, tall, proper, well-chosen Men; and almost as many of other different Nations; as *Amboineeses, Malabars, Malayers, Mardikers* and *Balingers.* These were all mixt into several Companies, which had their own respective Officers; and after they had all pass'd

Muster, they took the Oath of Fidelity in the presence of the General, and the Council. After which the General made a very Eloquent Speech to 'em, in order to encourage them valiantly to prepare themselves for the Action which was then in hand ; and to make his Speech more truly Rhetorical and perswading, he gave to every Man a month's pay *gratis*. Then one half of these Men were order'd to march toward *Bantam*, and to *Dangerang*, which is a Pass to it, which they found very well fortified. The other half march'd thro' the Castle to the Water-Gate, whence they were carried off in little Praw's, or small Boats, on Board the Men-of-War that lay in the Road, about half a League from thence, and so they were immediately embarkt. And the Wind blowing then just full East, as fair as they could have wish'd, they straight weighed Anchor, and steered directly to the Royal City of *Bantam*. But it will be proper to give you some account of that place, before I go any further, and to acquaint you with the causes and motives of this Undertaking.

First, Then you must know, that this large Kingdom of *Bantam*, being in it self of great strength, hath of late much improved it self, by the number of Foreigners that are come thither from all Nations ; and among them considerable numbers too of English, Danes, Spaniards, Portuguese and Dutch, which hath made it a very troublesome and dangerous Neighbour to the Dutch *East-India* Company ; insomuch that their Ships that came from *Europe*, or any other places thither, did not dare to come by the Road of *Bantam* ; but were forced to take a vast compass of three or four hundred Miles ; keeping to the Northward.

Moreover, the King of *Bantam* had made several Attempts upon *Batavia*, both by Sea and Land. Tho' he was always forced to retire with great loss, and without doing us any great damage. But tho' he could not accomplish his desire, and the Company could not fear a total overthrow ; yet they were still apprehensive, that he being so much more powerful than they were, would prove very fatal to them in the end, and by little and little bring his designs to perfection. Thus they were always very uneasie, by reason of their troublesome Neighbour : But not finding themselves able to declare open War against him, they endeavoured to gain him by Presents, and a specious shew of Friendship. These means did not prove altogether unsuccessful, but they were never at good understanding with each other long together. For the King of *Bantam*, besides that he was very fickle and unconstant in his Nature, having so many Foreigners about him, who were no Friends to the Dutch interest, he was easily perswaded by them, to break Friendship with the Dutch upon the least occasion. And this the English and Danes were the chief Instruments of, who made there a considerable Body, were rich, and enjoyed great freedom, and a most flourishing Trade; so that they with ease set the King upon us, in hopes of rooting the Dutch out of their holds.

The Dutch therefore were always forced to be upon their Guard; even while there was the greatest appearance of a settled Friendship; for they were sufficiently informed, that he was always contriving how he might at once fall foul of them, and drive them out of *Batavia*: Upon which, they on the other side, resolved to countermine his designs, and thought it the best Expedient to divert him from that Undertaking, by finding him some Employment with some other Neighbours; and accordingly made it their business to create an ill understanding betwixt him and the King of *Japara*, hoping that the silent Fire might in time break out in to an open Flame. This they effected at length; but it proved little or no advantage to them; for they lay so far asunder, that it never came but to a few little Skirmishes; which did not damage him much, nor profit them: So that they fell very short of what they had promised themselves; for they were fully persuaded that the Emperour of *Japara* would have soon been induced to pursue the King of *Bantam*, with the utmost vigour; especially, when there was so great a motive to spur him on, as the rejoyning of that Kingdom to his Empire, from which it had been divided. The Island of Great *Java*, of which I have already made mention, did likewise belong to him once, and altogether made but one Empire, under the Dominion of Great *Mataran*, but now it is divided into three Kingdoms, to wit *Japara*, *Bantam* and *Jacatra*, or *Kartiri*; of which *Jacatra*, the present *Batavia*, is a part, and did heretofore belong to the King of *Jacatra*; from whom the Portugueezes took it. After that, the *Spaniards* got it from them: And lastly, the *Dutch* from the *Spaniards*.

Now the *Dutch* having all this while made several Attempts upon the King of *Jacatra*, which have proved very advantageous to them; they at length subdued him: Having first made the Emperour of *Japara* unable to resist them, or to stand up in the defence of his Neighbour; over whom they carried a total Victory a little before I came to *Batavia*. And having all this while received fresh supplies yearly from

Holland, which, together with *Germany*, enjoyed a profound Peace, and therefore could, and did constantly furnish them with large Recruits of choice good Soldiers : The *Dutch East-India* Company thought they might be able to cope with *Bantam*, and accordingly made preparations against it.

Now while these things were in agitation, and they big with the design and hopes of infallible success, the fairest opportunity that could be wish'd for, offered it self to them unexpected, and therefore so much the more welcome, which was a sudden falling out between the old, and the two young Kings of *Bantam*. The occasion whereof was this : The old King being weary with the Burden of the Government, and desirous to spend his remaining days in ease and tranquility, made over his Kingdom to his younger Son ; the eldest having dedicated himself to a spiritual life, was a *Bangerang Babay*, something like an archbishop with us ; and having thus invested his younger Son with the Regal Power, he retired to an Old Castle called *Dortjasse*, the old place of his residence, about four Miles from *Bantam*.

The young King having Reigned some years, his People began to grow weary of him, specially the Nobles, the *Bourgerang* and *Kirria* ; and they made their Complaints to the old King that he oppressed his Subjects ; and that he over-burden'd them with his Recreations, and his constant Hunting ; and by his requiring so much Attendance and Service to be done him ; so that they were no longer able to bear the Yoke. He did not Govern as other Heathen Kings use for the most part to do, but after the Model he had taken from the European Countries ; some of which he had been in, as *Constantinople*, would have gone to *France, England, Spain* and *Portugal*, if his Law had permitted him ; and as far as that had given him leave he had Travelled, viz. in *Muscovy, Schiras, Ispahan, Japan, Siam* ; from which several places he had taken those methods of Government, which he thought most convenient to introduce into his own Dominions. But his Subjects being dissatisfied with these Innovations, conspired at last together, and Deposed him ; and set his Brother the *Bangarang Babay* in his stead.

Upon this the Old King came with a considerable Retinue, and his Main Guard, before the Castle ; which is in the middle of *Bantam*. The young King, having notice of this, commanded the Gates to be shut against him, and sent to know what he wanted. The old King sent him an Answer, which did not please him : Upon which, without more ado, he gives Orders to Fire the Great Guns from the Castle upon the City, and particularly that some of them should play upon his Fathers Quarters; against which sixteen Pieces of Demi-Cannon were planted, which were fired briskly upon him by his positive Orders, and some of them too by his own hand.

Being this satisfied, that his Fathers Intentions were to Depose him, he wholly forgot all Duty, and sent him word by one of his Concubines, that he did not reckon himself now bound to him in any Bond of Duty; and that he would pay him no other Homage but Powder and Ball, which he would not spare, for he had enough of it, and that should be at his service. Besides the Message that had made him so desperate, he relied much upon the strength of the Castle, which was very well fortified with very good Walls, lined with Earth, like those of *Batavia*, and very strong Bastions upon them, besides very large Canals round them, with Draw-Bridges. Neither did he want Provisions or Ammunitions; and the Bastions were provided with very good heavy Cannon. But the number of his Men was not above three hundred; yet with them he had resolved to stand it out to the last. So that his Garrison was not so considerable as his Court, which, as it chiefly consists of Women, according to the general Custom of Heathen Princes; so he had of them no less than one thousand two hundred that were his Concubines.

With this continual Firing, the City was miserably shatter'd, and lookt like a Wilderness; for every Man had got away that could, and all the English and Danes, together with the Nobility, and the most considerable Inhabitants, went over to the old King. And having formed a considerable Body, they went and beseiged the Castle, raised several Batteries, and plants their best Cannon upon them; and then fired briskly in their turn upon the Castle. Notwithstanding all these preparations, the young King remained undaunted, and only applied himself to get supplies and support abroad; and by Advice of two Dutchmen, who were of his Party, and who had formerly run away from *Batavia*, to shelter themselves from Justice, he resolved to send to the Company of Batavia, for Assistance. One of these Dutchmen was appointed for the Negotiation; and immediately was let down from the Wall of the Castle; and having pass'd the Canals in a little Boat, that used to lye there, he came to the Enemies Army, thro' which he was unavoidably to pass; but he being very ready in the *Javan* and *Malleish* Languages, having been fifteen years in those Countries, and having been Circumcised at his Abjuration of the Christian Religion, he easily pass'd thro' all difficulties, and came to the General at *Batavia*; and by word of mouth, without any further Credentials, delivered his Message to him in the young King's name.

This was an opportunity which the Dutch had long wish'd for; so that the Messenger needed no great Rhetorick or Art to induce them to take it by the forelock. But immediately orders were dispatched; and the Forces had their Rendezvous appointed. I my self had Orders to attend the Major General *St. Martini's* own person; and was in the whole Expedition, so that I may justly speak of the matter, and be the more particular in the relation of it.

The Major General above mentioned, commanded the whole Fleet; and one Captain *Harzing* of *Cassel* had the whole command of the Land-Forces. Both set out at one time, as I said before; the one march'd out straight upon *Dangerang*. The Fleet went directly to *Bantam*. Captain *Hartzing* was forced first to Attack *Dangerang*; by which means he reckon'd he should have drawn off the old King and his Army from *Bantam*; but found himself very much mistaken: For the place made such a vigorous Resistance that it appeared they neither wanted necessary Assistance, nor Courage. We lost there a great many of our best Men, insomuch that we found our selves forced to Intrench, lest they should have routed us quite; so we made our Lines of Approach, which we fortified with as good Pallisado's as we could, and so secured our selves, that the enemy could not come at us.

In the mean while we continued our Approaches with all the diligence that might be, till we came within Musket-shot of the Fort. There we made use of a cover'd way, with which we came up close to the Enemies works, and in some measure within them. And having finished our Mines, we set them on fire, with a resolution that as soon as they should blow up to any purpose, we would assault them. One of our Mines made a breach that three or four Waggons might stand abreast in. Upon which it was order'd we should immediately enter: And so we did, but with so much ado, that we had reason to fear we must have retired; but after a little resistance, they seeing us pour in so thick upon them, took their heels, and most of them threw down their Arms,

All this while we pursued them, and made the most heavy slaughter amongst them that ever any History can shew. For, the Gates of their Castle, or rather their Doors being so little that no one could not go under them without stooping, they were all forced, almost, to creep thro' them one by one; and as they were all in a cluster, and unarm'd, to the number of near five thousand, we fired continually upon them, so that they lay like heaps of Stones one on another, which made the most dismal sight in the World. And to prevent the Air being infested with them, we made our Blacks to carry them off, and throw them into the River *Dangerang*.

Having gotten this Post, we fortified our selves in the best manner we could; for we were sure that we should not enjoy our rest there long; and that we were to be upon our Guard.

In this six weeks time that we had beseiged this place, we had lost a great many Men, and a great many were fallen sick by reason of the bad Water, which had much of the taste of *Salt-peter* in it; which made Captain *Hartzing* at a stand, whether we should go on or not. At last he thought it best for us to stay there, till we could hear of the safe Arrival and Landing of our Fleet before *Bantam*, which we did in a few days after.

Major General *St. Martini* being come before *Bantam* with twenty stout Men-of-War, each of which carried between four and five hundred Men, besides a hundred Fire-ships, Tenders, &c. gave Orders for their Landing about two a Clock the next Morning: But first he took a general Review of the Men, and a Gill of Brandy was given to every one of the Soldiers; and after that six and thirty of the lustiest Soldiers were provided with a good quantity of Powder; and some hundreds of Sea-men were set out with Pole-Axes, or Hatchets, and eight or nine Hand-Granado's to each Man; all which were to Land with the Army.

We lay within Cannon-shot of the Town, and we could both hear, and see, the old King, who kept continually firing upon the Castle, and he had raised his Batteries above the tops of the houses that were in the City, so that the Enemy might see us with ease; so they immediately prepared to prevent our Landing, and for that purpose order'd the Main Body to march to the Sea-shore; and there raised Batteries to hinder our coming any nearer. In the mean while it was not a little satisfaction to the young King, to see our Fleet so near at hand, as well as to hear of our Forces by Land.

And besides, it gave him some time to take breath, and freed him from the danger he was in continually of a Storm, for the Walls being almost all down. But now the Enemy could not go on with that Design, having enough to do to look after us. They took most care of a certain place, where they thought we designed to Land, as indeed we did : But in the night time we weighed Anchor, with all the stillness that might be, and saild on about a League higher ; and drawing as near to the Shore as we could possibly, we let fall our Anchors again. Our Cannon on Board was all loaden, and all things were order'd to, so where-ever we Landed, we might fire them upon the Enemy, and upon the City. The Tenders, and other small vessels were all Mann'd immediately for Landing ; some with a hundred Men, some more, some less ; all which went with all speed to Shore. The Enemy having notice of this, were ready as soon as we, but had not time to raise any Batteries there against us, or to fortifie themselves ; for ere the day begun to peep, we had got all things ready for our landing.

Major-General *St. Martini*, with his Life-guard, which consisted of sixty Men, and the Surgeons, came into my *Schappon*, and stood ready to give Order for the Signal, by Drums and Trumpets, for the whole Body of our Army to Land all together : But the Enemy made a very vigorous Defence ; and being advantageously Posted in a Wood that was there, they charged us after so terrible a manner, that what with their Fire, and what with our Great Guns, that played all this while cross-wise upon the City, there was need of more than ordinary Courage to stand it out ; Besides that, we all this while being still up to the knees in Water, had a very great disadvantage.

In this condition we Charged them for three hours, and could not come to Land all that while ; at last five of our Companies were quite routed, and of the twelve Surgeons that we brought with us, there were but five left ; and we that did remain were not able to do any great feats, by reason that we all this while stood in the Water. When we saw that we could not get any ground, we got some small Vessels, which fetch'd us some *Haubitzes* [1] (which is a kind of Field-Piece to load with small Shot), with which we rattled so

[1] This is the German *Haubitz*, a Howitzer, or short gun throwing a heavy projectile at low velocity, used for high angle fire. They used to fire hail-shot to get the effect of modern shrapnel.

upon the Javians that we obliged them to give ground enough for us to get on upon dry Land ; and at last we forced them to quit the Wood, and to retire to their Breast-works ; so we remained Masters of the Field that night : And the next morning at break of day, we marched to Attack them in their Intrenchments.

The Major General, considering that the Dutch Companies were mightily weakened, commanded Captain *Jochem*, who led the Blacks, to march in the Front ; and he fell upon them straightway with admirable Courage and Conduct. The Major General behaved himself like a true Soldier, and gave such tokens of his Invincible Valour, Wise Conduct, and Indefatigable Diligence, as cannot be well described. And tho' he had the mis-fortune to have two of his fingers shot off from his right hand, as he was Riding to and fro to give Orders, he could hardly afford himself time to have his hand drest ; and I had no sooner done, but he straight mounted again.

The best of this Engagement was, that most of the Enemies Bullets flew over our heads. But I found that they did not all of them take the same course, and was a little surprized, when talking with the Sergeant of our Company, and jeering them for not being good Marks-men, a Bullet came and laid him dead at my foot.

In the mean while our Men made but little on't : And the Captain was not able to do any thing more than just to keep his ground against the Enemy. Wherefore the Major General having given some new Orders, and briskly encouraged the Soldiers, by telling them, that the beating the Enemy out of that place would be the chief part of their work, and the sure fore-runner of a total Victory, promising to the three first that should break into the Enemies Camp, an hundred Gilders, two Slaves, and a Pipe of Sack for a Reward ; and having by such like Speeches and Promises, infused, as it were, new Spirits into them, he took upon him the Management of the Front himself, and drawing out Captain *Bleutner* and Captain *Winkler's* Companions, together with some others, he led them in Person ; fell upon the Enemy with such fury, that we soon carried the day ; for he had so animated the Soldiers, that every Man was worth two. Our Men being now come too near to use their Muskets, took their Cutlaces [1]

[1] Old form of cutlass, a short sword with a flat, wide, slightly curved blade, more used for cutting than thrusting. In later times the term was chiefly used for the weapon carried by sailors.

in one hand, and their Hand Granado's in the other; and when the Blacks saw the Dutch drive so hard upon the Enemy, they took such heart too, that with their Sword and Buckler they poured in upon the Enemy, and drove all before them: So that the Slaughter we made of the King's Army in this place, was nothing less than that of *Dangerang*.

The Enemy was wholly put to flight, and left most of their Arms behind them. And we having gained that Post, the Admiral gave Orders that the Ships should no longer Fire upon the City, lest we our selves might receive some of their Shot amongst us.

All this while we push'd on forward to their Pallisado's, and came to the Fort which they called *Speelwick*, where we found a great many of the King's Men; but yet most of our Officers found that we should quickly become Masters of it. We sent for some heavy Cannon from our Ships, and batter'd it down in a very little time. The Seamen forced open the Gate with Hammers and Axes, and so enter'd, throwing of Granado's: But all the Javians being fled, we became Masters of it, without any further opposition.

This served our purpose mighty well, and saved us the trouble of any further Entrenchments, except a few Gaps that we made up with Wood, which our Blacks cut down and brought to us.

Here we took a little breath, and rested that night, and the following day; and a portion of Biscuit, Sack, and Brandy, was distributed to each Soldier in the Army. After this fine Refreshment, the Army was put into a new Order, and the Right and Left Wings formed anew, and provided with Field Pieces, loaded with small Shot. Then we march'd against the Enemy, who lookt at first as if they were able to have eaten us all up for a Breakfast, they being above thirty thousand of them. But our Officers were not in the least dismayed at their numbers, but very courageously Attack'd them on the two sides of 'em; yet taking such measures, that we could joyn together again at any time. I must own, I never expected the Dutch should have escaped a total overthrow, considering the vast disproportion of Men; and while I was in this contemplation, on a sudden the Javians sallied out upon us with such a terrible and horrid Outcry, as their Custom is, that one would have thought it had been a Hurricane, rather than a Body of Men. But for all that our Men stood their ground bravely, and gave Fire continually upon them. We had so order'd our Army, that behind each Rank of Musquetiers we had a Rank of Pikes lest they should break in upon us ; And all the while we played so thick upon them, with ten or twelve Field-Pieces, that they fell like Bees before us. Our other Wing observed the same Order ; and we at last joyned together again in to a Body. Having sustained this for near 3 hours they sent some of their *Muck Speelers* [1] amongst us, which are a sort of giddy, resolute Fellows, that are ready to be hired upon any kind of Exploit, how rash and mischievous soever it be ; be it to stabb a Man for any private Affront, or any thing else of that kind : And the more famous Cut-throats they be, the more they value themselves on their Reputation of being such. Before they go upon any such sort of undertaking, they eat of a sort of Herb which they call *Avion* [opium], which for a time makes them giddy, and altogether unsensible of any danger ; so that they are as fool-hardy, as they are dangerous. They rusht in upon us with an incredible Fury, and being incapable of consulting their own safety, they came running headlong against our Men, and spitted themselves upon our Pikes, and destroyed themselves without doing us any hurt. And in a little time, after having killed several thousands of the King's Party, we utterly routed them, and made them leave all their arms behind them. Upon which we fell from fighting to plundering.

After this, the Major General went, accompanied with his Life-guard, and others, to the Castle, where the young King was ; who immediately upon his approach, opened the Gates, came to meet him, and with all the humble acknowledgment fell down at his feet, and afterward embraced him, with all the demonstration of a grateful and sincere Affection.

Before this, the Admiral had given Orders for the Army to Encamp all round the Castle, and the Gunners to be ready in their Posts with the Artillery, which consisted of above three hundred Pieces of Cannon.

After this the Army having had 3 days rest, and all the refreshment that might be, was order'd to march into the City, and there they had the chief Posts in their hands, as the *Boom*, the *Speelwick*, and other Bastions, and the rest were quartered in the English, Danish, and French Quarters. Some were order'd likewise to keep Garrison in the Castle ; so that all

[1] Men who run amuck. A term used for Malays who madden themselves with opium or *bhang*, and cut at every one they meet until they are killed. For their use as professional bravoes compare the *berserks* of the Scandinavian sagas and histories.

places of consequence were sufficiently secured, in order to make the whole our own, when time should deserve a little more commodiously.

Here I received Orders to repair to the Hospital, where I had five Surgeons under me. But there being so many sick and wounded, that we could not well look after them; the best part of them we sent to *Batavia*.

The old King, after this Overthrow, retired with his shatter'd Army, to his Fort *Dorjasse*, where having made ready some hundreds of Prawen, and small Vessels, he resolved to be revenged on us. And having the conveniency of the two Rivers, *Dorjasse* and *Bantam*, which run from that Fort into the Sea; he Mann'd them in order to go as far as *Batavia*, and to do us some mischief, which accordingly he did. For being come into the Road of *Batavia*, they set fire on some of our Ships, and either kill'd the Men, or took them Prisoners, and went on Shore on the little Island call'd *Onrust*, and made sad Havock of the few Inhabitants that were there. To prevent their doing any further mischief some of the largest of our Men of War were straight got ready, besides a considerable number of Prawen, and small Vessels; all of which were as well Mann'd as we could wish: And with these we went in search of the Javians. In this Expedition I was made Captain of the Ship call'd the *Europa*; which had eight hundred Men and three Surgeons; and one Captain *De Ruyter* [1] commanded the whole Fleet. We straight put to Sea, and with our whole Fleet we made directly to *Bantam*, and *Dorjasse*, the two Rivers, which I told you, lay so conveniently for the Javians to run in and out at; and there we lay, to cut off their Pass, when-ever they should attempt to come in there for shelter.

Being come there, one half of the Fleet was order'd to stay there, and the other half of which number I was, went in search of the Enemy. The next morning, as we were come about the Island we call'd the *Toppers Hoadie*, we saw them about a League off of us, with more than a hundred Prawen, &c., cruising to and fro. Our Admiral *De Ruyter* judged himself strong enough to Engage them; so having call'd a Council, it was resolved to fall upon them. Upon this a Gill of Brandy (the best thing in the World to inspire Courage into a Dutch-man) was given to every one of them: And we were divided into two parts, with instructions that upon the

[1] Not the famous Admiral de Ruyter, who died in 1676, but possibly a member of the same family.

Signal given, we should fall upon them all together. All that day we lay still; but on the Evening we did so surround our Enemy, that they had no way left them by the next Morning, but to fight their way thro' us, or else be forced to shelter themselves on a little Island call'd *Schlepse*; but that being not above a League in compass, and besides, so barren, that it would not afford them any Provision or Relief; they were necessitated to Attack us; and indeed they were not long resolving upon it, having some times at least the number of Men that we had. They stood to the Windward off us; so that having the advantage over us, they came very briskly upon us with twenty Prawen well Mann'd, and with forty Double Haekken,[1] hoping with them to lay fast hold of our greatest Ships first, and so to board them, and then the smaller would easily be dispatched. The Admiral all this while did not let us fire one Shott, and had order'd a kind of Breast-works to be got ready upon the Deck by the Main Mast, and under Deck in the Fore-castle. Our Prawen and small Vessels kept behind us, ready to fall upon the Enemy, whenever he should attack us. We had planted some of those *Haubitzen* I made mention of before, behind those Breast-works, which we had made, which were to pour small Shot upon them; and there were Men ready besides these with their Granado's, Fire-Pikes &c. to give them a welcome at their entrance. All this while the Javians continually fired upon us, but did little Execution: And being come up close to us, they scaled us, and in an instant our large Ships were filled with Javians, who upon their Boarding of us, set up such a *Huzza*, or rather an Out-cry after their manner, that it made the Air to tremble. But we straightway falling to our works, opened our Breast-works, and fired our small Shot upon them, together with our Grenado's; so that never were Men destroyed after that rate. Those that were still coming up, and those that were in the Prawen, we swept down like a swarm of Bees, with our Fire-Pikes, and other Fire-Arms, and Hand-Granado's, into the Sea; all that remained begun then to provide for running off. But our Prawen and light Vessels followed them so close, that they killed infinite numbers of them, and took up some that were fallen into the Sea, and made them Prisoners; who were immediately hang'd up altogether upon the said Island. The sea all about us was pure Blood, and we were all in a Cloud

[1] Probably the same as the Hacker or Haaka boat, a one-masted craft employed in the South China Seas.

of Smoke, tho' we had not fired one Great Gun. There were no less than two hundred and sixty of the Enemy lay dead Aboard my Ship the *Europa*. The dead and wounded we threw one with another over-board; which caused a bitter Out-cry among those who were yet sensible, or but slightly wounded. After this great Victory our Ships came all together again, and upon a Review, we found our loss to be two Masters of Ships, seven Steers-men, eight Officers, and about three hundred and eighty private Soldiers, and seven hundred of our Black. We lost two Ships, the *Victor and* the *Ameland*, besides eighteen Prawen, three Galliots, and seven Fire-Ships; all which were burnt. But of the Enemies Ships, which were a hundred and twenty in number, there did not one single one escape; their Men were computed to have been 24,000.

CHAPTER V

The fleet comes together again, and falls upon the Javians at Sea. The Author is order'd to Bantam, to take care of the wounded, that were sent thither. The Council resolves to pursue the Javians. Their Malice and inveterate Hatred against the Dutch. Several Skirmishes with them. The Expedition of the Dutch from Bantam against Dorjasse, which was the old King's residence. A Bloody Fight maintain'd by the Dutch against the Javians, with a great loss of the former. Some Javian Nobles sent to desire a Peace, which was refused. The Garrison of Dorjasse set fire on Dorjasse and fly. The Dutch plunder what was left of it. The Author discovers a very considerable Treasure buried under ground, but receives little advantage from it. The Admirals Expedition in pursuit of the Enemy, where he meets with an unlucky accident.

HAVING put our selves into a pretty good posture again, our Men had all the Refreshment that could be, with plenty of Brandy, Sack, Biscuit, and such like. The next thing we did, was to dispatch a Ship to *Batavia*, to carry the news of our Victory to the General.

After this we went to joyn the rest of our Fleet again. The Javians all this while made several offers to come out of the River *Dorjasse*; But, our Fleet lying just in the mouth of it, they could not attempt it with safety; but were forced to make their way out at some other small Rivers; so that some of them came in sight of us; but we no sooner made towards them, but they retired. Yet were we obliged to keep Cruising between that place and *Batavia*, to prevent their doing us any mischief. So that there was continually some little Skirmish with them; but never any Engagement worth speaking of. In a matter of two months, the greatest part of our Ships, and the best of our Men, were sent again to *Bantam*, the rest of 'em kept still Cruising before *Dorjasse*.

Being come to Bantam, under the Command of Captain *Jochem*, the Men were put on Shore, and Quarter'd amongst the others that were in the Fort. It fell to my share to be of the number too. So I took my Lodging in the *Chineesen Straet*, where I was very commodiously seated for my business. There were also two Assistants with me, and three Under-Surgeons, who were Lodged in their several Quarters, for the better looking after their Patients. Those were obliged to come to me ever and anon to give me an account of those they had under their hands, and to fetch the Remedies, which were all in my custody, and to take my directions. Only those other necessaries, as Linnen for Plaisters, Arack, Sack, Salad Oyl, and such like, were to be fetched from the Steward, who had them in keeping; but they were never delivered without I sent an especial Order under my hand. The number of our Sick and Wounded was great, and that of the former increased, by reason of the Flux, which was very rife among them: And some were seized with a Lameness in all their Limbs; so that we had enough to keep us in employment.

All this while we were making all preparations for carrying on the War with utmost vigour, both by Sea, and Land: But we wanted Men; wherefore we were forced to stay till our Recruits came from *Batavia*. We had an especial Eye upon the Royal Fort *Dorjasse*; for we saw very well that we laboured in vain, while that stood; and we had reason to think, that if we did but once ferret them out of their strong hold, we should not find it difficult to give them a total Overthrow.

I must confess, that besides the pleasure I had out of a publick love for my Country, to see them in a fair way of overcoming their Enemies, and enlarging their Territories: I had also a secret satisfaction to see that they were the Javians that were the Object of our Conquests; they being the most faithless, treacherous and base of all the Indians. They are fit for all manner of mischief; but never fit to be employed in any action that's noble or generous. In short, they are skill'd in nothing, but in cheating, filching, and all manner of knavery. I have often found it to my cost, but that which was most notorious, tho' of no great moment, was the trick they put upon me at my first coming, which was this. When our Ship was just arrived from Europe, some of these Javians came to meet us, as it is their usual manner to come and meet all Ships that are newly come in, to welcome them, and to sell them fruits, fresh meat, and other refreshments. I, who was very much fatigued with my long Voyage, and quite tired with our Salt Provisions, was not long a fixing upon some of their things; and amongst others, I was so set upon some fine fresh Fish, that they had brought with them, that I was resolved I would have it at any rate.

Their way is to Truck for some of our Commodities, so I agreed to what they ask'd me for the Fish, which was some Nails, Thread and Tobacco-Pipes; which I immediately fetch'd for 'em, and gave to the Javian, who was then busie about something that others had bought likewise. I was so pleased with the thoughts of the rare Feast I was to have, and withal in such haste to be at it, that I could not stay any longer; but bidding the Fellow leave my Fish, with any of our Men, I ran down in the mean while into the Cook's Room, to get me some Water hung on ready, and I think never went so chearfully about any business in my life. But no sooner had I turned my back, but the Dog push'd off his boat, and went off with my Dish of Fish, and left me to Dine on my Water; and I must confess, that from that time I could never have a hearty love for one of the Nation. It was a sort of a satisfaction to me, that in three or four days after we were Landed, I had an opportunity to be revenged on a Javian, which I never let slip, for his sake, when ever it offer'd it self. They are generally very great lovers of Shooting, tho' they are so stupid, as never to understand it as they should do. And as I was one day Shooting at a Mark, one of them comes up to me, and wanted mightily to have a Shoot. I told him he should: So I shot, and loaded again with a double Charge of Powder, and a vast deal of Paper, which I took care to ram down as hard as ever I was able, and then offer'd it to him: He very joyfully received it, and went to fire it: But the Piece recoiled so furiously, and gave him such a knock on the shoulder, that down fell my Booby, and could hardly stir his Arm for a fortnight, or three weeks after it.

But to return to our purpose, all our Affairs were in a very good posture at *Bantam*: And there was a very good understanding between the young King, and our Major General *St Martin*. But the Javians were ever and anon upon us in small Bodies, and came quite up to our Rampiers: So that we had many Skirmishes with them; but so inconsiderable, that they were not worth the speaking of.

One would admire how quickly our Recruits were made at *Batavia*; for in a few months we had again a considerable Army on foot, and they had got together Men from all parts of the *Indies*, which were all sent to us with speed. And as soon as they were got together, it was resolved to go directly against the Royal Fort of *Dorjasse*.

Our Major General *St. Martin* left Captain *De Ruyter* to Command *Bantam*, in his absence, and himself went straightway with some of the best Ships thither ; and in some days after sent Orders for the rest of the Men to follow him, leaving only what was necessary in Bantam for the security of the Place, which had little to fear from the Enemy without, and less to suspect from the young King within, who had but a very inconsiderable number of Men of his own with him. So three thousand Men were order'd to be imbark'd, and of that Squadron I was, and had that time the Command of the Ship call'd the *Middleburgh*.

When we had joyned the Major General, we made together a very fine Fleet ; and indeed such a one, as had never been seen before in those parts of the World. For we had there fifty two fine large Men of War, besides some hundreds of Prawen Fire-Ships, Tenders, small Boats, &c. Major General *St. Martin*, soon after these were all come together, went back to *Batavia* ; and we continued our way under the Command of the General and Admiral, whose name was *Tack*.

As soon as we came to cast Anchor before *Dorjasse*, the Javians got together in prodigious numbers to the Sea Shore, and covered the ground for several Miles, which was all level from the Sea to the Fort, and all Fields of Rice. Just by the Shore were several Sconces at some distance from each other : Some big, some little, but all vastly strong, being all made with a double Row of Trunks of Coco-Trees, that were set very deep into the ground, and the space fill'd up with Earth ram'd down very hard. The space between each of these Sconces, was all Ditches and Rampiers, with Pallisado's. The Sconces were so broad, that two or three Waggons might drive abreast upon them. In the middle of them within, were the dwellings for the Soldiers : Some of them were built up square, and flat at top ; for the Soldiers to stand there and fight. From all these places the Javians were continually firing upon us, but to little purpose, because we were far enough to hear them make many hideous Outcrys, and to see their Troops hurry from one place to another.

In the mean time we made all ready to Land. Admiral *Tack* going all the while from one Ship to another, to give

Orders to the several Captains. Which done, we went to Prayers, and then the usual portions of Brandy, Sack, etc. were distributed with strict injunctions to be all ready. Presently after they brought us some *Schappons* or *Pontons*, which is a flat sort of Boat like a Horse-Ferry-Boat, which were fenced with a kind of Breast-work; and four Pieces of Small Shot to each, and to these, Gunners of a sufficient number, with some Sea-men with Hand-Granado's. Then went in the Soldiers. After this manner we kept our Easter, which was now come, but was none of the merriest for us. The third day after *Easter*, we unladed seven large Ships, and sunk them in the place where we had a mind to Land at: And upon them we raised Batteries, upon which we planted above forty heavy Pieces of Cannon, to shelter us when we Landed, and to annoy the Enemy and their Sconces.

The next day after, about two of the Clock in the Morning, the Signal being given, we all in general left the Ships; upon which I went down into the Boat with the other Surgeons, which were about seventy in number, upon our Vessel, which was attended always by two or three small Boats, that were ready in case of any wounded, that they might carry them off to any place, and upon ever so shallow a Water.

All this while we kept a hideous Shooting with our great Cannon, which was all we fired; under the shelter of which we drew all the while still nearer and nearer to Land, from whence the Enemy kept firing very hotly upon us. When we came to have no more than knee-deep of Water, we got out; and then our Gunners played the more freely from their *Schappons*, upon the Enemy, and the Sea-men could then make the better use of their Hand-shells.

In this manner we Charged for above two hours, and lost a great many of our Men: Their Sconces lying so high, that we on the other side could hardly reach them. Seeing that we could make but slow progress this way, the Council of War met and resolved to fall upon their Works altogether.

Upon this the Front marched forward directly towards the Enemy, and the Sea-men succeeded in our place, landing, and taking possession of the ground, which the Army occupied before. We carried some of their Forts by Storm in a few hours time, tho' with the loss of a great many of our Men. As soon as the Javians saw that they had lost some of their Holds, they set fire in most of the others, and betook themselves to their heels, but did not quite run away from us neither; for they kept moving in the Rice-fields on the sides of us, with a resolution to charge us all in a Body. We had yet a very considerable Army, tho' nothing in comparison to theirs; but we having by this time got together our Artillery, and planted it very advantageously, we were ready for 'em.

The Admiral gave Orders we should play upon them with our Artillery, without intermission, which we did. The Armies being now come in reach of each other, the *Javians* fell upon us with the greatest fury imaginable; the manner of which I could not see, being then in the midst of our Men; but I heard their usual Out-cry at their falling on.

Our Army opened it self to the right, and left; and then our Artillery, which was ready for 'em, was all at once discharged upon them, which made a hideous slaughter amongst them. After which our Men closed in again, while it was charging again: Our Front moving always with movable defence to our Men, and enabled them to keep their Order the better.

All this while, tho' thousands of their Men dropt, they would not give ground an Inch, nor did we. And the day was now so far spent, that we were both forced to give over; yet were we wholly set upon pursuing the Stroke, and hoped that the night should prove rather more commodious and successful than the day had done. As soon as the night drew on, we begun to play upon them with our Mortars, and sent such a quantity of Bombs among them, and at the same time fell on one of their Wings so furiously, that we gain'd ground; and pouring our Shot so thick upon them, we put them into such a consternation that they were not able to defend themselves, so that we thought of nothing more but to prepare to pursue them; but they did not design to put us to that trouble; for we could hear some of them in the front of their Army cry, "*Dida mou boggel ada orang Hollando*"; which is as much as to say, "I will fight no longer against the Hollanders." This was made known to Admiral *Tack*, and further confirmed by some of the chief Officers of the Enemies Army, which the Admiral had permitted to come to him, and were sent to parley, and to beg him to grant a Truce, or rather make a Peace. The Admiral durst not do anything in this matter of his own accord; but was obliged to send to the General at *Batavia*, who sent him word again that he should be sure not to hearken to any Proposals of Peace.

During this Suspension of Arms, I conversed much with those Javian Deputies, and I found them very inquisitive, and curious to know what our Army was composed of; whether of real Men, or of Devils in human shapes: We told them, they were only Men, but brave Men, and most Germans; and indeed they behaved themselves with such inexpressible Bravery, that it might have amazed a polite, and well-disciplined Nation, and much more it might do so, with a Barbarous, and Heathenish people.

When the Admiral had received his Answer from the General at *Batavia,* he told the Deputies that the Dutch would not hear talk of a Peace, and so sent them away; and bid them tell the old King, that they would now have as little regard for him, as he had formerly shewed for *Batavia.*

Upon which our Artillery was fired again, and we charged them with greater fury than before; so that we put their whole Army to flight, which they took directly towards *Dorjasse,* and there we put them all in confusion, totally routed them, and made a most dreadful Slaughter amongst them. We did not pursue them as we might have done; for we thought best to keep together, and to continue in our Entrenchments, while we made all the preparations required for a more effectual pursuit of 'em, and in order to Attack the said Town of *Dorjasse.*

Here our Men rested three days, and had all the usual Refreshments; and in that time our Dead were buried. But in the third night, about twelve of the Clock, we saw the City of *Dorjasse* in a blaze, and heard the blowing up of some of their Building and Fortification, great pieces of which fell into our Camp, which was half a Mile from thence; all which was very agreeable to our Admiral, and to our Army too, because it would have cost us a great many brave Men's Lives, if we had been put to fighting for it.

We sent immediately a Party towards the place, to see what they were doing there, and in what condition they were. But when they came near to the place, the old King withdrew with all speed, and passed over the River *Dorjasse,* with all his remaining Forces; and fled to the *Blawe Peperbergh,* which was about four Leagues from thence; so that our Men found *Dorjasse* quite empty, and the Coasts all clear. As soon as the Admiral had advice of it, he march'd thither with the greatest part of the Army. We found nothing more there, but Houses ruinated; most of them still smoaking, and no Inhabitants, but a vast parcel of Ducks and Hens, flying about the Streets to seek a habitation; which our Soldiers were very glad to see, and regaled themselves bravely with. I went to take my Rounds in the City, and as I came near to a parcel of Ducks, I fired amongst 'em, and shot a good many of 'em, and the rest ran into a House there hard by: So I followed them with my Fusil in my hand, designing to knock them down with the Butt end of it; But as soon as I came within the doors, I saw an old Woman sitting on a Bedstead, with a naked *Kriz* [1] in her hand. But she seeing me come with a Gun in my hand, fell down dead for fear.

Our Men found a great many Javians, that were hid in corners and holes, who could not flee away with the rest, being exceeding old, or otherwise disabled. Our Soldiers were Quartered upon the Bastions. The Admiral took his Quarters in the middle of the City, in the Court of the *Old Palace*, which before was the greatest place for Trade.

The chief of my care was, to see if I could not get some Plunder, which, while I was looking for, about the *Old Palace*, I discovered a place in a dark Entry, which was not Paved firm, but the Stones only laid loose; and knowing it to be their custom to bury their Treasures in time of danger, I went to examine the place more narrowly, and made shift to dig down a matter of two foot; but finding nothing but a few *Staefiens* or *Stiftiens*, which were about a quarter of a Yard long, I grew weary of my work, not knowing the value of 'em. Those I got I gave away to a Free-man, who went privately among the Free-men, and sold them for a Crown. As soon as ever I knew the worth of 'em, I went in all haste to the place again, and got a pretty good parcel of them: But as ill luck would have it, ere I could carry them off, the Admiral, who was come to take a view of the Ruines of the Palace, came just that way, and finding what I was at, engrossed it to himself, and sent for Men immediately to dig there; and there they found as many of them as filled eight Waggons, which were sold for 700,000 Gilders: All which went into the Admiral's Pocket. However, he presented me with a hundred Gilders for being the discoverer.

[1] The Kris, or Creese, is a Malay dagger with a blade of a wavy form.

In the mean while, others got several good Booties, as Persian Quilts & China Silks, with many other rich Furniture and costly Garments, that were left in the Palace. And I who had found the greatest Booty, came off with the least share.

By what I could see of the strength of this place, it is certain the Javians wanted nothing but Courage to keep us out; for if that had not been wanting, they might have defied double our number: For tho' the Town was four or five Miles in compass, yet there was but two Avenues into it, which was hardly wide enough for two Carts to go abreast, the rest being all Moorish grounds, where Rice grew, but where no Army could have come: And instead of a Wall, The Town was fenced with a Line of Coco-Trees set close to one another, and filled up with Earth; so that our Cannon would never have been able to batter it down, or so much as to make a breach in any part of it. The Buildings within were all built with Bamboo-Canes, except the Palace, and the Noble-Mens Houses which were of Stone.

Upon the twenty eight Bastions of this place, we found three hundred and odd large heavy Pieces of Cannon, tho' most of 'em Iron; but no Powder or Bullets: which gave us occasion to think, that thro' some carelessness the Magazine took fire, and so set fire on the whole Town, as indeed we found it true afterwards, by the account which some of the Inhabitants gave us.

The Fortification of this place was so strong that all the Canonading in the World could never make a breach in it; for the outside of it was all of Coco-Trees, set as close together as might be, and behind them was all Earth thrown up. And it is impossible for a Bullet to batter any of those Trunks of Coco-Trees, being of so spungy a nature, that a Bullet will stick in them, and go no further.

In this place was a high Hill cast up by the King's Order, and a few Hutts built at top of it; from whence he used to go, and spy the Army when it lay before *Bantam*, and take a prospect of the Fleet, the Country lying all level between those two places.

Two Rivers run thro' the Town, the little, and great, *Dorjasse*; which unite their Streams a little below the Town, and make up a fine River. It runs thence thro' the pleasant Vales of the *Blawen Peper Bergh* into the Sea, and divides the Kingdom of *Bantam*, from that of *Batavia*, or *Jacatra*, all along in its course.

When we had laid still here some few days, our Admiral went out with some Companies to visit some of their *Negeryen*, or *Villages*. We plunder'd all as far as the Plain of *Banta*, which is just by the River *Bantam*, and leads towards *Tangburang*, a Province belonging to the Kingdom of *Bantam*.

Here we saw some *Naekens*, or small Boats lying on the other side of the River; but neither saw or heard any body thereabouts. The Admiral had a mighty fancy to go over, and so had some others of the chief Officers: Wherefore he offer'd six Rixdollers to any that would venture to swim over and fetch some of those *Naekens* over. Tho' the River was about a mile wide, yet there were four Seamen that proffered themselves immediately, and several Blacks, who are generally excellent swimmers; but it was thought sufficient to send the Seamen only, and two of the Blacks, who brought over six *Naekens*; and having got some Oars to 'em, they went with them, and fetch'd all the others, which were twenty and odd. When they were all come, the Admiral went into one of 'em, and all the Boats were filled with Men. When we were got over, we found nothing but whole flocks of Hens, and Ducks; so that our Men divided themselves, some one way, and some another, to see if they could find any Body. One of these Parties met, by misfortune, with a parcel of Amboineeses, who were come out to get some Coco-nuts; and these going drest like Javians, our Men took them for such, and falling upon them, kill'd some of 'em, and would certainly have kill'd more, had not another party of ours come in of a sudden upon the back of these poor Amboineeses, who hearing them cry out for quarter, and discovering them to be Amboineeses, put a stop to the slaughter, and prevented further mischief being done.

We were all well provided with Powder and Ball, and kept on to the end of the Plain; where we found some little Works, Redoubts, &c. but all abandoned. In one of them were four or five pieces of Cannon, which we took, and carried over the River, and from thence drew them to *Dorjasse*.

Our Admiral was now thinking to get over the River again, and yet desirous to know what was become of the Enemy; but truly his curiosity cost us very dear; for we had not yet reach'd our Boats, when we perceived a great number of Prawen, full of Javians, making towards us, with such speed, that we could hardly get our Arms ready. All we could do was to fire upon them, and hinder them from landing just in that place. But they past by us quickly; and came to another landing-place, that was more convenient. As soon as they had got hold of the Shore, they came upon us in a trice, and so encompassed us, that we had no way left but to yield, or throw our selves into the River. The first of these could not please us, and the latter was almost as dangerous, for those who could not swim very well, so that they who had little or no hopes of swimming over, resolved to stand it out, and to fight till the last drop of blood. Our Admiral escaped with five Boats, and some others followed them as fast as they could, and swām over after them. I, for my part, threw away my Arms, and my Surgeons Box, and leapt into the River, tho' with little hopes of getting over; however it gave me a chance for my Life, and it pleased God to carry me over safe to Shore, where our Men were got, and stood spectators of the dreadful slaughter, the Javians were making among the poor Dutchmen that were left among them on the other side. There was no less than two hundred of 'em, who were all cut in pieces, but behaved themselves with an unparallel'd bravery, as Men in such desperate condition use to out-do themselves; and as they held it out a long while, so they sold their Lives at the dearest rate that ever men did.

The Admiral exceedingly concern'd at this sad misfortune, and desirous to revenge the loss of so many brave Men, took the rest who had made their escapes, and marched with them in all haste to *Dorjasse*, with a design to go over with a Body of Men, and pursue the Enemy. It was upon consideration found impracticable, being we had no way of passing the River, for it was very broad every where, and we had not above three or four small Boats: So that we were forced to quit our designs, but that we might not go altogether unrevenged, we set fire to all that remained standing in *Dorjasse*, after we had staid three or four days in it. The main Body of our Army continued along the Sea Coast, very well entrenched, under the Command of Captain *Harzing*; while the Admiral went, with some small Ships, and some Men, down the River *Dorjasse*, and so to *Bantam* by Sea.

CHAPTER VI

The Author, among others, going along the River Tangburang, meets with several Parties of the Enemy, and have several Skirmishes with them. The Town Anier besieged. Bravely defended by the Javians, by the means of two Renegade Dutchmen; one of which was taken, and immediately hanged. Anier plunder'd and sack'd. The Author shot in the Leg. The whole Country brought into subjection. The Young King's base dealing with some of the Chief Nobles, who came in to submit themselves to him, notwithstanding his Gracious Promises to them. An end of the Wars. The danger that a Man exposes himself to, that will take any of the Indian Commodities for his own private Gain. A very strange and barbarous Cruelty committed by the Javians upon some Dutchmen, who fell into their Hands. They are discovered, and punish'd after the most cruel manner that could be invented. The manner of their Death

AS soon as we were come upon the Road of *Bantam* the Young King came to meet our Admiral, and to thank him for his Signal Services; and after some Complements passed between them, they went both of them on Shore in the same Boat; and all the Men got ready, and landed soon after them; and were divided among the rest of the Soldiers that were in the place. I was order'd to go to my old Post in the Hospital: But another Order came, not long after, to me, to gett ready to go to Captain *Ruiter*, to view the Country along the River *Tangburang*, which runs thro' the Province of that Name, and comes by *Bantam*.

In our march we saw very pleasant *Negeryen* on both sides of the River, tho' all without Inhabitants. But one Night as we were very silent in our march, we were surprized with a sudden alarm, and outcry in one of the neighbouring Villages. We were not very much concerned at it, because we were 400 of us; however we stood all to our Arms, and moved, according to our Captains Orders, towards the

Village, and there we met with 'em upon the march, but it was not intended against us. Some of our Front only could fire upon them, yet that served to bring down several of the Javians; but the Blacks and Amboineeses, of which we had a Company with us, pursued them so long, that they brought us seventy Heads of 'em, when they came back to us the next Morning; according to the Custom of all those Nations, whether they fight for us, or against us; which is always to cut off the Heads of as many of their Enemies, as they kill, and to bring them to their Commanders, as tokens of their Valour.

Having had good success thus far, our Captain was for moving forwards, and pursuing our good Fortune; which we did, till we came to a small River that runs into *Tangburang*. There we found some Forts, and some Negeryen, well provided with Men. We were about going over to them, and we could have done it, the River not being very deep; but our Captain did not think it safe, because we did not know what Numbers there might be of the Enemy, or whether they might not lie there in ambuscade. He immediately dispatch'd some of our Men to *Bantam*, to Admiral *Tack* for Recruits; and according to his desire he had the very next day three Companies of Dutch sent him, and two of Blacks, that were Bandaneeses.

With this Reinforcement we crossed the River briskly, and marched directly towards their Villages and Forts: But we had not marcht long, before our Front, (which was hardly got in right order, after passing through the River), but a parcel of about a hundred and fifty of our Men fell in with a Party of near four hundred of the Enemy; they would at first have been glad to have been a little farther off, but there being no retreat, they engaged them so vigorously, that they killed above an hundred and seventy of 'em, and wounded several, and made the rest retire to *Tangburang*. As we pursued them, we took some of them, who had deserted the others, and hid themselves in the Woods; who all told us, that all the Enemies Force was within three or four miles of us, and more than eight thousand strong. That it was the same Army which had continually been commanded by the Old King, and that they lay there in order to hinder our coming over that River.

Upon this information, our Captain sent some Expresses with all speed to *Bantam*, to give an account of it to the Admiral, who, without delay, sent some hundreds of Men

THE PEARL FISHERY OFF TUTICORIN
(*From J. Nieuhof's "Voyage to the East Indies"*)

more, and some Field-Pieces likewise. Then were all the Officers commanded to take especial care that all their Men might be well provided with Powder and Ball. All our Body was divided into five Parties, each consisting of four Companies, and all the necessary Orders were given ; then all our Army went to Prayers, after which we marched straight upon the Enemy.

A Lieutenant with fifty Men was sent out before, to see what he could discover of the Enemy, and so to give us information. We had not moved half an hour, e're we had an account that the Javians were coming to give us battle, and that they were eight thousand strong. All our Parties put together, made but four thousand ; yet were we in hopes that we might encompass them, as indeed we did in a very little while, and made the place so hot for 'em, and sowed the ground so thick with their dead Bodies, that they betook themselves to their Heels and fled in all haste to *Anier,*[1] which is a strong and well-fortified place, about two miles from thence, and is the chief Pass into the Province of *Tangburang.* Wherefore we provided our selves immediately with Breast-Works, to secure us selves from the Enemies sallies. Every one that worked at the casting them up, had a Rix Doller as a present.

The next day, when we had hardly finish'd them, the Enemy made a sally upon us, which turned much to our advantage ; for being pretty well prepared for 'em, we made shift to cut off seven hundred of 'em, and took some of 'em prisoners, whom we gave quarter to for six or seven days ; and then took them into a Wood, and cut them in pieces. The next night we raised three Batteries, upon one of which we planted four large Pieces of Cannon, that were sent us from *Bantam,* together with two thousand Men. These were loaden immediately with Small Shot, in case of their sallies in the night-time ; and in the day-time we drew 'em out again, and loaded with Bullets, to send into the Enemy's Works.

When we had lain here about six days before the Town, we began to make our Lines of Approach ; and a General Assault was agreed upon. In three days time we put it in execution : We had a Water to go over, which we passed with great ease, by means of some Fascines which our Blacks cut and laid for us ; but we found so brisk a reception, that we were forced to retire with a considerable loss of Men

[1] Anjer, on Sunda Strait.

on our side. If the Enemy had made the best of their opportunity at that time, they might, with the greatest ease imaginable, have cut most of us off, and raised the Siege; but it pleased God they did not pursue us any further than their Works: And this was owing chiefly to some English, who were amongst them, and who persuaded them, that this was but a Sham-Assault of ours, and not the Body of our Army, and that that lay in the Trenches to cut off those that should sally out; which if they had done, they would have utterly routed us, for we were at first but five thousand strong, (reckoning the two thousand Men sent us with the Cannon) and of them we had above an hundred killed, and an hundred and twenty wounded. Notwithstanding this repulse and disadvantage, we still continued in our Resolution of carrying on the Siege.

In the mean while our wounded Men were carried to a place about a mile distant from us, where there were ten Surgeons to look after them; and those that were not dangerously ill were sent to the Hospital at *Bantam*, and with them Captain *Ruyter* sent a Letter to the Admiral, to desire him to send him a recruit of about a thousand Men; telling him, that with that he did not doubt but he should get master of the Town in a short time.

Three days after our Assault we begun still to make good our Approaches to the Town, being our number of Men increased; and being come pretty near to it, the Blacks came over to us in abundance out of the Town. We did not receive them into our Army, but posted them between our Lines and the Town: However, this gave us hopes that the besieged were weary of us. Wherefore we begun to make ready some Mines, which being finished, we again resolved to make another Assault.

While we were deliberating on these matters, an English Man, with his Arms, came over to us out of the Garrison, and gave us a good account of their condition, and withal told the Captain, that the Besieged seem'd now to wish for nothing more than that we would attempt another Assault; and that in order to receive us, they had pulled down the Houses in the Streets, and levell'd that part of the Town; that they had guarded all Avenues and Streets with double Pallisadoes, and that behind them they had planted several Pieces of Small Shot to receive us; And likewise that they had laid several Mines ready to blow us up. We on the other side were in hopes that we should surmount all these difficulties. We mounted upon our Batteries, and sent such a number of Bombs and Granadoes into the Town, that we thought it impossible they should keep with in it long, and so it proved; for by and by we heard a sudden Alarm, the Besieged having a mind to try the success of a second Sally upon us. But we, who were well prepared for 'em upon all accounts, did send such shoals of Hand Granado's amongst them, that we forced them to retire with very great loss, and all the while we pursued them to the very Town.

This being done, and our two Mines being finished, and having laid several hundred weight of Gun-powder in each of them: Orders were given to set fire to 'em, which was accordingly done: And in an instant, the Mines, having been dug very deep under the Town (as they might do easily, the Town being scituated pretty high), we saw half the Town in the Air, and some part of it, and of the Men came tumbling into our Camp; and within some thousands lost their Lives at that one blow.

No sooner was this done, but we, who stood all ready, and in expectation of this, rusht in furiously upon them, while they were in this confusion and disorder, and put all to the Sword that came in our way, except those that we saw were Europeans. Two of them we took, who were Dutchmen, that had deserted the Dutch Company, but these we immediately hung up without any further examination, as it is the constant custom, which the Dutch observe when-ever they catch any of their Deserters. But besides that they deserved this death by Law, they doubly merited this from us; for knowing that there was no pardon to be expected from the Company, they had been great instruments of the obstinate resistance we met with here; for their condition being desperate, so was the advice they gave to our Enemies, to hold out longer than they would have done. I could not but be exceedingly sorry at the fate of one of 'em in particular, being one of my intimate acquaintances, and who came over with me from *Holland*. He was of a very good Family, his Father was an eminent Merchant at *Bergen* in *Norway*.

Being now Masters of this Pass, we fortified our selves with the greatest diligence, it being the strongest In-land fortification, and the direct Pass from *Bantam* to *Batavia* by Land. We had already got the Sea-port Towns and Forts in our Hands; and having likewise possessed our selves of this, we did not doubt but the Javians would be obliged to come and surrender themselves, seeing they could not come at the Sea. Yet in case there should be some small desperate Parties abroad, Captain *Ruyter* commanded fifty Men to go and stroul a little about the Country, and I desired I might be one with 'em.

We marched about for a matter of an hour or two, thro' nothing but Woods and Coco-Trees, and then we came to a River, but we could not pass it; so we continued moving along the side of it till night; and then not meeting with a conveniency of passing the River, we took up our lodging there that night; but for fear of the Enemy, we hardly durst speak or stir all that night.

The next morning early we heard a noise not very far from us, and we began to fancy, that we might insensibly be got round upon our Army again; but when we were got a little further, we discovered the Enemy on the other side of the River, as busie as might be, cutting of Coco-Trees, with a design to go and raise some new *Bachers*, as they call 'em, that is, Fortifications. The River was very narrow, but very deep; and seeing they could not come at us, and that we could easily retire (if need was) to our Army, which was but a mile from us; we took a resolution, and fired so briskly amongst them, that we fetch'd several of 'em down off the Trees.

They, on the other hand, did not fail to make good use of their English Firelocks, and to give fire upon us; so that four of our Men fell. Two of them that were only wounded, I brought away, and appli'd what was requisite to their wounds; and having done that, I went forward to overtake the rest of our Men; but I was no sooner come up to them but I my self received a wound in my Thigh, from a Black, that was upon a Coco-Tree, and the Ball lodged within me. The small Skirmish being over, some of our Men took me up, and carried me to *Anier*, where the Army was; and from thence I was carried to the Hospital at *Bantam*. There I was the daily care of the chief Surgeon of that place, who was a very able Man, named *John Hanss* a Leydener.

He used his utmost endeavours to get the Bullet out of the wound, but all in vain; And after I had undergone a long and grievous pain, and had all the Splinters clear'd out, we were forced to leave the Bullet in, and to let the wound heal over it.

In two months time I was fully recover'd, and found no pain; nor did my Bullet ever trouble me, till I came into *Holland* again.

I was now again to my Employment, in the Hospital that was committed to my care, where we enjoy'd our selves with great security: Only for fear of the worst, we took care to man our outward Garrisons, and to fortifie our Frontier Places. But e're three Months were at an end, we were sufficiently satisfied that there was no great need of fortifying our selves any more; for the Javians came over to us in mighty numbers: And to convince us of their sincerity, and entire submission to us, they sent us some hundred of Carts full of Musquets, Lances, Pikes, Bows and Arrows, and other Warlike Instruments.

After this, some of their Nobility, and some Persons of greatest Note, who had great Estates in those parts, came to surrender themselves, and to beg for Pardon of the Dutch Company. But for that time the Company thought fit to leave that to the discretion of the Young King, who pretended himself willing to receive them graciously, and to pardon all that was past. But he having got some of 'em in his power, he forgot his Royal Word, and commanded some of them to be cast to Tygers, some to Venemous Serpents, some to be strangled, others were drown'd, others had their Throats cut by his especial Command; and all variously and miserably put to death. Things being come to this pass, the Company thought it was high time to put a stop to such Barbarity: And therefore they acquainted him with their resentment of this his base dealing, and made him sensible of the great imprudence, as well as the baseness he had been guilty of; seeing he ought to have been glad, to have seen these Persons come to submit themselves to him, and furnish him with Subjects which he was now like to want; and that so he might have his Towns and Cities once again raised, and filled with Inhabitants. The rest of them that came in, being hereupon more civilly used, and kindly treated; insomuch that in the eighteen Months time that I was there, all the Places were rebuilt, and made finer than they were before. For then the Chineeses, who are willing to be under the Dutch Government, came and settled there in greater numbers than ever. For as they love to live among the Dutch, because of the Priviledges they give them; so the Dutch are very glad of their company, because where-ever they are among them, they cause a brisk Trade, which turns to the advantage of the Dutch, as well as of the Chineeses themselves.

The Country being now again pretty well Peopled with

Neighbours and Forreigners, and by the coming in of the Javians; I thought it high time to look about me, and to try to recruit my Pockets, which were now very low, all Provisions being exceeding dear; and I had had no opportunity in a great while to get a Farthing by my Profession, any other than what my Salary brought me in. So I applied my self to the Javians, among whom I thought there might be a great many wounded, and accordingly I found pretty much practice amongst 'em. With all this help I made shift to live handsomly enough, but truly it was as much as I could do: For considering the scarcity there was, and the great fatigues I had born, as well as the rest, I thought it the prudentest way to look after my Health, and to afford my self what my Constitution required, rather than pinch my self, and contract a fit of Sickness, as several, and indeed most People do, who go over to the Indies with no other design but to enrich themselves at any rate. Tho', by the by, after all the pinching, saving and scraping together, that is not so easily done, as People imagine: For nothing is more common than the vulgar opinion that there's no more to be done to get an Estate, than just to go to the Indies; from whence they reckon they may come home with a burden of Gold, Pearls and Diamonds, as if it was but picking them up and come away. But it may be worth the while, seeing we are speaking of this Vulgar Error, to shew that these precious things are so far from being thus easie to come at, that it is even a very dangerous thing to attempt to carry off any of those things, if a Man hath got any of them in his possession.

I my self went once to *Amboyna*, and got intimately acquainted there with a Sergeant, that had lived about nineteen years in that Country, and was an Overseer over several Blacks, that work in *Press-Mills*. We came to trucking at last, and I exchanged some of my Cheese, Tobacco, &c. for some Oyl of Cloves; of which I purchased seven Bottles of near two Quarts apiece. This exchange of ours was to be kept as secret as any Robbery one should commit in Europe, for both our Lives lay at stake. Fortune favour'd me so far, that I came away undiscover'd, and brought 'em safe into the Road of *Batavia*; where I began to have some hopes of running it ashoar and pleased my self with the thoughts of what it would yield me among the Chineeses, and the English. But I reckon'd without my Host there; for no sooner was I got into the Boat, in order to get to Shoar, with one of our Seamen, whom I had made privy to the business, and who understood that Trade, but the *Fiscal* made towards us with his *Caffers*. The Seaman had so contrived the business, that the Bottles were under water well stopt, and tied to a Cord; but when we found the *Caffers* came directly to us, the Seaman who stood ready with a knife in his hand, cut the Cord, and dropt the Bottles into the Sea. The *Caffers* were immediately with us, who searched our Boat very narrowly, and then with their Hooks groped all round the outside: They found nothing but the end of a Cord, which made them give us an Ugly Look, but it was not sufficient to bring us into any further trouble. But immediately upon this a poor Gentleman had much harder fortune than I had; for these *Caffers* going from us to a Ship, that was come along with us from the Western Coast, they caught a Lieutenant there, that had got a piece of Gold of some pounds weight: And the *Fiscal* carried him strait away to *Batavia*, and in two days time he was hang'd up in the *Galgeveld*. This poor Man's hard Lot made me not regret my loss so much, I rather hug'd my self that I had let my Tartar go. But it cured me from ever attempting any thing of that nature. This may serve to let you see, how dangerous such undertakings are; and that such Contraband-Goods are not so easily brought off. So that if Men have no other end in going to the Indies, I advise them as a Friend, to stay at Home while they are well.

But now to return again to where I was: I ought not to omit giving the Reader an account, which will not be unacceptable, tho' the action will rather amaze than delight, and must needs fill the Reader with horror. For of all the Cruelty I ever heard of there, I never met with any that could compare with this, which was committed in my time, tho' I must confess I think the Punishment that was inflicted on the Malefactors did in some measure out do it.

Some of our Men went one day a little way up into the Country, rather out of necessity than for pleasure, designing to shoot some Birds, &c. notwithstanding they might know well enough, that it was not very safe, being we were not altogether reconciled with the Javians. They were expected back at night, but three days past, and no news of 'em, which occasioned many conjectures; but most were of opinion, that some Javians had faln upon them, and murdered them. Upon which *Minheer Tack* commanded a Lieutenant, with some Men, to go in search after 'em. Having wander'd a matter of two hours, they came to a lonesome place, where as they were thinking to go back, and take some other Road, they heard a piteous outcry, which made them go forward to see what it was, and there they found 'em all six, and discovered the most dismal Spectacle that ever was.

One of them was stretch'd out between two Trees, with his Arms tied to the one, and his Legs to the other, about three or four yards high from the ground, with a great Fire still burning under him; but he was quite roasted when we came.

Another hung by his Privities upon another Tree, with his Arms and Legs tied together under his Back; this was dead also.

The third was spitted upon a Bamboo-cane, in at his Fundament and out at his Mouth; he was dead too.

The fourth was buried up to the Neck, his Eyes put out, and his Nose and Ears cut off; this was not quite dead.

The fifth and sixth were tied fast Back to Back, each of them had their Right Eyes put out, and their Privities thrust into the holes; both these were still alive.

Our Men were so surprised at this sight, that they were ready to sink down; and finding no other remedy, they came with all speed to *Minheer Tack*, to give him this tragical account, who sent straight some Blacks with a Barrow to fetch these poor Creatures, and bring them to *Bantam*.

We were not a little concerned at this strange accident, but what was an addition to our trouble was, that we could not learn from these Men how they came to be thus served, because they were deprived of their Instrument of Speech.

Admiral *Tack* sent immediately some Messengers to the Young King to acquaint him with all this, and to desire him to have a search made among his people, and to use all means possible to discover the Authors of this Fact. This he did, and with such good success, that in less than a fortnights time, we found the Rogues out; and all of 'em (being sixteen in number) were apprehended, and eight of them were forthwith condemn'd to be thrown to Serpents.

The manner of these Serpents destroying of Men is thus. They catch hold of a Man, and swallow him near half up, and then suck all the Blood out of his Body, then they tear him peace-meal, and eat him up.

The other eight were confined to one Room, where they had very good Diet afforded them, but that was only in order to prolong their Pain; for there were Men always attending them with Scourges; and as soon as ever these Criminals begun to nod, they lashed them severely, and this continued for a fortnight; and then they begg'd that we would knock them on the Head, or put 'em to any speedy death they pleased, tho' it were the most cruel they could invent.

But all their begging was in vain, for the Young King was wonderfully pleased, that he had found out such a Punishment, as would probably terrifie the rest from committing such frequent Murders as they used to do.

Thus they continued in that misery, and lived till the fifth Week; then they fell asleep inspight of all their Whipping; and continued so notwithstanding they were pincht with red hot Tongs, and so they ended their miserable Lives. So, that how barbarous soever their Fact was, yet it met with such a Punishment, which, I think, did rather out-do the Fact it self in Barbarity.

CHAPTER VII

How insolently the Javians behaved themselves at first towards the Dutch, and how civilized. The Dutch get the total Government of the Country into their Hands by consent of the Young King. The Old Kings Surrender, Confinement and Death. Rebuilding of Bantam, and its flourishing Condition. Its Traffick, Commodities, Fruits and Provisions. Tygers there in great numbers, how catch'd. Elephants taken after a like manner in Ceylon and Aracan. The several Games and Pastimes at the Weddings of the Chief Javians, together with some Customs and Ceremonies used on those occasions. A description of Pepper, and its growth. The Author's departure from Bantam to Batavia, and thence to Banda

THE Javians could hardly bear the *Hollanders* for a great while, and truly their antipathy against us was not altogether without some grounds, seeing that we, being Forreigners, had invaded their Territories, and taken possession of all they had, and then lorded it over them. They being a very silly sort of people, had no other way to shew their Spight and Resentment than by making Mouths at the Dutch as they passed by, and sometimes Spitting upon them. To break them of that ungainly Custom, we made a resolution amongst us, never to let any pass by that did so, whether Old or Young, Man or Woman, without giving them a good Box on the Ear. This cured them of their incivility so effectually that you'ld have wonder'd to see how courteously they behaved themselves towards us; for all of a sudden there was so great an alteration, that there was no passing by 'em, but they would greet you very civilly, give you good morrow, (in their Language, "*Dobidis Sinior*") clapping their Hands together, and holding them up to their Forehead; and when they were willing to shew themselves more courteous and officious, they would add, "*Manna Bigi Sinior,*" that is, Where are you going Sir? which was much as offering their service and assistance, which we frequently made use of.

Admiral *Tack* was all this while lodg'd in the Apartment which belonged before to the English, where the Young King used to come to visit him almost every day, and maintain'd a faithful Friendship with him. In a little time, things being settled, a Proposal was made to the Young King by the Dutch, that if he would resign intirely all claim of Power and Jurisdiction over his People, custom, &c. and turn over the whole Government into their Hands, they would allow him such a Sum as would enable him to keep up his Grandeur, and live like a King, (a titular one, that is) and would be obliged to pay him some thousands of Gilders every Month. To this he condescended; whether thro' fear, or thro' indifference, I cannot well say; and a certain Pension was likewise settled upon his two Young Princes, all which was duly paid according to agreement. The rest of the Nobility, and Chief of the Land, remained in the possession of their Goods and Lands, as before, only that they were now subject to the Dutch Government. Thus the Dutch compassed their whole design by force and policy; and by fair means became Masters of that Kingdom, which was, and had been so long flourishing, and famous for its vast Trade and traffick; and that in so little time, as from 1682 to 1685, that I believe History will hardly afford an instance of a more sudden change of Affairs in so great a Kingdom.

The Old King all this while having wander'd up and down on the *Blawen Peper Bergh*, whither he had been forced to retire when he was defeated; and being there forsaken by most of his People, resolved also to come, and submit himself to the Dutch Company; and accordingly, after near two years he came and surrendered himself, having first sent some of his Servants to Admiral *Tack* for his Pardon, which was granted him. Upon which he appeared in Person, and came to *Bantam*, with a very small Retinue; there they assigned him a Lodging, and set Guard upon him, and in a little time after sent him to a small Island, where he ended his days.

Thus all being quiet, all Hostilities ceased, and all reduced to one Government, Bantam flourished again in a more perfect manner than it had ever done; and did, like a Phœnix, spring up out of its own Ashes, but more beautiful and strong than it was before. Its Borders were now vastly enlarged, by reason of the vast number of Foreigners which daily flocked thither, and were all indifferently received, except the English, French and Danes, which were not admitted, but were sent with their Ships to *Batavia*, where they were permitted to trade, and to take Houses and Ware-houses, &c.

The chief Traffick of *Bantam* consists in *Pepper*, *Salt-Peter*, *Salt*, *Ginger*, *Cotton-Cloth* plain, and wrought with *Silver* and *Gold*; also *Fine Linnen*, and *Flowered Stuffs*, which are the common wear of the Inhabitants.

The Country about it is exceeding pleasant, and produces all manner of necessary Provisions. There are all manner of tame Fowls, Hens, &c. and their Eggs very cheap. All sorts of Fish. Great store of Cows and Buffels, but the Fat of these last is not much eaten, because it tasts so much like Tallow. Many Wild Boars there are also, but the Tamest of that kind that ever was, because that the Javians never hunted them, by reason that their Law doth not permit them to eat the Flesh of 'em; so that they used to come so close up to our Works, that I have shot three or four of 'em in one day, and sold them for little or nothing.

But the worst Cattle thereabouts is the Tygers, which are in great numbers near *Bantam*, which the Javians used to be frequently sent out to catch or kill. And they did it after this manner.

Thousands of Javians go together to the place where the Tygers lie; and there they spread themselves round the place in about three miles compass, and so march gradually to the center and meet upon the Tyger, keeping still their *Nassingayen* [1] before them; so that if the Tygers come out towards the circumference they make, they are so frighted that they run back again; and so they keep them running to and fro, and retiring, till at last they are so closely encompassed, that they must of necessity be forced to throw themselves into some of their Traps, which are something after the manner of our Wheel-nets, but incomparably stronger and bigger; for they are of strong Wood, made less and less, and several Partitions; and in each Partition a Trap-door that shuts upon 'em, till at last they come into the narrowest of all. There they let him alone a good while without Meat, they then get a Rope about his Neck, and put him into a small Coop, upon a Cart drawn by Buffels; and these are always brought to

[1] These were Javelin men, and the word comes from assegai, which originally meant a slender lance or spear used by the Berbers, but was applied by the Portuguese to light javelins used by African natives generally; hence its application to the characteristic Zulu weapon. The Dutch borrowed the word from the Portuguese.

the King, who keeps always some of 'em in his Palace, and looks upon that as a piece of great State. And when one of them brings forth a young one, it is so much taken notice of, that all the Cannon round the Castle are discharged, and great Rejoycings and Pastimes are made upon the occasion.

They do breed very often, but tho' one might expect to bring the young ones to be perfectly Tame, as indeed some do pretty well come to it, yet it is never safe to trust them too far; for while I was there, two of 'em, which they thought as tame as they could wish, broke loose and run thro' the Town, and tore several People to pieces, and would have destroyed several more, had not some Javians come upon them, arm'd with their *Nassingays*, who killed one of them, and took the other.

There is another way of catching them in Traps, laying a Bait for 'em, but then you can't have them alive; so there is shooting of 'em but not without very great danger.

In *Ceylon*, *Pegu* and *Aracan* they use to catch Elephants much after the same manner. It is worth while, upon this occasion, to undeceive those simple and credulous People, who believe that the way to catch them is to saw some Trees almost thro', against which the Elephants come to lean to take their rest; and so the Tree falling, they likewise fall, and are not able to get up again, being very clumsie, and without Joynts in their Legs. Whoever gives credit to this Fable, is easily imposed upon, for considering the Bulk of 'em, there is not a more nimble and active Creature than they are; and nothing is more sure, than that when they are used in War, there are never any Ladders made use of, to help up the three or four Soldiers, which they carry; but they are taught to kneel, or rather couch down, while they get upon their Backs. But their Agility is so observable from what we have seen some of 'em do in Europe, that I will not go about to describe them any further. But for one instance of their Nimbleness, and Aptness to be taught any thing, I cannot but set down here what I was an Eye-witness of my self, done by an Elephant which one of the chief Merchants of the Company kept of his own, that had abundance of Tricks. And when he had a mind to divert himself, or some special Company, he would have him brought out by the Men that lookt after him, and knew how to manage him. This Elephant once was brought out upon a Bridge, which was over a very deep River, and a great Loaf was given him in his Mouth. The keeper gave him a sign, and fell a beating upon a Copper Instrument; upon which the Elephant went back, as in a fright, and tumbled down backwards into the River, with a most hidious plunge, and kept so long under water, that he eat up his Loaf there, and he staid so very long under the water, that no body expected ever to have seen him come up again, except those that were used to this trick; at last up he came and swam to Shore, and having paid his respects to his Master, he threw up the Bread he had eaten, and near a Barrel full of water. Many other Tricks he shewed, but this is the only one that I thought worth relating, as being somewhat strange and uncommon.

I used to frequent many Javians of my acquaintance, to pass away the time, and to observe some of their most particular Customs and Humours, and to share of their Diversions. Of the latter none pleased me more, than to see their *Balliar* Dances, performed by Women who were kept for that purpose by Persons of the greatest Quality. These Women are of an extraordinary small size, but of the most exquisite Form and perfect Shape that ever was seen; Their height is but between five and six Spans, their Skin as white as the driven Snow; and taking them all together, one would sooner take 'em for Angels, in the likeness of Women, than for Women themselves; for besides their natural Beauty, there is all the artificial Dress that can be conceived. Their Garments are of the finest Silks, wrought with Silver and Gold, and their Tresses neatly adorn'd with the rarest Orient Pearls, all which doth still add to their lustre. Their manner of dancing is in Masquerade; they have in their Hands some Ebbony Balls strung upon a String, with which they keep time very exactly with the Musick, instead of our Castanets; and sometimes they sing with their dancing, which is yet more charming than the rest, their Voice being wonderful sweet. One of these Women costs generally two or three thousand Gilders, they are fetch'd out of the Province of *Babylon*, about forty miles from *Jerico* the less; and no other Women are fit for these kind of Pastimes and Dances but they: So they are much made of by the Indian Kings, and Nobility, who spare no pains nor charge to get 'em. Some of these I have seen also at *Surat* and in *Persia*, when I lay before *Wond Artz*, with the Ship called the *Gelderland*, where we took in Silks in lieu of our Pepper and Spices.

Another sort of Sport they have is Cockfighting, which being so common here, needs no further description.

The Sports and Pastimes are frequently seen amongst 'em,

but especially at their Weddings, which are never held without them, together with several other Recreations, and strange Ceremonies, of which I will give you some account.

In the time that I was there, a young Gentleman, Son to one of the Principal amongst 'em, was married; and being intimately acquainted with him, I was invited to that Wedding. His Wife's Portion was considerable, and proportioned to the Young Gentleman's Fortune. The Father gave with his Daughter, thirty Men, forty Women, and twenty Young Maids, all Slaves, besides two hundred thousand *Cujax*[1] which amounteth to about sixteen Rix-dollers, for twelve thousand *Cujax* are only the value of the piece-of-eight. All these Women-slaves the Man may lie with if he pleaseth, but the Children that are thus born, are not at his disposal, but at his Wife's, who may sell them or dispose of them as she thinks fit. But those Slaves' Children which are given in Dowry to the Wife, are in the power of the Husband to order as he will.

When a Marriage is on foot among them, both the Young People confine themselves within, for about six Weeks or two Months: The Parents in that time set out their Servants and Slaves, and make 'em as fine as they can against the Wedding. The Bridegrooms Apartment is all strewed with Flowers. Then on the Wedding-day he mounts on a Fine Horse, which is set out in the finest manner, and thus goes to his Bride, where all her Friends meet him, attended with the Slaves, Presents and Household-stuff, &c. Then a great Dinner is prepared, where each of the Young Peoples Parents are to be present, and to make merry. In the mean while the Young Couple are lead to a Room with a fine Bed in it; where they are shut in, and left to their liberty, after which the Bridegroom comes out to the Guests, but the Bride is not seen of any Man after that time.

These Rejoycings usually last four days, during which there are some Comedies acted after the Chinese manner.

Among all their Sports, there is their baiting of a Buffle, which pleased me very well, but that it so frequently occasions much mischief; because their way is to leave them loose, and to set several English Dogs upon them. I saw my self once two Buffels let loose in a small inclosed piece of ground, with five Dogs against 'em. One of the Buffels defended himself very well of the first Dog that came to him, and tossed

[1] Possibly the Chinese Cash.

him up a vast height; but a second coming upon him, before he had well rid himself of the first, and seizing him fast by the Testicles, it so enraged the Buffel that he run directly to a little Shed, that stood there in a Corner, upon which three Blacks and two Dutchmen had got, the better to see the Sport; and throwing all down before him, and the Dogs still holding him fast, three of them, viz. two Javians, and a Dutch Carpenter, were trampled to death, and indeed almost all to pieces: And the other Javian, with the Admiral's Baker, came off luckily with no other wound, than what they got by their fall: They had no other way to put an end to this, or to part 'em, but by firing them altogether; for now the other Buffel was deeply engaged too: So that with their Musquets, they killed the two Buffels, and two of the Dogs, and unfortunately another Javian. So that this Sport ended very tragically, and it generally proves so, thro' their want of management.

The next day another ill accident happen'd; for as there was in that place a great Mast, which the English had taken formerly out of a Ship, and set up there, in order to get up, and spy the Ships a-far off at Sea. One of our Seamen would needs go up for a frolick, and being come almost to the top, one of his holds broke, and let him down, and was (as you may well imagine) killed with the fall. Upon which Admiral *Tack* immediately ordered this Mast to be cut down, and another to be set up upon the *Speelwick* Bastion, which was much less than the other, and not near so high, but commanded a farther prospect, the bastion it self being very high, and upon a much higher ground.

While I resided in the Hospital at *Bantam*, which was some Months, several of our Company, which we had left at *Dorjasse*, dropt in by degrees, having destroyed all in their way; and being all come in, they were almost all sent back again to *Batavia*, especially all the Blacks; so that there were not left, both within, and without the Castle, above five thousand Men to keep the Garrison; which was little enough for so great a place, it being as far as I can judge fourteen or fifteen miles in circuit: and the number of its Inhabitants was computed to be 700,000 besides the Foreigners, which might amount to half the number more.

Towards Land the City lies open, but to the Sea it is guarded by a very strong Wall six yards broad; besides some hundreds of Bastions, little Forts, Redoubts, &c. all which are very well provided with Cannon.

All things were now in good order, and the Government very prudently managed, so that all those that were in the Companies Service, even the Soldiers themselves, had no reason to complain. But their Condition was much mended, their Provisions were cheap and their Usage and Treatment very civil; and I must confess that I had all the enjoyment I could well wish: But notwithstanding all this, I was still dissatisfied and restless, and wanted to be going to visit some other parts of the Indies. But it was in vain to wish, for I was under Obligations not to move yet.

The time now drawing near that our Captain was to return to *Batavia*; a Council of War was held, where it was resolved that a general Muster should be made, and that those who had served out their time should come out and claim their liberty. But withal notice was given them, that if they would engage themselves afresh, they should not only be kindly received, but should have their Pay raised by four Gilders.

Then our Captain *Tack* went back to *Batavia*, to be President of that City, and Captain *Harzing* succeeded him in his place of Governour of *Bantam*.

About this time the *Muck Speelers* were very troublesome about the City, and daily committing great disorders. Their way is to make themselves mad by eating of the Herb they call *Avion*, *i.e.* Opium: Then ye shall see 'em run about the Streets, like Men distracted, and kill all they meet. But our custom was, as soon as we spied them a coming, to cry out "*Amuck, Amuck*," upon which every body stood ready with his Weapon in his hand; and these Blockheads would run themselves upon a Pike, or upon a Musquet, and be shot through, and in the heat of the Fury, run it may be a hundred or two hundred paces before they dropt. And these Disorders could not by any means be prevented, tho' the Company had made it death for any one to be found with any of that Herb about him, in any part of the *East-Indies*.

There being now no more Action here, nor any Novelty that this Place afforded me, I was very desirous to be gone. But I found the only way to attain my wish, was to get some Sea-Surgeon in the mind to exchange Places with me. Wherefore I waited patiently for the coming in of any Ships that were to go to *Batavia*: And in a little time the *Tidor*, from *Bali*, came into the Road of *Bantam*. She had no sooner cast Anchor, but I was with her to welcome her, and to feel the Pulses of her Surgeons ; but I found their Designs were much the same as mine, and they were all dispos'd for a longer Course ; so that I found no hopes there of success. But being told that they expected another Ship in toward night, if the Wind did not cross 'em, wherein were four Master Surgeons ; my hopes quickly revived, and I resolved to stay there that Night. In the Evening the Ship came in according to their expectation, and the next Morning early I went on board of it ; and after the usual salutations, I applied my self to the Master Surgeons, and freely declared to 'em my Intentions. One of 'em, a Gentleman of *Delf*, at first liked my Proposal, and after some further discourse, was fully in the resolution of changing with me, which did not a little rejoyce me. The thing being thus agreed upon, he asked leave of the Captain, after having acquainted him with his design ; and having got his leave, he came away with me to Shore. My business now was to have leave my self, which indeed I had moved for at a distance before, but not doubting of having leave given me when-ever I should desire it, because I had behaved my self well ; and what made more yet on my side, I had now and then greased the Chief Surgeons Fist : I had deferr'd speaking for it directly, till I had met with one that would change with me. No sooner had I declared my Mind to the Chief Surgeon, but he gave me an ample and honourable *Testimonium* to carry to the Governour, who with a Complement of Thanks, gave me a Pass, and entred the other in my Place. So I took my leave of 'em all ; and having got my Chest and Hammock ready, I got me a-board my new Ship called the *Enckhuysen*, it was laden with nothing but Rice, and had but twenty eight Seamen, besides the Officers and us four Master-Surgeons.

I parted very cheerfully from *Bantam*, the only thing that I was loath to part with was, a little Summer-House I had order'd to be made in the Garden of the Hospital, which was very delightful. It was made of Bamboos, and so contrived that I might have removed it very well ; but being I could not move that with it, which made it so extream pleasant, I left the whole standing for my Successor to enjoy, but not without grudging it him heartily. The Top of it was cover'd very neatly with Fig-leaves, and the Sides were sweetly shaded with Pepper-plants, which hung like a Vine over the Windows, and made it extreamly agreeable. But now that I am speaking of this Pepper, it will not be amiss to give you a description of its growth &c. This part of *Java* is the most famous for it, and the great *Blauwe Peper Bergh*, which I have so often mentioned, hath its denomination from it, and signifies *Blew-Pepper-Mountain*, it being full of it; there the best of all grows. Indeed *Malabar*, *Malacca* and *Sumatra* do produce vast quantities of it too, but it is all white and long, like the *Canary* Pepper, and is not to compare with the *Javian* Pepper for goodness; and for that reason hardly any but the latter is transported into *Europe*.

They plant it at the bottom of other Trees, to which it clings in the nature of our Hops, and winds round as that does, but higher. Its Leaf is like that of the Orange-Trees, but less, and of a more pleasant Green, and tasts pretty sharp if one bites 'em. The Fruit grows much like Grapes, tho' (every one knows) much smaller, and closer to one another. They are ever green till they dry, which is in *November*, *December* and *January*, at which time they gather 'em, and spread them upon Mats in the Sun to dry; then they run 'em thro' a Sieve, and pack 'em ready for the Merchants to take away.

Now, tho' Pepper is as plenty in *India* as Stones in the Streets, and only serves for the Ballast very often, and to pack up other Goods tite; and altho' sometimes several whole Shiploads of it be thrown into the Sea, and many hundred thousand pound weight of it burnt; yet dares no Man in the service of the Company take one single Corn of it, but every one is obliged to buy it of the Indians, who deal with the Company for it: And the same rule is observable in respect to other Spices. But now the *Enckhuysen* lay still but one day, so that the next morning after I had boarded her, we weighed Anchor and sailed to *Batavia*, with a half wind. It lies but six Leagues from *Bantam*, yet were we seven days before we could reach it, for we were ever and anon forced to cast Anchor and weigh it again, which fatigued our Men mightily.

Being now come before *Batavia*, our Master went immediately on Shore, and the next day our Ship was unlading. I went to Shore too with all speed in a Chineese *Praw*, and went to wait upon the Head Surgeon there, one Mr. *John Streckelberger*, who was my old Acquaintance; but I found him now raised to the highest pitch of Preferment the Profession is capable of there, which was the place of Overseer-General over all the Surgeons in the whole Indies, in the place of Dr. *Kleyer*. I told him upon what design I had left *Bantam* to come to *Batavia*, which was in order to get me a Deputation to some other part of *India*, that I might travel farther still. He seemed very ready at the first, but afterwards he desired me to come again in three or four days time.

In the mean while I went to visit all my old Acquaintance in the Fort where I once lived, and to divert my self with 'em. But unhappily I took out an old Gentleman with me, one day, to go to a small Island hard by, where there were a great many Oysters; we had got a good many, but as we were coming back, it blew at so excessive a rate, that our Boat was turned over. The poor old Gentleman could not reach the Shore, meerly for want of strength, and so lost his Life within a hundred yards of the Land, but the old Chineese and I came safe to Shore, and the Boat was driven quickly after us, so that we took that up. Instead of paying the Chineese, I beat him soundly for being the main cause of all this. And from that time I never saw him more; without doubt he run away for fear the *Fiscal* should call him to an account for the death of my Companion.

This was the fourth time that God in his infinite goodness delivered me out of that Element of Water, once in my own Country, once in *Africa*, once in the River of *Bantam*, and this time at *Batavia*.

It was now time to go and wait upon the Surgeon-General, to know what was determined as to my affair. When I came there, I was surprized to find a Deputation to go and Board the *Phœnix* for *Banda* and *Amboina*, for besides that it crossed my design, which was to go to *Japan*; I knew that those two Countries were the most unhealthy of all India. However, after a little pause I resolved to go thither or any where, rather than to stay there. So taking my Orders with me, I went aboard the *Enckhuysen*, and told my Brother Surgeons how I was serv'd, who instead of condoling with me, laught at me very heartily.

I was now to be gone in two days time; so I made haste and provided my self with *Arac*, *Tobacco*, and Long-Pepper *preserved*; all which are found to be of greater use in those unhealthy parts than in any other: And having made all other necessary Provision, I went on board the *Phœnix*.

The next day we weighed Anchor, and sailed from *Batavia*, the wind N.E. passed the *Streights of Sunday*, and in three Weeks time we arrived before *Banda*, which is reckon'd to be three hundred Miles from *Batavia*. There fell nothing out worth any notice in our passage thither, but that a poor Seaman was blown down by a sudden puff of Wind from the Fore-Mast upon the Anchor, which tore his very Guts out of his Belly.

CHAPTER VIII

Their arrival at Banda. The Author falls very ill there, how recovered. Description of the growth of the Nutmeg and Mace. Departure from thence for Amboina. An account of Clove-Trees and Cloves. Return to Batavia. The Island Onrust, why so called. A vast quantity of Tortoises there ; The manner of taking them. They are a mighty Food amongst them. How Sharks are taken, and the use of that Fish's Liver. A Voyage from Batavia to Ceylon. Columbo the Chief City there. The Stratagems which the Portuguese used in that Country to get footing there. An account of the growth of Cinnamon there. The Root Borrobone as good as Saffron. The manner of fishing for Pearls there ; many Lives are lost by diving after them. One Oyster had near three hundred Pearls in it. Mother of Pearl. Departure from Ceylon. Arrival at Batavia, where their Ship takes fire. Kastizen and Mastizen, what sort of People. A Voyage from Batavia to Japan. Pass by Formosa, and come to Pangato in Japan. They are forced to put away all their Books ; the reasons why.

AS soon as we were come into the Road of *Banda*, our Master went ashore. My Legs which had been swell'd for three or four days were now so sore, that I could not stir, else I would have gone with him with all my heart ; but my Indisposition augmenting, I was forced to be carried ashore. There my Swelling increased, all upward, and my Belly was now swell'd to the highest degree that I could be ready to break : And in this condition I continued the space of three weeks (so that I was left here very comfortless, for the *Phœnix* was obliged to be gone) and after that the Distemper seized me so in all my Limbs, that I wholly lost the use of them ; and during a quarter of a Year I could not bring my Finger to my Mouth ; so that I truly despair'd of ever recovering the use of my Limbs, (altho' I was not sick inwardly) and therefore I often prayed to God to take me to himself. I was carried every day to the Bagnio, where several other Patients with me were set upon Seats, all in a ring, with Blankets wrapt round about us so close that nothing but our Heads stuck out; there was a great Fire of each side of us, which made the heat intolerable, and then we were held over the steem of some medicinal Herbs, which were boyl'd for the purpose; into which infusion they threw thirty or forty red hot Cannon Bullets, which raised such a steem, and made such a smother, that not one in a hundred was able to bear it, but they were forced to be taken out, and carried away upon Quilts made for that purpose. I was taken out thus in the beginning, but when I came to be used to it a little more, I bore it out bravely, and found it very helpful. So keeping to this for some weeks, I recover'd apace, and then they begun to anoint my Feet with *Oleum Terræ*, and prescribed me to drink frequently a small Glass of Bitter Brandy, or Arac infused in Bitter Herbs; by which method, with the help of God, I prefectly recover'd.

After this I went to satisfie my curiosity, (which was the occasion of my coming) and to see the Country. But I shall decline giving any description of it, because it hath been done already sufficiently by others, especially by *Johan Hugen Van Linschooten.*[1] Only I will give you a short account of the Noble Fruit which this Island is famous for, viz. the Nutmeg and Mace, which the Inhabitants, whether Dutch, or Freemen, or Slaves, are obliged to deliver yearly to the Governour, and is sent afterwards to *Holland*, and other parts of *Europe*, and to *Persia*, and other places of *India*.

The Tree on which the Nutmeg grows, is almost like the Pear-tree, but doth not spread so much, and its Leaf is somewhat rounder. The Fruit is much like a Peach in bigness and looks, of an extraordinary fine taste and delicate smell, when it is ripe: On the out-side is a thick hard Shell, like the Bark of a Tree, over which the Flower grows. When the Nut begins to be ripe, it swells so much, that the first Shell bursts open. The Flower is of fine Red, and very agreeable to look on, especially when the Tree is pretty full of Fruit. Sometimes the Mace comes off of it self, and when it sticks to the Fruit, they gather all together;

[1] John Huyghen van Linschoten, whose travels gave a great impetus to the trade of Holland and England with the East (*see* Introduction).

and in the drying of the Nutmeg, the Mace drys and falls off, and changes its lovely Red into that brown Yellow, which we find it hath here in Europe. The whole Fruit is very proper to preserve, and is an excellent Confite.

While I was at *Banda* a couple of Fellows were executed for having killed their Mother; the death they were put to was very terrible; they were fasten'd upon a Wooden Cross, and their Limbs were broke with an Iron Bar, and there they were left to expire.

After I had spent three Months here, in pretty good health, the Ship called the *America* came to *Banda*; so that having now the opportunity of compleating my Voyage, which my sickness prevented me to do with the *Phœnix*, I embraced it readily, and went in her for *Amboina*. I was glad to leave that unhealthy Country; and tho' I had, and shall ever carry with me severe tokens of the Plague of that Country, I was glad to come off so well as I did. In four days time we came before *Amboina*, where our Ship was straight loaden with *Cloves*. I went there on shore to look about me; and while the Ship was lading, I had time to examine how they grew, and what I could not be an Eye-witness of, I had from my old Friend the Serjeant, whom I made mention of before, from whom I got those Bottles of Oyl of Cloves, which cost so much care and trouble, and at the last I was forced to drop them into the Sea.

The Clove-Tree is much like the Laurel-Tree, the Blossom is White at first, then it turns Green, and after that Red. While it is green it smells so fine and sweet, that nothing can be compared to it. These grow mighty close to one another, and many of 'em together, all within the Blossom; when they are ripe they gather 'em, and dry them; then they are of a brown Yellow. Those Cloves which they do not gather, as not being ripe, hang on till the year following; and those they call then *Moeder Nagelen*, i.e. *Mother Cloves*. Where these Trees grow, there grows no kind of Grass, or any green thing nigh; their nature being such, that they draw all the moisture about them to themselves, and so do the Cloves likewise, as I have often seen my self, that a Tub of Water being set in a Ware-house that had store of Cloves laid up in it, after they were pickt and cleans'd, in three or four days time after the Water would be all gone out of the Tub. The smell of 'em is so strong, that some People have been suffocated with it when they have been busie with too great quantities of 'em, and in too close a place.

Our Ship having taken in all her Lading, we left this place, and made directly for *Batavia*, and arrived there happily in a Fortnights time; where our Ship was immediately unladen, and all the Cloves put aboard the *West-Friezland*, in order to go for *Holland*.

Here an Order was sent to me to change my Ship, and go in the *Old Europe*, the same Ship that brought me from the *Cape* to the *Indies*. I went with her to the Island *Onrust*, which is a place fit for careening of Ships; where she was to be fitted up, being very old. The Island hath its name very justly, *Onrust* signifying *no rest*, by reason of the continual disturbances which the Sea causes to the Inhabitants, who are only Carpenters, Smiths, and other such Artificers for Shipping. For the Island being very low, and the Sea Ebbing and Flowing every two hours, at very uncertain heights, gives the Inhabitants no rest or security: And every new and full Moon, the Sea drives 'em up a vast way; but so unfixt are its Bounds, that they are forced to be continually upon their Guard: Which besides the great labour, and great quantity of work that lies upon their hands, makes it truly very restless for them.

There were two Master Surgeons besides me belonging to the same Ship, and we had all our Patients ashore. The only pastime we could have, was catching Tortoises, of which there are vast numbers there. When it is fair, and the Sun shines bright, they come out of the Water, and lie in the hot Sand. So when they were all very quiet and settled, we came upon them of a sudden with Sticks and Iron Bars, and turned them upon their Backs, as fast as we could, for then they cannot stir. When we had done catching 'em so, we took them out of their shells, and put them in Pickle, and kept them in Barrels or Ports, with Salt and Vinegar. This was our daily Food, and very good, but some of 'em are far better than other some. The biggest we caught was more than three Men could compass, and a loaded Wagon might safely have gone over it without breaking it.

Besides these, there are also a great many Sharks, which do much mischief; of which I gave you an instance before in the poor Chineese, that was diving for Iron, and was devoured by 'em. There is much fishing for 'em. And the manner of catching them is, by baiting several very large strong Hooks, with the whole Liver of some other Fish, which the Sharks will not fail to swallow Hook and all, being extream greedy, and so they are taken. The Tail is all that is eaten of this Fish, and that is not very palatable neither; but the whole is eaten sometimes by Seamen, in case of necessity, for want of other meat: But its Liver is very useful for many things in Surgery.

Our Ship being now thoroughly refitted, we returned to our old Anchoring Place at *Batavia*; where we found a Ship newly come from *Holland*, that had not yet cast all her Anchors. I took in all hast a Chineese Praw, and went on board of her to see if I could not meet with any old Aquaintance there, and to hear some News from our Country; And there I heard the first account of *Stransbourgh* [1] being taken by the French, which was a very great surprize to us.

As soon as our Ship had taken in all Necessaries here, she was ordered to sail for *Ceylon*, at which I was mighty joyful, and accordingly I recruited my self with Provisions, and went on board: Then we left *Batavia* with the first fair Wind, and in five Weeks time we happily arrived before *Columbo*, which is the Chief City of the Dutch in *Ceylon*. It is one of the most commodious Ports of any in the Indies, where Ships may lie safe many years, and come in at will, with the Sea-wind, and run out when they please, with a *Land-wind*. Yet there are a great many Rocks there, but they are only dangerous to Strangers; for which reason, when a Ship comes thither, that hath never been there before, she is obliged to fire three Guns; where as if he is acquainted with the place, he need fire but one. This is straight answer'd by a Gun from a Watch-Tower, that is on one of the highest Rocks, about two miles distance from the City, where there is always a Pilot, and his Men ready, who as soon as they spy a Ship coming, display a Flag in token that they must come no further, and then they go and bring the Ship in.

At the Mouth of the Haven lies a Fort or Castle, called *'t Swart*, i.e. the *Black Fort*. It was first built by the Portugueze, under a specious pretence of building a thing of very different nature. For when the King of *Candy*, who could at that time have prevented their work, sent to know what they were about; they told him they were only building a

[1] Strassburg: annexed by Louis XIV in 1681.

Play-house, and under that colour carried on their work, and provided it with large pieces of Cannon, which they brought to Shore in great Hogsheads; and so became able to maintain themselves there.

I do not design to enter upon a description of this Island, because it hath been done very particularly by others, and especially by *Chr. Schwitzer*, whose Relation is now published with mine, to which I refer you.

While our Ship was lading with Cinnamon, and several other Rich Commodities, I went on Shore most of the time; where I took my diet at a Freemans House, where I had it extream good, and well ordered, and for a very small price.

The great Commodity of this Island is Cinnamon, which is the Bark of a Tree, much of the bigness of an Olive-Tree; the Leaves are much like the Laurel, but somewhat smaller; the Flower it bears is white, and the Fruit is like the Black Olives of *Portugal*. The Tree hath two Barks, the Cinnamon is the inner one of them, which is peeled off the Tree, and cut in square pieces; then laid in the Sun to dry, which makes it rowl up together, as we see it in Europe, and changes its colour, which is at first near upon Ash-colour, into what we find it of here.

When the Trees are peeled in this manner, they are let alone for three years, in which time they have regained their Coats as before. The Trees grow wild, without planting and cultivating, and make a sort of Coppice of themselves; and require no other hand than that of Nature to make them beneficial to Man.

There is besides this, a sort of Cinnamon, that grows in *Malabar*, and is called *Canella de Matto*, but it is a bastard kind, and nothing near so good.

None of the Spices, neither the Cinnamon I have been speaking of, nor the Cloves, Mace, Nutmegs, Saffron, &c. may be carried away by any private Person upon pain of death: And it hath cost some Men their Lives for attempting to bring them over; as I saw an instance of one who had got a small parcel of *Borrobone*, in order to take with him home, and was executed for the fact. This *Borrovone* is a Root growing in great plenty in *Java*, and is made use of instead of Saffron by all the Inhabitants; and it hath all the Vertues of the best Oriental Saffron; it is cut and dried, and looks like Ginger.

The other Great and Rich Commodity of this Place is

Pearls, which they fish for after this manner. The Company hath some thousands of Divers for that purpose, which are divided into so many Companies, and to each of them there is an Overseer. These men are all divided, so many to each Boat, and so they go to the Oyster-Banks; where stripping themselves, every one of them tie a small Basket round their middle: Then they bind a piece of a certain Root they have, that is very hollow, and of an Oyly substance before their Mouths, so that it resists the water a good while, and gives them some time to breath. In this manner you shall see 'em all go down with wonderful quickness to the very bottom; where they fill their little Baskets with Oysters, then come up again as nimbly as may be; and when they have a good quantity of 'em, they carry them to Shore, where they lay 'em out in the Sun; there they open of themselves, and in them are found sometimes many Pearls, sometimes none at all.

Some of these Divers, more skilful than the rest, will, without the help of those Roots, keep under water almost as long as they that use them.

When their days work is over, they come to Shore all together in good order, delivering faithfully all the Pearls they have got to the Officers that are appointed by the Company, which finds all these Men with Provisions, and other Necessaries, and allows some of them pretty good Salaries besides.

In the whole fishing Season it cannot be but, there must happen several accidents, and that many Men lose their Lives in the Sea among the Rocks; you hear almost daily of some such misfortune, and every day gives subject of lamantation and complaint to some new-made Widow or Orphan. Yet notwithstanding all this, there is no want of Men, ready to take to serve in this dangerous employment, some being forced into it by the Dutch, and others by their necessities.

The Oysters in which the Pearls are found, are fine, white and smooth; I have known 'em find three hundred and odd of Pearls in one of 'em. When they have a mind to give them a fine colour, they take Rice, and beat it to dust with Salt, and rub them with that, and it makes them as bright as Christal, and so they will continue.

There is another sort of Oyster in *Ceylon*, which is called by the Inhabitants *Changa*, by us *Mother of Pearl*; this they polish very fine and make fine drinking Cups of it.

It is also of great use for many Ornaments, especially that which comes out of *China*, *Bengal*, *Ormus*, *Gammaron*,[1] &c. as we see most frequently on those pieces of work, that come from thence into these parts of *Europe*.

There is likewise another manner of fishing, which is more tedious, and therefore less used. Yet I have seen it practised in a River that was thirty or forty Fathoms deep. Two Ships were laid aside of one another, at about eight or ten yards distance; and a Beam being laid across them, whereon there is a large Pully fix'd; they hang a large Bell thereon, in which the Man sits, (upon a cross Seat fix'd within the Bell) and so the Bell is let down; there is a little ringing Bell fixt upon the top of the Beam, and the Man hath a Cord with him fasten'd to that, and to his Body; as soon as he finds the Air begins to fail him, he pulls that little Bell, which is a token to the rest to pull him up; and when he hath clear'd that place, they move a little further, and fix there again till they have got all they can.

Having spent my time ashore, I went on board again, and then the other Master-Surgeon took his turn, and I went no more on shore, but only once, when my Comrade sent me word, that there was an Elephant of the Governor's was to shew a great many Tricks, of which I have given you a relation before.

In a matter of five Weeks time, all our business being done in *Ceylon*, we all got aboard, and set sail for *Batavia* again, where under the Almighty's Protection we arrived safe, after a kind Voyage of three Weeks. But we were no sooner arrived, and cast our Anchors, but we fell into an extream danger. Our Butler, according to custom, and by the *Skipper's* Order, went down to fetch some Arack for the Seamen, and as he was drawing it out of the Bung-hole, with a sort of small Pump, which they had for that purpose, either by a Snuff of the Candle, or by the Candle itself, the Arack took fire; and that spreading, like Lightning, set the whole on fire; for the European Brandy doth not burn near so violently as Arack doth. All our Men were immediately at work to put it out, but all in vain: It got a head after so furious a manner, that it set fire in the Ship it self, and it was not long e're that was all in a flame. We had then nothing more to do, but to

[1] Gombroon, now Bandar Abbas on the Strait of Ormuz, where the English, Dutch, and French had factories for the Persian trade.

look after ourselves, and to endeavour to save our own lives; and it was a great mercy we could do that, for we could not save the least parcel of our Goods, nor one of our Chests, much less any of the Company's Goods. This was a mighty loss to the Company, who had abundance of Cinnamon, and rich Cinnamon-Oyl on board, all which helped to its own destruction ,and increased the Fire: For no sooner had we left the Ship our selves, but the fire took in the Powder-room, where there was some Tuns of Powder, which blew up the Ship and tore it all to pieces, and threw some of its Cannon above a quarter of a mile up into the Air. Thus, when we thought our selves secure, and past all danger, and pleased our selves with the thought of our success, we were all on a sudden mortified with this great accident, and all our Joys destroyed, with the utmost peril of our Lives. But God be praised, that no Man got any harm, but every one of 'em were saved by means of a good number of Small Boats that were sent to our Relief. The Butler, who had been the occasion of this, was seized by the Judge Advocate, and for ought I know, was forced to serve the Company all his life long for nothing.

After this I had Orders sent me to go upon the Fort, called the *Hollandia*, which is by the New Gate. There I had the care of the Sick and Wounded; and was set over a Young Man, whom I had formerly known at *Dantzick*, and was here married to a Daughter of one of the *Kastizen*.

These *Kastizens* are those that had a Dutch Father, and an Indian Mother. When an European marries one of these *Kastizees*, and hath any Children by her, they are called *Mastizees*; and these may wear the same Garb that the Dutch use. Of this latter sort, there are many thousands in and about *Batavia*.

An Old Freeman, whom I used to converse with frequently, and was very intimate with, undertook once in friendship to advise me to marry one of those *Mastizens*; who, as he told me, was worth above forty thousand Gilders. This proffer did not much displease me, but it was an Old Woman, he told me, and the Widow of an European Officer, who had served the Company. Hearing of her Age, made me not so eager to see her as I was at first, when he proffered to carry me to her. But the very seeing of her disgusted me so much from Matrimony, and my Friend, that I never had a charitable thought of him ever after. I thought at the first sight of her, that it was an

Ape of the larger size, that had been the wonder and pastime of Mankind for some hundred years. And asking him, whether he thought me fit for nothing but the procreation of Baboons, I left him in a mighty passion, and would not so much as speak a word about the matter.

When an European designs to marry any of those People, he and the Woman must appear before the President of the Council, and bring their Contracts, (which are to be drawn up and signed by a Publick Notary) to him, to have his consent to the consummation of the Marriage; likewise a Memorial of the Goods of each of them must be shewed him, and registered: And when they have obtained leave, the Wedding is generally kept about a fortnight later.

Besides, that this baulk had turned my Stomach for some time against Matrimony, I was not very much inclined to it, because a Man is obliged to settle, and spend his life in India. For I had a design to be going further still; and by the means of some Presents, now and then, to obtain leave to go to *Japan.* For which purpose having made some close applications, and used the means I mentioned just now, I after some time had orders to get me ready to go thither, on board the Ship called the *Asia,* which was to go in a fortnight to *Formosa,* and from thence to *Japan.* So I went and provided my self with all necessaries for that Voyage, it being no small one.

According to the Orders given, we set sail in the Name of God, on *St. Steven's* day, with so fair a South-wind, that by the next morning we were got three miles beyond the great Island *Java,* and passed by the small Island *Carousing.*

The next day we saw the famous Coast of the Island *Borneo,* and leaving that on the right and *Temaho, Tumbolan* and *Ananibo* on the left, we steered our Course between them, till we came into the open Sea of *Paragoa*; where leaving *China* on the left of us, we sailed directly upon *Formosa.* But e're we could reach it, we had very bad weather for some days, and were in extream danger; for besides that, the Sea it self is one of the most dangerous by reason of the many Rocks there; we went thro' one of the dreadfullest Storms that was almost ever known; insomuch that we lost both Bolt-Sprit, and Sprit-sail[1] and

[1] "A sail attached to a yard which hangs under the bowsprit" (Falconer, *Dict. Marine.*

one other Sail. As we were drove to this extremity, our Master and Steersman advised together, whether they should not make what way they could to an Island that lay on the right Hand, and within sight of us, to see if by that means we might not save the Men and Cargo. So it was agreed upon, that we should make thither with only our Mainsail. But the night coming upon us, before we could come near it, we lost all hopes of safety; for the Tempest increased with the darkness of the night, and we were most of us in despair of our Lives, and for my part I never was less fond of Travelling, than at that time.

Yet my hope was, that as God had often preserved me from Eminent dangers before, so he would not forsake me then in this Condition; Thus we Continued till near Morning, when our Seamen conceived some hopes of attaining to Land, and accordingly by break of day, we discovered the Island *Manilha* within two Miles of us, and by the help of the Light we made shift to weather the Gulf of *Manilha*, which as soon as we were got into, we gave God Almighty thanks for his great Preservation.

Here we refitted our Ship as well as we could expect, and got a new *Mast*, and in Eight days time we set Sail again with a fair wind Early in the morning, so that by next day we left *China* on the left, and the next Morning were in sight of *Formosa*, whither we came on safe, and cast our Anchors before the Fort called the *Zealand*.[1]

Our Master went ashore, and did all his business in a fortnights time; during which time I was most upon Land, but it being needless for me to give any Account of that place, which hath been so Amply described by others; I will wave it, and pursue our Journey.

We set Sail again with a fair wind, and sail'd for Three days along the vast Coast of *China*, which we had still on the left of us, and when we came before *Cucheu* [Kowchou] we cast our Anchors, and lay still Two days there.

And then continued our Course, so that the next day we passed by the Island of *Chanquoish*, and Steering between the Island of *Fuego*, &c. We in a few days came before the City of *Nangato* [Nagasaki], where we again returned God thanks for having brought us thro' that dangerous Voyage. Notwithstanding that our ship was so tattered,

[1] Fort Zelandia was on the south-eastern coast of Formosa, on the site of the present Taiwan.

and that we had lost 14 of our Men; and had 20 sick, among those of us that were left.

We were forced to leave our Chaplain behind us at *Batavia*, for the Javians [1] will not suffer any Nation to bring any of their Teachers along with them into their Territorys. So that we were forced to make use of one of the gravest of our Company, who was Assigned to read Prayers daily in the Ship, and as soon as we came to cast our Anchors we had strict Orders given by the Master to hide the Book very carefully that had been used in the Voyage; and to keep all other Religious Books close out of sight, lest we should go in danger of our Lives, if they should discover any of 'em about us.

[1] A mistake for "Japonneeses."

CHAPTER IX

How foreign Ships are receiv'd, and visited in Japan. Women proffered to them for their use while they Stay. Some of the Japonneses exceeding Nimble at shewing Tricks. Strange variety of Birds, in the Port of Nangato. A Ship takes Fire, by means of the Men drinking of Arack. Account of the Manners, Customs, Religion &c. of the Japonneses. Departure from Nangato. Near being Shipwreckt a going back to Batavia, yet arrive thither. Departure thence again, to Malacca, and Achem, with an Account of those Inhabitants, and return again to Batavia.

WE had scarcely dropt our Anchors before *Nangato,* but we had some Japonneses Boarding us with their *Canows.* They visited our Ship from Top to Bottom, by Order of the Emperor; and according to their Custom, secured all our Sails, and all our Powder and Bullets; dismounted our Cannon, and took off some of the Principal Tackle of our Ship, and carried them on Shore with them. Thus they serve all the Ships that come thither, and thus they had done to 3 or 4 English and French Ships that lay there: But every bit they take away is faithfully returned, when they are ready to go off again.

When we had begun to unlade, a parcel of Japonneses came to us to offer us some Women, and ask us, if we could not have some of 'em while we stay'd there: But no body hearkned to their Proposal but the Master, and the Book-keeper.

The goods were unladen by the Japonneeses, of which a certain number is allotted to each Ship: So that our Men had little or nothing to do. The Master went on Shore, as soon as the Ship was come nearer to the Town and lay'd up there: But he came back every day an Hour at least, or Two, before night: For all the while that we lay here, the Japoneeses held a continual Watch aboard all the Ships that were in the Port. I cannot undertake to give you a large Account of *Japan*, because it would require a larger Volume than I intend ; nor do I think it necessary, because so many have done it before me ; but what I observed most particularly amongst 'em, will, I hope, be sufficient to satisfy the Readers Curiosity.

When I came on Shore, the first place I entered into, was a publick house, where they drunk Tea, and that very plentifully ; having rested there a while with my Companions, we went to take a view of the Town ; where we saw abundance of Joyners, and Japanners Shops, set out with Wonderful variety of rich and Exquisite work, as *Scrutores*, *Cabinets*, &c. inlay'd with silver and gold, and most admirably lacker'd, all which made as fine a Show as ever I saw. Some of these pieces of Work were valued at some Thousands of Gilders. In that kind of Work they out-do all Indians whatever, and indeed in all manner of Ingenuity and Cunning, insomuch that it was a Proverb among the Dutch, that *tho' a Dutch Man was Cunning, he might go to School to a Japoneese*.

They do not trouble themselves with Linnen or Silk Manufactures ; by reason that they are brought over to them in such abundance from other Countreys, that they have 'em as Cheap, as in the places where they are made.

Our Ship the *Asia*, was laden with such kind of things, and took in Exchange, what *Japan* affords, as Copper Stafetiens, Silver, Gold &c.

Their manner of Saluting us seemed very strange to me at first ; whereas the Chineeses, and other East-Indians used to shew their respect by clapping their hands together against their Breast or Forehead, these People pull'd off their Shoes, and set themselves down on the Ground, for they look upon it as a greatest piece of Incivility to receive any Person Standing.

Whereas other Nations think fair Hair, and white Teeth great Ornaments ; these are of a quite different Opinion, and think none agreeable but those who have the Blackest Hair and Teeth : and they use all the Art they can to make them so ; their Notion in this being directly opposite to ours, taking Black to be the Livery of Mirth and Pleasantness, and white of Grief and Mourning. They have but little Hair on their Heads, being always carefull to pluck it out by the Roots from their Youth. In short, all their

Customs, Language, Dress &c. is as different as can be from all other People.

There is a certain Antipathy between them and the Chineeses, they cannot bear with one another; when they go to War against the *Tartars* or the *Chineeses,* they never give Ground, and will sooner be Cut into a Thousand pieces than Fly: and if Thousands, 10 or 100,000 are Cut down, they are immediately Recruited: For their Law forbids them to yield to, or Flee from, any Enemy. Their Countrey is so Populous, that one who hath not seen it cannot hardly believe it.

The Sea Port of *Nangato,* was at our first coming so full of Birds, that it was almost covered with 'em, and all the Ships that lay there as it were Blockt up with them; they were very Tame, insomuch that as our Boats went to and fro to Land, they would but just give us way: the Reason of that vast Quantity is, because they never kill any of 'em to Eat, for their Law forbids them strictly to Eat any thing that is Tame, as Oxen, Cows, Hens, &c. But any thing that is Wild, they may and do Eat. So that these Fowls being harmless, as well as Tame, they do not so much as disturb them; which makes 'em Increase to that prodigious number. They are in Shape and Colour much like our wild Pigeons, and have the same feet with Ducks.

The night before I was resolved to go on Board again, there fell out an unlucky Accident in our Ship. Some of the Seamen had saved their Portions of *Arack* for some days, designing to have a good Quantity together for Punch, and the place where they were to drink it being very dark they got themselves a Lamp, which they lighted, and Imprudently hung up upon one of their Hammocks. One of them being a little Intoxicated, and lazy, lay'd himself down in that Hammock, and the rest of the Company pressing him to drink in his Turn, he did now and then take his Cup, but at last his hand growing more and more unsteady, he spilt part of his Cup over the Lamp; which by Misfortune hung over their Bowl. So that the whole taking Fire, and they not in a Capacity to look carefully about them, the Fire took hold of the Hammocks, and burnt several of them. But by the Assistance of the other Seamen it was happily stopt from doing any further Damage.

The men who had occasioned this were immediately clapt into Irons. And some days after they were brought to publick Punishment, according to the Custom of the Sea:

Which was to receive from every Person of the Ship 90 Blows on the Breech, with an Anchor Rope.

And had the Master not been very favourable, it would have fared much harder with them. However, as mild as the punishment was, it made them in such a Condition, that they were forced to keep their Beds for several Weeks; and most like to Die. Neither could any of 'em ease Nature, or make Water, for several days.

While we lay here, I was Invited on Board an English Merchant-Man and there had great proffers made me if I would have gone along with them; the proffer was the more Advantageous, because they had lost their Surgeon in the Voyage, and had but a Young raw Boy with them that could hardly spread a Plaister. But I would by no means hearken to their Proposal, because it was as much as my life was worth, and what was yet more, I should have been Perjured if I had accepted it, and forsook the Company.

In this Port dyed three of our Men, and a Carpenters Boy. Some Japonneeses carried them out of the Harbour in a small Boat, into open Sea, where they threw 'em over: For they are so far from suffering any Foreigners to be Buried among them, that they will not permit them to be thrown so much as in the Water that is near them. We had here such a Terrible Storm all on a sudden, that if our Ship had not been well provided with Anchors, and the Tempests lasted but a very little while; it had certainly been lost. For in that little while, of four Anchors that we had, we lost Two.

The English Ship I was just now speaking of, foundered at that time, 7 of her Men were drowned, and the rest very hardly escaped. The next day they refitted our Ship again; during which time, I had an opportunity of going on Shore again for three or Four days.

In that time there happened to come some Jugglers to *Nangato*, who shewed the finest and the most dextrous Tricks that I ever saw, both of Legerdemain, and of Activity of Body; but of what they Showed of the latter an Instance or two, will not be unacceptable. One of these Fellows had a Bamboo-Cane, of about 6 foot length tied to his Middle, and as he was Standing still, another Fellow leaping on a sudden with his feet upon his Shoulders, climbed up to the top of the Cane; and there lay'd himself out at length upon the Knob, which was on the top of the Cane, of about the bigness of a Goose's Egg, stretching out his Arms and Leggs, and whirling round 3 or 4 times. The Man upon whom the Cane was tied fast, walking all the while to and fro, and never offering to touch the Cane with his hand.

After this there came a second who stood upon his head, with his feet directly up on the Air, and then a third came and got up and stood upon the Soles of his feet.

Then another set himself firm upon his Leggs, and there came one of them and stood upon his head, with his feet up in the Air.

Lastly, they took a Board all stuck with sharp Nails about two spans length; over which a Fellow raised himself upon his hands so neatly, that his head did not touch one of the Spikes. These tricks being somewhat extraordinary, and far more surprising than what I have yet seen in Europe, I thought it might not be amiss to give you an Account of them, tho' I am sensible that some who think it Impossible which they have not seen, will be apt to censure it, rather than believe it.

This last time of my being ashore, I chanced to come by one of their Religious Assemblys, into which my Curiosity led me to go in hopes of seeing some strange Custom: But there was nothing very peculiar. There only came in one of their Priests, who set himself down in the midst of the place, and a great many People being gathered about him, he made a kind of Sermon or Oration to them, which I hearkned to very diligently; but could not understand a word of what he said. Nor would any one of that Assembly give me any answer when I asked them what it was that he had been saying to them, but all went off like Mutes, they do not at all care to enter into any discourse with Christians concerning Religion, which I often attempted to bring them upon; And indeed it is not safe for Christians to talk to them on that Subject, as we had all sufficiently been Informed 'ere we came to Land there. Yet I could not forbear to touch a little upon't sometimes with one particular Acquaintance I had got there, who was a grave, sober, understanding Man: And he would often express very favourable Sentiments of the Christian Religion, and did not stick to tell me once (fetching a deep sigh) that he wished he could be at liberty to Embrace it, but withal conjuring me not to discover him; because it would cost him his Life, if it was known that he had such a desire.

My time now grew short; and I made haste to buy what

I wanted; but when I came to look about in their Shops and Ware-houses, I was so Tempted with the sight of their Fine-works that I bought a great deal more than I at first designed to do. What I bought, tho' of the Finest-work, I had exceeding Cheap: Which was another Encouragement to me to lay out my Money. These Work-men are but very poor, as indeed all the Trades-men in the Country are. Some of 'em do not live better than Beggars, and a little Charity Transports them into such humble Acknowledgments, that if at any time I gave any of 'em the value of Two-pence of our money, I could hardly keep them from falling upon their knees before me to thank me. There is no middle Rank of Men among them, of any value, even the Merchants being not lookt upon: But on the other side, their Gentry or Nobility are valued and Respected at a more than ordinary Rate: And in their gate and behaviour one may observe such a Grandeur, or rather Haughtiness, as is scarce to be seen any where else.

Our Ship being now full laden with Copper, Lacker'd work, Jappan-money, and other Commoditys, the Japponeeses came again to us, first to visit the Ship, and then restored us all our Cannon, Powder and Bullets, and our Sails; all which they brought us on Board again, and the next day, we set sail out of the Port, tho' it snowed hard, and the Wind was somewhat Rough.

The next Morning we saw three Suns in the Heavens; but the Brightness of the two unusual Phœnomenas the two seeming Suns was not comparable to that of the real Sun; all three of them were seen within a large Rainbow.

The 2d, 3d, and 4th day we sailed by the Island *Ximo*, and coming to a small Island of about 6 miles compass, we cast Anchore, to wait there for a Wind. Some of our Men went on Shore, and brought back some Eggs with 'em, which Water-fowls lay usually about the Shore. They were as large as Geese eggs, and we found 'em extraordinary good.

The next day we went off with a good Wind, 2 or 3 days after, we were all of us surprized to see something Floating, hundreds of Fowl upon it; but coming nearer to it, we found it was a vast big Fish cover'd with those Birds.

We found here but 18 or 20 fathoms Water; so that we were dayly and continually forced to use the Plummet: Till a fresh Storm came upon us which obliged us with all speed to hand all our sails.

The Tempest was so furious for a time, that we thought no otherwise but we should have been swallowed up: But God Almighty, whose Compassions never fail towards them that call upon him faithfully, was pleased to deliver us out of our distress, but stilling the Winds, and after some time we came to a small low sandy Island, called *Kruys Island*, where we dropt 2 of our Anchors.

In this stress of Weather we lost one Man, who was Tossed off the Maintop Mast into the Sea. The Billows carried him quite out of our sight, else we had been obliged by our Sea Articles to have put out the long Boat and to have gone after him, tho' we run the risk of loosing all the Men of the Ship. But being we could not see him, we were not obliged to seek after him; and it was more prudent to give him over for lost, than to venture 7 or 8 Men more when there was no Prospect of doing any good.

It Snowed very hard: so that we lay still here 2 days, and on the 3d day, we set sail directing our Course towards *Formosa*. In our way thither we came by a large Rock almost cover'd o're with Fowl, we went up to it with our long Boat, and caught above a hundred of 'em: if we would have stayed a while we might have caught thousands, for they hardly fled away from us: But most of 'em crept into their nests, which were nothing but the natural Cavitys of the Rocks, without any straw or any kind of Lining in them, they being so easy to come at, made us conclude, that they had hardly ever been disturbed by any Man.

At Noon our Steers-man took the Suns altitude, by which we found that we were within 40 Leagues of the Island *Formosa*, whither we were Steering. It was as fine Weather, as we could wish; but the Wind being against us, we were forced to clap upon the Wind to make the best of it, and get a little forward, till we came to have the Wind upon the beam, which in 3 days time brought us before the Road of *Zealand*. There we put some Rice ashore, and stayed but a day and a half, and at night we put out of the Bay, Firing 3 Guns to take our leave. While our Gunner was doing this, he had left a measure of Powder in the Boys hands who stood behind him, and a Seaman coming by with a Pipe of Tobacco let fall some of his Tobacco amongst it, which burnt him dreadfully, and threw the Boy backwards to the ground. It was well this did not happen in a greater parcel, and that there was no more harm done. But for this the

Seaman was taken, and was severely punished: That is done by laying 'em flat on their Belly, and stricking them with a rope across the Breech.

The next day we Steer'd between two high Rocks, that were about half a League asunder: The Wind from that time continued fair for us during the space of 8 days, in which we passed by the Island *Manilha*, then we came into a Wind, which was very troublesome to us; for it filled the Air with nasty stuff as thick as Snow, this Wind came over some small Islands that lay 2 Miles on the South of us, which are called the *Stof Elyanden*. When the Wind is pretty high, and fits in that corner, if a Ship goes too near them, it is almost enough to Smother Men. But God be thanked, we came safe thro' it, and with a favourable Wind came into the Sea of *Paragua*; we kept on our Course to *Borneo*, and from thence to Great *Java*, whence we quickly reach'd *Batavia*; which happily compleated our Voyage in 5 Months.

Being Arrived, our Ship was unladen: Our sick Men carried to the Hospital, and I at the same time went on Shore, and took all my Medicaments with me, but we had not been here above a fortnight, but an opportunity offered it self to me, either to go along with a small Fleet to the Straight of *Sunda*, or else with another which was to cruise between *Malacca* and *Sumatra*. I had my choice, and having declared my desire rather to go with the latter, I received my Commission. The reason why these two small Squadrons were sent thither was, because we were informed, that the *French* and *English* being disgusted at the disturbance we had given them in Bantam, were coming out against us.

After we had been some Weeks a Cruising there, now toward *Sumatra*, then towards *Mallaca*, sometime to the Island *St. Maurice* and *Madagascar*, without Meeting with any either French or English, Captain *Vander Bors*, who was our *Commadore* or *Admiral*, resolved to go with the Fleet to *Achem*, and to lye still there, only he ordered that one Ship should be Cruising about and bring Intelligence, and the whole Squadron which consisted of 11 Ships should take it by turns.

While we lay here we had a most dreadful Storm for the space of 6 days. The *Sciam* was cast away, Men and all, except a few of 'em. The *Zealand* having lost all her Anchors, was drove upon a Shelf, where she stuck. We went in haste to help her Men, and we did save some of 'em : But at last the two long Boats which we had sent to their Relief being Tossed violently against each other, Split in pieces, and all the Men in them were drowned, which were about 130.

As for our Ship, we were forced to Swaddle it with a four double Cable Rope, lest it should have Split, by the violence of the Waves, and to keep constantly Pumping, six and six at a time, changing Men every quarter of an hour. And whereas one Man used to suffice at the helm, we were forced to have to keep our Anchors from twisting altogether and breaking. The worst of this was, that we were not far from Land, and we were just of the Windward of'm : For we had been much safer if we had been in open Sea. But that is safe enough every where which God takes into his keeping, and it pleased him at the end of 6 days to send us a fine Calm again, wherfore we went immediately to Prayers, and gave God thanks that he had thus delivered us.

The next thing we did was to give the Men some Refreshment, one chief part of which is always a good portion of *Arack*, and that being done we sent word to *Batavia*, what a poor condition we were in, to which we had for answer, that we might come away for *Java* again : For that two Ships were lately come thither from *Holland*, which had brought information, that there was no report there of any likely-hood of War, and that we needed not to fear it in those Parts : But only that *England* required some Millions of Money from *Holland* for the damage the English had sustained by their means in *Bantam* ; and that in case the Dutch did not come to a Composition, a War would most certainly follow.

While we lay still before *Achem*,[1] I went often to Shore to refresh my self with the excellent Fruits of that Country. The Religion, Manners, Customs, &c. of that People are much the same with the *Javians*.

In a village not far from thence, where none but Fishermen live, I saw Men that had one of their Leggs as big as most Mens middles ; when they used to hold them up, it would Shade their whole Body from the Sun, and yet would these Men run as fast as Horses. I sometimes layd my

[1] Atchin, at the North-western point of Sumatra, where the Dutch had a settlement.

hand on those Leggs of theirs, and they felt just like a Spunge.[1]

By that village runs a very fair and pleasant River, which empties itself into the Sea, near the place where we lay at Anchor, along the side of which are a great many strange Trees, which bear a Fruit they call Wild Ananas 3 times a year, when the Fruit is ripe it is extream pleasant.

Our Fleet, which consisted now of no more than 9 Ships, set sail for *Batavia*, where we Arrived in a fortnight : And found the other Fleet come three days before us. I had changed my Ship, and was in Business in the *Hollandia*, where I had a great deal of work, and most of my patients Afflicted with sore Leggs. The Surgeon that did belong to it dyed in this Voyage, and I the rather chose that Ship, because it had already received Orders to go to the Isle of *Bali*.

Before it went off I went to Shore to take my leave of my old Acquaintance ; and there met with one that was lately come out of Europe, a Native of *Ulm*, a place I was well acquainted with ; and it being a day which was kept there as a Festival, we kept it here also amongst our selves, and diverted our selves very well : Among other news he brought over with him, the most considerable was, that the *Turks* were beaten from before *Vienna* ; which did not a little contribute to our Joy and Satisfaction.[2]

[1] These were undoubtedly men afflicted with elephantiasis of the leg, a disease not uncommon in the tropics. *Cf.* " Elephant-Legged St. Thomeans," Fryer, "A New Account of East India," Hak. Soc., Vol. I, 1909, pp. 116, 138.

[2] The relief of Vienna, on 12th September, 1682, by John Sobieski, with a combined Polish and Imperialist army, was one of the great turning points of European history. Sobieski's victory and the War of the Holy League which followed finally removed the menace of Turkish invasion.

CHAPTER X

Their departure and Arrival at Bali. Arrows used by the Inhabitants which are Mortal. They sell themselves for Slaves. Their strange Idolatry. Women Burn themselves with the Corps of their Husbands. The Island Susu Inhabited by Men-Eaters. Departure from Bali, and arrival at Batavia. Observations on that place. Account of his Voyage to Surat, and return to Batavia which he leaves again to go to Bengal, Pegu and Aracan. Roses of Jericho.

IN two days time we set Sail with a fair Wind: And the same day before Sun-set we passed by the Island *Onrust*, then came between the Island *Toppers-hoedie*, and *Bantam* along Great *Java* into open Sea: And in 18 days time we reached the Island *Bali*, and cast our Anchors before the Capital Town of the same name.

In our former Voyage to *Banda* and *Amboina*, we passed by this place and came within 8 Miles of it; But the Wind being then so fair for us, we would not touch here, but made the best of our way forward: Otherwise we should have called here of Course, as most Ships do, to take in fresh Water, and other Refreshments.

Here we unladed our Ship, and exchanged the Commodities for those of the Countrey: Which were chiefly, Silk and Cotton wrought, most of the People here being employed in Spinning and Weaving.

They are a very Strong sort of People, somewhat Blacker than the generality of other Indians are. They use no other Weapon when they fight but Arrows, which they carry always about them in a kind of quiver. These Arrows are so contrived, that when the Man who is Wounded with 'em goes to draw them out, they break; besides that, they are so Artificially Poyson'd, that it is present death without any Remedy.

They permit themselves to be sold, to any Nation over all The Indies, for Slaves; while I was there I bought a young

Girl of a Merchant, for 18 Rixdollers, and took her with me to *Batavia*, where I could make her earn me two Shillings or 18 Pence a day.

They are exceeding Brutish People, and the Simplest of Heathenes. Their God is what ever they first cast their Eye on in the Morning, so that it is still variable, sometimes a Cow, sometimes a Tree, sometimes a Dog, or a Bird, &c. This they keep in veneration for all that day, and pray to it with great earnestness upon all emergencies.

They know nothing of Marrying amongst 'em. But as it is among Brutes, Men and Women are in common to each other, which makes the Country very Populous. Yet each man hath always some one whom he looks upon as a Principal Consort, and by the Custom of the Country she is obliged to such a severe and Rigorous Ceremony upon the death of her Mate, as would very ill go down with those who make a profession of more faithfulness and a more Honourable observance of their more solemn Engagements: And I have seen them acquit themselves of it with the greatest Resolution imaginable; I mean the Burning themselves when their reputed Husbands Corps is committed to the Flames. The manner of it is thus. When the Man is dead, they sew him up in a Cotton cloath, and carry him up to the Top of the House, where they keep him four or five days; during which time the Woman hath time to prepare herself, that is, to take her leave of her friends and all the while some old Women who are hired for that purpose, are sitting at the door, crying and howling. Then they dig a great hole near the River side, which they fill with Wood, and having laid the Corps upon it, they set fire to the Wood. The Woman all this while having taken her farewell of all her Relations, and having got a whole bundle of presents and recommendations to their friends in the other World, she binds up all her tokens together in a Cotton Cloath, and when the Fire is thoroughly lighted, she throws her self therein.

These tokens are different according to the Condition, Inclination, or degree of Relation of the Person they send to; as one Man shall send his Wife Money, the other Flowers, the other some other small present, all which she promises to deliver faithfully. There stands round the Fire several Persons with their Instruments of Copper and other Metals, on which they make such a horrid noise, that there is no hearing of the Womans Shreeks, besides there are Men ready with Vessels of Oyl to pour into the Fire to make it Burn more vehemently, that she may the sooner be out of her pain.

When they are thus consumed to ashes, they are taken up very clean and thrown into the River with another consort of howling and crying. I know there hath been several Accounts of this given by others after a different Manner, but what I have here given is as I have been an eye witness of it my self.

Here grows some of the finest Fruits in the World, and in great plenty, so that I eat my fill of 'em. These Fruits are a Refreshment of no small value to an European, and it makes him have a much greater esteem for those remote and Barbarous Isles, and it is very often the only thing for which one would value them; it is as observable, that the more Barbarous the Country is, the more it excels in choice and delicate Fruits, as this place may well serve for an example, and all the Isles thereabouts, which are Inhabited by the most Brutish sort of Men. And some of 'em by Men who devour one another, and make a feast of their Victory; as at *Susu*, which lyes here hard by, and likewise in the Country of *Hottentots* near the *Cape of Good Hope*. I have often wisht for some of them since I parted with them, and that they had agreed more with our Climate, so that we could have them in Europe.

Our business being done, we left *Bali*, and quickly gained the Coast of Great *Java*, from which *Batavia* lyes but eight Leagues distance; and in eight days sail we arrived at *Batavia* again. We had all the way the sight of the Island we left, and sometimes could see over it in a very clear day, it not being above sixteen Miles in compass.

When we came to Shore I was very kindly received, and placed into the Hospital at *Batavia*, there being just then a vacancy by the death of the chief Surgeon of that place, the Council was pleased to choose me in his stead, and to give me the care of it. Here I had five Master Surgeons under me, and my Station was every way much more agreeable than hitherto it had been; but that which pleased me the best, was that I had both time, and opportunity to serve God; and tho' it was only the Reformed Religion that was exercised here, yet I took a great deal of Satisfaction in going to serve God with them, when their Assemblys met; which was three times a Week. But I could rather have wished there had been a Church of my own perswasion (which is the same that *Luther* maintained and profess'd) for then I believe I should never have troubled my self to have come back to *Holland* again, and I dare say that thousands more would willingly continue there, rather than undertake such dangerous Voyages to come back, if they could but have the free exercise of their Religion, as they have in *Holland*, where all Religions are tolerated; and it was ever a wonder to me, that the same liberty was not granted in *Batavia*, which is as wisely and politically govern'd as any City in the World, and keeps as good an order in all things, notwithstanding the great variety of its Inhabitants; having within it, besides the Natives of the several parts of the Indies, vast numbers of *Turks, Persians, Tartars, Chineeses, Siamers, Moors, Japoneeses, Armenians, Arabians, &c.* Yet there is no other Religion allowed, but that of the Reformed, and at their Assemblys are all the Soldiers obliged to be present, of what perswasion soever they be, and forced to be there every *Sunday* by Turns, under the Eye of an officer, and then they put their Shoes on, whereas they wear 'em but rarely otherwise.

There are besides the Church in the Castle two other Churches, where they Preach in the *Portugueeze* and the *Maleysh* Languages, the first for the conveniency of the Burghers, the other of the mixt Nations who generally speak that Language.

Yet for all this liberty of Religion is not given, there are many hundreds who when their time is expired, bind themselves a fresh rather than venture the danger of going home again, tho' they lay their Religion aside for ever for't. The frequent news of Ships being cast away, and loosing one half of the Fleets, and sometimes the whole ones, increases their fears daily. While I was at *Batavia* my self, I sent a letter to my Relations, by one who intended to pass thro' *Ulm*, where they lived: And of this Fleet he went in, half was lost by the way, tho' he got safe home, and to my great surprize brought me an answer to it himself, about two years after that: Just as I was preparing to come into *Holland* my self, he told me he was come over again to end his days there, for he found that the Air of his Native Country would no more agree with him.

While I was thus settled here, I got very considerable practice among the Free-men, besides my fixt employment; and especially among the Chineese, whom I found by much the most generous sort of People and best to deal with. It was common for them to give me three or four Rix-dollars for letting of 'em Blood, and forty or fifty Gelders for curing the least Wound. But of all the Patients I ever had, I cannot but mention one, who for the odness of the Punishment which was inflicted on his Adversary, is well worth the Relating.

I was once in a Chineese's house drinking of *Tea*, which is drunk in great quantitys there in *Tea-houses*, very good and very Cheap. On a sudden two Chineeses fell to high words, till at last one of 'em took a pot full of Boyling hot Water, and threw it all upon the other, and all Scalded his Face, and some other parts. I took the Man home, and cured him in a few days, for which he gave me thirty Rixdollars ready Money and did me all the kind services he could, often inviting me to his house, and treating me very civilly. The other who had used him this basely, was Condemned to have twelve of the longest Hairs of his Beard pull'd out, or else to pay thirty Golden *Cubanz* which is in value 300 Rixdollars (each *Cubanz* being worth 10 Rixdollars, and the Golden Coyn of the Great *Mogul's*) but this Chineese being a Man of Substance, chose rather to pay the Money than to part with so many precious hairs out of his Beard, and they are all of them so fond of that Ornament, that it would have been as Reasonable to have asked him for twelve of his Teeth. Besides this, he was obliged to defray all the charges my Patient had been at, and to stand to all damages.

There was all this while a fine Ship preparing for a Voyage to *Surat*, and I having a great desire to go that Voyage, because it is lookt upon as very safe, and hardly ever attended with bad Accidents, I ordered my affairs so as to get leave to go : Upon which I sent my things on Board the *Gelderland*, for that was the name of the new Ship which I was to go in.

On Easterday in the Morning, all things being ready, we set Sail by break of day, and took our farewell with three Guns, but we reacht no further by night than the Island *Onrust*, and for want of a Wind, were forced to lye still there four days. At last we weighed our Anchors, having a small gale of Wind, which carried us past the Isle *Sumatra* : And as we came by the Island of *Engano*, it ceased and left us without a breath of Wind. Thus we left the Ship to run a drift, and our Men were all idle for three or four days, during which time we had *Engano* still in sight of us, for we moved but very slowly.

In this while many of our Men took notice that one of our Souldiers (for we had fourteen of them a Board besides

DUTCH SHIPS IN A STORM OFF THE COROMANDEL COAST

(From F. Valentijn's "Oud en niew Oost-Indien," 1726)

Seamen) a Venetian Named *Nicolao*, used to be frequently with two Boys that belong'd to the Ship, and those three would meet in private ever and anon. The Boat-Swain took a particular notice of 'em, and watcht 'em narrowly; at last he discovered the end of their Meeting, and surprized them in the Act of Sodomy; Upon which he went and informed the Master of what had passed. Immediately after the Venetian, and both the Boys one of about eighteen, the other about twelve year of age, were seized, and layd up in Chains, and upon Examination they all confess'd that they had been guilty of that abominable Sin ever since their departure from *Batavia*. I and the other Master Surgeon were then of the Council, and by them, we were ordered to visit them, and we found it but too true, upon which the Sentence was pronounced against all three of 'em, viz. that they should be cast into the Sea, and accordingly early the next Morning after Prayers, the Venetian was brought forth: And one of the Boys tied to his right side, and the other to his left, and in that Manner thrown in altogether, and were never more seen by us.

The boys were very penitent, and much affected with their guilt, and Prayed with the Chaplain very heartily, and shed Tears in abundance: So that there were but few of us, that could refrain weeping at the sight of 'em: But the Venetian was not at all concerned; and when he stood upon the Plank, ready to be thrown off, he begged for nothing but a draught of *Arack*. The Master told him, he should have drink enough in an Instant, and desired him to consider of his latter end, and to provide for futurity, but all Remonstrances were in vain to the last, and so he was thrown over.

There was another, who was suspected of the same crime; and upon Examination he confess'd he had intended it, but never was guilty of the act, him the Council order'd to remain in Chains, and to be set on Shore on the next Wild Island we should come to, which was *Ouro*, which was accordingly done; when we Landed him there we left him some Water, Bisket and Tobacco to serve him some days, and a Gun; he begged heartily that we would rather take away his life: But it was not granted.

So we went forward with so fair a gale of Wind, that we lost sight of that Island before night. We passed on between *Ceylon*, which we left on the right, and the *Maldivy* Islands which lay on the left, and Steering round the Coasts of *Malabar*, and *Bisnagar*,[1] we came with good speed to *Surat* after five Weeks sail, where we cast Anchor.

Our Ship was immediately unladen to make room for other goods: And our Merchants went on Shore to their apartment, which is always ready for 'em here, as it is in all those places, where they have Factories: And there they have all necessary Warehouses; Apartments, Servants, &c. fit to receive them when ever they come.

Surat lyes about 800 Leagues from *Batavia*, and belongs to the Emperor of *Indostan*, otherwise called the *Great Mogul*, who calls himself Lord of all the Indies.

It is remarkable and strange to observe how the Seasons of the Year are here divided, their Winter only shows it self by its constant Rains, for half a year in one part of the Country; during which time it Rains almost daily more or less; and while this sort of Winter lasts in one part, it is Summer and fair in the other parts of the Countrey, so that they have it by turns. The days and nights are always near equal, of twelve hours each, what difference there is, is not perceptible.

All this while our Ship was taking her lading in apace, but it was not great, most of it was *Persian* Money; when she had all in, we set sail without delay with the first fair Wind, and in fourteen days time we passed again by the Coast of *Malabar* now on the left. Thence we sail'd about the Cape of *Gomori* [Cormorin], which lyes extended to the South, and after that, we came to *Punto de Galle*, which is very commodious for all the Ships that pass that way to take in any Refreshments. There we took in fresh Water and other necessarys. We found there an English Ship, called the *Sina*, come from *Bengal*, and bound for *Cameron* [Gambroon] in the *Persian* Sea.

We laid four days here, before *Punto de Galle*: And then the Wind blowing fair for us, we run out of the Haven, and passed the next day by the *Maldivy* Islands, of which it is computed that they are above a thousand in number, and in seven days sail we came to the Island *Ouro*, where we had left the Souldier. We cast Anchor there, and sent out the long Boat with some Men to look after him, but they could not hear or see ought of him: So we continued our Course towards Great *Java*.

[1] This was the Hindu Empire of Vijyanagar in the Dekkan; by this date it was overrun by the Mohammedans and Mahrattas.

While we were in open Sea about 100 Leagues off *Malacca*, we had during three Weeks time such a Calm, that we thought we should never have had a breath of Wind more. So that in all that time we did not get a League forwards, only the Sea Wind moved us a little to and fro, but did us no good. For, tho' it may seem strange to those that are ignorant of it, it oftentimes happens that the Main Sea, especially that part of it, where no Bottom is to be found, is in a very great agitation, tho' there be no Wind at all to be perceived : and I my self have often seen in the stillest Weather, the Waves heap'd up on Hills, and so furiously high, that no Storm can raise them higher, and often times there is as great Danger, and as many Ships are there cast away ; especially those that are not well laden.

During this Calm, we suffer'd more than ever we could have done in the most Terrible Tempest, for we were under the Line, and the excessive heat caused several to fall sick, and what was worse still was, that we had made no great provision of Water by reason it was lookt upon to be but a short Voyage ; So that with heat and thirst, we were all in danger of being suffocated. Our Water was now so far spent, that a draught of it could not be had under a couple of Rixdollars. At least it came to that pass, that there was a necessity of setting two Centinells to guard the Water-Cask ; out of which they used to distribute every man his portion, and to set four Locks upon it. And when the Portions were given out in the Morning, it was not above one quarter of the measure that it used to be.

In this miserable Condition I have been forced to give two dozen of my Silver Buttons off my Waistcoat, for one draught of Water, and to gnaw bits of Wood, hoping I might suck some moisture out of it. In short, it put us all upon trying all the ways we could imagine to allay our excessive drought ; we had now but six Barrels of Water left, and we saw no prospect of Relief, so that many of us often wish'd that our Ship would sink down right with us, we neglected not to call upon God, and to send up our Prayers to him constantly thrice a day, that he would have Compassion on us ; and as this was more becoming Christians than the rash wishes which our desolate Condition forced from some, if not the greater part of us ; So it was that undoubtedly which was most effectual, for our merciful God sent us a seasonable relief, and surely because we cried unto him in our trouble, he delivered us out of our Distress.

The Moon, which shined very bright, was all of a sudden a little over cast, and at length a Black Cloud came, which deprived us wholly of the sight of it, and gave us mighty hopes that we were going to have some Rain. This gave us all new life, and set us all at work to spread out our Sails ready, fastening them by the four corners, with a Bullet in the Middle to receive the Water; thus we stayed between hope and fear for about three hours; at last the weather grew very cool, and the Clouds gathering together, the Sky was all darkened, and suddenly the rain came pouring down upon us: But never were Men more heartily glad to be wet to the skin. The first Water that came thro' the Sails was very bitter; so we threw that away; and then we fell to filling our Vessels, which done, we hoysted up our wet Sails, and run briskly before the Wind.

One may Imagine what Joy it was to every one of us to have our miserable Condition brought to such an happy End, nor did we fail to give due thanks to the great Author of it, who had so mercifully heard us. With this Wind we were not long 'ere we reach'd the Island of *Engano*, so that we after three Months Sailing passed the Streight of *Sunda*, and arrived happily on the Road before *Batavia*.

The Master and the Steward, who had been so imprudent as not to provide our Ship with more Water, was called to an Account for it, and punished for their carelessness, and had a good round fine laid upon them, which was to be deducted out of their wages, by little and little till the whole was payd.

This same Ship being design'd for *Bengal*, *Pegu* and *Aracan* in a very little while, and some of the goods being ready to load, I left all my things on Board, designing to go that Voyage too. And having provided my self with what Medicaments I wanted, in about a Months time we left *Batavia*, and came in nine days before *Pegu*, where we cast Anchor. We had but very little business there, so that we stayed there but three days, and set Sail again, and came to *Aracan*; and thence went to *Bengal*, which is but eight Leagues further. There we cast Anchor just at the mouth of the River *Chaor*, which mixes with the *Ganges*, about a mile before it throws it self into the Sea of *Bengal*. About eight Leagues up that River, lyes *Verma*, a Town of considerable Trade: Some of our Merchants sailed up to it; But I went not with 'em.

About forty miles from *Bengal*, between the River *Ganges*

and *Perselis* lyes a place, called *Lobanack* ; where there are whole Fields of those Flowers called Roses of *Jericho*, or the Rose of *Jerusalem*, and the Lady's Rose. They are quite green ; when you gather them, they close together straight and keep so, while they are dry, and when you put them into Water, they open as at first. They are good for many uses ; but excellent for Women in Labour, and facilitate the Birth by being only put under the Woman. I could have had abundance of 'em for little value, of the Inhabitants. They say the seed of these was brought over by a King of *Syria*, where they grow in abundance about *Jericho*. I do not find they grow anywhere, but in these places I have mention'd ; they have endeavoured to Transport them into several places, especially in Great *Java* ; But they die and come to nothing, the ground ought to be very full of nitre.

As to what Relates to *Pegu*, *Aracan* or *Bengal*, I will not undertake to give a description of either of the places, because I did not stay there long, and besides they may be seen at large in Linschooten's Travels, who hath been very particular in his account of 'em.

CHAPTER XI

Masulipatam its Inhabitants call'd Jentives. Account of the Climate. The Isle of Nicoporas. Arrival at Batavia. Chineeses sumptuous in their Burials. A pleasant quarrel between the Author and one of his Patients, for which both were called to account and Punish'd. The Author goes to Bantam, gives an Account of the young Kings Retinue there, and of his return to Batavia. And likewise of several Customs and Humours of the Chineeses

AFTER our Ship had got in her Complement of Sugar, Salt-peter, and Opium, we set Sail and went from *Bengal* to *Masulipatam*, belonging to the King of *Golconda*, whose Son keeps his residence at *Pentipoli*, lying not far from thence.

The Inhabitants are most of the *Mahometan* Religion. The Air is very healthy one half of the year, when the Northern winds blow constant: But the Southern winds, which blow the other half of the year, fill the Country with distempers. We were there during this latter Season, and felt the dismal Effects of it. We had already lost nine of our Men, and the rest were most of 'em ill of Agues or Dropsies. But blessed be God, I was not at all indisposed. The ill State we were in, made us make all the haste we could to be gone, and hoysting Sail, we departed, and came in four days time before the Island *Nicoparas* [Nicobar Islands], here we sailed in very great danger; for all the Sea there abouts is full of Rocks that lye three or four fathoms under Water, and little small islands, some of which are almost cover'd with Water. A little before we came by there, the *Lion*, a Ship of 470 Tun, run upon one of them, and was Split in pieces: But we past them all safe, and Steerd between *Sumatra* and *Malacca*, and thus got to *Batavia*; where I return'd to my former post. I used to go and visit the other Surgeons that had the care of some small Forts about us, and when they had any Patients that were dangerously ill, and their case desperate; they were sent to the Hospital at *Batavia* by vertue of a warrant from the Governour, which they used to get for that Purpose.

Near the Fort *Jacatra,* where I used to go often, is a piece of ground which the Chineeses bought of the Dutch, and cost them abundance of Money, in which they bury their Corpses: It was called the Chineeses Church-yard. I remember there to have seen a Grave made for one of the Richer sort of 'em, that amounted to three or 4000 Gilders, neither are they raised high, or costly in the Ornaments they bestow on 'em, but only they dig them of such a vast depth, and line the Grave from the very Bottom with fine square Stone cut for the purpose, and so strong is the Work, as well as neat, that it is as if they did design never to move from thence. I omit the other particulars of their Ceremonies, &c. because others have done it before me.

All the way from that Fort to *Batavia,* is so pleasant and diverting by reason of the continual variety of sweet Walks, Curious Gardens, &c. that it is a perfect earthly Paradise, and there is none comes to *Batavia* but goes to see it, and is exceedingly Charm'd with the sight of it.

A pleasant accident befell me there once. An officer, who was at that time a Patient of mine, a loose debauched Fellow, who followed no prescriptions, and therefore made all my remedies ineffectual to him, being at the head of a Company exercising the Men, and having got I suppose a cup in his head, seeing me come towards him to be a Spectator among the rest, saluted me at first sight after a kind of an insolent manner, and then gave me some Scurrilous Language, and told me, he thought I understood my business but very indifferently, since I kept him so long under my hands. I told him he talkt like an Impertinent Fellow, and that all the means of the most skilfull Surgeons in the World would be in vain to him, while he was alway drunk and lived such an intemperate life, and observed no rule. In short, I told him that my Art was to cure Men, and not Beasts, and that he might seek a cure elsewhere; this enraged him so, being spoken at the head of his Company, that he came and struck at me with his Cane with all the eagerness that might be, but 'ere the blow fell upon me, I closed in with him; and having no Weapon in my hand, I wrested the Cane out of his, and flung him upon his back, as he was getting up again, the standers by parted us, and there was no more heard of it for that time.

This spread about among all the Officers, and the Account of it being little to his advantage, and giving sometimes occasion to some to jeer him with his adventure, it made him stark mad ; and set him upon thinking of revenge. I expected it, and therefore avoided him, when ever I could handsomely do it. But one day we chanced to meet in a Chineeses house, where we dined ; nor did I see any tokens of his Resentment all the while we sat together, so that I was apt to think he designed to pass it by. But when he had drunk a little largely, and the ill humours were set a Floating, he begun to make little insolent Reflections upon me which turned at last to down right abuses. This did not suffice, but he must needs urge me to come out to him in the Street, and going out first into it himself, with his drawn Sword in his hand, he vapoured and call'd me all the Cowards he could think of, who durst not come out to meet him. I wore no Sword, as indeed none of our profession did : But I had a tuck Cane in my hand, which I used to wear ; but especially since my first quarrel with him : and being forced to it at length I came out to him, and with my unwieldy weapon after some passes on both sides, I struck him into the left side, but glancing against his ribs, I just larded him, and that was all ; but he keeping his ground, I made another pass at him, and fortunately run him into the Shoulder, and disarm'd him ; upon which he was carried into the Chineeses house.

As soon as this was made known at *Batavia*, we were both of us taken and brought bound into *Batavia*, and there had before the Judge Advocate, who, having examined us and our Evidences, passed Sentence upon my Adversary in an instant, which was that he was to be kept in Chains for three years, and to work among the Slaves ; and to forfeit his Salary for the time, which was to be distributed among his Company, which was accordingly put in Execution, as soon as he was perfectly recovered, and that was in a few Weeks time.

My cause being much more just than his, and my Sentence being suspended for a while, I thought I might come off Tolerably well ; but when I consider'd with what severity they had dealt with him, I could not but expect something proportionable would fall to my share. But it was not long 'ere I was put out of doubt, and my Sentence was pronounced. I was to stand before the *Corps de Guarde* at *Jacatra* three days after one another, with six Muskets hung about me, and to forfeit three months Salary to the Judge-Advocate, and to do for that time the Duty of a private Centinel, standing such hours as were allotted me, with a Musqet in my Hand.

This was tolerable, and better than I expected; but it seems it was rather contrived for me, that I might not go altogether unpunished than as a punishment deserved by, and suitable to what I had done. One may see by this punishment that was inflicted on me, that a Martial Genius reigns there; and that they are much given to a Military Discipline; for there was no manner of relation between the Musqet and me, nor indeed did it agree with me at all. But some of my Friends gave me hopes that they would soon get me released; and by their means, orders were sent me to return to my Post, after I had exercised the Musqet during two Months; by which a Month of my Sentence was remitted me.

A little while after I was restored, Orders were sent to the *Sumatra*, the Ship I was last in, to get ready in eight days to go to *Bantam*. I put my self in readiness to go with her, being desirous to see how the Place stood since its great disorder. The last day we were to be in Town, being *Sunday*, I went to Church, and heard a most admirable Sermon preach'd by the worthy Mr. *John Conradus*; after which I took my leave of my Friends, and then took a *Praw* to carry me aboard the *Sumatra*, which had her full Lading in, which was all Provisions, and most of that Rice. The next Morning the Wind being very fair for us, we set sail, and came that very Night into the Road before *Bantam*. I went on Shore with the first Boat, and was much pleased to see all the Parts of that City so neat, and in so good an order, that there was not the least sign of its late Misfortunes to be seen. I staid there that night, being told that the next day eight *Javians* were to be executed for killing some *Dutchmen* in the Country; and accordingly four of them were broke upon the Wheel; the other four were tied fast together, and turned down headlong off the Castle-Bridge into the Water.

While this was doing, there was a vast out-cry of a sudden of Fire: The Houses being all of Cane, the first House had in an instant set fire to several others; so that the Uproar increasing, the Magistrate set double guard upon all the Convenient Posts and Gates of the City, to prevent further harm; and lest this might be intended to serve for an Insurrection: But both the Fire and Noise ceased quickly after.

I went on board again, and hearing that the Young King was in a few days to make a Visit to the Governour, I desired a Friend to give me notice the night before the day on which it was to be; and notice being given accordingly by my Friend, I went to Shore.

The manner of his Pomp and Magnificence was, I thought, very well worth my sight; and it may not be disagreeable to the Reader to have a short account of it. As soon as ever the King had set his Foot out of the Castle, all the Cannon were discharged, great and small, all round the place.

The first that walked before him were four *Amboineeses*, carrying Bucklers and Swords in their Hands; next to them went a Company of *Javians*, then a Company of *Balingers*, with *Assagyen*; after these came six *Javians*, who carried a Chair finely wrought and gilt: then followed six Persian Horses, with Trappings richly covered with Gold and Silver; after them four *Amboineeses*, with Escutcheons and Swords in their Hands; then the Young Prince, or King's Son, of about eight Years of Age, on Horseback; his Horse was set out after the noblest manner I ever saw: He was attended by some hundreds of Women, each of which had something in their Hands; some, Golden Cups; some, Flowers; others, several Fruits of the Country; these were followed by the Company of *Dutch*. Then came the King himself, riding on a very fine Persian Horse, sumptuously accoutred, and sitting with that Majesty that one would have thought him Lord of the Universe. Next to him went a great Company of Women; then another Company of Dutch; and a Company of Javians, with their *Krizzen* and *Assagyen*, which ended the Procession. All this mighty Shew and Formality, was a very great surprize to me, considering that King's Station, and that his Dignity was meerly titular. But that Pomp and Grandeur did not give him so much lustre as it did those under whose subjection he was forced to live: And in that consideration, I suppose, the Dutch were willing enough to amuse him, with this vain shew of Power and Greatness. When the Guns were fired, one of the Men, not being so careful as he should have been, had one of his Arms shot off, as he was ramming in the Powder. As soon as the young King heard of it, he came into the Hospital himself to see the Man drest, and to charge the Surgeon to take great care of him, and ordered an hundred pieces of Eight to be given him; promising withal that if he cured him, he would give him a Pension of two hundred pieces of Eight yearly; which was an argument of a good tender Nature and Generosity, notwithstanding some of his Actions, before-related, might represent him as one of a cruel and barbarous Disposition.

It was not without Wonder, as well as Pleasure, that I beheld the great Restauration and Improvement of this Famous City, which once lay in so ruinous a condition; and to see such plenty and abundance there, where some time before there was such a scarcity of necessaries, that many Men were e'en famish'd. And certainly of all the hardships of that War, none was to be compared to that which we underwent for want of Water. I was once forced to give as much Money for one single draught of it, as would have bought a Butt of Wine in some places. And such was our lamentable condition, that a Man would have given his Life the next hour for a draught of Cold Water to prolong it till then. So that when Water could be got at any rate, those who had the greatest share of Plunder, would give all they had for one single Cup of it; and thought themselves happy they could purchase it upon such easie terms: And thus after all their Labour, they were but little the better for all that Booty they had gotten.

But what was the most dismal of all was, that it was not to be gotten sometimes, tho' one had had the World to give for it: And in those extremities, many of our Men drinking out of some Pools that were not wholesom, some being *Nitrous* or *Salpeterish*, and others being poisonous Water, it threw them into such Distempers, and put 'em into such Tortures, that it would have grieved any one to have seen the miserable condition they were in.

In the Wars with *Kartiri*, which were a little before my coming to the Indies, the poor Soldiers were in as bad a condition to the full. So that a Man would wonder, that the same Persons should willingly expose themselves to such difficulties a second time; as most of our Men did, who were in both Expeditions. But what will not necessity put a Man upon, especially when it is a little enliven'd by the hope of some fortunate Success? And I believe, that the good Fortune of a certain Drummer in those late Wars, served in a great measure to animate the whole Body of our Army. For this Drummer lighted fortunately on the King of *Kartiri's* Crown, for which the General at *Batavia* gave him thirty thousand Gilders of Dutch Mony; and gave him his Freedom, and a Pass to go into *Holland*, where he was to have his Mony paid, tho' the Poor Man ne're liv'd to enjoy it, for he died in the Voyage; but the Mony was duly paid to his Sisters, who lived at *Middleburgh*, according to the agreement made with the Deceased. And I make no doubt but every one of our Men, that knew this, were in hopes of getting at least a Crown for their share too.

I was one of four who had almost got as considerable a Booty, but we lost all by our want of curiosity; for three of the Admiral's chief Attendants, and I, being just come into *Bantam*, after a little fatigue, we went to take a Nap in a Warehouse that stood open, we laid us down upon a great Chest that stood there, and never dreamt that there was any thing of value within it; but we had not been there above half an hour, when an Officer was sent from the *Admiral* to demand our Bed from under us, which we readily yielded. We were strangely surprized when we saw a Party of Men ready to convoy it to the Admiral, before whom it was open'd; and out of it came seven hundred Leather Bags full of *Cubangs*, which (as I told you before) are pieces of Gold, worth ten Rixdollars apiece. You may imagine then how silly we lookt upon one another, when we heard this; and how angry we were with our selves, that we could complain of the hardness of our Bed, and were not so wise as to shake up the Feathers. But to be short, we lost very simply a Treasure which we might have had very fairly, and without opposition, if we had but been so prudent as to search into it at first.

But it is time to return to the *Sumatra*, which was now ready to go off; so that with the first fair Wind we set sail, and got safe to *Batavia* again, where we found a Fleet of seven Ships in a readiness to go home, *i.e.* to *Holland*. (as the custom is to send some such number of Ships home, every Year, sometimes more, sometimes less at a time). I was glad to have the opportunity to send some Letters by 'em, and I did so; but charging only one Friend with 'em, my Friends in *Holland* never received any of 'em. But what made me the more negligent was, that I was near the time of my freedom, and in full design of going over my self in a very little while. As soon as that Fleet had hoisted sail, I went to Church to join with the Prayers of the Congregation for the Fleets Prosperity and good Voyage, as there is always on those occasions.

Our Ship lay still at Anchor here for three Weeks, which made me very weary of it ; at last we had Orders to go with a smaller Vessel, call'd the *Bali*, to a small Island, about four Leagues from *Batavia*, to fetch Timber to repair the Ships that lay at the Island *Onrust*, and to carry it thither. This Isle hath nothing but Timber upon it : Here we spent our time in catching of Tortoises, with which we feasted our selves rarely ; and having carried what was requisite to the Isle of *Onrust*, we return'd to *Batavia*. The *Bali* being but a small Vessel, we ran up the River with ease, to the very Gate of the Castle. The Chief Surgeon of *India's* Lodging being very near to us, I took the opportunity to wait upon him, and desired him to take care I might be appointed to go with the next that should be sent to any distant part of the Indies, where I had not been ; which he promised to do, seeing it was my desire.

He represented to me sufficiently, and I knew it well enough, that I had a better Post already, and that any Post at Land was more considerable than the best at Sea ; and that those who had a settled charge there, were more regarded, and better esteemed. But I was for seeing of strange Countries, and variety of Things ; and besides, a continuance upon Land, required a continual expence, which the Sea doth not give opportunity for. But, in a word I would not have been penn'd up in one Town only, as some are there, for all the Credit and Advantage they can propose to themselves, or attain to ; and indeed except in *Bengal*, *Surat*, *Camron* in *Persia*, *Japan*, or some few other places, it is hardly worth a Man's while to rest in hopes of being advanced ; for Preferment goes there by Favour, as well as in these parts of the World ; And when it doth so I think no wise Man will depend upon it.

Thus I continued upon the *Bali*, and as soon as she had taken in her lading of Linnen and Striped Stuffs, together with some Chests of Money ; we fell down the River and set sail for *Bantam* ; whither she was bound. We were above two hours sail ; but we were forced back by a contrary Wind, which blew so excessive hard for the space of two days, that we were very happy, that we riddled our selves out of it so luckily. As soon as it was over, we set sail again, and in forty eight hours we reached the Road of *Bantam*, where we immediately unladed.

When we went to Shore there, we saw some thousands of Javians got together at the Mouth of the River: We were a little surprized at first, not knowing what the meaning of it should be; but coming nearer, and seeing several Hollanders amongst 'em, and then discovering their Nets, Hooks, and other Instruments, we found they were only catching of Crocodiles. When we landed, we saw several they had caught and knock'd in the Head already; their King was amongst 'em to see the Sport. No body can think what a strange kind of Noise these silly Javians made, and how they rent their Throats at it. Whereas my Comrade and I had caught almost as many without any kind of Noise, and not half that Trouble.

The *Bali* was only to unlade here, which being done, we set out for *Batavia* again; and as we came by the Island *Onrust*, we heard all the Cannon fire, both in the Castle, and in the City; we could not tell then what it was for, but we kept going on; and not long after, when we came to cast Anchor, we heard that the Fleet from *Cameron* in *Persia* was safe arrived, and had brought the good news with 'em, that all the Old Differences between the Viceroy there, and us, were perfectly adjusted; and that there was a Good Correspondence settled between us. And another Ship was come in from *Holland*, which had also brought the good news of the quarrel being made up between the *English*, *Danes* and *French*, and ourselves concerning the Injury done to them at *Bantam*: Which good news coming together, could not but make us all exceeding joyful. So that all the Streets of *Batavia* were all illuminated with Bon-fires, and Fire-works. The latter were chiefly the work of the Chineeses, who delight much in them, and are so ingenious at 'em, that one would wonder, especially being a People who never have any Instruments of War, where Powder is used. They likewise entertained us with their Comedies, which are very diverting, if seen but seldom. We Germans ha[illegible] over and above these good news, that which more nearly concerned us, which was, that of the good success of the Emperors Arms against the Turks; so that some of my Countrymen and I joined so much the more chearfully in the common Rejoicings, which continued all that Night. The next Morning the General *Camphuysen* [1] went to the *Maleysh* Church, where publick thanks were

[1] Johannes Camphuijs, Governor General, 1681–91.

return'd to God for our Prosperity; then the Service being over, the Guns were again fired round the City and Castle.

Three or four days after, as I was returning to see my Patients on board the *Bali,* I met with a Company of Soldiers that were going on board the *Flessingen.* These were very prettily accoutred with Silk-Stockings on their Legs, and Shoes made of Sail-Cloath: These Men were designed for *Camron, Surat* and *Macaran,* to fill up the vacancies there of such as keep Guard before the Houses of the Company. But I would not have a private Soldier to fancy by this, that they are all to meet with such treatment there; for this good usage is only to a few, that are to credit the Factories in those places; and those are some of those that have a great many Friends, and great Recommendations: Whereas many a brave Soldier is forced to spend his time in *Bantam, Amboina, Banda,* and other unhealthy Islands, where they must trudge it without either *Shoes* or *Stockings,* and it may be perish miserably.

Our Ship was once again order'd to go to *Onrust* to carry Rice, and other Provisions; which we did, and returned in four or five days.

As we were come back, it was my fortune to fall once more into the Sea; for as I went to ease Nature on the outside of the Ship, according to the usual way, I held fast by the Rope, which broke, so I dropt. The Ships Crew was more ready to laugh at me, than to lend me their Hand; and I was doubly put to't, to swim with my Breeches down; but at last my Comrade threw me out a Rope, by which I got up, and praised God for my safety. This made me more careful for ever after; and that the Boatswain might be more diligent to see for the future that such things were firm and strong, the Master gave him a severe reprimand, and laid a Fine on him.

After this I went to pay another visit to the upper Surgeon; and from thence went to Sup with an Acquaintance of mine in the Castle, and took a Friend with me. I was to go into the Town to lie; so my Friend and I took a Praw to carry us thither up the River. In the way we came thro' the Boom, which is a String of Trunks of Trees chained together, which block up the River from one side to the other, so that there is no passing thro' without an Officer, who stands there to let you thro', who first visits and searches you, and then too you must pay so much, according to the bigness of the Vessel; and this goes to the Company, who make some thousands of Gilders yearly out of it.

The next day we went to the Lottery, to see what Gaming there was; that was most full of Chineeses, who, as I said before, are the greatest Gamesters in the World. Whoever is a loser there, the Company is sure to be the winner; for there is a Money-Changer appointed by them, who sits to keep order amongst 'em, a kind of groom-Porter; and every throw that is thrown with the Dice, there is two pence paid to him for the Company. And notwithstanding that some of those who ruin themselves at play there, might be supposed to fall into a passion, and cause some disorder, yet there is never any disturbance heard of; it being no less than Death to make any in that place: For without that severity it would never be free from it, especially when poor Soldiers lose sometimes their whole Pay in one Night, which they have done very hard service a Month or two, or may be more; or when a Chineese loses all that he is worth, even his Wife and Children, nay his very Beard; nothing being more natural, than for Men in that condition to fall into excessive Passion. But they dare not give it any vent there, nor make the least noise.

I could not refrain neither, but ventured six or seven Ducatoons, which were gone in the twinkling of an Eye; but I presently gave over, and took my leave of it for ever.

Thence I went to reside for a few days at a Friends house, and a Countryman of mine, one Mr. *Buschbach*, who had got his Freedom, having compleated his time in the Company's Service, and was in very good Circumstances. He was a Man of an exceeding kind and generous Temper, and a constant Patron of all the Germans that came to *Batavia*, and never weary of doing them all the service that lay in his power. I was a little indisposed at his House, so that I sent word to the Ship, that if they were ordered to go any Voyage before I got better, they should give me notice of it, that they might be supplied with some other Person to go in my stead. But blessed be God I recovered in a few days, which I think verily was in some measure owing to my Friend's care, and his facetious diverting Company; for I never met with more agreeable Company in my life.

His House stood upon the *Vierkant*, a place so called from its being a Square, where the Rice Market was kept, and several other Provisions, being just at the Mouth of the River, and therefore most commodious for all the Country

People to bring their Fruits by water, as well as for the Fisher-boats to bring their Fish thither. There is also a small Dock for building of little Vessels. And all Vessels whatsoever that come by here, must come to Shore, and be visited by a Centinel that stands there for that purpose, and is relieved every hour ; and in case any of 'em should attempt to slip by, his Orders is to fire upon them.

CHAPTER XII

The Author's Voyage to Macassar; goes in his way to Japara; passes by Pater-noster Islands, &c. Description of Macassar: The Natives are the most faithful Soldiers the Dutch have, and the best Slaves. Moors, some black, and some very white: Their Nobility: The Author cures the Son of one of their Noblemen, and is generously rewarded. Comes away from Macassar, and finds Japara in an uproar; the Authors of it seized and punished. The great power of the Dutch Government in the East-Indies. Arrival at Batavia again. The manner of Fishing at Batavia. By a Flame which they saw afar off at Sea for two Nights together; they concluding that something extraordinary had occasion'd it; they went and found several Men reduced to the greatest extremity that ever was, and brought them into Batavia. Departure in Siam: Description of that Country, and the Dutch Factory there. Return to Batavia, where one of their Ships, by a mischance, is blown up, and all the Men killed. Ceremonies usual at a Wedding amongst the Javians

BEING pretty well recover'd, tho' as yet somewhat weak, I return'd on board, where I spent my time but after a melancholy manner, and most of it lying in my Hamock; yet I gathered strength apace, and in some days got perfectly well.

There an Order came to me to remove on board the *Tyger*, which was to go to *Macassar*; this I received with a great deal of satisfaction, and accordingly went out with her. We had not been three hours under sail, but such a violent Storm came upon us as brought our Main-Mast by the Board with such a force, that we thought our Ship was dash'd in pieces; and this continuing for some time, we were obliged to cut our Gears, and hand in what we could of our Sails.

Our Master was not for going further, so we went back to *Batavia*; and being there refitted, we set Sail out again;

and in three days came before *Japara,* which lies likewise in great *Java,* seventy Leagues eastward of *Batavia.*

This Place, which was once the Residence of the mighty Emperor of that Empire, is as much under the Dominion of the *Dutch,* as *Bantam* is. And that Emperor likewise is no more such than meerly in Name and Title ; and is as subject to the Dutch Government as the King of *Bantam* is, of whom I have given you an account. So that this whole Island, which is about five hundred miles compass, is almost all in subjection to the *Dutch* Company The Religion, Manners, Customs &c. of the Inhabitants of *Japara* are much the same as of those of *Bantam.*

Here we provided our selves with Water, and Wood for Fuel ; which being done, we wound up our Anchors, and set sail : The next day we passed by the six Islands of *Luboce,* leaving them on our left, and *Java* on the right ; and arrived to the Island of *Madura,* which is about ten Leagues from *Java.* There we staid a while, and then we set forward again with the first Gale of Wind, and passed by some hundreds of little Islands and Rocks, which are called *Pater noster,*[1] some of which we went over, whilst the Sea beat most terribly against those Rocks which stood a little above the Water, and made us very much afraid, we having no other way, but thro' them : So that we were continually sounding with the Plummet. We fell foul of the Rocks four times notwithstanding all our care ; but God be thanked, without any damage. The best of that course is, that there is scarcely ever any stormy Winds there, by reason of the great heat the Sun gives. A few days after we got before *Macassar.*

Macassar is a considerable Kingdom, and well govern'd. The *Dutch, English* and *Danes* have all freedom of Traffick there, as well as the Indians of all parts. It lies on the Island *Celebes* to the South, and reaches about an hundred Leagues ; under the Line, it hath *Borneo* on the one side, and the *Molucca* Islands on the other.

Here lay an English Ship, which had lost both her Surgeons in the Voyage, and were in great want of one to take care of their Men. They applied themselves not only to me, but to the Resident, to permit me to leave my Ship, to go with them, but it did not lie in the Governours power to free me from my Engagement in the Dutch Company.

[1] In the Flores Sea.

However, they being drove to such necessity, I went and lookt after their Patients. I left all that was proper for 'em with one of the Ship, together with written Instructions, how, and when to make use of 'em, for which they thanked me heartily, and gratified me very generously.

There happen'd a Fire one Night in one of their Negerys, which was all consumed in an instant, being built with nothing but Bamboos, and gave so great a light, that we thought it was the Day breaking upon us again, and put us into a kind of Consternation, till we knew what it was.

The People, Natives of this Island, are scatter'd thro' all parts of the Indies; and all Nations are desirous of 'em for their Slaves, because they are exceeding faithful, diligent, and good natur'd, and make the bravest Soldiers, as I have seen it my self in the whole time of the War of *Bantam*, where they daily signaliz'd themselves, both by their Courage and Conduct. They are likewise the most profitable sort of Servants. I have had two of them, who have got me half a Ducate on a day; so that these are lookt upon as the most valuable of all the Indians; and they are used with the greatest care and humanity that may be. The hardest and most slavish part of their Work, is generally put upon the *Malabarians*, who are an ill-lookt sort of People, like the *Caffers*.[1] They are so black too, that they are often taken for *Moors* [2]: Whereas it is a Nation of *Asia*, but dispersed here and there over all the Indies, as the *Jews* are in *Europe*.

The right *Moors* are those of the great *Mogul's* Country, and the places adjacent, as *Bengal*, *Surat*, *Golconda*, &c. but they very seldom or never go out of their own Country; nor doth any body dare to take them for Slaves. As there is some of 'em as black as Coal, so there is some as white as any *European* whatever. They are most of 'em very civil, handsom and well shaped, courteous and genteel in their Behaviour. They are great Merchants, and very sincere in their Dealings; and those I have had to do with, I have always found very generous and grateful. I had once the Son of a rich Moor under my hands, while I was at the Hospital of *Bantam*. He had broke his Leg, and had been

[1] The Portuguese frequently applied the term Kaffir to non-Mohammedan natives; but there had been a considerable importation of Africans, both by the Portuguese and Dutch.

[2] The Dutch, following the Portuguese, called all Mohammedan Asiatics Moors.

left to the care of some Surgeons of that Nation, who had done him no good. The Father at length despairing of the skill of his Countrymen, sent for me, and shew'd a great deal of rational concern for his Son's condition. I went to the Boy, and having examined the Fraction, and found it be better than I imagined; I told the Father he might take Courage, and that I did not doubt but I should in a little while set his Son upon his Legs again, with the help of the Almighty Creator of Heaven and Earth; (making use of those Terms, because it is in that Idea especially, that the *Moors* worship God :) Upon which he bowed and lift up his Eyes towards Heaven. I sent for my Boy, and with the assistance of a *Moor,* I set the Bone of the Boy's Leg; and having done all that was necessary for the present, my Young Patient found ease immediately. This gave the Father much satisfaction, and he immediately presented me with twenty *Spanish Matten,* telling me that was nothing of my pay, but to encourage me to take what care I could of his Child. Thus, with God's assistance, I cured his Boy entirely in six Weeks time; and without asking me, what I expected, he gave me thirty *Cubanz* into my hands, which amount to three hundred Rixdollers, and ask'd me whether that satisfi'd me. I told him it did extreamly well; and truly well it might, for in our Country we knew nothing of such large Fees as those are. If we had but a few such Patients there, it would keep a great many at home, who are now forced to ramble abroad, meerly to get their livelihood.

But I return now to my Ship, which was ready to set sail again for *Batavia,* and waiting only for a Wind. Therefore with the first Easterly Wind, we set out of the Port of *Macassar,* and running happily thro' the *Pater-noster Islands,* we came to Anchor before *Japara,* where we found three Ships come from *Batavia,* three days before us; and had brought some Soldiers from thence to quel an uproar that had been made at *Japara,* in which above twenty Dutch had been killed by the Inhabitants, who attempted to throw themselves into the Fort *Sambura.* But by means of the Governor, and this Auxiliary Force, all was quieted, and the Ringleaders sent away to *Batavia,* where they receiv'd their due reward. Some of them were broken upon the Wheel, some had their Ears and Noses cut off; and were sent chained together to some Islands to spend all their Life in burning of Lime; and there to remain perpetual Slaves.

I landed before those Wretches were sent away, so that I saw 'em go along Chain'd together : But that which was the most dismal to see, was the Lamentation and sad Out-cries of these poor Fellow's Wives and Children, who conducted them to the Water-side.

All being this settled again, the Company augmented the Garrison, and fortified those Places which needed it most, to prevent any such Disorders for the future. It is a wonderful Thing, that such are not more frequent ; and that whenever they happen, they are so soon Calm'd, considering the vastness of the Dutch Dominions, which are so scatter'd here and there, and so far asunder ; but it is to be ascrib'd to their vigilant, and wisely Model'd Government ; without which, they could not support the weight of their several Dominions, which contain several Empires, Kingdoms, and large Provinces, (all which would be too tedious to set down) and it would amaze one to think, what a vast number of Deputies, Presidents, Governours, and Officers, they are forced to maintain for the Preservation of their Power ; besides some Hundreds of Ships : And, I dare say, by good Computation, they have above a Hundred thousand Men by Sea and Land. But as their Expence is great, so their Wealth is unaccountable ; for where-ever you go, you shall not see one Thing in a thousand, little or great, but if you ask whose that is, all the answer is, the Company's.

We departed from *Japara*, and came the next day into the Road before *Batavia*, and an hour or two after us, came in the Ship that had those Rebels on board : so that there we saw them Executed, and disposed of as I have said already.

Before our Ship was quite unladen, here arose a most terrible Hurricane, which tore most of the Ships off their Anchors, and drove two of them upon some of the little islands, that lie near there ; one of which being old and decayed, was dasht into pieces. It lasted but half an hour, and so the Damage was the less, else there would hardly a Ship have escaped : Ours had cast out five Anchors, two of which we lost ; and two of our Men being in the Long-Boat, the Storm coming upon them so suddenly, could not make to the Ship, but the Rope breaking, were torn off from us. When the Wind ceased, we went to see after 'em, and found our poor Seamen still alive, but that was all, tied fast by cords to the Boat, which floated with the bottom upwards ; So that all were recover'd : But it was a Miracle, that being so far spent as they were, and not able to help themselves, their Brains were not knockt out against the Boat ; or that they were not devoured by Sharks. Besides all this, abundance of small Vessels, Prawen, &c. were cast away ; and many Persons drown'd.

The next day I went to shore with the Master and the Doctors, who design'd to stay there all Night, and ordered the Seamen to go back to their Ship. I desired they might stay till the Evening, because I had a mind to go with 'em. But it being pretty dark, and the Wind very high, our Seamen keeping up the Sail without Fear or Wit, we were all over-turn'd, within a Stone's throw of the Ship ; but by the Blessing of God, and the speedy Assistance of the Ship's Crew, we were all took up Safe.

The next Morning I return'd to Land, where I was no sooner come, but a *Muck Speeler,* who had done a great deal of Mischief, and put the People in an Uproar, came running by me, and by good Fortune did me no harm ; but kill'd a Boy within 20 Steps of me, and was presently Shot himself in the Head, and dropt down ; but it was after he had kill'd five or six People ; Nothing saved me but the corner of the Street, by means of which, as he run so furiously, he over-shot me, and got past me before I could get aware of him ; and so, God be prais'd, I was safe, but ever since I was always upon my guard at Turnings and Crossings of Streets.

Here I spent my time with a great deal of variety of Diversions, as Fishing, Walking, Shooting, going by Water, and chiefly seeing my Friends : Most days I took a Praw, and went to some small Islands that lie hard by there, where the chief Fishing is to be seen. Upon one of these Islands lived a rich Chinese near to the *Chinese's* Temple. He having a numerous Family of Children and Servants, I had frequent Business in his House, and got a great deal of Money by him. One Night, as I had taken my leave of him, and was going home, I saw a bright Flame at a mighty distance, and heard some Shooting : Being Landed, I took some of my Friends with me to a high part of the Shore to see it. We were all amazed to think what it should be, and in giving our several opinions, we spent all the Night looking upon it. In the Morning the Flame could no longer be seen ; but we hearing still a Gun go off now and then, we went and acquainted the General with it, who order'd a

Boat to be set out with 20 Men and an Officer, ready to go at Night, in case the Flame appeared again, and the Shooting continued. As the Day shut in, the Flame begun to be seen more and more, and somewhat nearer than the Night before. I desired the Officer that I might go with him, which he readily granting, we set forward, and made directly up to the Fire. Coming nearer, we saw it was a small Bark and People in it, we Hail'd them, upon which they gave over Shooting, but made us no Answer. This made us the more Earnest to get up to 'em, and to Board 'em, which we did: And there we saw a most lamentable Sight, eight poor Englishmen, three of 'em Dead, and the five others little better, not able to speak one Word, but endeavouring to mutter. We took them into our Boat with us, together with some Chests of *Tanges* and *Larines*, (which is a certain Money of that Country) which they had in their Boat with them; we used them as gently as we could, and made all speed possible to the Place from whence we came, and there gave them all Kind of Refreshment. It was five or six hours 'ere they came to themselves, so as to speak: At length they gave us an Account of themselves; and told us, they belong'd to an English Ship that came from *Bengal* richly laden, and was Bound for *Batavia* to joyn the English Merchant-men that lay there; but coming by the Island *Engano*, it being hard Weather, they were thrown upon a Shelf, where their Ship was sunk, so that of 78 Men they had on Board, but 15 got into that little tatter'd Boat, and that of them there was but those we saw left; the rest having perished one after another for want of Water, which they had not had a Drop of in 15 or 16 days time.

When we had this Account from them, we took them to *Batavia*, and carried them to the English House, where we were heartily thank'd, and treated with great Civility: Besides all which, the next Morning a Reward was sent to every one of the Soldiers, and to the Officer: And as for me, Having been very Helpful to them, and managed them with some Cordials, and taking Care lest their sudden Refreshment should do them an Injury, I had 20 Ducatoons [1] sent me as a Present.

While I remain'd here, there happen'd nothing more

[1] "*Dukaton*, a Ducatoon, a silver coin worth LXIII stivers, and in English money nigh VI shillings" (Sewel's *Dutch-English Dictionary*, 1766). Other reckonings make it from 5*s*. 3*d*. to rather more than 6*s*.

worth taking Notice of: And now Orders were sent me to repair on Board the *Bergen in Norweegen*, which was to go Commadore, with two other Ships bound for *Odia*,[1] the capital City of *Siam*; so that I went and provided my self with all that was necessary for the Voyage: Which being done, I went on Board my Ship, the Fleet being ready to go off, and we should have set Sail the very next day, had not the *Ekersloo*, one of our three Ships, sprung a Leak, which obliged us to stay while they took all the Goods out of her again, and mended her, which was a whole fortnight.

This done, she had her Lading put in again; and then we went under Sail with a favourable Wind, and next day pass'd by the Isle of *Lucapara*; and thus we continued our Course with good Success for about eight days: But as it is almost impossible for two or three Ships to make so considerable a Voyage without some Lett or Misfortune; the *Ekersloo* struck upon a Bank of Sand, which frighted us all very much. As soon as she gave us notice of it by firing a Gun, for we were a good way before her, but had happily Steer'd aside and miss'd the Bank, we immediately set out our Shallops, and went to her, and found there was no Remedy but Unlading her; which we did with all speed, and bestowed the Goods, partly on Board of our Ship, and partly on the other: It was a great happiness that the Wind was not very high, else we could never have done this. When all the Goods were out, we made shift, by means of casting Anchors, to get her off the Bank; and having examined her within, and found she had no Damage done to her Keel, we put the Goods on Board of her again, and continued our Course, thanking God we had escaped such a great Danger, by the favour of the Wind, which still continued good for us.

This happen'd to us in our Course to *Tumbolan* and *Ananibo* as we sailed between *Borneo* and *Malacca*, from which in three days we reach'd the Island *Matuna*. As we pass'd by it, we saw some Ships before us, which we concluded were *Chinese Jonckers*; About night they pass'd by us directing their Course towards *Borneo*, which made us think they came from *Cambodia*. At break of day we saw five more, who likewise past by us about Noon, and steer'd their Course towards *Malacca*.

[1] One of the variant spellings of Ayuthia, the old capital of Siam.

When we were come up to the corner of that Island, we took the Elevation of the Pole, and found we were to Sail more to the Northward; and in a short time we came to the River, which runs through the Kingdom of *Siam*, up which we sailed as far as the Town *Bontempia* [Bangkok], and there we cast Anchor. Our Master and the Factor went straightway in the Long-Boat to the Chief City *Odia*; which is 30 Leagues up the River; as soon as they were come back they went to Unlading.

I then went on Shore too, and visited the Dutch Factory there. The House which the Dutch Factors have there, is amazing both for its Largeness, Beauty, and Strength. Above are all the Lodgings, which are wonderful Stately both without and within: Under are the Warehouses, which are of a vast bigness; and richly stored with all manner of commodities.

The city of *Odia* is very large; but most of the Houses are very low: So that all the Towers of their Temples (which are computed to be above Five thousand) being rais'd much higher, and being all easily seen by reason of the other Buildings being so low, seem altogether like a Forest in Winter. It is impossible for any one to conceive what vast numbers of People is continually moving about in that City, insomuch, that a Man who is newly come, would be apt to ask what's the matter, and take that for a gathering of the Mob, or an unusual Croud, which is but the usual Concourse of the Town. It is seated upon the River *Menan*, which is likewise filled with Ships, Praws, &c. This River is of the same Nature with the *Nile*, the *Niger*, and the *Ganges*, and like them, overflows all the Fields about *Odia*, and makes them very fruitful; spreading it self over great part of the Country, by means of several Arms or Creeks which Providence hath ordered for that purpose. And besides this Advantage which this Inundation affords to the Country, it is a mighty Fence to the City *Odia*; because the River over-flowing at certain Seasons, no Enemy can Besiege it but for some Months, during which the City is always able to defend it self, being extraordinary well Situated and Fortified.

Through most of the Streets run fine Channels, as at *Rotterdam*, so that one may go with a Boat from one part of the Town to the other, which renders it mighty Commodious for Trade; I may say, that considering all things, there is not a finer City in all *India*.

Our Ships having now been in little more than a Fortnights time unladen, and taken in their full Lading, which consisted of several Commodities, as Buck and Roe-Skins, Jappan-Wood,[1] &c. we fell down the River, and with a fair Northerly Wind set sail homewards again.

The next day it Snowed so hard, and the Wind was so high, that we were drove almost upon Land 'ere we could be aware of it; but by good Providence we came off without any hurt, and in 11 days came up with the Island *Puloaura*; where we lay still three days refreshing our selves, and then continued our Course. We arrived at *Batavia* in three weeks: We were hardly come into Harbour when we saw the most dismal Spectacle that can be. The Ship the *Elephant*, which rode at Anchor hard by us, laden with Powder and other Ammunition design'd for *Bantam*, by some Accident took Fire; and in an instant blew up into a thousand pieces; so that of above 80 Men that were on Board her, there was not one left alive to tell how it came. It was the most dismal sight methoughts I ever had seen, to behold so many human Bodies toss'd at such a vast distance into the Air, for some of them went over our Ship, and so did several large pieces of the Ship likewise; and what made it the more dismal, was, that no manner of help could be afforded them.

Instead of going ashore with the rest, I went on Board a Ship that was come hither some days before us from *Cameron* in *Persia*, because the Chirurgeon which belonged to that Ship was a Countryman and intimate Acquaintance of mine, and we had been together in several Expeditions in the Wars of *Bantam*. He was over-joyed to see me, and I was no less pleased to find him well. After many Questions past on both sides, we came to give one another an Account of our Adventures since we parted, which gave him occasion to tell me, that he had had pretty good Fortune in all his Voyages, but that he had narrowly escaped Death in a place where he thought himself most secure: "For," saith he, "When I first went to Shore at *Cameron*, I went with some of my Companions to the Factor's House, and having spoken with them I had Business with, we went into a *Cabaret* or publick-House; whence, after we had staid an hour or little more, we thought to go back to our Ships; but ere we could get to our Boats the Night catcht us, and

[1] A mistake for Sapan wood, a wood yielding a red dye.

we were set upon by a company of Cut-throats. They out-did us in number, and were well Arm'd, whereas none of us had any Weapon about us, so that we could make but a fruitless Resistance. Flight being the best Remedy, I presume we all attempted it; but three of us only escaped their Hands, yet not altogether neither; for I had several Blows from 'em, and was run through in two places; the two others had their share too; but neither of us three got any further hurt, and we have great reason to thank the Almighty God who delivered us out of their Hands; for whatever they did with the rest of our Company, which were five more, we never yet could learn what became of 'em."

He likewise speaking of *Cameron*, told me, That while he was there, there had been such an Earthquake as had thrown down several Houses, and kill'd several hundreds of People.

Our next talk was about our own Country, to which we having both of us an Inclination to return, we agreed there in an instant to take our Measures about it; for both of us had served the Company our due time, and some Months over. So we went together on Board my Ship, and from thence we took a Boat to Shore, and went together to wait upon the Head Chirurgion, to acquaint him with our design, and to desire him to employ us now on land till the Fleet went off for *Holland*. He received us with great Civility, and did what we requested of him; and gave us part of the Hospital in Charge, as I had had before. This being done, We went each of us to our respective Ships to take our leave of 'em, and to fetch our Things, and return'd in the same Praw to Batavia, where we repair'd to our Post, and proposed to our selves to take such Care, that there might be no Cause of Complaints least they should prove an obstacle to our Designs, as it frequently happens.

We had not been long here, but a Ship arrived from Holland. All the People that came in her, which were above 200 Soldiers, besides Seamen, were presently landed, and drawn up before the Castle-Gate, till an Order came from the General for them to march up to his Apartment in the Castle. I went up to see them for as the Reader may well suppose, every Body is desirous to hear how matters stand at home, and is in Expectation to meet with some Acquaintance. I found one there whom I had some Knowledge of, a Merchant's Son of *Suabia*, but had lived a long time at *Amsterdam*, where I had seen him.

When I had given him a Welcome, and he me an Account of his Voyage, he rejoyced me with the good News of our Victories over the Ottomans.

While we were Talking, the Order came from the General to let them march into the Castle; where they had each of them their several Posts and Stations assign'd. But as all New-comers have three several Days liberty to refresh themselves, I took my Acquaintance with me, to shew him the Civility of the place (which is commonly speaking, not very great). I took him out designing to go to a *Negery* about two miles from *Batavia*: But as we were going up the River in a Praw we had taken, we met some *Javians* coming down in a small Boat, making a mighty noise with some little Bells. We ask'd them the meaning of it; they told us that it was a Wedding, and that that was their Musick. So we resolved to go back with them, and see the manner of 'em: They went to an House about a quarter of a Mile out of the City. We were invited to come in. The House was all set out and strewed with Flowers, and several Mats made of Rice-Straw were laid upon the Ground, on which they were to have their Dinner.

After a great many Ceremonies were past, which I have given an account of already, a Buffle was brought, which the Bridegroom knockt down, and the Bride took a Knife and cut his Throat. Then they by turns cut pieces of the Flesh, which they gave to the Cook to dress, giving him at the same time Instructions how they would have it done, and Herbs to do it with. Some of it was ordered upon our Account, but we neither of us cared to be Sharers of such a tough Entertainment, and they being but a meaner sort of People, we thank'd them for the Civility they had shewn us, and so left 'em.

From thence we return'd to *Batavia*, for the day was shutting in; and no New-Comer may absent himself from his Post the first Night, wherefore we deferr'd our designed Walk till the next day.

That night one of the Castle-Gates was open'd, (which is a thing seldom known) to let out the President of the City; who, together with some others of the Council, had been at Supper with the General.

CHAPTER XIII

They go to the Negery; An Account of their Diversions there with Tumblers and Javian Baliar Dancers, and of the strange Tricks they shew'd; The Charges of their Entertainment. Pyrates infest the Streights of Sunda: Ships sent out against them, and meet with them: Some of them taken, and how punished. Strange sort of People of the Island St. Galle brought to Batavia, where they soon died. A Javian Hermit comes to Batavia, and makes a discovery to the General of a Plot which the Javians were hatching at Bantam. The Account of his Life, &c. The Author going a Hunting, with others, meets with a poor Runaway Slave, a Dutchman, whom he takes home with him. Ships sent to Discover an Island, which by a Magnetick Force draws the Ships on Shore; to prevent which, some were Built with nothing but Wood. Some of the Javians blow up one of the Bastions by Bantam, their Punishment, &c.

THE next day we took a *Chinese* Praw to pursue our Design, and went up the River to the *Negery*. In our way, we came to a strong Current, which being very shallow, the Head of our Boat struck upon a Rock and turn'd us over. We were in no danger of our Lives because it was not deep, but we were Duck'd over Head and Ears; but we got up and drew our Praw to Land, and so got in again, and went forwards.

We went there into a publick House that stood not far from the Water-side upon an Eminence, which afforded us a very agreeable Prospect, and sat us down in a very pleasant Arbour, with Cedar-Trees, Limon-Trees, and other Green-Trees of that kind all about us. We caused a Dinner to be got ready for us of what the Country afforded; which was Fish and Fowl, Eggs, Herbs, &c. Our Liquor was Suri, which is a Juice drawn from the Coco-Trees; with that, we made very good *Massack* and *Lemonade*, by the help of some Sugar, Spices, Limons, and Oranges, which we had in good plenty.

I having a mind to make my Friend merry, and to divert him with variety, I sent for some *Gomgomers*, (the Musicians of that Country) and some *Javian Baliar* Dancers, who made us a great deal of Pastime. The *Baliar* Dancers, which come from *Babylon*, I have spoken of before; but these were *Javians*, which are a sort far inferior to them, and differ from them much in the same manner as there is between a Dance performed by a Dancing-Master and one danced by a Rustick: But what was most Diverting to us, especially to my friend, was some Tumblers and Jugglers that were amongst 'em, who shew'd us several Tricks, which do usually so much surprize, even those that see them, that I know a Man runs some risk in relating of them. However, some of their most considerable Tricks of Activity I cannot wholly pass by.

They were five in number: One of 'em laid himself flat down upon his Belly, upon a Mat they had spread on the Ground, and in the twinkling of an Eye, raised himself upon his Legs; then laying himself down again as before, he rais'd himself after the same manner, and stood upon his Head only: After this he laid himself on his Back, and gave several Leaps in the Air like a Fish. The other four did the same Tricks over, one after the other, and still better and better. After this they took a Ladder of about 12 Rounds, and set it against one of 'em; one of the other four got up to the top of it, and laid himself a cross it; the second went up, and sat a-cross the other's Shoulders; the third climb'd up and pitch'd himself on his Head, upon the Head of the second, and there stood with his Feet directly upwards; upon which, the fourth came, and stood upright on the Feet of the third; And after playing several Tricks there, he leapt down to the Ground, and stood still; the next Fellow, that was still standing on his Head, gave a spring upwards, and falling down, lighted on the Shoulders of him that stood below; the next, who was on the Ladder came down likewise with a Leap, and fell a-cross the Shoulders of him; and so did the fourth and last, who had been the first on the Ladder: He that had stood all this while, and held the foot of the Ladder, climb'd up with it to the top of the other four, and there made a sort of Harangue to us in *Japponnese*, which concluded the Sight. There was a great many other Tricks intermixt with these, which were well worth the taking notice of; but I thought these would suffice to shew you, how far these Men out-do any thing we commonly see in *Europe.*

This being over, we call'd for our Reckoning in, which came to no more than Two thousand *Butgis.* An *European* at first is frightned at such a reckoning as this, and thinks that such a Sum of Money should be enough to Treat a King and all the Nobility, or to defray the Charges of a Lord Mayor's Feast; but he must understand, that these *Butgis* are little thin pieces of Lead, with holes in the middle of 'em, a certain number of them is put upon a String to save the trouble of telling them over upon every occasion, and three Hundred of 'em are worth but Two Pence of Dutch money; so that our Dinner amounted but to 13 or 14d. Besides this, our Musick and Dancers cost us a Shilling, and we gave a Ducatoon to the Juglers and Tumblers; having paid all, we went back again down the River to Batavia.

At this very time the Streight of *Sunda* was very much infested with Pickaroons; They had only Praws or small Boats of their own, with which they run with ease in and out of several Rivers of the Kingdom of *Bantam,* and did a great deal of mischief about the Islands of *Toppers-boedie, Dwarf-in-de-zee,* and others. They used to wait there for their Prey, and when they had gotten their Booty, they made immediately to their lurking holes, where finding safety for a great while, they were at last so bold, that not a Ship could escape them; and the more, because the Company never concerned themselves about it, nor took any Measures to suppress them. But at length, the *Bali,* (the Ship in which I had been some time before) coming that way, bound for *Jambi* on the Coast of *Sumatra*; and being obliged to cast Anchor near the aforesaid Islands, these Pyrates, joyning their Forces together, came and surrounded her, and notwithstanding a stout Defence made on Board the *Bali* for some hours, they made themselves Masters of her, killed all the Men they could come at; and having taken what they could conveniently carry away, set it on Fire.

While the Ship was all in Flames, a Ship from *Malabar* coming luckily by, made towards the Fire to see what it was. Two Men, who in the Engagement had hid themselves below Deck, and were now got out, but knew not how to dispose of themselves, stood upon the Fore-Castle ready to throw themselves into the Sea to avoid being

THE CORA-CORA, ONE OF THE LARGER TYPES OF MALAY WAR-CRAFT

(*From F. Valentijn's "Oud en niew Oost-Indien,"* 1726)

burnt: But they sent them a Boat, by which means these poor Creatures were preserved; and being brought on Board the Ship, they continued their Course to *Batavia*, where they gave the General an Account of what had happen'd.

The Company now being Sufferers by this, thought fit to send after these Pyrates, which they never minded before, while they came by no loss themselves; and while the Fishermen only, &c. were in danger, Immediately two Men-of-War were ordered to go after 'em, together with eight small Boats well Mann'd, to give them Chace. It being requisite there should be Chirurgions more than ordinary in those Ships, and this being like to be a short Expedition, and near home, my Friend and I, who could not be employed in a long Voyage, were appointed to go with them. We were very well pleas'd with our Commission, and accordingly we got ready our Chests, and went on Board the *Ceylon*, which carried 300 Men, and 48 Guns; The other Ship was about the same Rate. The Boats had each of them from 60 to 70 Men, and about 16 Patterero's.[1]

When we were got past the Island *Onrust*, we kept along the Sea-shore till we came beyond *Bantam*, and there we lay before the Mouth of some Rivers, as close to the Land as we could: And so as to lye to the Windward. At Night we divided our Fleet, and sent two of our Boats out Sea to entice the Pirates out after them, if they should chance to see them, and we stood ready to clap in between them, and the Rover; so to cut off their Pass, and hedge them in. We lay two days close to the Shore, within a Stone's throw of Land, but very safe, with no less than 60 Fathom Water. At length, about Sun-set, we saw five Boats making Sail towards our two Boats, at about two Leagues distance from us; upon which we moved altogether forwards, along the Shore; and by that time it was quite dark, we made directly towards 'em, taking still care to be between the Shore and them.

The next morning we saw them by break of day sailing by a small island. They having found out our Design, were endeavouring to make their escape, for the two Boats we had sent after 'em were farther from 'em than we were

[1] Patteraro or Pedrero (from Petraria, a stone-throwing engine, med. Lat.) was originally a gun throwing stone-shot. Later, any small swivel used for man-killing at close quarters.

with the whole Fleet: So we joyned together again, and our eight Boats sailing much faster than the Men-of-War could, persued them so tightly, that notwithstanding these Rovers had several Oars with them, (which they use to make use of in a Calm or in case of pursuit) yet by Noon our Boats were all got within a quarter of a League of 'em; so that the last of 'em were forced to yield or fight. We with our great Ships were within a League of 'em all, and turn'd round a small Island, during which we lost sight of them; But our Boats all this while having got ground, they begun to thunder amongst 'em; so that in a little time, two of the Pyrates Boats were seized. Then we came in sight again, and took these two Boats into our Charge, and brought the men on board of us. Our boats having made some stay, while they engaged these two, the other three were got away again pretty far. However, ours were not long 'ere they came within shot of 'em, and so pursued them that they came to a close Engagement, and after a sharp resistance, at length became Masters of them.

We lost in all 28 Men, and had 30 wounded; but we kill'd 200, and wounded above 50 of theirs. The rest we carried to *Batavia*.

There was at first near 900 of 'em; of which nine were Dutchmen, and two Danes; one of whom had been a Captain in a Man of War. We caught both the Danes, but we had but three Dutchmen, the six others were killed in the fight.

Being come to *Batavia*, they were all put into Prison, and Examin'd. They confess'd, that they had their Habitations in some *Negery's*, about the *Blaw Peper-bergh*, and discover'd several of their Companions thereabouts: Upon which they sent Soldiers both by Sea and Land towards those places; and in three weeks' time they brought back with 'em some thousands of 'em, most of 'em being *Javians*.

Of the whole, one part was broke upon the Wheel, some were Quarter'd, some were Whipt, some had their Ears and Noses cut off, and some were burnt in the Forehead. The three Hollanders were Hang'd; The two Danes beheaded: and a great number of others were sent to several Islands; to burn Lime, Hew Stone, &c. and there to remain Slaves all their Lives. Their Wives and Children were served after the same manner, that it might more effectually prove a terrour to others.

About this time came into the Road of *Batavia* a Ship

from *Madagascar,* which brought with her two and twenty Savages from the Island *St. Galle.* They were much uglier and much more brutish than the *Hottentots* at the *Cape of Good Hope*; their Speech was hardly articulate, but confused like that of Children, and as if they Sung. They had no Hair on their Heads, only a rough scabby Skin. They were strong, tho' excessive Lean, and had scarce any thing but Skin and Bones. Before their Privy-Parts they had a Wild Cat's Skin, which reach'd down to their Knees; for in *St. Galle* there are multitudes of Wild-Cats.

They were shut up all together, like Beasts in a Stable, and were fed with nothing but raw Rice and Water, which it seems was too good for 'em; for in a little while they all died. A nastier sort of Men I never saw; for as I said, except their Head, they were Hairy all over to their very Hands and Feet. Their Face was very red; but their Teeth were very fine and white: Their Eyes were very large; and their large Ears slit in five or six places. About their Neck and Feet they had some Twists of Sea-Rushes, which their Women made use of likewise to bear up their long swagging Breasts. I believe the World doth not afford a more Savage Wild sort of Men. *St. Galle,* from which they came, lies about 1300 miles from *Batavia,* and about 300 from the Cape, on the side of the Island *Madagascar.*

Some time after this, a *Javian* Hermit, who lived in a Cave on the *Blaw Peper-bergh,* came to *Batavia* to speak with the General; and refusing to deliver his Message to any of his Attendants, he was admitted and brought before the General, with whom he spent some time alone. His Business with him, was to make a discovery of a Plot, which several Javians had laid to surprize the City of *Bantam* and to put all the Dutch Garrison to the Sword: Upon which the General dispatch'd an Express to the Governor of *Bantam,* to Command him to be upon his Guard, and to let him know that he should have a Reinforcement sent him speedily by Sea and Land.

The Company upon thus conceived a great Suspicion that the young King might be in this Conspiracy; But it was upon a close Enquiry, found to be a meer surmize; and all his Actions shewing so much the contrary all along, they continued to treat him with the same Respect as before: For all the Ring-leaders of this Plot were detected; but not the least thing could be found that might any way reflect on the young King.

The Hermit did not Care to return to his Cottage again : So the Company promised him, that he should never want if he would continue wth them ; which he accepted of readily.

He spake seven languages ; to wit, *Turkish, Arabic, Persian, Moorish, Chinese, Maleish,* and *Javian* ; and had Travell'd over most parts of *Asia* and *Africa.* He had lived 15 years in that Cell ; and it was a wonder how a Man should continue there so long with any thing of safety ; considering the many Tygers, Leopards, Serpents, and other devouring Creatures that are in great numbers all about that Mountain.

His Dress was very much like that of the *Armenian* Women ; so that one would not have taken him for a Man ; and besides that, one might have mistaken him, even tho' one was near him, because he had pull'd his Beard out by the Roots : He was very thoughtful, spake but seldom, and very gravely. He had about twenty pairs of Shoes made of Pastboard, hung about his Girdle. Instead of a Hat, he had a sort of Turban wrapt about his Head made of strip'd Cotton, about twelve Ells long, as the Moors usually wear.

As to his Diet, he Eat moderately, but loved to have all very good. Whatever he Drank, he poured part of it upon his Head, which was as bare as the Palm of a Man's hand. The Lodging that was appointed for him was over against mine, so that I had some Conversation with him in the *Maleish* Language. But he was not free of his Discourse, except sometimes in the Relation of his Voyages, and the Description of the Countries he had seen ; as to the rest he seemed reserved. I ask'd him one day, how he came to be a Hermit ; to which he replied, "just as you come to be a Surgeon." But to have done with my capricious Gentleman.

I was sent for to one of the General's Servants, so that I had once more an opportunity of seeing the General's Garden, which was one of the finest that ever was seen, for all kind of Asiatic or Indian Trees and Flowers, in which were two Parts set aside, the one for manner of Wild-Beasts ; the other for all sorts of Birds, of all which, an account would be too tedious : In short, I can hardly think of any rare Creature that was not there to be seen.

Two days after this, my Companion and I, and two more, went a shooting, about two or three Leagues into the

Country, along by the Powder Mills, upon the River *Jacatra* : And as we had pretty good sport, and kill'd a good quantity of Pigeons, Rabbets, &c. we were going to a *Negery* to refresh ourselves, and make Merry with our Provisions, we spying a Rabbet making towards a little Wood ; two of us went after him, while the others went forward to get that Dress'd which we had kill'd. As were in pursuit of our Game, my Friend one way, and I the other, I came to a narrow River's side, where I saw a Man sitting in a Melancholly posture, with his Eyes on the Ground. Hearing him groan and sigh, put me to a stand, and ask him what he was ; to which he answer'd me with a deep sigh, that he was a poor Hollander. I askt him what he did there, and whither he design'd to go. "Ah ! Sir," says he, "I know not where I am, nor which way I am to take, but surely Providence hath sent you to my Relief ; and seeing I have the Happiness once more to meet with a Christian, I beseech you to direct me, (if there's any way for't) how I may come to you." Saying this, he fell upon his Knees ; so I told him, I would get him over, and bid him stay there. My Companion had made his shoot, and was gone to the rest : So I went up to the Village, and got a Praw, which I sent to bring him over to me ; and as soon as he came over, he gusht out in Tears, and Embracing me, thank'd me most passionately for my seasonable Assistance. I desired him to go along with me to some Company I had, which he did ; and gave me a short account of himself by the way. My Company wondred who I had got with me, but when they were informed what he was, we all help'd to Comfort him, and treated him as we did our selves. In that while he inform'd us of the particulars of his Misfortunes : The sum of which was, That being come over from the Delft, in the Company's service as Carpenter, he had been employed in the *Kartirian* Wars ; and as he, with three more, were sent out to take a View of some part of the chief City of that Kingdom, they had the ill Fortune to fall into the Hands of the Enemy, who carried them away Prisoners to *Tuban,* and there Sold them to a rich *Chinese,* who was just come thither in a Ship of his own : That Chinese carried them all four to *China,* to the Sea-Port Town calle'd *Quancheu* ; where after seven years of hard Slavery, they found an opportunity, and made their escape from thence in a small Boat to the Island of *Manilha* ; where they luckily met with a Ship that was coming to

Batavia, but as they were got almost within reach of it, and within four miles of Land, their Ship struck upon a Shelf, and there sunk; and he knew of none that had saved themselves but he alone. The Relation of this dismal Story did affect us so, that we were as Melancholly as himself.

Our Dinner being over, we return'd to *Batavia,* and took this poor man with us, and presented him to the General, who appointed him a Post under the Gunner of the Castle, till further Orders.

I need not give the Reader the particular Account which he gave us of his Slavery, it being much the same with what we used to hear concerning that Condition, and may be found in most Books of Travel, especially in those of *Ferdinandus Mendez Pinto,*[1] who gives an Experimental Account of all sorts of Slavery, having been himself, taken 13 times, and 17 times sold, in the space of 21 years.

About this time three Ships were getting ready to go and make a discovery of a certain Island which lies Northward of *Japan.* There had been some Ships sent thither some years before, but they had all miscarried; some by the way; others (as it was reported) by the attractive power of the Magnetic Mountains were drawn violently to Shore; so that to avoid that danger, they contrived the Building of these Ships, without Nails or Iron Work. When they were ready, they Beat up for Volunteer Seamen, promising them for an Encouragement a Twelve Month's Pay over and above their Wages; half of it to be paid presently, the other half when they came back. This raised Men in abundance, and as fast as they could wish; and in three weeks time the Ships being ready, went under sail with 220 Men on Board of 'em.

It is said that Island was first found out by the Portugueses, but that they were forced to abandon it by reason of the excessive Cold and multitude of Wild-Beasts; for it lies Northward of *Tartary.* But the Gold, which as it is reported, comes in great store down several Rivers of that Country, was (I presume) the only Motive which set the Dutch upon making these dangerous Attempts, and upon venturing a second time, after such bad Success. What

[1] This was Fernão Mendes Pinto, 1509–83, whose travels in India, China, Tartary, and Japan form one of the earliest masterpieces of Portuguese prose. He was the friend and travelling companion of St. Francis Xavier.

became of this last Expedition I never heard; for there came no News of it to *Batavia* before I came away from thence.

Soon after this, a great piece of Roguery was carried on at *Bantam,* which unhappily proved successful. The Dutch had there under one of the Bastions, a great Magazine of Powder, and they had unfortunately at that time above 100 Tun of it in the Magazine. A Javian undertook to get in by breaking of the Wall, which he was forced to do by digging a way under Ground quite to the side of it. Every day he closed up the entrance into his Hole with earth, so artificially and so softly, that no body perceived it, and that neither of the two Sentinels that stood on the Bastion heard the least Noise at any time. When he was got in, he took a Bamboo-Cane that was hollow and filling that with Gun-powder, lighted it at one end, and the Fire coming to the Powder in the Cane gave a great Blow, with some Flame, without doing any further harm for the present. This alarm'd all the People, who presently went to search every corner of the Bastion, to see what the matter was, and there the Bamboo-cane was found, and the Powder that was in it was consumed: But no sooner had they open'd the Vault-Door, but the Wind finding a free passage, took some sparks of Fire along with it, which lighted among the Powder, and in an instant set that on Fire, and blew up the whole Bastion with 16 pieces of Cannon, and above 200 Persons.

An Account of this Accident was quickly sent to the General at *Batavia,* who presently sent Men thither; together with Orders to the Governor, and to the young King, to make a diligent Enquiry after the Authors of this Villany: And in a short time, three Javians were discovered to be the Men; who were brought bound to *Batavia,* and confess'd, That they were the only Contrivers of that Action, upon which they were all three Condemned to Die. He that had set Fire to the Cane, was brought upon a Scaffold erected for that purpose, and there Pinch'd with red-hot Tongs from the morning till towards the evening, at which time he was cut into Quarters; so that that day was spent in Torturing of that Fellow only. The next day the second was served in like manner; the third was Broke upon the Wheel.

We thought the time long now 'ere the Ships went off to *Holland,* or at least till the time was fixt for their going;

which we expected daily should be done: However, we had got our Names upon the Roll, and having time enough, we ventured to take a small Journey together to visit the Hermits Cells; for which purpose we took some Javian Guides with us. The Road, we found as it was told us, very commodious, having a great many Inns, and good Accommodation, till we came to the Wilderness where these Hermits dwell. Within six or seven miles of which, we came to two Villages, one on one side, the other on the other side of the River; in the middle of which was a very high Rock, upon which was a Javian Temple. We went to see it, and found there only one Reverend Bard, who resided there all the Year round. That Temple was used only two days in the Year, viz. Their *New-Year's Day*, and the *Feast of Mahomet*, whose Sect they follow; And on those Days, there is much Praying and Worshipping, and great Processions made.

Having taken a View of this, we went on, and came to a Village that is near the *Blawen Pepper-bergh*, from which we had not above 2 or 3 miles to the place where the Cells are. In that Village we staid the latter part of that Day, and all that Night, in order to spend all the next day in satisfying our Curiosity; and accordingly we got thither early the next morning. There we saw a great many pretty Caves, cut out of the Natural Rocks, and very Artificially contrived. We had been told, that they were poor little miserable Holes that were not worth the seeing; but we were not a little surprized to find them so neat and delightful, nor less pleased to see how successfully they had imitated Nature; insomuch, that it was hard to judge, whether Nature or Art had had the chiefest hand in the ordering of 'em. These Cells were most inhabited by a sort of Men, who in imitation of their Founder, Devote themselves to a perpetual Austerity, Mortification, and Self-Denial, as he himself had set them an Example; assuring them, That the Chastising of the Body, would conduce very much to Felicity, and would infallibly draw down God's blessing upon them; so that he was look'd upon as a great Saint; and his Followers are valued at no less rate all over that Country.

They wore long Gowns after the manner of the *Armenian* Priests, or the *Bonzen* in *Japan*. They spend all Day and Night in lifting up their Eyes and Hands, intimating, That they Desire nothing here below. The Javians that were our Guides told us that they used to eat nothing but Boil'd Herbs, Beans, Roots, and such like Fruits; And that on some Day, which they call their Feast-Days, they eat Flies, Mice, Scorpions, and Spiders, drest with a Juice prest out of a certain Herb that grows there in abundance, which looks very much like our Sorrel. In this poor Condition they live and die; but in the highest Esteem and Veneration among all the Javians: So that they never fail to be Canonized after their Death, and their Bodies are burnt with great Solemnity, and with all the respect imaginable; every one thinking himself happy, that can but come and throw in a Bundle of Sweet Herbs upon the Corps.

Some of those Hermits, thinking that the more they mortifie the more they are acceptable to their God, eat nothing but the green Herbs and Roots, and that very sparingly; which makes them look so nastily, that it frightens one to look upon them, and kills them quickly too.

When we had seen all we could see, we came away time enough to reach the two Villages again before Night; where we staid that night; and the next morning we set out early, to get into *Batavia* as soon as we could; because we had a mind to share in the Rejoycing that was to be that day, it being the General's Birth-Day; wherefore we took a Praw, seeing the Wind and Tide was for us, and with a very quick passage down the River, came to *Batavia* just as the People began to move. All the Burghers and Freemen were in Arms, and drew up before the General's Lodgings in the Castle, where after the Discharge of all the Cannon about the Castle and City, they saluted his Excellency with several Vollies of Shot. Each Nation then came in a distinct Body with Presents to the General; at first, the *Chineses, Siamers, Japonneses, Macassars, Amboineses, Bandaneses,* &c. and even the *Javians,* who are not permitted to set a foot in the Castle on any other time, were then let in; but all these come but after the Company of Burghers and Freemen, which is composed of Dutch, Germans, English, Danes, French, Portuguese, and other Christians, born in the *Indies,* who altogether make one Body. These Presents are Magnificent, and one may judge they must needs be very considerable, when the very Soldiers who stood to their Arms under the Castle-Gate had some Hundreds of Guildens given them.

Besides this, all the Streets were full of Lights, Bonefires, and Fireworks; wherein the *Chineses* employed their utmost Art and Skill: And for three or four days there was nothing but Feasting and Treating one another.

The time now being come that the Fleet was to go to *Holland*, and the day fixt, viz. the 12th of *February*, (in case the Weather should permit it) my Friend and I made our Applications to be ordered on Board of our Ship, if it might be thought convenient: And according to our Request, we were assign'd on Board the Ship called the *Exchange*; which did not as yet lie before *Batavia*, but was refitting in the Island *Onrust*, and was ordered to get ready to go Commadore of this Fleet, as she was to have gone with the last Fleet which went on the 22nd of *November*, 1684, but that she was disabled. Thus we had time enough to make Provision for our Voyage.

The Ships being come into the Road before *Batavia*, some days were appointed to Address our Prayers in the most solemn manner to the Almighty for his Protection, and to Beg of him that he would preserve us from all Dangers; which was Religiously observed in the Dutch and Maleish Churches.

After this, the General gave Order that the List of those who had served out their time, should be called over; and publick notice of it being given by the Clerk of the Musters, those who were to go, appeared all with their Arms in good Order, and by Beat of Drum were led into the Castle, where they deliver'd their Arms into the Hands of the Armourer: Upon which every Man of 'em was presented with four Rixdollers, as a Gratuity over and above each Man his Half-year's Pay. Those that wanted more Money, and desired to have it might be furnisht with it, so it was less or not more than what the Company owed them, abating or allowing 20 per Cent. and giving an Acquittance of his Money so received aforehand, made and signed before a Notary Publick.

CHAPTER XIV

The Author's Departure from Batavia for Holland. Orders observed among the Ships: They come and lie before Bantam; where the Author going on Shore, is left behind, but by good luck overtakes the Ship again. They come to the Cape de Bon Esperance. Observations on the Place, and on the Hottentots there. They leave the Cape. Come into the Sea which they call the Graz-zee; They meet with a fearful Storm, which lasted four days. They come to the Briel; thence to Amsterdam, where the Author is forced to lie, in great Pain, and at great Expence; and at last, with much ado, gets home to Ulm.

I HAD made Provisions of all things necessary for my Voyage, but especially of preserved Pepper, Arack, and Tobacco, which are the chief Things for such a long Voyage as that is. I took with me a good quantity of *China*-Ware, some pounds of Tea, and some *Murus* and *Parcallen*, (which are a sort of very fine Linnen) off the Company, upon my own Account, which amounted to a great deal of Money. After this, I went to take my leave of all my Friends, and amongst others, of our Countryman, of whom I made mention before, who entertain'd my Friend and me with all the Expressions of Love and Friendship that could be imagined. He gave me a Seal-Ring and a Letter, desiring me to deliver them to his Wife at *Ulm*, in case I got safe thither; so we parted with Tears in our Eyes all three of us. He conducted us two to the *Vierkam* or Square, from whence we took a Praw, and went on Board the *Exchange*; where a Review was made the next day, to see if there were no body wanting. All being found there, Orders came the next day, that we should weigh Anchor, and go a Quarter of a League into Sea, and there cast Anchor again.

Then was there again a Day appointed to implore the Blessing of the Almighty; which was duly observed, both at Land, and on Board our Ships. Then the Masters of the

Ships and the Factors were invited a Shore to take their Farewel Dinner with the General, and to receive his Orders for Sailing, and to take their Oaths of Fidelity : After which, they repaired every one to their several Ships, with Orders to set Sail with the first fair Wind ; but the Wind was so changeable for three or four days, that it made us weigh our Anchors, and drop them again four or five times. Some of our more debauch'd Seamen, and others, did so fret and fume at these frequent Disappointments, and grew so very impatient, that they could not forbear venting their Rage in very undecent and prophane Expressions ; for which, the Master, a good old Man of near 90 years of Age, reproved them very sharply, and threatned them severely if they did not refrain from such Words ; telling them, that this was not the way to obtain their Desires, but that they ought rather to Pray to God to send us a favourable Wind, and patiently wait his Will and Pleasure.

About 12 of the Clock, in the 5th Night, the Wind came good for us ; whereupon our Master as Commadore, ordered a Gun to be fired as a signal for the two other Ships to weigh Anchor with us. So we all went under Sail together, for in the Voyages homeward, the Ships are always obliged to go together ; and tho' the one may be a quicker Sailer than the other, yet she must not run away before the rest ; but she is forced to Furl some of her Sails, so as the slowest of 'em may keep pace with her ; and nothing excuses their parting from each other but a Storm, or hard Weather ; after which they are to rejoyn as soon as possible.

The next day we came and Anchor'd before *Bantam*, about a League from Shore near the place where we lay when we went in pursuit of the Pyrates. Our Boat went on Shore, and I went with it, to see some of my Acquaintance there, and to take my leave of them. Notwithstanding that the Steward had given me very strict charge not to stay, and told me two or three times he was just going, I could not part from my Friends readily, and when I came to go, I found my Spark gone : and was told he was gone off half an Hour before, with eight Cows, and other Provisions that he was come for. When I heard this, I was ready to die with Fear and Grief ; and had no other Remedy, but immediately to Hire a light Praw with 16 Oars ; When we came out of the River of *Bantam* into Sea, we saw our Ships just ready to Sail ; for the Wind was very good, and then they loose no time : However, I pluckt up a good Heart when I saw 'em, and encouraged the Javians to pull stoutly, and promised them six Rixdollers amongst 'em over and above the Bargain, in case they overtook our Ship. This made them Row like Tygers, and by that time it was Night, as the Ship was got up to the Island *Dwars in the Zee,* we came in reach of her, at which the Javians set up a full *Huzza,* and I was so transported with Joy, that I could not but joyn with them very heartily. As soon as we could come to fasten by her side, I went to get up; but unfortunately made a false step, and tumbled down again in the Boat, and so Sprain'd my Leg, that I was forced to be drawn up into the Ship, and lie still for some days.

The next day, three of the Cows were kill'd and distributed among the Ship's Crew. Some days after we passed the Streights of Sunda, and came to the *Prince's Island,* where we parted with our Convoy Ships, and sent them back to *Batavia.*

As we came by *Prince's* Island, which lies at the furthest corner of *Great Java,* we came into open Sea, and the Wind being right good for us, we continued our Course forward, not being willing to loose so fair a Wind as we had then; so that we did not put in there, nor would we stay to send in our Boats for a Recruit of fresh Water, as it is Customary; but made the best of our way, and fired three Guns to wish each other a good Voyage.

We steer'd our Course now directly towards *Cape de Bon Esperance,* Hall'd in our Long-Boat and Shallop, and took in our Anchors, and fitted our selves for the Voyage.

When we were got out of sight of *Great Java,* a second Review was made of all our Ship's Crew, which amounted to Eighty eight Persons in all, viz. the Master, the Upper Steersman, two Under Steersmen, and two Mates, to relieve them from Duty; two Quarter-Masters, to Order to Watches, which I have given an Account of in the beginning of this Book; a Factor; a Book-keeper; and a Clerk or Assistant; An Upper Chirurgion, (my self) and an Under Master-Chirurgion; a Steward, who distributed the Allowances of Meat and Drink to every Person according to the Master's Orders; a Cook and a Scullion; a Gunner with four Men and Boys, who were likewise to help the Steward; a Serjeant; two Master Carpenters, and three Mates, a Boatswain, and his Boy, a Schieman [1] and his Boy; a

[1] Boatswain's mate.

Provost; four Boys, the eight Soldiers, and 32 Mariners: We had no Chaplain, but we had Prayers duly read by the Book-keeper: There was another Master of a Ship and a Master Chirurgion; but neither of them has any Post in our Ship, they were only Passengers.

We came safe with all these People, till we got past the Island, called *St. Paul of Amsterdam*: After which our greatest concern was, to pass safe through the Latitude of *Madagascar*, or *St. Maurice*; which, as I have already told you, is very subject to dreadful Storms and Hurricanes, most Seasons of the year; insomuch that more Ships are lost thereabouts, than any where again.

Having escaped this place likewise, tho' we met with hard weather, we came at last, after nine weeks Sail, in sight of the great promontory of *Africa*, the *Cape of Good Hope*, which rejoyced us much. One of the Carpenter's Men had the good fortune to spy Land the first of any; for which good Tydings, the Master presented him with two Ducatoons and a Quart of Canary, as it was ever the Custom on Board our Ships, to gratifie those that first discover Land. We immediately loosned our Anchors, and fasten'd them to their Cables, and made directly towards *Tafel-Bay*, which lay about 20 miles from us. The next day we were within two Leagues of it, it being a very great Snow, and the Weather being very Calm, which was very extraordinary, it being for the most part very Blustring there all the year round. We hall'd out our Boat, and Long-Boat, into which having sent some of our Men with Oars, they hall'd our Ship into the Haven. This took up half a day, and when we were come to a place where we could cast Anchor, we did so; and hoisted up our Flags, after which they at Land did the same likewise upon the Tower of the Castle.

Then our Master went to Shore, and gave the Governor of the place on account of our Success thus far on our Voyage. Here we found three Ships from Holland, and one English Fly-boat, riding at Anchor. We were immediately supplied with some Sheep, Fruits, and Herbs, which were very welcome Refreshments, and many Hottentots came on Board of us; some of which, our Men made several little Presents to. Our Men were likewise permitted to go on Shore by turns, to refresh themselves: Some of our Crew were sent on purpose, that they might go into the Wood to fetch some Fuel, and others were sent for a Recruit of fresh Water.

When I went ashore, I found the place extraordinary full of People, but mostly of those Soldiers, which belong'd to the Dutch Ships that lay there. They were brave lusty Men, and very brisk, having met with nothing but good Success in their Voyage thither. Some of their Men were Sick, and carried into the Hospital, which was pretty full. I went to see it, and told near 200 of them there; most of which were forced to be left behind, not being recover'd before the Fleet was obliged to go on, on their Voyage. These Ships being gone off, the Town was left as thin as might be, and every thing was as cheap again; so that we had more conveniency of making our selves Merry. I spent here some time very pleasantly, my Landlord being a very honest Fellow, and extraordinary obliging. He was of *Newrenberg*, and by Employment a Brewer. He having some Knowledge of me before this, seem'd daily to increase his good Opinion and Esteem for me; and his Daughter, I observed likewise, to become every day more and more obliging, which I look'd upon as a design between them of staying me there: But I was so heartily set upon my Return home, that I might once more again Enjoy the free liberty of my Religion, that I could not be gain'd upon to alter my Mind upon any kind of Consideration whatever. A few days later, I found, that what I had surmiz'd was true enough; and the Father very kindly made me an Offer of his Daughter, and told me what he was ready to do for me if I would stay there; and withal, that he had a great inclination to go into his own Country, which he was loath to do, unless he could by such means as this, make over his Lands to his Daughter, and put her into Possession of them: For a Freeman cannot otherwise dispose of what he hath: and if he is desirous to leave the Country, he cannot Sell his Estate, but it must fall of Course to the Company; so that he can take nothing over with him but his Personal Estate. But neither the Daughter's Beauty, nor the Sweetness of his Habitation, could have such an Influence upon me as to make me break my Resolution. So that without hearkening to him any further than just to thank him, I made all necessary Preparation, and made me ready to go back to my Ship. But I wonder'd that my Landlord could ever have the Heart to part from so pleasant a place as his was to return home, seeing he had that only thing which I wanted, the opportunity of Exercising my Religion publickly.

One day I went out by my self to fetch a walk, and as I

went musing along, I found my self before I was aware of it, within a quarter of a Mile of the *Lewen-bergh*, between which and the Sea, I saw some of those Hutts which the *Hottentots* dwell in. Upon sight of which, my Curiosity led me to go and see what kind of life those People led. I went into one of 'em, and there I saw a parcel of 'em lying upon the Ground like so many Hogs, and fast asleep: But as soon as they awaked and saw me, they sprung up and came up to me, making a noise like Turkies. I was not a little concerned; yet seeing they did not go about to do me any harm, I pull'd out a piece of Tobacco and gave it them: They were mightily pleased with that Present, but the way they took to shew their Gratitude, and to thank me, was so odious to me, that I wish'd I had not given them any occasion of returning me Thanks. For no sooner had I given them this, but they all lifted up those Flaps of Sheep-Skin which hang before their Privy-Parts to give me a sight of 'em. What with this beastly Behaviour, and what with the nasty stench of their Kennels, (as I think I may properly call 'em) I made all haste to be gone. Some of 'em I found at their Dinner, or rather, Eating (for that is a word of too much Order and Decency for them). They had only a piece of Cow-hide, laid out upon the Coals a Broyling, and to make the Carbonnade more pleasant, they had squeezed the dung out of the Guts, and spread it finely on the Hide to moisten it, and to give it a relish; and this they take when it is broyl'd, and chop it, and so Eat it. The very ordering of it in this manner, turn'd my Stomach so, that I could not stay to see the Eating of it: But I made all the haste I could to be gone. I went from thence directly to the *Lewen-bergh*, which is a fine pleasant Hill, not at all Rocky, but cover'd over with Grass, and affording a most pleasant Prospect. Here I sat me down, and took a view of the Country all round me. After I had been there a while, I espied at Sea a Ship making to the Port with full Sails; and presently after I saw the Flag hoisted up in the Castle. Upon this I came down to go towards the Fort, and as I was going along the Shore, there stood a Servant maid, who was come to fill a little Tub with Sand: As soon as she saw me, she cry'd out to me as loud as she could, Maridi fini Senior: Oh Sir! Pray come and help me. I ran full speed towards her to help her, and when I came up to her, she shewed me a dreadful long Serpent, that had just then been devouring a young *Hottentot*, and had swallowed him all up but the Legs, which still stuck out of his Mouth. This had put the Maid into a great Consternation, and made her afraid that she should be his next Prey : And truly being much in the same Apprehensions my self, I betook my self to my Heels, which the Maid seeing, she gave a dreadful Shriek, and began to run too. That great Shriek she gave brought out some *Hottentots* that were thereabouts, who came running towards us. As soon as they saw what was the matter, they got themselves ready to catch the Serpent ; and having brought out some long Ropes, they threw them with wonderful Dexterity about its middle, and drawing the Ropes, some at one end, some at another, as hard as they were able, they held him so fast, that I expected they would have cut him in two. All the while the Serpent Hiss'd in a fearful manner, and Twisted it self strangely, but could not slip away. At last came some of the Men with great Poles with which they knock'd him on the Head. This dreadful Creature was very near 16 Foot long. They fastened it to a Stick, and let it dry.

This being done, I return'd to the place from whence I came.

In my return I met with some Wild *Hottentots*, who come down thither from the *Cafre's* Country, about 100 Leagues from thence. They, as I observed, are almost Blind in the day time, at least extream Dim-sighted ; so that they do most of their Business by Night. In the time that I staid in the Cape, I saw once one of these Wild People executed for theft : He had some time before stolen some Cows and Sheep from some of the Freemen, without the Approbation of their King, (which is a dignity they confer upon some one amongst 'em ; and wherever they are, tho' but to the number of five or six together, they always make them a King or Captain to Rule over them, without whose Consent no kind of thing is to be done ; and in this the Company doth not at all interpose, but leaves them to their own Customs). The Criminal was tied Hand and Foot, and stretched out betwixt two Posts, about half a Man's height from the Ground ; after which some Men came with great Sticks, and beat him to Death. If they hit him on the Head or Breast he is soon dispatcht ; but they never give over so long as they find any Breath in him. When he is expired, they carry him to the Wood, and there fasten him to a Bough, and leave him for a Prey to Wild Beasts.

The Ship that I espied coming from the top of the Hill, was an English Fly-Boat, which came and cast Anchor by the other English Ship that lay there before. The Master gave us an Account of his Voyage, which had been thus far very prosperous. He was bound for *Jappan*, but was to call at several Places by the way. He put in here to Treat with the Governour, but about what, I could not be informed.

After we had staid here full three Weeks, which is more by a Week than Ships generally do, every body was ordered on Board in a readiness to be going. Our Master being Commadore, call'd a Council to settle the Orders of their Voyage. The next day a Review was made, where all were found in very good Order, except two that were very sick; but yet, as ill as they were, they would not stay there, but would venture on their Voyage.

The next day, after the Review was made, our Master and Factor, together with the other Masters of Ships, went once more a Shore to wait on the Governor to take their Leave of him: They came back that same night in order to go out of the Bay with the first fair Wind; which happen'd that very night, being the 23th of *May*; and then we steer'd our Course North-West.

All next day we had the African Coasts in sight. Our Water Vessels were shut up again, and dealt out by Portions: which was, a Can to each Person once in 24 hours; and half a Quartern of Brandy, or Arack. When we had been a while under Sail, out came a Seaman from under the *Hatches*, who had hid himself there till we were got out in full Sea. He was but just come to the Cape with an English Ship; and being sent ashore to fetch in fresh Water, he so contrived his Business as to get in with our Men, being resolved never to go with the English again. He was an Hamburgher, a brisk active Fellow: In the hardest of Weather, he was first and last on the Mast, and extreamly serviceable. So that he got the love of every body, and generally had a larger share of the Distributions than any of the rest.

Having now sailed about 10 days, we came up to *St. Hellens* [St. Helena], where the Ships that are homeward bound from *India* seldom fail to call; but our Master did not think fit to put in there, partly because we had already made great stays, and partly because we needed no provisions.

In 14 days we found our selves under the Line, and the Sun stood Perpendicular over our Heads. This was the twelfth time that I passed under it in my Voyages to and fro. As soon as we came there, our Master commanded a White Flag to be hung out; which was the usual Token for all the Masters and Steersmen in the Fleet to come on Board of him. When they were all come together, they open'd their Instructions to them, which were That contrary to the Custom of the *East-India* homeward bound Ships, (which was to Steer their Course betwixt *Scotland* and *Hitland* [Shetland], in their return to *Holland*) they should now go round *Hitland*, and pass betwixt *Fero* [Faröe] and *Filo*, and so keep along the Coasts of *Norway*, where they should meet with a Squadron of Men of War for their Convoy. And this was accordingly done. But now being our Voyage was made so much the longer by these Orders than otherwise it would have been, they began to shorten each Man's allowance to make it hold out the better.

All this while we got (Blessed be God) all safe from under the Line, and were not above seven days a passing of it. Whereas it is common for Ships to lie there two or three Months, and cannot stir for want of a Wind, so that what with the Calm, and the excessive heat, they loose abundance of their Men: But we had but five Men sick all that time.

From thence we pass'd to the *Gras-Zee*,[1] or Grass-Sea, so called from the *Grass* which grows there, so that the Sea appears just like a Meadow, and it lookt to us as if we were already with one Foot upon Land. This held for near 100 Leagues together. We pass'd through it with a very good Wind, and were very glad to get out of it, notwithstanding it was a pretty Sight enough. When we pull'd up any of that Grass, we found it had very long small Roots.

Soon after this we came in sight of the Islands Corvo and Flores, and at the same time of the North Star. Being got thus far, each Seaman's Allowance began to increase again. But before this Order was given, the Master sent to Examine all the Provisions, and had an Account brought him of what quantity there was left of each particular. He finding there was a good store of Arack left, and that we had a very quick Passage so far, and the Wind continued so very fair for us, that it gave us hopes of being quickly at the end of our Voyage, was willing to let the Men enjoy themselves a little

[1] The Sargasso Sea, a tract covered with floating weed, between Lat. 25° and 30° N., and Long. 38° and 60° W

more, and so order'd that a pretty good share of Arack should be dealt out to every one of 'em. But there being several that were sick, and could not use their Arack themselves, disposed of it to those that were well, who having then too much of that strong Liquor, made themselves exceeding Drunk, and committed a great deal of disorder: For tho' there is very severe Laws on Shipboard, and those are generally Executed with Rigour, yet such is the Seamen's Temper, that they ever grow more disorderly and ungovernable as they come nearer home. Wherefore our Master being a very good honest Man, resolved to let none have any more, but those that were in a fit condition to Drink it themselves; And that this might be observed punctually, he order'd the Under Steersman to stand by every day, and to see every body Drink their own Portion: By this means he put a stop to those Disorders, and prevented a great deal of Mischief.

When we came more and more in sight of the *North-Star*, we began to be very chearful, and fell a Singing of the Hymn,

Hoe Schoon light ons de Morgen-Star.

But by that time we got a little beyond the Island Fero, the Weather began to seem very Cold to us, tho' it was in the very middle of the Summer, that we could not bear to sit above Deck, till we had got some more Cloaths on. What made us so very sensible of Cold was, that we came from so Hot a Country as the *Indies* is. Here we observed, That the day was 20 hours long, and that in the four hours that the Sun was below our Horizon, it still gave so much light on the one side, or the other of us, that a Man might shift to Read any Book of a fair Character any time of the Night, by the help only of that refracted light.

The next day our Master, and Steersmen, judged that we were not far from *Hitland*. Then we saw continually great Flocks of Birds and flying Fish, which fell down in great numbers in our Ship. So Orders were given to watch on the Main-top-Masthead, and about the Evening one cry'd out Land. The Mountains assured us sufficiently that it was *Hitland*; therefore we bore directly upon it with a brisk Gale, and no small Joy it was to us, that we were thus happily drawing apace towards our Country

Thus we kept sailing all the next day along that Coast, within about a League from it, and so past it. Quickly after that we spied four Men of War, which we concluded were our Convoy ; and being come something nearer, we perceived them to be so by their Colours : Upon which, we hung out ours, and fired some Guns for a Signal. We likewise Hall'd out our Boats to go on Board them, but the Wind hindred us from doing it. All the while we came nearer and nearer, and the Convoy having a small Tender with them, they loaded it with Provisions, and sent it towards us ; as it is always the Custom to meet the homeward bound Ships, and to bring them fresh Victuals, &c. to refresh them after such a long Voyage. They brought some Vessels of Beer, Sack, Butter, Cheese, Tobacco, Pipes and Brandy.

When these things were brought on Board of us, one Vessel of Beer was put on the one side of the Main-Mast, and another on the other side ; and those were free for any body to go to, and Drink at Discretion.

But we did not long Enjoy our selves thus ; For as we were just coming to a pitch of Mirth and Jollity, such a dreadful Wind arose, as we had not met with any thing like it in our Voyage ; and it terrified us so much the more, because we were near home, where we thought our selves secure, not dreaming of any farther danger. The night came upon us, and our Ship being very old and crazy, began to spring several Leaks, so that we were forced to keep continually a Pumping. The Weather was so cold, the night so dark, and the Wind so very boisterous, that we were past all hopes, except what we had in God's Gracious Providence, and to that alone we committed our selves. The morning came, but gave us but a small Relief, for the Wind was as terrible as before ; and so it pleased God to hold on for four days together without Intermission ; at the end of which, God was pleased to Calm the Wind and Seas, and restore us to our former Peace and favourable Gales ; for which we all heartily offer'd up our Thanks to the Almighty.

Here we lost our Upper Steersman, who had been sick most of the Voyage, and we threw him overboard.

We had after this hard Weather, a pretty good Gale of Wind which brought us quickly in sight of the Northern Coasts. We sail'd all along by them, and steer'd our Course directly upon *Holland*, reckoning to reach the *Maes* in three or four days more. In our Course we met with some Fishermen, who came a-board of us, and sold us some fresh Herrings. This was to me the greatest Feast I had had a great while, and I think I never liked any thing better in my life. Among those Fishermen, there was one, that was as he said, 142 years old; and because we scrupled to believe him, he shew'd us an Extract of his Birth out of the Register-Book: He was as Active at his Business as any of his Fellows.

Shortly after this came a Pilot on Board of us, and by Orders from the Company, took the Government of the Ship on himself, and dismist the Master: So we came to cast Anchor before the *Briel*. As soon as we had cast Anchor here, the deputies of the Company came on Board of us: They are generally two of the oldest that are Deputed for that purpose. These Gentlemen call'd all the Ship's Crew together, and thank'd them in the name of all the Company for their Faithfulness and Diligence in their Service; from which they immediately freed them, and promised them that they should be paid with speed: After which, every one was at liberty, and was carried to Shore in some small Ketches that came for that purpose.

Immediately upon this, came other Seamen on Board the Ship, which they call *Sjouwers*.[1] These Furl'd in all the Sails, and took them down; fired all the Guns and charged them again. All the Provisions they found remaining was theirs. Every one of us was forced to leave his Chest on Board, they being all to be brought to the *East-India* House, and there to be Search'd.

The Wound I had received in the Wars of *Bantam* had of late been a little uneasie to me; and the two Bullets which were ever since that time in my Leg, began to be a little troublesome: But now my Pain increased so fast upon me, that in a very little while after we came to the *Briel*, I was no more able to walk at all by my self; but was forced to be carried into a House by a Couple of our Men. I was sorry I had not a little more time to Ease my self here; but the rest being ready to go for *Rotterdam*, I was obliged to be gone along with them.

Being come to *Rotterdam*, and having within 3 days time received my Chest back again, as all the rest likewise had. I was forced to go from thence to *Amsterdam*, that being the Chamber where I had engaged my self; and from which I was to receive my Money. Thither I went partly by Land, and partly by Water; but either way with so much

[1] " A Drudge on a ship's dock or aboard " (Sewel, *op. cit.*); " Porter, jobber " (Calisch, *Dutch-Eng. Dict.*, 1875).

pain and uneasiness, that all the Hardships I had undergone in all my Voyages were not to be compared with that: Yet I was full of acknowledgment to Almighty God, who had deliver'd me out of so many Extream Dangers to which I had been exposed, from the merciless Sea, fierce and cruel Serpents and Beasts; and from several Heathens of many Nations more barbarous than them all, and had brought me again into a Christian Country. And though I was not in Health of Body, yet it was an exceeding Comfort to me, to have so good Opportunities again of making better Provision for my Soul, and to participate of that Holy Sacrament from which I had been absent during seven years. Wherefore being in this weak Condition, the chief thing I desired was to have a Minister, and to receive the Communion. My Landlady help'd me to one who was the Minister of the German Lutheran Church at *Amsterdam*, from whose Pious Discourse, and Absolution, together with the Blessed Sacrament, I received an exceeding great Comfort, and then very chearfully resign'd my self up to the Almighty's Pleasure. I thank'd my Ghostly Father for his Kindness, and made him a Present of six Ducatoons, some Roses of *Jericho*, and some *China* Ware.

My Pain encreasing rather than diminishing, and I growing daily worse and worse, I sent for a Doctor and two Chirurgions, not willing to trust to my own Skill only. And being I was not able to go and receive my Money my self, I was obliged to send a Person to the *East-India* Chamber to receive my Money and Goods, by Virtue of a Letter of Attorney which I gave him. The Money that was Due to me from the Company did not amount to more than 4 or 500 Ducatoons, which was all the Fruit of my Labours; except some considerable *East-India* Goods I had brought over on my own Account, which I had to Sell: But by that time I had satisfied my Attorney, my Doctor, and the two Chirurgions, and defray'd the rest of my Charges, I found my Bag very light. My doctor did not cost me above Forty Dutch Gilders: The two Chirurgions, who were two of the most famous Artists in the whole city of Amsterdam, had Eighty Rixdollers; They had taken out my two Bullets, and cleared the Bone of above Twenty Splinters, great and small: For my Lodging, I paid Two Rixdollers a week, and had but a very poor Accommodation neither. The Apothecary too came in with a hideous Bill. In short, I should have been but in a miserable Condition if I had not had Money: And that went after such a Rate, that in less than Three Months time I had spent above 300 Ducatoons. However, I began to recover a little, and my pain was not sharp as before; tho' I could not go or stand as yet: But as soon as I was able to stir, I was resolved to continue my journey, and set out of this place, and endeavour to get home, whatever befel me. And in order thereunto I took a Coach to carry me to the *Utrecht-Poort*, where I took Boat for *Utrecht*, and from thence went to *Nimeguen*, and so passed through *Cleveland* to *Cologne*. By that time I got hither, I was so fatigued, that I was not in a capacity of moving any further; and therefore I was forced to lie still here for near three Weeks; during which time, I spent a great deal of Money again, and was so weak that I had hardly any hopes of ever reaching so far as home; nor did any Body think I should ever have recover'd. But it pleased God to Bless human Endeavours, so that I recovered a little again; upon which I immediately got my self carried to the *Rhine*, and there went on Board a Ship which carried me to *Mentz*, and thence to *Franckfort*. Some Relations and Gentlemen of my Acquaintance were so kind as to come to meet me before I got Embark'd on the *Rhine*; but I was not in a Condition, to take notice of them. However, they were so Civil, as to Convoy me along the Shore. When I was come to *Franckfort*, I was forced to stay without the City two days before they would permit me to enter, and the Weather being very Cold, I made but a poor shift in the Ship all that while: till at length the Chirurgions came to me, and went themselves to the Burgher-Master; upon which I was let in to the City that very night, tho' late. It being hard to get a Lodging in an Inn at that time of night, some good Friends of mine carried me to a private House, where some of my Acquaintance came to visit me. One of them got me a Coach, which in seven days time brought me to the place where I so earnestly desired to be, the City where I was Born. There I found all my Dear Sisters alive and well, who received me with all the Demonstrations of that sincere Love and Affection they had for me, and were extreamly Serviceable to me.

Thus I finish'd my Travels, which had taken up Nine whole years. And by the Faithful Relation which I here give of them: Thou mayst not only see, what Dangers and Difficulties I have been exposed to in so many various Adventures, but also thou oughtest to Admire the wonderful Goodness of God, who so wonderfully delivers Men, and never forsakes those that put their Trust in him. And not being able to Praise him sufficiently my self for his great and signal Mercies to me, I heartily desire that every thing that hath Breath may Praise the Lord.

THE END OF MR. FRYKE'S VOYAGE

A RELATION OF A VOYAGE TO AND THROUGH THE EAST-INDIES, FROM THE YEAR 1675 TO 1683

BY CHRISTOPHER SCHWEITZER

CHAPTER I

The Rise of the Dutch East-India Company. Many go to the Indies induced by a foolish hope of growing Rich there. Kidnappers send many thither. The Author's going off from Amsterdam to the Texel. What Ships were sent out. Ice and hard Weather detains them some Weeks in Texel. Orders given in case they meet and should fight with the French. The Allowance distributed to the Ship's Crew. They meet with Turkish Pyrates. Sentence given on a Criminal. The Equinoctial Line. Great Mortality under it in the Ships. A Remarkable Accident that befel the Author. Northern Pyrates. The Devil's Mount in Africa. Arrival to the Cape of Good Hope.

IT is about sixty years since some rich Merchants and others in *Holland*, as at *Amsterdam, Enckhuisen, Rotterdam, Leyden, Delft, Hoorn, Middleburgh*, and *Flessinguen*, having joyned Stocks, made up a Company, Rigg'd out some Ships, and Manning them with Officers and Seamen, sent them to the *East-Indies*. They have from time to time mightily increased their Strength there, and at length made themselves so powerful as to wage War, not only against some Kings of *Europe* as of *England* and *Portugal*; but to be able also to Curb several Kings and Emperors of the *East-Indies*. And hereby they are already become much more Wealthy than some Kings are, and grow every day greater and greater.

The rich Things which several Persons have brought with them out of the *East-Indies*, the great Booty which several opportunities offer to Men, the just and exact Pay of those who are employed in the Service of the Company, on the one side ; the desire of seeing strange Countries, and the Customs and Manners of People, so far distant, on the other, induce many Men to undertake this Voyage : Besides that, there are many Strangers that come into *Holland*, who are drawn in by a sort of Kidnappers, to engage themselves in the Service of the Company, allured by the hopes of great Profit and Advantage.

These Buyers and Sellers of Men are People that entice Strangers to their Houses, if they see they have but little Money, or are in perfect want, or if they come of themselves through Necessity, receive them, and provide 'em with Meat, Drink, and Cloaths plentifully, till the Ships are ready to go, and the People Embark ; Then each Kidnapper brings his Men, sometimes Ten, Twenty, Thirty, to the *East-India* House, and there gets them listed. Some days after this, he receives for each Man, for his Pains and Charge, a Note of 150 Guldens, and Two Months ready Pay, which the Soldier or Mariner, whatever he be, must Earn out. And the Note is not paid till it comes to be Due in Monthly Wages. An Account of what Pay is due to every one is sent every year out of the *Indies* to *Holland*, and may be seen upon the Books there. But if one of these Men happens to Die in the Voyage, the Kidnapper looses all his Charge ; for in such a case, the Company doth not pay him his Note, because it was not workt out.

These Men, to Entice Strangers to go, make them believe strange stories of the *Indies*, promise them vast Things, and are not ashamed to go so far as to put a Hammer into their Hands to knock the Diamonds out of the Rocks they shall meet with. Many of these poor Fellows Ruin themselves Body and Soul, by Marrying Indians, and running over from the Christians to some Heathenish King, when they have Habituated themselves to their Customs and Manners : Others meeting with untimely deaths, amongst Drinking, or other ill Company, which often happens : Others committing what Costs them their Life by a Sentence of some Court of Justice. And because these Men trapan that sort of People to go a Voyage that commonly proves their Destruction, they are generally call'd, *Ziel-Verkopers* or *Kopers*, that is *Soul-Buyers* or *Sellers*.

I for my own part was forced, for want of Money, to be some Weeks at one of these Jack-Call's Houses for Entertainment, paying 170 Guldens, the two Month's ready

Pay being reckon'd in; and I was accepted by the *East-India* Company on the 15th of November 1675 as a Volunteer, and was made Steward of the Ship call'd *Asia*: My pay was 20 Guldens *per* Month of Dutch Money; and I was to serve them five years in the *Indies*.

Upon these Conditions, I, with several others, went off from *Amsterdam* in a little Smack to the *Texel*, on the first of *December* 1675. There the Fleet lay that was ordered to go to the *East-Indies*; which consisted of Five Ships, viz. the *Asia* Admiral, the *Macassar* Vice-Admiral, the *Utrecht*, the *Cortgeene*, the *Tidor*: We saw besides a great many English and Dutch Men of War and Merchantmen, that staid for a good Wind.

The 2d of *December*, I Embarkt on Board the *Asia*, together with several others, engaged in the same Service.

The 3d *Ditto*, The Dutch Gentlemen that were Owners came on Board of us, with a very rich little Yatcht, wish'd us a good Voyage, and took their leave of us.

The 4th there came a Muster-Master, to see if all those that belong'd to the Ship were in it. There was in ours, the Chief Merchant, the Master, the Chaplain of the Reformed Religion, with his Wife and four Children, four Steersmen, one Book-keeper, five Barbers and Chirurgions, two Mates, two Stewards, two Cooks, two Gunners, four Carpenters, three Coopers, two Sail-Makers, two Quarter-Masters, one Serjeant, two Corporals, two Under-Corporals, 150 Soldiers, and 93 Foremast-Men, nine Boys to swab the Ship every day, and one Boatswain; the whole number was 297 men. The Muster-Master having taken a view of all, wish'd us a good Voyage and a good Wind.

The 5th, The Wind blew very strong at North-West, so that we were obliged to drop four Anchors at one time, of which each weigh'd 36 hundred Pound.

The 12th of *January* 1676. The greatest Trouble we had was caused by the Ice that came against us in great Flakes from the North, and encompass'd us on every side, striking continually against our Ship, and did our Cables a great deal of Damage. Therefore our Officers having consulted what to do, resolved, That if the Wind did not change in three days, we should leave the Ship and Goods, and go back to *Amsterdam*, with the light Vessels; that the Men as well as Ships might not perish, as it happen'd 15 years ago, when 15 founder'd about the same place.

The 13th *Ditto*, At Eleven a Clock at Night the Wind

changed and blew very fair for us at S.E. upon which a Gun was fired from our Admiral, all the Ships in the Fleet being to be govern'd by it, and was a Signal that every one was to weigh Anchor, and make ready to Sail.

The 14th, early in the morning, sailed first the Admiral, with Flags and Pendants on the Mainmast; after him the Vice-Admiral, with a Flag on the Foremost; and then the *Utrecht*, with a Flag on his Mizen-Mast, and then the other common Ships.

The 15th, An English Fisherman came to us, and gave us information that there were 16 French men of War cruising near *Calais*, with two Privateers and two Fireships laying wait for our Fleet. We sent out immediately a Yatch for true Intelligence, which came back to us on the 16th, and brought us word, that the Enemy was making up to us. Then we fell back to the Rode of *Duyns* [The Downs], and lay under the Cannon of that place, while we prepared our selves for Fight, and to Consult what we were to do: Upon this we had these following Orders agreed on.

I. That all Captains, Seamen, and Officers, should carefully observe what Signals and Commands were given by the Admiral, and Obey them punctually.

II. That as soon as the Enemy came in sight of us, we should draw into the Form of a Half-Moon.

III. That if we should happen to find a strange Ship fall'n in amongst our Fleet, we should give the other Ships notice of it by firing off three of our Demy-Cannon.[1]

IV. In case a Ship should be ready to sink, it should give notice of it by hanging a Lanthorn on the Foremast, if it were night; or by hanging out a Yellow Flag, if it were day.

V. Being the Admiral upon Pain of Death, must not yield himself, nor his Ship, into the Enemies Hand; The Vice-Admiral was (in case of a Fight) to be nigh, and second him.

VI. The Admiral was to put up two bright Lanthorns, and the other Ships but one, that they might distinguish and follow the Admiral.

VII. Upon all Occasions, the Officers and common Soldiers were to behave themselves briskly and

[1] The Demi-Cannon was a 30-pounder. Schweitzer probably uses the term in mistake for demi-culverin.

honestly, and to observe very strictly these and all other Articles relating to the Fleet, upon their Peril.

The 17th, We lay still, and a French Privateer came up the English Road, and passed by our Fleet, narrowly viewing it, and struck in to Sea again.

The 18th instant, in the morning, Our Admiral shot off one piece and hung up a Blue Flag, for a Signal to hoist up Sail, which was done accordingly, with many discharges of our Cannon in Honour to his Royal Majesty the King of England, which were answer'd from *Dover*-Castle.

The 19th, We saw the French Fleet about a League distance from us, but when they saw that we were so strong, they did not dare to fall upon us, but made home to *Calais*.

On the 20th, We lost sight of *England* and *France*. The Sea that lies between them two is call'd the Channel, and is 96 miles long. After this we came into the Sea of *Spain*. The Water there looks extreamly blue by reason of its being so vastly deep. About Noon, the Admiral sets up a white Flag, and fires a Gun, to give notice to all the Captains, Masters, and Stewards, belonging to the Fleet, to come aboard his Ship, which they did; and whilst he treated them, and all were mighty merry, the danger of the French coming upon them being over, the *Macassar* fell foul of our Ship, and gave us a terrible shake. The *Macassar* got a great Hole in her side by it, but it was easily stopt again. Towards Evening, our Guests went to their respective Ships, and the Cannon kept firing all the Night.

The 21th in the morning early, the Ships, that till then kept together, parted, each taking their several Course to the Places where they were Bound for. Some went to the *West-Indies*, others to *Smirna, Spain, Italy*, and *Portugal*. We that were bound to the *East-Indies*, being five Ships, kept on to the South-West, having a very good Wind at N.N.E.

The 22th, our Men aboard the *Asia* were divided into two parts; the one call'd the *Prince's*, the other *Count Maurice's Quarter*, one of these Quarters was to watch by turns four hours a piece at Night; when the Watch on the one side wanted to be relieved by some body of the other, two Men sung a Song to awake them.

In the Evening of this day, the *Rantsoen* (as we call it) began, that is, we came to set Allowance, which was, to every Person three Pound of Bisket a Week, half a Pint of Vinegar, a quarter of a Pint of *Lisbon* Sallad-Oil, and every day a

Gill of Brandy. On some days we had Stock-Fish and Pease boil'd in Water, upon which we us'd to pour a little Oil and Vinegar : But the next morning we had a Wooden-Dish full of boil'd Barley allowed to every seven Men. On Sundays, Tuesdays and Thursdays, our Dinners was Pork, or other Flesh.

From the 23th of *January* to the 24th of *February,* nothing remarkable happen'd, except that the cold Weather had quite left us ; And we saw the Fish sometimes driving one another to and fro, and particularly the flying Fish, about the bigness of a Herring, always in fear of being devoured. The longest Flights they could take was about a Musket-Shot, and then they were forced to light on the Water to wet their Wings again : By this Flight they escapc indeed from their greatest Enemies, the Dolphins and the Porpoises ; but then they often become the Prey of Sea-Birds, call'd Boobys ; Here we saw Birds and Fishes flying together.

The 25th of February we saw *Pico de Canaria,* or the *Canarie* Mountain : We steer'd our Course thither, and came pretty near it by the next day ; and then we found that we were 20 Leagues off when we first discover'd it. Otherwise, upon a smooth Sea, we could not see farther than five Leagues in a streight Line. This difference happens from the extraordinary height of the Hill above the surface of the Water.

The 26th, 27th and 28th *Ditto,* we had good Weather.

The 1st of *March,* early in the morning, We spied two Ships with Dutch Flags and Pendants, that were Roving about ; but we would not trust them, for we knew the Turkish Pyrates used to Lurk about this Mountain of the *Canaries,* or the Southern Island. After a Council of War held, our Admiral, about Noon sailed foremost to take better notice of them, and he quickly found them to be what we suspected.

We were not the only one who made our selves ready for a Fight, but our Four Ships that came after at about a League distance, did the like, and gave us notice by an appointed Signal, that they were prepared. We expected them, and towards the Evening, the Enemy came somewhat nearer to us, yet not within shot ; all that Night we kept a very strict Watch.

The 2d *Ditto,* very early in the morning, the Wind blew hard at North-West, by which means we lost sight of the Turkish Ships about Twelve at Noon ; and about the Evening it ceased.

RESIDENCE OF THE DUTCH GOVERNOR-GENERAL AT BATAVIA

(From J. Nieuhof's "Voyage to the East Indies")

The 3d, we made vast way with a good Wind, and about four hours after we espied a Ship, and found by her running she was one of the Turks we had seen the day before ; our Master being a very brisk Sea-Soldier, (his Name *Peter Vander Woetstiin*) found that he could not possibly outsail this Pyrate ; so he lower'd his Sails and staid for him, as much as to say, that he did not fear him. The Turk sailed by us with his Dutch Flag up, as near and swift as he could : He pretended to be a Friend of ours, and set a Renegado to Hail us, and ask us in Dutch, What Ship ? And whither Bound ? Our Master ordered the Gunner to fire, and the Men fired so briskly with the lower Tier, and batter'd the Mahometan so sorely, that they made all the haste they could to get away, and found work enough to mend the Holes our Guns had made.

The 4th in the morning, about 7 of the Clock, this Turk, batter'd as he was, came up to us again ; his Design was to clap us on board, and to Storm us. We having a sufficient Force on Board, defended our selves so bravely, that the Enemy was obliged to run again at night, with no small loss. On our side, we had Twelve kill'd and Twenty wounded, Soldiers and Seamen : The wounded were all cured. In the mean while, the Carpenters were employed in Repairing what Damage the Enemies Shot had done us, and stopping the holes.

The 5th *Ditto*, our Chaplain Preached a Thanksgiving Sermon for the Assistance God was pleased to give them, delivering them through his Mercy out of the Hands of those Cruel Tyrants : And after that, our Master and Admiral thank'd his People for the help they had given him with so much Gallantry ; and ordered a Bottle of Sack for every man.

From the 6th to the 24th of *March*, we had very blustering Winds, and a dreadful violent Storm, so that we often thought our selves at the very brink of Death.

The 25th, While that Tempestuous Weather still lasted, the Mate and his Boy were catch'd together acting the abominable Sin of Sodomy: A Council was held upon it, and Sentence was given that they should be tied back to back, (which was done by the Boatswain), and tied in a Sack, and thrown alive into the Sea. As the Minister was doing his Duty towards these Malefactors, representing to them the hainousness of their Crime, and directing them to prepare for Death, the Boy, about 14 Years of Age, wept bitterly : But the Mate, being an Italian, about 40 years old, shew'd himself right ready to Die, saying : 'Twas better he should be punish'd alone for his horrid Sin, than that the whole Ship should suffer for his sake.

The 26th, the Wind ceased ; But we hardly knew where we were, nor had known it for 20 days time, having not been able to make an Observation since the 6th day : And,

On the 27th, it being very fine Weather, we found that the Storm had carried us under the Equinoctial Line. Here it is extream unhealthy, and a certain Distemper seized most of our Men, which made them raving mad : In one day five Persons died, one of which was our Chaplain, and other four Soldiers. These Dead Men, were (according to the Custom of our Dutch Ships) sew'd, each Corps by itself, in a sheet, and after our usual Morning or Evening Prayer, (with a Psalm sung at the end of it) thrown into the Sea.

The 28th, we had no Wind : On this day, one of our Barbers, and two Seamen died ; and two Soldiers, in their raving Fit, (caused by the intollerable Heat) leapt into the Sea ; which two of our best Swimmers perceiving, leap'd in after them, and brought 'em into the Ship again : But one of 'em after all this, hang'd himself that very night by his Bed-side.

On the 29th, the other Soldier that had leapt in the Sea, died, having no regard to any good Advice that was given him, and could not be made to Pray. We had not a Breath of Wind this day, nor

The 30th and 31st : These two days we threw over-board our late Chaplain's 4 Children, 4 Chirurgions and Barbers, a Carpenter, and 10 Soldiers.

The 1st, 2d, 3d and 4th of *April*, the Calm held us still ; and in those days we lost a Steersman, two Carpenters, the Serjeant, and 30 Soldiers and Seamen ; so that we expected every Soul should Die out of the Ship.

The 5th *Ditto*, it Pleased God to deliver us from that fatal place by a favourable Wind at West and by South. We had still a great many sick Men, and not enough in health to be able to Brace our Main-Sail, tho' the Mortality ceased ; so we were forced to make shift with our small Sails. That day we caught with a Hook one of the great Fishes called Sharks, that rowl'd and toss'd about our Ship. We design'd to dress him, and refresh our selves with it ; but when we cut it open, we found in the Belly of it our Serjeant that we had thrown over-board, not yet digested. The sight of this so turn'd our Stomachs, that none could find in their Heart to Eat of the Fish; so that we threw Man and Fish into the Sea again. It is observable, that these great Fish have always some small ones to go before 'em, that are called by the name of Pilot-Fishes, and swim in and out of the Shark's mouth. And when a Shark is catch'd, they cleave to his Back like a Burr.

But I must not omit what happen'd to my self. As I fell ill and was in a Swoun, he that look'd after the Sick, took me for Dead, and fetch'd a new Shirt out of my Chest, and was putting it upon me; The Sail-Maker too was going to sew me up; and he handling me a little roughly, after all his pushing and tossing of me, I open'd my Eyes: Those that were about me were not a little startled; and said, it was high time for me to open 'em; for if I had winck'd but a little longer, over I had gone. Our chief Merchant gave me a Glass of Sack, which refreshed me very much.

From the 6th to the 18th of *April*, we had a very fair Wind and good Weather. In that time we saw some of the Northern Capers, and a great many Whales, which kept us Company till we came on

The 20th, within sight of the *Devil's Mount* in *Africa*, which is very remarkable for its height.

The 22th, We came happily into the Road near the Land call'd *Cape de Bonne Esperance*, or the *Cape of Good Hope*. And here we met again with two of our Ships, *Cortegeene* and *Tidor*, which had been parted from us, and we had not seen, since the 2d of March. They gave us an Account, That they had been busie with the Turkish Privateers that fell upon us, and that they had wetted their Feet; which was, that they had sunk 'em. However, They took up 36 of their Men that could Swim best, and brought them along with them. This News gave us a great deal of Joy. The Prisoners we sent hence immediately to the *Robin-Island*, to gather Mussel-shells, and others, for the burning of Lime.

CHAPTER II

The Cape, how far from Amsterdam. Fruitfulness of that Country. Its fullness of Inhabitants, call'd Hottentots, their Customs and Manners. Its Wealth. Their going off from the Cape. The day of Humiliation kept in the Fleet. A certain Merchant's son falls into the Sea and is drown'd. Two more drown'd. Their Allowance lessned. Arrival at Java Major. The Road of Sunda: Bantam. A Man swallow'd up by a Crocodile. Arrival at Batavia. Description of its Fort, with four Bastions. Custom of the Chineses there, when one of them dies. What Heathens live at Batavia. Amboineses great Conjurers. The best Soldiers sent to quell the Inhabitants of Jappara. The Dutch land, but are beaten. A remarkable Accident. Ships arrive from Holland to Batavia. Account of the troublesome Voyage of one of 'em. A Pellican of a Purple colour. A strange Bird call'd a Casswari. Great Execution of Malefactors. A Crocodile 22 foot long, catch'd. A Huntsman tore in pieces by a Tyger. A wonderful Leap given by a Man. Twelve of the Heer Spelman's Slaves that were run away brought back and broke upon the Wheel: How that is done at Batavia. The Square in Batavia, why so called and by whom built. By what means the Dutch took Batavia from the English. A very Comical thing that happen'd by one of the Casswari-Birds, that were kept in the Fort of Batavia. A strange Accident between a Peacock and an old Chinese that had game'd away all his Money and Goods. The manner of living of the Chineses at Batavia. The rich Chinese

THE 23th of *April,* early in the morning, I went on Shore of *Africa* with our Admiral: From this place to *Amsterdam* they reckon usually 2000 miles. At this Cape we lay still nine days, and in that time provided our selves with Water, Wood, and other Necessaries. As to the Qualities of this Land, by what Observation I could make of it, I found it to be : First Fruitful ; And for that Reason, our *East-India* Company hath caused some years ago, many very strong Places to be Built there by the Water-side, close under the *Duyvel's-bergh, Lewen-bergh,* and *Tafel-bergh,* well stored with Soldiers, and all things necessary, and are sufficiently provided against the Incursions of the Wild-Men ; so that their Ships going to and from the Indies, may safely, and without any danger, put in there at any time, and take in Provisions, whether it be of Cattle, Water, Wood, or other Refreshments. And here are already a great many Boors [1] that are come from Holland, and by reason of the great Priviledges that are granted them, have settled there, and have Tilled the Land and made it very fruitful, for a matter of 20 or 30 miles round about those Places. Secondly, Very populous : The Inhabitants are called wild Africans, or *Hottentots.* Their Colour is like that of the Egyptian Heathens, or we call them corruptly, Gypsies. The Hair of their Head grows entangled in one another, like the Wool of a young Lamb ; upon which they hang for Ornament all manner of Sea-shells. They are of a middle stature, and well proportioned, only that they have their Noses a little too flat and broad.

They wear no manner of Cloaths, only a Sheepskin or Calf-skin on their Shoulders (and that's besmeared with Grease to make it soft and pliant) when it is a little cold, or when it rains. They wear the tail of a Fox, or of a wild Dog hanging before their Privy-parts. The Women among these *Hottentots* have a different Ornament from the Men, which is the Gutts of their Cattle fresh killed. These they wrap about their Legs, not minding the inconveniency it puts them to, which is such that they can hardly go, and they leave 'em there till they are quite dry.

These People have a very strange Speech, and make such a disagreeable Noise with their Mouth, as other Nations cannot imitate ; but a great many of them that live near to the *Cape of Good Hope* can speak some Dutch. They have no manner of Religion, Prayers, or Laws, only they Worship the Moon. The first time that they see it ; they spend that whole Night in Dancing, Singing, and Bawling Ha, ha, ha, ha. They do not at all trouble themselves with Building or Planting : So that they have no constant abode,

[1] This is another form of Boer, a term applied to Dutch settlers at the Cape.

but move from place to place with their Children and Wives, where they can find Pasture for their Cattle. They Eat all sorts of Fruits and Roots that grow either above or underground. They make no difference, whether their Meat is kill'd, or dead with any Distemper, or whether it be Man's Flesh : Whatever it be, they throw it upon some Coals, leave it there a little while, and so Eat it.

They lie in small Hutts or Holes, every one with his Wife. If any of the Women have two Children at one Birth, they kill the weakest, that the other may have the Breasts to himself, and grow stronger and lustier. As soon as the Boys come to be above Twelve years of age, they cut off his right Testicle, that he may be fitter for Running.

They have some Kings amongst them, and a great many Captains, and have cruel Wars between one another. They shoot Darts, and are excellent at hitting a Mark with a Stone. The Women too will come in often and carry their Husband's Arms : If they take any of their Enemies, they kill 'em and eat 'em with great Joy and Satisfaction. And in the same manner they use the Europeans too, (who come often to Truck a little Tobacco or Bracelets, for a good parcel of Cows and Sheep) if they can get them into their Hutts.

Thirdly, Rich. They have all manner of wild Beasts. For here are the furious Lions, which regard no Man, and when Hungry, fall upon Men and Beasts and Devour them. The Grinning Tygers. The vast Elephant for Bulk and Strength. The Angry Rhinocerous. The skipping and clambering Ape : Besides, Wild Dogs, Bears, Wolves, and wonderful fine Wild Asses, all in great numbers ; As also Ostriches, which have indeed Feathers and Wings, but cannot fly by reason of their bigness and weight. Their Eggs are hatch'd of themselves, and not (as some misinformed Persons have given an account of it) by their continual looking after them. Sea-Cows, that lie in the fresh Rivers all day, and at night come on Shore to feed : Their Flesh is better than that of Swine. Stag and Deer, Wild-Boars, Partridges, Peacocks, Geese, Wild-Ducks, and other sort of Poultry, too long to give an account of, all which are here very plentiful.

The 1st of *May*, towards Night, the *Asia*, *Tidor*, and *Cortgeene*, put off together to go forward, and continue our Course (with the help of God) to *Batavia*.

The 2d we had a General Day of Humiliation in our three Ships. For tho' we were now out of Danger of sea-Robbers, we were not so from Storms and Tempests, and other fatal Accidents.

The 3d, The Wind blew very hard at N.W. tho' it was Serviceable for us to set us forward.

The 14th, The Wind grew higher still: And in the afternoon, a Merchant's Son of *Franckfort*, *Morel* by name, going, (as it was usual) to the fore-part of the Ship to ease Nature, fell into the Sea; and all our Endeavours to help him were in vain, by reason of the boisterousness of the Waves, and our swift Sailing: That same day the two Ships of our Company, the *Tidor* and *Cortgeene*, parted from us.

From the 5th to the 10th the same Wind lasted.

The 11th, We felt it very Cold.

The 12th, We had a mixture of Hail and Snow, and two of our Seamen fell in and were drowned.

The 13th, 14th, 15th, 16th, 17th, 18th, 19th, and 20th *Ditto*, We hoisted up but one Sail, and ran very swift, the Wind blowing almost a Storm, and made commonly 70 miles, or more, in 24 hours.

The 21th, We reach'd the Altitude of the Island *St. Maurice*. This Island was not long since Invaded by the Dutch *East-India* Company, before which time it was not Inhabited. It is fruitful, and has great store of Wild-Deer; It produces Amber Greese, Ebony, and other fine Woods.

The 22th, A Seaman of ours fell unluckily from the Main-Mast upon one of our great Anchors, and from thence into the Sea, and sunk immediately, his Breath being gone with his first fall.

The 23th, We came again into a warm Climate, and we had a very favourable Wind to the end of this month.

The first of *June* it was very still, but very Rainy Weather.

The 2d, Our usual Allowance of Flesh, Bread, and Beer, was lessened, which did not please most of us very well.

From the 3d to the 20th, We had nothing remarkable, save that suffer'd in some measure both Hunger and Thirst, tho' that contributed much to our Health, according to the Proverb, which says, *That Hungry Men will not over-sleep themselves*; and much Sleep being unhealthy, the sharpness of our Stomachs would keep us from any such indisposition.

The 21th, Our Master promis'd Twelve Crowns to any

one that should discover Land, upon which we all look'd about us very sharp, and kept very strict Watch, taking great notice what Colour the Water was of, by which we often have notice that we draw near the Land; in the mean while we were busie with getting of our Anchors ready.

The 22th, in the morning, One that stood on the top of the Main-Mast, cry'd out, Land, and being ask'd which way he spy'd it, he answer'd, Directly in the East, and that it was a high Land. This was about Sun-rising, and about Noon we found that he had not been mistaken; for it was the very Land which we were to go to, viz. *Java Major*, or *Great Java*; This occasion'd a very great Rejoycing, for now we had bread and water allowed in abundance.

The 23th, We came into the Road of *Sunda*, which is about 36 miles long: Here we were obliged, by reason of the Calm, and the fierceness of the Tide against us, to cast out our Anchor. While we lay there, some of the Inhabitants of Java came to visit us, and brought us all manner' of Indian Fruits; such as *King's Apples, Mellons, Figs, Citrons, Bananas, Sugar, Rice,* and other-like things; all which Refreshments we had of them in exchange for old Iron and Tobacco. They came in little Boats, but oddly made, and very ill put together, but they sail very fast with 'em.

The 24th, Two of them were sent over to us out of *Bantam*, laden with Fruit from *Java*, Ducks, Goats &c. This day we made some of our way with a good Wind, but towards the Evening we cast Anchor, the Wind being changed.

The 25th, in the morning, betwixt 9 and 10 a clock, we saw at the right Hand of us, the Royal City *Bantam*; In the afternoon, about 4 a Clock, we came into the Road before *Batavia*: Our Cabin-Boy swimming very well, and having a mind to refresh himself in that Water, was unexpectedly catch'd and devour'd by a Crocodile.

The 26th, in the morning, we were fetch'd to Shore in a small Skiff to *Batavia*, to our great Joy: Thus we did (by God's assistance) compleat this great Voyage from *Amsterdam* to *Batavia*, in five months and 12 days, and in less than 24 weeks, made 3636 miles.

The 27th, came in the *Tydor* and *Cortgeene*, which came out with us from the *Cape of Good Hope*, and which had not been seen since the third day after that until now. This made them all very glad in *Batavia*.

This day at night, all the Soldiers that were sent here from *Holland*, were brought, well Arm'd and in good Order, before the Dutch General there, called *Maetzuycker* :[1] He welcom'd them ; and after that, the Officers divided them, and sent them some into the City, and some into the Fort. I went to see the Fortification : It has four Bastions, viz. First, the *Diamond*, where a Major, with 40 or 50 Soldiers keep constantly ; Secondly, the *Ruby*, kept by a Captain, and as many Men ; Thirdly, the *Saphire*, which is commanded by a Serjeant ; And Fourthly, The *Pearl*, commanded also by a Serjeant.

The 28th, 29th, and 30th, We had three days liberty to go up and down, in and out of the City ; and here we much wondered to see the Chineses, (of which several live here upon the account of their great Trade) carry Meat and Drink to those that are Buried in the Church-yard, in Vessels of fine *China*, lamenting, and asking them, Why they Died, and what they wanted ; and telling them, it was unkind not to let their Friend know of it ; But the Dead there, as well as here, are very silent. This good Chear of theirs is generally carried off by the Dutch Soldiers and Seamen, who Feast themselves with it, when they have Gamed away their Money, or otherwise spent it. Besides these Chineses, there are several other East-Indians, and other Heathens, that live at *Batavia*, and drive a great Trade there. They are all oblig'd to joyn together in the common defence of the City, in case of Necessity ; chiefly the Javans, the proper Inhabitants of this Island : They are very Tawny, and wear only a Girdle about their middle, of fine Linnen or Silk : They are Circumcis'd as the Turks : Some of them Worship an Image with a Lion's Head, the Sun, and the Moon, &c.

Besides Amboineses, Tarnatans, Malleyers, Machaffers, and other like Nations, each of these have their Kings ; are very skillful with Weapons, which are Bows, Arrows, Javelins, Spears, and Poisoned Darts. When they go into the Field, they adorn their Bucklers with a great deal of finery, wearing on their Head a very fine Bird, call'd the *Bird of Paradise*, which is found in *Amboyna*, about 500 miles from *Batavia*. Their warlike Musick is an Instrument made of Mettle, called Gum-Hum, much in the Nature of our Drums ; It makes a greater noise than a good large

[1] Joan Maetsuyker, Governor-General 1653–78.

Bell. The Amboyneses are great Necromancers; and hence it is said, Doctor *Faustus* got his Master, and was carried thither through the Air riding upon a Cloak.

From the 1st of *July* to the 9th, We were daily exercis'd in the handling of the Musket and Pike, &c.

The 10th, Some of the stoutest and briskest of all our Men were pick'd out and sent.

The 11th, Under the Command of Major *Poolman* a Brandenberger, Captain *Harzing*, Captain *Roodbol*, Captain *St. Martini* a Frenchman, and Captain *Dack*, each with his Company, and Embark'd in one Ship to go to *Japara* to quell the Insurrection there, and to help the King of *Bantam* against the Inhabitants.

The 12th, Our Seamen too, belonging to our five Ships were divided into Companies, and provided with Hand-Granadoes, sharp Cutlaces, Pikes, Bills, and other Weapons useful in War: Their Officers were the Master as Captain, the Mate was made Lieutenant, the Boatswain a Serjeant, and the Quartermasters Corporals.

The 13th and 14th, We past by *Bantam*, and afterwards by *Toppers-boedie*, and the *Prince's* Island.

The 15th, We saw our Enemies in an innumerable quantity of little Skiffs. They had notice of our approach, and designed to keep us from their Wall; so they came to meet us, and quite surrounded our Ship: Their intent was to get on Board, then Storm, and Rob us. All this while, our Granadiers and Soldiers were employed, and fought so briskly, that that day we destroy'd about 1100 of their Skiffs, little and great. We had but few of our Men killed, but many wounded. We could not tell the number of the Enemy that was slain; for supposing there were as many of their Boats sunk, as I said ev'n now, the number of the Men is uncertain, for they hold according to their bigness from 6 to 30 Persons. And besides, As their Boats sunk, abundance of them were Swimming to Land, like so many Water-Spaniels for about a mile's space, and so saved their lives. Our Booty was but small; for the Indians had nothing about them but Provision and Arms, the best part of which fell into the Sea.

The 16th, early in the morning, We were put ashore all together to pursue the Enemy, whilst they were still terrified with their late loss. We expected to make an easie work of it, but they understood, and we found it otherwise. They fell upon us like Mad-Dogs, in vast numbers, and of all sides. The *Opium* that they use to take always before they engage, had made 'em stark Mad; so that they kill'd the flower of our Officers, and 150 private Soldiers: And at last, the rest of us were forced to Flee and Swim for our Lives to get into our Ship.

The 17th, All our sick and wounded were put into a Ship, and sent to the Hospital in *Batavia*; And a Letter sent to the General, and the Council, to acquaint them, that we wanted a fresh Assistance and Recruits to go on in our Enterprize.

The 18th, We sent out a large Boat, with a Lieutenant, and Soldiers and some Seamen, to go ashore and view the place, and give us Intelligence; but the Enemy fell upon them, and slew every one of them, except one Seaman: who,

On the 19th, came swimming to our Ship very quick, having the stream with him. He gave us an account, how they were fell upon by four Boats full of those Japarians, who killed all his Companions; and as for his own safety, he had made his way through 'em with a great lighted stick of Wood, that he snatcht up from under a Kettle, and with that kept them at such a distance who were half Naked, that he had room and time to throw himself into the Water and Swim for his Life, tho' they continually shot at him with their Arrows. Our Master order'd him immediately a Glass of Sack to refresh him, for he was sadly weaken'd, having been almost a day and a night in the Water.

The 20th, After a Council held, Letters were written to the General *Maetzuycker*, in Batavia; and I was one of those that were order'd to go with them.

We sailed all the 21th, 22th, and 23th, and arrived happily at *Batavia* on the 24th, and delivered our Message and Letters.

The 25th, An Advice-Boat was sent with a Letter to the Fleet at *Jappara*, to order them to come all back to *Batavia*.

The 26th, A new Ship from *Holland* arrived here, and brought us an Account, That they had been 9 months a coming, and that 18 of their Men died in their Voyage.

The 27th, Came another Ship in, which the Hollanders had given over for lost, having been gone from *Zealand* above 18 months, and they had no news of it all that while. The Master of it told me, They had undergone a great deal of Hardship; (which one might easily see by the Ship and her Crew). Amongst other things, he told us, That they had been driven so far Southward by a continual Storm, that their Compass did 'em no more Service, the Needle turning from one side to the other irregularly. At last, they had discover'd in the night, a high Land, which appear'd to them like Fire; but they turn'd their Backs to it, and sail'd so long, till they came at last by meer good Fortune, to get the use of their Compass again.

The 28th, a Ship came from *Malacca* to *Batavia*, which brought a great many Spiauters [1] and Pellicans of a Purple Colour, as also a Casswari: This is a great Bird that has no Feathers on his Body, but Hair, like a Hog's Bristles. It will Eat red-hot Coals, Tobacco-Pipes, Iron, and leaden Bullets; but doth not Digest any of 'em: It hath no Tongue, but makes a Noise as Shrill as that of a little Gosling. Of this Bird we shall take an occasion to tell you a very pleasant story by and by.

The 29th, Four Seamen were publickly Beheaded at *Batavia*, (which is here the common Death of Criminals) for having killed a Chinese. At the same time, six Slaves that had Murthered their Master in the night, were broke upon the Wheel. A Mulatto (as they call those that are begotten betwixt a Black-a-Moor and a White) was Hang'd for Theft. Eight other Seamen were Whipt for Stealing, and running away, and were besides this, Burnt on the Shoulder with the Arms of the *East India* Company. Two Dutch Soldiers that had absented themselves from the Guard two days, ran the Gauntlet. A Dutch Schoolmaster's Wife that was caught in Bed with another Man, (it being her frequent Practice) was put in the Pillory, and Condemn'd to 12 years Imprisonment in the *Spinhuys*.[2]

During the time of Execution, the Gates of the Fort, and of the City, were shut up, and all the Garrison in Arms.

The 30th, Came 32 Javans with a Crocodile, 22 Foot long, which they had caught with a great Crook, and brought into the Fort to shew it to the General, who having taken a view of it, gave the Fellows that brought it 6 Rixdollars for their Pains; So they carried it away again.

The 31th, A Javan came into *Batavia*, and gave an Account

[1] The translator is at fault in this passage; the correct rendering is "much spiauter and a Pelican." Spiauter is Spelter, or zinc.

[2] "*Spinbuis*: The house of correction for naughty women" (Sewel, *op. cit.*).

of the General's Huntsman's being fall'n upon by a Tyger, and torn in pieces by him.

The 1st, 2d, and 3d of *August*: The Dutch Burgers and Soldiers, as also the Indian Inhabitants of *Batavia*, drew up in the *Galge-Veldt*, each by themselves, and made a very fine shew. Many of the Indians here shew'd their Activity in Leaping, and in exercising their Arms, *viz.* Shields, Bows, Arrows, and Pikes. The most remarkable Leaper amongst them all, was one Captain *Joncker*, who Leapt cleverly over a Dutch-Trooper, that was mounted on a Persian Horse. We Hollanders were Posted, (about the House where our General and the Lords of the Council of the *Indies* were, with their Wives and Children) with four Companies under Arms, ready in case the Indians (who were in great numbers) should attempt to Rise or to make a Rebellion. This shew was made to entertain the *Heer Rycloff Van Goens*,[1] a Dutch Admiral, that was newly come over, and was then one of the Lords of the Council, and a short time after was made General.

The 4th, Twelve Slaves of the Heer *Speelman's*, one of the Council of *India*, run away; they had taken a Boat and got to *Bantam*. The Muster-master of *Batavia*, went with six Servants, all Guinea-Gaffers, well provided with Cutlaces and other Arms, in a Yatch in pursuit of 'em. They soon met with them, but the Slaves so well defended themselves, that they kill'd the Muster-master and all his Company; and went on to *Bantam*: where they thought themselves very safe, but to their Grief, they found themselves mistaken; for as soon as they Landed, they were known to be Fugitive Slaves, and seized and sent back.

On the 7th, All the Twelve were broke upon the Wheel in the place call'd the *Galge-Veldt*. The manner of doing it is thus: There are four Posts drove into the Ground, and stand out about two foot: To these they Tie the Malefactor's Hands and Feet; Then comes the Executioner with a Bar of Iron, and breaks his Limbs one after the other, and at last gives him one Blow on the Breast.

The 8th, A Seaman was found in the Square (the Dutch call it the *Vierkant*) cut most dreadfully with a knife. This Square is a very large place, and is so called because it had four Angles. It was built by the English about 60 years

[1] Rykoff Van Goens, Governor-General 1678–81. He had played a prominent part in the conquest of Ceylon and wars with the English and Portuguese (*see* Introduction).

ago. Afterwards the Dutch got it from 'em, by this means, (as I am informed). Some Dutch Ships came close to this Square; Their Admiral begg'd the favour of the English Governour, that he might be permitted to bring in his Men, (who were very sick with their long Voyage) for recovery of their Health and for Refreshment; which the English Governour generously granted out of Pity and Compassion. The Dutch sent two Boats full of their best and stoutest Men, arm'd privately with such Weapons as might not be discover'd, as Swords, Knives, and Pistols, and with a feigned groaning and grunting, were let in at the Water-Gate; and being got in, fell upon the English, and slew one part of 'em, and took the other Prisoners, and plunder'd all their Goods (vid. Van Hesse's *Account of the taking of Batavia in his Voyage*). Since that time, the City and Fort was built by the Dutch, who have now made it so strong both within and without, with Walls and Ditches, (which never are frozen up by reason there's no Winter here) that the place is inaccessible, and is able to resist all their East-Indian Enemies. The Fort, with the 4 Bastions, (which I have an Account of already), commands all the Streets of the City, the Square, the Water-Gate, and the Road where the Ships lie.

The 9th, Our Armourer sent Orders to all the Guards, That those who wanted Musket-Balls should come to the usual place at 4 a Clock in the afternoon (after they had been Exercised), and fetch 'em. He sent out before-hand, a Box full of 'em by two of his Slaves from the Store-house, and bid them set it down in the great Court. A while after, coming to given 'em out, he found his box empty. He runs immediately to our Captain, and complains, That the Soldiers had stole away his Bulletts: The Captain sets him Sentinel for his Negligence; and then had all the Soldiers searched: But on

The 10th, They found out that the Casswari Birds (of which we have made mention above) that run all about the Fort, had swallowed all the Bullets, and dropt them here and there, as they wander'd about, whole and undigested. Our Armourer was forced for his Carelessness, to go all over the Fort to pick up the Bullets that were fall'n, and to hunt the Birds about to make them restore the rest.

The 11th, As an old Chinese was coming along the said Fort, with two Vessels of Milk to sell; a Peacock that belong'd to the General, seeing him, flew up upon his Head, and had certainly pickt out his Eyes had it not been for some Slaves that beat him off. This old Chinese had once been the richest Man in *Batavia*, and worth some Tuns of Gold, which he had play'd away at Dice, and lost the very Hair of his Head which was his last Stake.

The 12th, I went into the City to a Chinese's House to drink a Glass of their Grass-Beer, which is made of Sugar, and is very pleasant. There I saw their manner of Eating: Seven of 'em, all Men, sat at a Table by themselves, for they will not trust themselves among the Europeans, nor will they let them see their Wives: Besides their Wives, they keep several *Malleyers*, that are fine Women, tho' of a tawny Complexion, and broad Noses, whom they Buy for their use. These Women have the liberty of shewing themselves abroad: Their Masters lie with them at their Pleasure; but besides these Women, they frequently keep Swine for the same purpose, and make the same use of 'em.

In the middle of the Table stood a very large *China* Dish, with a great many little ones in it, which were filled, some with Fish, and boil'd Rice instead of Bread; some with a sort of a Mess made of Citrons, which they call *Arochbar*; and others, with a pickl'd sort of Fruit like our Barberies, which they preserve in Juice of Citrons and Vinegar. Each Man had a Wooden thing in his Hand like a pair of Tongues, which they use instead of a Fork, to eat their Meat with. After they had done Eating, they took every one a Whiff of Tobacco out of a Pipe (which they call *Gur-Gur*) the Bole whereof is so large, that it would contain half a Pint of Water.

At the time of their Meals, they did not forget their God, which was an Idol made of Wood, and stood very finely adorned upon a Table, with a Lamp burning by it. Him they served first with their best Fruits and Meats, and laid it all decently on a Board that stood by for that purpose. I was so intent upon observing them, that I never minded my Drink, tho' it was excellent, and continually expected to see that Devil Eat the Victuals that were set before him; but I found, I might have staid long enough, for he was so modest, he would not offer to touch them, so I came away: For I saw they did not like my standing so near their Door to observe 'em as I did, and they knew me to be a Dutchman. What the Devil did with his Meat afterwards I cannot pretend to give you an account of.

On the 13th, I went to visit the Rich Chinese. Any European that goes there, is treated very liberally with as much strong Drink as he pleases; which sort of Drink is Distill'd out of the *Suri* that comes off from the Coco-Trees, and they call it *Arack*. The Richest Chinese hath all the others under him; and as soon as he hangs out a red Flag, they are all obliged to appear immediately. He furnishes also all the Dutch Ships with a sufficient quantity of *Arack*, and Vinegar; of which he makes a Bill, which is abated out of their Contributions.

CHAPTER III

Bats as big as Geese, good to Eat, and esteem'd a great rarity. A Sentinel kill'd by a Javan drunk and mad with Opium. Great mischief done by the Lightning. Robbers very dangerous, who are a sort of Dutch Soldiers that have Deserted. A Serpent of a dreadful bigness being 26 foot long. Wages of the Officers and Soldiers. The Ship call'd the Utrecht burnt. An Earthquake in 1674, that destroyed part of a very rich Island. What may justly be judged the Causes of it. King of Siam's Present to General Maetzuycker. Elephants taught to stand firing. The Author goes for Ceylon from Batavia. The Prince's Island. Their Allowance at Sea. The Coast of Sumatra, very unhealthy. Storm and Tempest. Catching of Sharks. They met with strange Men whom they could not understand. Two Seamen quarrel and fight with Knives; both of 'em punish'd, and how. What Hunger and Thirst they all underwent in the Voyage. Their arrival before Columbo. Lions sent to the King of Candy. The Author is sent to the Fort of Galture.

THE 14th of *August*, came two *Javans* to *Batavia*, and brought Twelve Bats as big as Geese for a Present to our General. They are reckon'd there a very delicate Food; and I was told, they were brought to the General's Table as a Rarity, and fit for a great Entertainment. They fly out at Night as ours do, and haunt the Coco-Trees, and there suck the *Suri* that lies in the Coco Nuts, so long, till they tumble down, and so are easily taken up with one's Hand; in the Day they keep in the Woods and hollow Trees.

The 15th, A Javan [1] that had eaten some Opium struck a Soldier that stood Sentinel with a half Pike upon the

[1] See more of him in Christopher Frike's and Elias Hesse's Relation. (Note in original.)

Bridge, between the City and the Fort, with a Poisoned Dart, and kill'd him. This mad Fellow went on with a Design to fall upon the next Centinel also which stood next to the Gate; But he being aware of him, presented the Point of his Half-Pike against the Javan, who ran furiously upon it, and so killed himself. His body, was, for an Example to the rest, dragg'd about the City by the Executioner's Men, (who are *Caffers* of *Angola*,) and after that Hang'd up upon a Tree by *Jacatra*.

The 16th, We had a great deal of terrible Lightning that set fire on many Chinese Ships, and consumed them. It look'd all that day, as if the Cannon had been perpetually firing. The reason of which is, That their Masts and Ships (*Jonckers* [Junks] as they call 'em) are of Bamboo-Canes, the Knots of which, when the Fire comes to crack them, give a very great Bounce in the Air.

The 17th, Two Soldiers and one Seamen deserted out of the Garrison, and went to joyn with the Robbers that dwell on the *Blaewbergh*, that is, Blew-Hill, about 12 Leagues off here. These Robbers are a parcel of Soldiers and Seamen that are run away from the Dutch Service, and live about the *Blaew-bergh* with their Wives that are Javans, and much annoy the Passengers.

The 19th, Twelve Javan Wild-Horses were brought over from *Bantam* for a Present, to the Heer *Maetzuycker* our General.

The 20th, Some Javans brought a Dead Serpent 26 foot long, before our General's Lodgings. When the General had seen this dreadful Creature, he order'd it to be carried to his Physician Dr. Kleyer, who had it cut open by one *John Otto Helwigh*, a Saxon Doctor of Physick, (that came over with us as a Soldier) and had his Skin stuff'd up, and kept for a Show.

The 21st, Three Month's Pay was paid to all the Garrison, in Money, Silks, Stuffs, Linnen from *China*, Shirts, Shooes and Stockings; instead of Victuals here, we are allowed Board-Wages. The Pay is as followeth :—

A Captain's, 80 or 100 Guldens *per* Month Salary, 10 Rixdollars, and 7 Cans of Wine, and two of Oil, Board-Wages.

A Lieutenant's, 50 Guldens *per* Month Salary; and 6 Rixdollars, Board-Wages.

An Ensign's, 36 Guldens *per* Month Salary; and 6 Rixdollars, Board-Wages.

A Serjeant's, 20 Guldens *per* Month Salary; and 4 Rix-dollars Board-Wages.

A Corporal's, 14 Guldens *per* Month Salary; and 4 Guldens, Board-Wages.

And a Private Soldier's, 10 Guldens *per* Month Salary; and 4 Guldens, and 40 pound of Rice, Board-Wages.

The 22nd, The *Utrecht* that was come some days before from the Western-Coasts, and loaded with 400 Lasts [1] of Paper, was burnt in the Road of *Batavia*. The Cannon and Anchors were hall'd up again, by reason it was not very deep, and all the Men saved.

The 23rd, Our Major *Poolman* order'd a Lieutenant, with 60 Soldiers, to go with the *Asia* to the Western Coast.

The 24th, Two Ships happily arrived before *Batavia*; the one from *Siam*, loaden with Spiauter; the other from *Tarnate*, loaden with Cloves, Nutmegs, and Mace. They brought us the News of a great deal of mischief that had happened in *Amboyna* and *Tarnate* about 500 miles Eastward from *Batavia*, by the Earthquakes, that are very frequent there, and commonly every year. Amongst others, a part of an Island that was sunk by an Earthquake in the year 1674, which at that time was saved, and was very rich in Clove-Trees, was now wholly sunk.

Those that know the way of living here, need not much wonder why that Island should have such severe Misfortunes fall on it. The Spaniards heretofore found this Island, and seeing it abound so much in Spices fortified it with Castles and Towers, and adorn'd it with Churches, Cloisters, and Schools: But they exercised an excessive Tyranny over the Inhabitants. For after they had treated with them and establisht themselves in Peace, the Don's carried themselves so haughtily and cruelly, that if an Inhabitant chanced to meet 'em, and did not go 10 or 12 steps out of their way, and then stand still, till the proud Spaniard was gone by, *Sinioro* made no more on't, but thrust him through the Guts with his Cinque-Palm, (a Sword five Spans long) and laid a certain piece of Money, call'd a *Perdau*, upon the Dead Body: After which, the Murtherer was free from any Punishment, nor was he liable to be accused or reckon'd a Murtherer. And in this manner they have dealt with abundance of poor Indians upon any

[1] The word "last," meaning "load, burden, weight" was used in several scales of measurement. A last of corn was about 4,000 English pounds.

slight occasion, and oftentimes out of a meer insolent Humour. This Tyrannical Spanish Yoke hath been somewhat lighter to 'em by the assistance of the Dutch; but the latter too, often plagued them sufficiently, tho' not so bad as the former; and being once become Masters, turn'd the Churches, Schools, and Cloisters into Warehouses, Inns, or Taverns, to save the Charge of Building new ones. To this excessive height of Inhumanity and Irreligion they were come, till in the year 1674 they were overwhelm'd by an Earthquake, and their Forts, Walls, and Houses sunk, together with a great number of the Inhabitants.

The 25th, Two Elephants passed by our Fort, which the King of *Siam,* who keeps his Residence in *Odea,* sent as a Present to General *Maetzuycker*; besides 35 hundred weight of Spiauter: With this His Request was, That we should lend him a Man to make him some Gun-Powder; promising that he would send him back again to *Batavia* in two years time.

The General received the Present, thanking the Ambassador; and desired him to return his Thanks to his Master for his Favours, and to tell him, That he would heartily have fulfill'd his Majesty's Desire, but that he could not possibly do it then, because he had but one of them himself, which he could by no means spare; but that he had some Powder that was at his Majesty's Service.

From the 26th to the 31st, We were obliged to appear every day upon the place where we used to Exercise, with our Companies, and fire against two Elephants that were newly come from Ceylon, which were brought every day to that place, that they might stand firing, and be useful in fight.

From the 1st to the 30th of *September,* I did not stir out of the Fort, by reason of a terrible Head-Ach that seiz'd me, and such a terrible one, that it fetch'd all the Hair off my Head; nor was I able to bear the excessive heat of the Weather. I us'd no other Remedies but Bathing and Refreshing my self every night and morning (after Sun-rising and Sun-setting) in the Water that runs about the Fort, tho' that was very dangerous, by reason of the Crocodiles that are there.

The 1st of *October,* Three Companies of the Garrison of *Batavia* were order'd to Embark in three Ships, call'd the *Macassar, Polsbroeck,* and *Polran* to go to the Island *Ceylon.* They were all to be ready the next day to go off: I being one of the Company that was to go, took my leave of my Friends, and made my Provision of Fish, Sugar, Dates, Citrons, and other Necessaries for my Voyage.

The 2d, about 10 a Clock in the Forenoon, each Company went to its appointed Ship; We and our Lieutenant (called *Henrick Rentzen Van Oldenburgh*) went to our Admiral-Ship, call'd the *Macassar*; In the Afternoon a Muster-Master came to visit the Ships, to see whether all the Men were on Board or no. If at any time one absents himself after Orders given, and is found on shore, he is condemn'd to remain in Chains till the Ship in which he was to have gone is come back again.

The 3d, early before day, The Master order'd the Gunner to fire one piece, which was the signal for our two other Ships to weigh Anchor, and to hoist up Sails. At break of day, (the Sun rising here all the year round at 6 in the morning, and setting at 6 at night) we sail'd with a Land-Wind by *Bantam*: In the afternoon, when we came to have a Sea-Wind, it blew very hard, and quite against us; so we were forced to cast Anchor, and lie there still till,

The 4th, about two at night, The Tide and Land-Wind turn'd for us again, which carried us as far as the *Prince's* Island, where we were to take in Wood and fresh Water.

The 5th, 6th, and 7th, I went ashore with five Soldiers, well provided with Arms, to defend those that cut the Wood, from the Tygers; and to shoot some Fowls, such as Peacocks and Ducks; for this Island being not much inhabited, does very much abound with all sorts of Fowl.

The 8th, at break of day, We weigh'd our Anchors, and pass'd that day through the Road of *Sunda*, and came about the evening into the Sea. The Wind was S.E. and by S. our Course lay most toward the North.

The 9th, We were divided into two Quarters, for the better regulating the Watch, that every one might know when to Watch, and when to enjoy his Humour: Till this time we had Water to Drink, and Rice enough, but boil'd only in Water.

The 10th, We had a very favourable Wind, And this day we came to an Allowance, which was, To each Person half a pound of boil'd Rice every day, half a Pint of distill'd *Arack*, and a Pint and a half of Water: Two Pound of Bisket a week, and half a Pint of Vinegar, and half that quantity of *Lisbon* Oil. Sundays and Thursdays three quarters of a pound of Flesh: On Tuesdays a Quartern and a half of Bacon; Mondays, Wednesdays, Fridays, and Saturdays, Gray-Pease, which we Eat with Oil and Vinegar.

The 11th, 12th, 13th, 14th, and 15th, We had still a good Wind, and we began to draw pretty near the Western Coast. In the night, about the 2d Watch, which is between 10 and 2 of the Clock, we saw a continual Lightning shoot through the Clouds, which look'd like a mixture of black and red, and made the most dismal sight that Man ever saw. In the 3d Watch, called the Day-Watch, about 3 of the Clock, we chang'd our Course from West and by North, to North and by East.

The 16th, It was a very serene Calm; But on

The 17th, 18th, and 19th, We had nothing but very unconstant Winds and Weather, and very dark Clouds all about us.

The 20th and 21st, We saw neither Sun, Moon, nor Stars; from whence we concluded that we might expect a great Storm, and for fear of it we took in our Sails, and prepared our selves for it.

The 22nd, We had a smooth Gale of Wind at West: Our Course being Northward, we saw continual Lightning, and heard much Thunder: I was Amazed that it lasted so long, and I enquired of our Master, and some of the oldest Seamen, what could be the reason of it. They told me, That it was dark in that Country of *West-Kust* [West Coast of Sumatra] six months together; that the Country afforded great store of Pepper, and some Gold was to be found in the Mountains of it. For that Reason, the Dutch, after a long War, had built there some Fortifications, and kept Soldiers there, which hold it to this day. That the Europeans cannot bear the Climate long, it being very unhealthy; and unless they are fetch'd away within three years time, they generally Die. To prevent which, they send fresh Men thither every year. That those that Die there are commonly taken away suddenly, as they are Eating or Drinking at Table. Their Food is Rice instead of Bread, Bufflars Flesh, Beef and Pork, and Fish in abundance: Their Drink is Suri that comes from the Coco'd, and Sugar-Beer, 3 or 4 years old, which they keep under Ground.

The 23rd, The Wind blew hard at West. We saw an infinite number of Fishes, called *Springers*; their length is generally about 6 or 7 foot, and about as much in thickness. Their Flesh is very firm; they Swim always against the Wind. When they Leap very high out of the Water (as they did then) the Seamen expect a very great Storm and Tempest. We catch'd several of 'em with a certain Instrument, which they call an *Ellegaer*, striking it into their Bodies. This night the *Polran* parted from us, but we could not tell whether it was done designedly by the Master, or whether it was by the Carelessness of the Helms-Man, whose turn it was to Watch.

The 24th, We were forced to take in our Main-Sail, by reason of the hard Wind, and defend our Deck all over with pitch'd Canvas from the Waves that were so boisterous, that they almost overwhelmed our Ship.

The 25th, 26th, 27th, and 28th, We had stormy Winds, but yet so tollerable, that we made 25 or 30 miles of our way in 24 hours.

The 29th, The Wind increased. The *Polsbroeck*, which still kept us Company, gave us a Signal, that she was so full of Water, that she stood in need of our help. When we came to be somewhat near, the Master told us, that his Pumps were good for nothing, and begg'd of us to lend him some of ours, which we did; for our Ship was so strong and close, that it receiv'd no Water, and we did not want 'em our selves; but that night this Companion of ours lost us too.

The 30th, We took in all our Sails, and lower'd our Yards, and made our selves ready for a Drift; that is, to bind the Helm fast, and commit our selves to the Winds and Waves to drive us where they pleased. This Drift we held out in, till

The 4th of *November*, five days together. Upon Consultation held, we cut down our Main-Mast, which, with the force of its fall, was like to have sunk our Ship. Till that day we had not taken the height of the Sun, so that we could not tell whither, or how far we were cast.

The 5th, The Wind fell, and changed to the S.E. Then we hoisted up our Sails, and took the height of the Sun, whereby we found that we were close by the Equinoctial, and not cast yet away so far as we were afraid we had been. We sailed N.E. and by E. all this Voyage we had that kind of Birds flying about us, that lived upon the flying Fishes; but upon the great Heat we were now come into, they left us.

The 6th, We had a brisk Wind, and from six in the morning to six at night we made 20 miles of our way, and found the next day, being

The 7th, That we had pass'd the Line. Two Soldiers and

three Seamen died out of our Ship that day, and were thrown, after Prayers, into the Sea, And we had about 20 sick.

The 8th, The Wind changed to the South ; and we were directly to go Northward. The Boatswain's Mate catch'd a large Shark, in which they found four Boys, and some Bones of Men.

The 9th, We saw a little Vessel that made towards us ; in the afternoon it came near to us, and we were big with the hopes of some News they brought, but they were all in vain : For our *Orlamen* (as we call them that have been before in the *Indies*) spoke to them in the *Malleyers, Amboineses, Cingalaish, Malabarish*, and *Maldavish* Languages, but neither would do ; and they answer'd us in a Language that none of us could tell what to make of ; but they made us to understand by Signs, that they were in great want of Drink : Our Master had their Vessel boarded, and in it we found 24 Indians, with long Hair ty'd up on the left side of their Heads. They had with them 12 Muskets, some Gun-powder, and Iron-Balls ; pretty good store of Rice, Pepper, and dry'd Fish, but no Water. We supposed them to be some Indian Robbers come from the West-Kust, and drove thus far into the Sea by the late Storm. Our Master order'd them to be taken into our Ship, together with their Provisions, and we drew their Vessel along after us, ty'd with a strong Rope to our Ship. We allowed them Bread and Water, and we made them Pump the Water out of our Ship, and Swab it.

The 10th, 11th, 12th, and 13th, The Wind continued directly for us at South, we going on still Northward.

On the 14th, We changed our Course to the N.W. and by W. the Wind kept where it was, but something weaker. This day one that sate on the Foremast, holding by a Cord, the Cord broke, and he fell down Dead into the Ship.

The 15th, We observed, that the Water begun to change colour ; at night we used the Plummet to sound the Water, but we could find no bottom, tho' the Line was 200 Fathoms long.

The 16th, The Water changed yet more, and seemed whitish ; we made our Anchors and Cables ready, if occasion should be to use them.

The 17th, Our Master promised six Rixdollars to the first Man that should spy Land, and a Flaggon of Wine.

The 18th, We had a lovely Wind and good Sailing. A

Seamen that stood on the out-side of the Ship to draw Water, was wash'd of by a Wave. We immediately tack'd our Ship, and back'd our Sails, and threw out our Long-Boat to go and take him up ; which they did, and in about two hours time brought him safe to us.

The 19th, We had a very fair Wind and fine Weather. Two of our Seamen quarrel'd, and fell at last to their Knives, and wounded each other. As soon as the Master knew of it he had 'em both Duck'd from the Main-Mast, as wilful Transgressors of the Laws of the Ship.

The 20th, about 6 in the morning, our Boatswain, a very expert Seaman, climb'd up the Main-top-gallant-Mast, which is the highest part of the Ship ; no sooner had he look'd about him, but he cry'd out aloud, Land, Land : The Master ask'd him which way, and he told him to the North-East ; straight we changed our Course from North West thither. The Helmsman threw out the Plummet, and found a sandy bottom at 80 Fathoms. In the afternoon we got sight of the high steep Mountain call'd *Adam*'s *Pick*, and by that we knew that this was the place we wanted to be at, viz. the Island *Ceylon*. Towards night we changed our Course again to the East, and sometimes to the E. and by N. for we had no mind to be near Land that night, and we could not have reach'd the Road that day. In the first Watch, between 6 and 10, we could feel ground still, but in the 2d and 3d we could not.

The 21st, in the morning, at break of day, We chang'd our Course again, and went directly towards Land lying South-East of us, with the Wind at S.W. About 10 a Clock before Noon we saw the Ships that lay at Anchor upon the Road by the City of *Columbo*. In the meanwhile, the Wind veer'd four Points more to the W. and so much the fitter for us. About Noon, we felt a sandy ground at 40 Fathoms, but we kept Sounding still, till we were quite out of the deep, and in full sight of the Land. This day every one had plenty enough of boil'd Rice, and the Water Vessels were free to any body. We had suffer'd a great while Hunger and Thirst, notwithstanding that we had Coarse Diet enough, and above 40 Barrels of Dutch and Batavian Water. The Soldiers now begun to Equip themselves, to make a shew at their Landing, and dress'd themselves very fine with great Joy and Satisfaction. Their Arms, which till then had been kept up in the Gunner's Room, were delivered to 'em, to go out Arm'd, as is usual, to Shore.

All our Flags were out till about three in the afternoon, when we cast our Anchors, and found still 12 Fathom Water. The Gunner was ordered to fire one Gun, and one Seaman was to strike our Admiral's Main-Mast Flag before the City of *Columbo,* but immediately again to set it up. After this, we fired all our Guns, to which the Fort of *Columbo* answer'd with seven of their Cannon. The Governor of this City sent two great Sloops of *Ceylon* to fetch us ashore ; in which our Lieutenant and Men went up to the Governor's House, who welcomed us all very heartily, and gave all our Men three days liberty to refresh themseves after their hard Voyage. The distance between *Columbo* and *Batavia* is about 500 Dutch miles, which we had reach'd in 49 days, from the 3d of *October* to the 21st of *November.*

The 22nd, I went to Board with an old *Cingulaish* Woman, because she could speak a little Dutch ; and she got her living by keeping a House to entertain the Dutch, of which she had generally 20 or 30 in her House. I paid 15*s*. a Month, and 40 pound of Black Rice. We had every one his own Dish served up with Flesh, Fish, Figs, and such like Diet, twice every day, at 8 a Clock in the morning, and 4 in the afternoon. Our House was only a Hut, made up of Boughs of Trees. And here I met with three of my old Aquaintance : who,

On the 23rd, took me Abroad to a very large Orchard, call'd *Tang Salgato,* where we drank some *Sury* fresh from the Coco-Trees. This was in the morning, and about noon we bespoke a hot sort of Liquor, called *Massack,* which is made in the following manner. They put into a Vessel 8 Quarts of *Suri,* and to that, one Quart of *Arack* or Brandy. All this boil'd together, and about 20 or 25 Eggs and broke into't, which gives it substance, and a good colour. Then they add to all this some *Kings Sugar,* (which they get from some certain Trees there) and some Nutmeg, and Mace : All this came to half a Rixdollar. We had some Women to wait upon us, which they call *Bulliatoses,* who diverted us with various Leaping and Dancing. Their Ears are about a Soan long, with Golden Pendants in them : They saw by my Dress, that I was newly come from *Europe* ; and I found they had a great mind to Converse with me, but I not understanding them, made them understand by shaking my Head, that I did not Care for their Company.

The 24th, We took a walk about two or three miles out of *Columbo,* to see some tame Elephants that were kept in

Orchards there. And having seen them, we went into the House which belong'd to a Portuguese, who treated us very nobly; and at night had us home upon an Elephant of his. This day an Ambassador, named Myn Heer *Bucquoi*, was sent from *Ceylon*, with a Lion, for a Present to the King of *Candy*.

From the 25th to the 30th, Our Men were daily Exercised, and at night our turn began to be upon the Guard, where my Post obliged me to be, till

The 25th of *April* 1677, which was five months, in which time I learned the Cingulaish and Portuguese Languages, finding them not only useful, but necessary to those that are to stay there.

The 22nd, I was sent with 30 Soldiers to the Fort of *Galture*, 8 Leagues from Columbo, to have some new Ramparts added to it. Of this Fort I intend to speak by and by, designing now to give an Account of the Cities, Inhabitants, Cattle, and Fruits of the Island *Ceylon*, as far as I could observe of them while I staid there.

CHAPTER IV

A Description of the Isle of Ceylon, its Cities, Forts, and Inhabitants, which are chiefly of two sorts. An Account of the King of Candi's Court, Officers, Counsellors, and his other Subjects: Their Customs, Manners, Religion, &c. Their Houses over-run with Fleas and Pismires; Their manner of Eating and Trading. The King of Candi's a Cruel Tyrant. The Cingulayans Customs in War; Their Arms and Exploits. The other Inhabitants of Ceylon are Malabarians, who are Subjects of the Dutch: They Worship the Devil, Crocodiles, Serpents, &c. Their Burials. The Dutch took Columbo, and other Cities of Ceylon from the Portugueses, and the King of Candi, tho' he had help'd them against the Portugueses. The King of Candi's Resentment of it to this very day. Unhealthy Climate of this Country.

THE Island *Ceylon* is about 200 Dutch miles in compass. It lies in the Indian Sea, not far from the Maldivian Islands, and the Wild Coasts of *Cormandel* and *Malabar*. It was found out about 200 years ago by the Spaniards, who invaded the Kingdom of *Cotta*, which the City of *Columbo* belongs to, in this following manner.

They came with two Ships, and landed at the place, where now *Columbo* is: The Cingulaish King, being informed of it at *Cotta*, came out with an Army to meet them, but in vain; for his Men could not abide the smell of Gun-Powder. The Spaniards fell to Building some small Fortifications, and to settle themselves in the Country: As soon as they were able to get some Assistance, being well pleased with the Land and their Success, they carried on the War not only against the said King of *Cotta*, so as to beat him out of the City where he resided, and lay it waste, (as it is now to this day, a place where wild Elephants are catch'd) but in time reach'd farther; and at last, of seven Kings that had possession of this Island, they destroyed six. But the seventh, who resided at *Candi*, in the middle of the Island, being vex'd to see with what Tyranny they used his Subjects, begun to carry on a War very vigorously against them, and continually Plagued the Cities and Forts, which they had built on the Sea-side and for about 20 miles into the Land, How this Country fell from the Spaniards to the Portugueses, and from the Portugueses to the Dutch, I will give an Account hereafter.

Their chief Fortifications, are, the City and Castle of *Columbo*; eight Leagues Westward of that lies the Fort *Negombo*; 20 miles further, the Fort *Calpintin*; again, 22 miles from thence, another call'd *Aripen*; and between those two, the *Paerl-Bank*, heretofore so famous: Six miles further, a very strong Fort on the Island of *Manara*, very fruitful, and seven miles in compass. This Island of *Manara* is divided from *Ceylon* by an Arm of Salt-Water, about a Cannon-shot wide. *Jafnapaparnum*, a fortified City, lies 22 miles distant from *Manara*, and is secured with Bastions, call'd by these Names, *Pas-Piil*, *Pas-Beschatter*, *Pas-Elephant*, and *Punt de Pedre*. Six and thirty miles farther, is the Fort called *Trinconamale*, built by the Dutch against the French. This Fort the French had taken Possession of; as also of the Bay, where Ships ride very safe, under the Command of Monsieur *de la Haye*, as Viceroy, till the Dutch drove them away again. There is another Fort call'd *Battacolo* 40 miles from that. Thence to *Punt de Gala* 30 miles. Thence to *Alecan* 11 miles. Thence to *Galture* 5 miles. Thence round back again to *Columbo* 6 miles.[1]

The Description I have given here of these outward fortifications makes the Circuit of this Island to be in all 206 miles.

The inland Fortifications are; *Maluane*, 6 Leagues from *Columbo*; *Hanguelli* or *Gourwebell*, 2 Leagues from *Malvane*; *Sittawaca* 4 miles farther; *Ruenell* also 4 Leagues farther; *Saffrigan* and *Bibliogam*, 8 Leagues from *Ruenell*: And 12 Leagues on this side of *Columbo*, you have *Auguradotten* and *Caudingellen*, lying upon two Rivers that run out of the King of *Candi's* Country, very rich in precious Stones.

The Island of *Ceylon* hath chiefly two sorts of Inhabitants.

[1] Schweitzer's description goes round the island clock-wise from Colombo. The forms of most of the names have altered little. Jafnapaparnum is a mistake for Jafnapatam or Jaffna, at the extreme north of Ceylon.

Those of *Columbo*, from *Columbo* to *Gala*, are called *Cinguleeses* or *Cingulaians*. They are very well shaped, part of a black, and part of a yellowish Complexion. The Men have long streight Hair, and wear their Beards very large, like the Suiffers. They are generally very Hairy upon their Breasts, and they are very proud of it. They wear a piece of Linnen about their middle, from the Navel down to their Knees : But they make a very great distinction of their Apparel, according to their Dignity, and Quality.

Their King dresseth himself as he pleases. His Cap is of Silk, wrought with Gold about a yard high, with a great Carbuncle before, and Rubies and Saphires all round about it, and at the top a Bird of Paradise. His Shirt and Wastcoat is made of the finest Cotton, with Golden Buttons, and he wears a Garment of colour'd Silk, that goes 4 or 5 times round his middle, and hangs down to his knees. His Stockings are fastened above his Knees with a string, whereon is fastened a silver Plate as large almost as a Trencher. His Shoes are only Leathern Soles with strings, one of which comes up between his Toes, and the other comes round his Foot, and ties the Sole fast to it : And all these strings are set out with Saphires and Rubies. He wears a Sword close under his right Arm, tied to a Silk Ribbon : It is very heavy, being in a massy Silver Scabbard ; it is made like a Hanger, and about a yard long ; the Handle is ordered with fine precious Stones. On his left side, between his Shirt and his Wastcoat, he wears a long Knife, besides his Sword, inlaid with Gold and Jewels, and by that a sharp Pen, (wherewith they write upon Leaves of Trees) in a Silver Sheath.

Those of his Council, called *Pisare*, and his Generals, may also wear Silk, Gold and Silver, but they are not permitted precious Stones for Ornaments ; and it is as much as their Lives are worth, to offer or pretend to wear any of 'em, tho' they are of little or no value ; Nor do they dare so much as take up one of them when they find them any where ; and the greatest, as well as the meanest Persons throughout all the Kingdom, are equally obliged to the Observation of his Custom.

His *Corals*, which are Governors over some one *Coral* or County, may wear Silk, but neither Sword nor Stockings. They wear a Staff tipt with Silver, with the King's Arms on it ; they wear a sort of Slipper or Shoe made of Wood, mighty neat, and very curiously wrought.

Next to these *Corals*, the *Apohami* or Nobles are rank'd; They go drest as the *Corals*, excepting that they may not tie, like them, the Caps they wear on their Heads. These are to be known, when they come into the City, by their having a Slave always behind them to carry a *Talpot* Leaf after them, which serves as an Umbrello when it Rains.

The next in Rank are the Scriveners and Husbandmen, who Manure the Fields of Rice. They must wear nothing but Linnen, no Swords, Shooes, Stockings, nor Caps, only a Knife they may, and an Iron Pen. Their Wives, and those of the above-named Persons, may have their Garments from a handful above the Navel down to the Ground; but nothing upwards, but a short *Bajuwan*, as they Name it, which doth not come so low as to cover their Breasts.

After these, are the Handicrafts-Men, as Carpenters, Goldsmiths, Blacksmiths, Potters, Barbers, Burners of Chalk, &c. These and their Wives may wear a Linnen Garment from the middle downwards, and set out their Wars with Gold. After them are the *Trivitors*, who gather the Drink from the Trees and boyl the Sugar: *Tschallias* that peel off the Cinnamon: The Fishermen and the *Laserins* their Soldiers: *Mainets* their Washers: *Borrowayen*, their Drummers: *Cubin*, who are a sort of People that will carry People where they please for Money: the meanest of all are the Batins and *Zubies*; These may not lay down upon the Ground, but must always have a Fan with them to lie in; Nor are they permitted to lie under any Roof. All their Women are obliged to go Naked all upwards upon pain of being whipt.

To give you a specimen of the *Cingulaish* Language, they express their numbers thus:

1	Eckai.	8	Attai.	15	Pahallohai.
2	Deccai.	9	Nahahai.	20	Wishai.
3	Dunai.	10	Dahahai.	30	Dihai.
4	Hattarai.	11	Eccollahai.	40	Hattalishai.
5	Paurai.	12	Dollahai.	50	Paswichai.
6	Hasai.	13	Dahattunai.	100	Sihai.
7	Hattai.	14	Dahattarai.		

But it is to be observed, That there are Diversity of Dialects, as in the several Provinces of other Countries, and so the Inland Cingularians differ from the Borderers;

which makes *Rob. Knox* [1] in his Description of Ceylon, give a different Account; and generally writes with an *o* what I put down with an *a*; as *Echoi, Dechoi, Tunhoi, Hutterhoi, Panhhoi, Hoyhoi.* Their Salutation is in these Words, *Deo wardende Sacradende Neinde;* and is answer'd with the same, both clapping their Hands to their Foreheads. *Whither go you, Gandi Jannade. I don't know, Dutwanetti. Fire, Genere. Water, Diwere.* They write upon the Leaves of Sugar-Trees; when they read, it is with a very unpleasant Accent, and very long Tone, as if they sung. They write to each other on these Leaves, which are about an Ell long, and two Inches broad, and can fold them up so artificially, that none can open them, without discovering that they have been open'd. They teach their Children to write upon the Sand or Ground with their Fingers. As to their Religion, they believe, That God, whom they call *Deine,* governs in Heaven, and that the Devil governs on Earth. Wherefore they Religiously serve him, giving him the Name of *Jacie*; and that not only by Offerings, and Songs in their Temples, but with Meetings in the Fields, under a sort of Tree, which I cannot compare to any Tree so well as a Lime-Tree. There is a Wall built round it of about half a Man's height; Here they Dance, Leap, and Sing, to his Honour: He comes to them in their Dance, and gives them Answers to their Questions about things to Come: As whether it shall be a plentiful Year, dry, or wet, and other things of this kind. The Soothsayer too, that receives the Answer, hath great Honours paid him. But because the Devil torments him too much, they are forced to carry him away home. They believe, that those that Die are turn'd into a Bufflar, wherefore they give the Bufflars the name of *Apetie,* which signifies Father; and to the Cows, that of *Amme,* which signifies Mother.

When the mean illiterate People (who cannot Read) have a Child born, the Father Plants a young *Jacken* or *Jager-Tree* by his House, by which he can reckon up the Child's Age. I have been at some of these Men's Houses to buy Goods, and happen'd to ask the Age of some of their Children that came about me, and they shew'd me a Tree, and told me,

[1] Robert Knox was a seaman who was shipwrecked in Kottiar Bay, in 1659, and detained for nearly twenty years by the King of Kandi. He managed to escape in 1679 and made his way to Colombo. Two years later he wrote "An Historical Account of the Island of Ceylon." *See* also page 254.

THE TIGER'S GRACHT, ONE OF THE PRINCIPAL STREETS OF BATAVIA

(*From J. Nieuhof's "Voyage to the East Indies"*)

he was of the same Age as that. But they have there a Proverb, the cursed Allusion of which they verifie in earnest, which is, That it is fit a Man should Eat the first Fruits of the Trees they Plant; so the Father always deflowers his Daughter as soon as she is come of Age.

They have a New Year's Festival, which lasts six weeks, and begins about our *Easter.* In the first three weeks they wash themselves every day; the other three weeks they pass away in Singing and all kind of Mirth.

Their dwelling houses are made according to the conveniency of the Country; some are near one another, after the manner of our Villages, which they call *Aldeen.* Others stand by themselves upon some rising Ground, to be secure from the Water, which sometimes rises very high, by reason of their great Rains: They are cover'd with Leaves of Trees. There is commonly but one Room where they Eat and Lie, and another to Dress their Victuals in, which they besmear every week with Bufflar's Grease, to free themselves from Fleas and Pismires. Their Money they generally Bury in a Pot under the Hearth, or sometimes under the Devil's Tree, in the Field, where it is Sacred.

Their Victuals is Rice boyl'd instead of Bread, and what they Eat with it, is made of all kinds of Herbs, Roots, Fruit, dry'd or fresh Fish, which they Boil with a deal of green Pepper, or else with the Milk that comes from the Coco-Nuts. Every one takes his share of Rice upon a Fig-Leaf, (instead of a Plate) and takes his other Meat, and mixes it together with his Hand, and so eats it.

They wash their Hands and Mouths very clean before and after Meals. They chaw *Betel* all day which they prepare after this manner. They take one or two of the Leaves, about as broad as one's Hand, they call them *Bular*: They grow all round about, against Fruit-Trees, as Ivy does. They take some very fine Chalk, made of small Mussel-shells burnt, and of it they scatter about as much as will lie on the top of a Knife over those Leaves, and then rowl them up, and put into the middle a fourth part of an *Arek* [Areca nut], which is a Fruit like a Nutmeg; and to this Composition they give the name of Betel, which they keep continually in their Mouth; And this is to prevent the Scurvy. They Smoak Tobacco too, not out of Pipes, but wound up in a dry Leaf.

In their Trade, like other Nations, they love to Buy as Cheap, and Sell as dear, as they can. They have no particular Traffick amongst them, dealing almost all in the same Goods. One thing which seemed mighty strange to me, was, That when I, or other Europeans came to buy any such things, as Butter, Pepper, Sugar, Honey, Figs, Fowls, Rice, &c. and ask'd them if they had any, they used to say *Netti*, which is to say, *No*. So that we were forced to give them very good Words, and insinuate our selves into their favour by giving their Children some Tobacco, or some little Trifle : Then they would ask their Children, even the smallest of 'em, whether they had best Sell any thing to these Persons ; and according to their Answer, they either sold to us, or refused us, and would not have sold us any thing without their Consent, tho' we would have paid ten times the value of their Goods. When they had sold us any thing, and received their full Price, they would beg of us, that we would give them some of it again, tho' at the same time they were well stock'd with the same Commodity.

Theft, tho' but inconsiderable, is punished with Death. All their King's Commands must punctually be observed upon Pain of Death ; and that not of the Person only that hath Transgressed, but of his Kindred, to a third Generation. This King of *Candi* is a very cruel Tyrant. Some Europeans, that had been Prisoners at his Court for about 20 years, have told me, That he had order'd no less than 300 in some years, to be drawn in pieces with Elephants, for a very small Fault, or sometimes a meer Humour.

We will now give you some Account of their Military Exploits and Discipline. They have a General, which they call Dissave [1]; next to him some Sandis. Then the Araski, which are as Captains over 20 or 30 men each, with an Ensign. Their Artillery is only a sort of Muskets, which stand upon a frame with three Feet, of which the hindmost is broad, and shorter than the two foremost ; Having no Lead they shoot with Iron Bullets. These Muskets, the Nobility, which serve the King, carry with 'em in fights.

They come into the Field, 30, 40, or 50000 strong, all barefoot. Their Arms are a heavy Iron Cimiter about a yard long, and a light Half Pike. Few have Muskets or Fire-Locks ; or if they have, they do little Execution with them ; tho' they have never so much room to draw up, yet they never advance but in single Ranks, for fear the

[1] *Disawa* : the Governor of a Province or *Disawani*.

Hollanders should take too many of them off at once with their Field-Pieces. Their Drummers are very much despised, being taken from a sort of People, (tho' *Cingulaians* too) that live upon Bufflars Flesh, and the Flesh of any kind of Beasts. They call them *Borrowayen.* They tie to their Body, two little sorts of Drums call'd *Tamelins*; others have but one of 'em, but then it is bigger. They beat distinct Marches, with a great deal of Art, and the Soldiers understand them very well. They beat morning and night, but differently. Their Pipers use both a straight and a crooked sort of Pipe, and make pretty Musick with them both together.

Any Dutchman, that are taken by these People, are never to be ransom'd at any Rate ; but must remain amongst them in great Slavery all the days of their Life ; and all the ways are so strictly guarded that there is no escapying by any means. The Dutch that sometimes desert us, and go over to the King of *Candi,* are maintained in Necessaries, but are not trusted in any Employment.

The other sort of Inhabitants of this Island, are those of *Gala Batacolo, Trinconomala, Jafnapatnam, Manara, Aripen, Calpintin,* as far as *Negombo*; and are called *Malabars.* These are all very well shaped, and very black. They are all under the Government of the Hollanders, except those of *Wani,* who have a King of their own. But he is obliged to pay to the *East-India* Company a yearly Tribute of many Elephants, and Money besides.

These *Malabars* come originally from the Wild Coast of *Malabar,* lying by *Manara,* and from the Kingdoms of the great *Samerin, Calicut, Cananor,* and others. They are all Infidels, and of different Opinions. Some of 'em, who are call'd *Vitzliputzli* or *Joosie,* Worship the Devil ; others, a Serpent, a Crocodile, or an Elephant, and commonly what they please themselves. They neither Eat the Flesh of Bufflars, nor Swine. They hire old Women to Mourn over their Dead a whole night, and cry over the Corps all the time : *Ajo aniate, ariate, inguwarre,* which is as much as to say, Why did you Die, Come, come live again, &c. Then they Bury him, and leave the Hutt out of which the Man died, and build another. They are a little more Civil than the *Cingulaians,* and their Dress is a little more comely. The Women never let themselves be seen uncovered by the Christians. When they go abroad, they are all covered with white Linnen, and so close, that they can but just see their way with the corner of one Eye: Their Arms and their Legs are all adorned with Silver Rings, and their Ears, about a Span long, with Gold: Their Fingers and Toes too are all richly set out with several sorts of Rings, most of Silver and Gold.

Their Numbers are; 1 *Onera*, 2 *Renda*, 3 *Muna*, 4 *Nala*, 5 *Anse*, 6 *Ara*, 7 *Ola*, 8 *Orta*, 9 *Otta*, 10 *Padda*, 11 *Paddona*, 12 *Padda-renda*, 13 *Padda-muna*, 14 *Padda-nala*, 15 *Padda-anse*, &c. The manner of their Salutation is, Laying their Hand on their Forehead, and saying Damrian Amadran, which is returned the same way. They write likewise upon Leaves of Trees with an Iron-Pin, and make whole Books of 'em. We will now give you some Account How the Hollanders came to Conquer this Country, and make themselves Masters of it.

I have already told you, how it came to be in the Power of the King of Spain, and fortified by the Spaniards: It remained a great while in their Hands, till the Portugueses Rebelling in Spain, chose a King to themselves, with whom all the Spaniards that were in the *East-Indies*, joyn'd. And thus the King of *Spain* lost all his Pretensions in those Countries, which was no small loss to him. The Portugueses would be improving their Conquests, and try their Strength against the King of *Candi*, and thought by Fire and Sword, and their barbarous Slaughters and Murthers, to frighten him out of his Kingdom, but all in vain. For the King of *Candi*, finding himself in a great Extremity, call'd the Dutch to his Assistance; who together fell upon the Portugueses and became at length Masters of all their Cities and Fortifications above-named. The last that was Beseiged by 'em, was the Capital City of Columbo, which is about 28 years ago.

The King of *Candi* was now free, and had an Army of 50000 Men. The Dutch General on the other side, (call'd Min Heer *Vander Hulst*) had an Army of 12 Companies of 80 Men each, together with a Fleet of 8 Ships. Both these, tho' the one a Heathen, and the other a Christian, agreed very well together, put things into very good order, and made a Treaty; That when the City of *Columbo*, both the old and the new, should be taken, the King should have the Old one for his Residence, and the Fort *Negombo*, lying 8 Leagies from thence, towards the Kingdom of Candi, in his full Possession: The Dutch for their part should have the new City of *Columbo* without any Molestation, with all the other Fortifications they were already possest of; and besides this, should have Priviledge to Trade in any part of the Kingdom whatsoever with its Inhabitants.

The City of *Columbo* being taken at last by the Dutch Admiral *Ryclof Van Goens*,[1] (the above-mentioned Heer *Vander Hulst* being shot Dead in the Trenches) and by the Assistance of the King's Forces, who did not suspect any Falshood after the Treaty made. The Heer *Van Goens*, having gather'd together the King's Army under pretence of giving them a Treat, and the Streets being filled with them, he sets all his own Men upon them, (for what Reason I cannot tell) who cut the best part of them in pieces, and put the rest to flight. The King, whom they thought to have taken Prisoner, made his escape upon his Elephant, and got over high Mountains, Rocks, and Wildernesses, and at last into his Kingdom of *Candi*, where being secure, he swore never to forget the Falshood and Treachery of the Christians but to continue in a perpetual War and Emnity against them.

And in that he hath so constantly kept his Resolution, that in these 28 years, he hath taken Prisoners, and put to Death some thousands of them. Therefore this Island of *Ceylon* is not unjustly called the Dutch Soldier's Slaughter-House; and when they are commanded thither, they reckon themselves going to Execution. For the Cingulaish Soldier or Inhabitants are not the only Enemies they have there but the Blood-Suckers, or Hedge-Hogs, which the Ground is cover'd with after a show'r of Rain, will suck the Blood out of 'em; Besides this, there are other Dangers; which are, First, Being very often Pinch'd with Hunger; and then the Unwholesomness of the Air, by which those that are not used to the Climate, fall into many Distempers. Some are seized with a Stiffness in their Limbs, others with a Dizziness and Swimming of the Head, and cannot endure to look on the Light. Others are killed by the Bloody Flux; and with these Distempers, I have seen more Soldiers at one time in the Hospital than in the Garrison: Besides many others, who in pursuit of their Lustful Desires, destroy themselves by Venereal Distempers.

[1] *See* Introduction, p. xxiii.

CHAPTER V

Giving an Account of the sundry sorts of Beasts, Fowls, &c. that are in Ceylon; a more particular one of the Elephants, concerning which, many things very wonderful are attested, upon the Author's own Experience. The manner of catching them, their peculiar Qualities, &c. Wild-Bufflars, Tygers, Bears, Jackalls, Bitsche-Vergunie, or the Devil of Degombo, very rare; Levers are lazy sort of Beast, Wandura or Apes. Wild Cats. And many other sorts of Beasts. Of Fowls, Parrots, Batts, &c. Crocodiles, will live 300 years. Different sorts of Serpents; of Pismires; Blood-Suckers; Sword-Fishes; Sharks; Sail-Fish; St. Peter's Fish; Sea-Swine; Sea-Devils; Tortoises. The manner of the Malabarians Fishing with their Netts.

I COME now to give a short Account of the Wild and Tame Beasts that are in this Island of *Ceylon*.

Among the Wild ones, I will speak first of the Elephants. They are finer and more Docile than in other Countries. Therefore they catch a great many of 'em, which they make Tame, and fit for War, and send them to the Kingdoms of *Persia*, *Surrat*, the *Great Mogul*, and several other places; and the Dutch themselves made use of them in the Field.

I have been very curious in Searching into the Nature, Disposition, and Qualities of these Elephants; and for that purpose conversed much with those that Catch them, when they are young, and have my self help'd to catch 'em. I have found in them all a great deal of Cunning, and a good Memory, in which they seem to be almost Rational Creatures. They never forget a Master's kind Usage; but that of a rough and cruel one, they on the other side, never leave unrevenged. They never Couple together in the sight of Men, but first they search round about the Wilderness to see if no Body is there hidden in any Tree to spy 'em; and if they find any, woe be to them. The Male hath his Testicles inwards, and the Female gives Suck between her fore Legs.

When they are Catch'd and Tame'd, they never Couple together. They carry their young ones seven years, and this has often been manifest by the Wild She-Elephants that have been taken, and kept in the Stables which they have for 'em at *Gala*, and have brought forth young at seven years end, after they were catcht, The young ones are, at first, about the bigness of a Calf half a year old. They feed on Grass, Figs, Leaves, and Coco-Nuts, Rice, and other Fruits, and Bread if one gives it them. This they reach and hold faste with the end of their Trunks, and then thrust it into their Mouths. Before they Eat any Grass, they throw it and toss it about, to shake out the Pismires, by which they are mightily tormented sometimes. If these little Animals chance to get in their Trunk, they walk about there and tickle them intolerably.

Tho' they have no Hair, except on the Tail and Ears, yet they swim very well. They'll live above 200 years, as has been seen in some whose Age has been desiredly mark'd. They go together in the Wood some 8, 10, or 20 in a Company. They have a sort of King, or Master-Elephant, which they follow ; the young ones go in the middle. In the day time, they keep on the Mountains in the shade, but towards the Dusk of the evening, they repair to the Meadows and Water-side. They break their way through the Boughs and Bushes with their Trunk ; so that by the Noise they make, one may hear them coming a Mile off. Then the Inhabitants, and the Keepers of the Fields, cry out to one another for help, to keep them out of their Grounds, where they destroy all when they come. They holloe first, *Hu, Hu,* and then they cry for help, *Alia innuwate, The Elephants are coming* : Therefore, when they come near their Hutts, Orchards, or Fields, they light Torches, which they have on purpose made of long dry Wood, and with this they drive them away, making a great deal of Shouting and Noise. Those that watch the Fields of Rice, sit and sing all night in a little Hutt raised upon four Posts ; and when they hear the Elephants coming, they holloe and light their Torches.

There is two different ways of catching the Elephants. Among the *Malabars*, from *Trinconomala* to *Batacale* : There are some that Worship the Devil, by whose help they Charm these Creatures, after having Sacrificed to him a Cock for an Offering. After they have Caught 'em with their Hands, they tie them with strong Thongs of Bufflar's Leather, and Tame 'em : But neither the *Persians*, nor the *Moors*, care to Buy those that are catch'd this way.

The other way of Catching them, is in a Pound prepared for that purpose, as I have seen one in the Kingdom of *Cotta*, two Leagues from *Colombo*, near the *Aldee* or Village *Battalamuda* : And I have been my self at the Catching of 50 of them, young and old ; which is done thus.

When the Inhabitants have notice where they are, and what place they frequent most, the Governour of *Columbo* gives a general Order for a Hunting Day ; on which every one high and low, even the Nobles themselves, meet at the appointed place : Besides this, the Governour takes all the Soldiers, Drums, and Burghers, along with him ; being all met, they spread themselves in a Wing a League or two long.

Thus they go holloing and shouting along the whole day, thro' the Woods and over Mountains : At Night they rest, and for fear the Elephants should get out back again, they light Fires all along about a Stone's throw from each other, which the Elephants are very much afraid of. The next day they go on again, and draw the Elephant's into a narrower compass. If any of 'em offer to go back, and break through, they fright them with Drums, and shouting and holloing. If one of them should chance to break through, all the rest would inevitably follow. When all the Hunters have in 3 or 4 weeks time ranged over 20 or 30 miles Ground, these Wild Elephants are at length, by the means of Tame ones that serve to decoy them drove into the Pound, which we mention'd above. Then they tie a Wild one to a Tame one, or if it is a very lusty one, between two. Then they make 'em so Tame by giving them neither Meat nor Drink, that with a certain Instrument they use, a Child may manage them. Notwithstanding there are some which they can never Master, and those they turn out again to Breed and Increase.

The East-Indian Kings and Merchants buy the Elephants by their height, which they measure to an Inch (as we do Horses here) from the Ground to the ridge of the Back. According to their height, they are worth 7, 8, 900 or 1,000 Rixdollars. Sometimes they buy them (when they are of an extraordinary vast bulk) for shew. Otherwise they use 'em in War, and to draw Baggage, and great Artillery. The *Great Mogul* hath frequently with him 4 or 500 in the Field ; and we used them in all Expeditions : Each Company had an Elephant, as we shall tell more largely hereafter.

The two Teeth that stick bending so long out of their

Mouth, are sufficiently known by the Name of Elephant's Teeth. The Flesh of Elephants is not fit to Eat, and their Hides are made no use of, by reason of their wanting Men to dress and prepare them. They are extream thick. The Flesh is Spungy, and Rotts in two or three days. The Hair that grows upon the Tail they hold very good against the Cramp, and as an approved Remedy they wear it made up in Rings on their Fingers.

When they are to draw a Load, they go side long and look steadily upon the Waggon, to see that no Body lays anything more upon't than what is usual ; and if one doth, they will not wag a foot further till it be taken off again : But what is more strange than that, is, what I have often seen at *Columbo* and *Jafnapatnam*. That these Elephants when they were drawing a Load of Stones for the Fortifications, would stand stock still at 11 a Clock, which is the Dinner time allowed to all the Slaves and Workmen, and would not draw an Inch further, tho' they were just at the place, and the Drivers encouraged 'em never so much.

There is great store of Bufflars in *Ceylon,* especially in and about *Calpintin.* They are about the bigness of a Podolian or Hungarian Ox, but stronger. Their Horns are about two yards long : They are of an ash-colour. In the day time they lie in the Water up to their Nose, and at night they come to Graze in the Meadows. Their Flesh is Eatable, when it hath lain 2 or 3 days in Salt ; but very hot, and gives the Bloody-Flux to most People that Eat of it. They are very dangerous to go near, especially to the Europeans, and chiefly if they have any young ones by them.

Tygers are here also in abundance, and very pernicious to Man and Beast, and particularly to Stags and Deer. They are about the bigness of a large Ass, but something longer ; they are spotted with yellowish and whitish spots, and in their Make exactly like a Cat. Their Flesh is white, and many People Eat of it. Their Skins serve to make Belts, Holsters. &c. and are most used for covering of Trunks and Boxes. They have so much of the Scent of Musk, that the Huntsmen, if they take the Wind right, will find them out by it, and so in their pursuit of other Beasts, avoid them.

Bears are likewise found here in several Parts, and are dangerous Creatures : Yet they are not so much fear'd here, as the Wolves are in Germany.

Jackalls are of shape and bigness like a Fox, only a sharper Snout : They keep all day in their Dens, and at night they gather together a hundred of them or more, and come to the outside of the City of *Columbo*, in quest of Dead Bodies, and fall sometimes upon a Man, if they chance to find him asleep.

There is a sort of Creature here, that is not very well known, because it is rare ; it is called *Bitsche Vergunie*, and by the Dutch, the *Devil of Negombo*, which Name they have given it, because of its Qualities, as I am going to tell you, and because they are most frequently about *Negombo*. It is about a yard high, and three yards long. It hath a sharp Snout, and very sharp Teeth. The Body is as it were Harnass'd over with thick round yellow Shells. When it is pursued, it can winde it self up into a Ball. At night it makes such a dismal frightful Noise, that it hath often scar'd the Centinels from their Posts.

The *Lewer* is another, called by the Dutch, *Luiste Dier* ; i.e. Slow-Beast. These Beasts are made like an Ape, with Hands and Feet, look very ghastly, and as lean as a Skeleton, wonderful slow in their Eating, Drinking, and Going ; tho' Dogs, or any Wild Beasts come towards 'em, they will not hasten their pace in the least ; and when they come near 'em, they turn themselves to 'em, and with their glaring Eyes, fright away the fiercest Dog that can be. Their Eyes stand quite out of their Heads, and appear very terrible ; When Men come after 'em, they do the same : But it hath not the same Effect, for Men have a Snare, which they clap on their hinder parts, and so catch them as they do Monkies. After they are catch'd, they are still slow as before, and would not go above a League in a day, if one left 'em to themselves. They are kept in Cities for a Rarity, but they are too tender to transport into other Countries.

Wandura, or Apes are here in abundance ; they are black, excepting a whitish Ring about the hinder part of the Body, and a great gray Beard, which makes them look very much like some of the old Cingulayans. They are about the bigness of a Mastiff, and have a very long Tail. They skip about the Woods from Tree to Tree, making a great noise, their young ones hanging all the while about 'em. If you shoot 'em, the young ones fall with 'em, and then you take 'em off to keep and breed up : But this is not a true kind of Ape for keeping, so that few People take the trouble to Catch them ; for they do not take any thing that's taught 'em, as others will. If a shot wounds them so as to fetch out a part of their Guts, they work out the rest with both their Hands (if I may so call 'em) and so fall down. Those that are Catch'd will never Couple together, tho' one keeps them ever so long.

Wild-Cats; there are of two sorts: One of which is as large as our common House-Cats, and live upon all sorts of Fowl. The other is as small as our Squirrels, and are called Suri-Cats; because they keep about the Coco-Trees, whence the Suri comes. Their Hair is of a grey colour; and they make a noise like a young Turkey.

Stags are bigger than the Stags in *Holland*.

Deer are somewhat less, and full of white spots.

Wild-Goats are a little bigger than our Hares.

The Hares less than with us.

Wild-Boars here as in *Africa*.

All these are in vast numbers, because but few People Hunt 'em; there being so great a quantity of Wild-Beasts there that are better.

Wild-Horses are very plentyful in the Isle of *Manara* and not far from thence in another Isle towards *Jafnapatam*; but they are less than our Horses in *Holland*. Sometimes they catch some of the finest of 'em, which they Break for the Saddle, or else they use 'em for Carts and Waggons.

Among the Tame Beasts and Cattle, Oxen and Cows are in so great plenty, that one of 'em is not worth above two or three Gulders.

Bufflars are in abundance; the Country Fellows use them in their Rice-Fields: One of them is worth three or four Gulders.

Three sorts of Sheep there are amongst 'em; one which comes out of *Persia*, which for Wool, &c. are like those in *Holland*, excepting that their Tails are so vastly big, that some of 'em will weigh 20 or 25 Pound: Another sort comes out of *Africa*, with Horns about a Span long, but no wool, only Hair like Calves: A third sort hath Wool like the first, but very long Ears.

Goats are in good store here, and Swine, such as in *Holland*. One of the biggest and fattest in the Island *Manara* is not worth above a Rixdollar.

Now for the Wild-Fowl. There are Peacocks of the same colour as here; and besides these, there are many as white as Swans.

Wild-Cocks and Hens are about the bigness of ours.

Water-Fowl, Snipes, Stock-Doves, and others. Two sort of Herons, one of 'em bluish, the other half black. Geese and Ducks in great numbers. I will not make any mention of their small Birds, &c. I will only give you some Account of the Parrots, which are here of three sorts. The largest are of a green colour, mixt with blue and red, with a black Ring round the Neck, and are accounted the best. A lesser size there is, all green, with a red Ring round the Neck, which is but little valued; and a less than that which is less esteemed too, because it is the least docile. They Eat Rice and Figs. They are best to be taught when they are young. They are tied to a Cord or Chain, and morning and night, while it is duskish, one talks to 'em half an hour or thereabouts, till they get 'em at last to speak any thing after them.

There is also a great many Birds of Prey; as Falcons, Hawks, and Ravens, with a white Ring about their Neck.

Batts are of two sorts; the one small as ours here, that fly by night; and the other as high as those I have spoken of in Java. There is another sort of Bird, which is call'd a *Navi*, (because it maked a noise which sounds like that word) which when the Portugueses hear, they expect the arrival of some Ships in a short time.

They have but few Geese, except such as are brought hither from the *Cape of Good Hope*; they have a Bunch growing on their Bill: They cost a Rixdollar a-piece.

Other Tame Fowl is there in such plenty, that one may Buy a Pullet for a Peny, and 40, 50, or 60 Eggs for the same price. Ducks that lay 200 or 300 Eggs after one another, without one days intermission, will cost but Two Pence or Two Pence half peny. Many keep Pigeons likewise, which comes from *Holland*, which they Buy for 10d a pair.

Among the four-footed Animals, in the Rivers; There is the Crocodile which devours many Men that live near them, as they are Fishing, Washing, or Bathing themselves; if they do not take especial Care: But I will in short describe something of the Nature of them.

The Crocodile is not so very furious as some People imagine. He seeks his Prey alone; but when he is hungry, he Devours any living thing he can Eat, whether Man, Fish, Beast, Dogs, &c. shews himself commonly, and swims any part of the day at the top of the Water, like a piece of Timber. He sets open his Mouth for a certain Bird to pick his Teeth with his Bill, which is about the length of one's finger. At night he comes upon Land to seek out for Meat. These Animals lay their Eggs upon the bare Sand, and leave the Sun to produce the young ones out of 'em, who as soon as they come out, are about half a yard long ; The Egg itself is about twice as big as those of a Goose. They continually keep growing as long as they live, and come to be some 20, some 25, some 30 foot long : The Body is armed all over with a thick Scale : Their Teeth are exceeding sharp ; and so much strength is in their Tail, that they'll kill any Fish or other Animal with a blow of it. Upon Land they can run faster than most Men ; but in a short turning, a Man may have the Advantage of 'em, because they must take a great compass ; and being so long and thick, without any bending in their Backs, they are forced to take a large turn, which affords a Man fair time to escape out of their reach.

Here is another sort of Beast, much like the Crocodile, which is call'd a *Caprigoy* ; but it hath neither Shells, nor Scales on it, and its Tongue is very long and pointed. The longest I ever saw of these was not above ten foot.

Another not much unlike this, but less yet, call'd a *Leguwan,* the Flesh of which many People eat.

Now of Serpents there are several sorts ; one of 'em is called *Worgers,* they are 10 or 15 feet long. They will seize a Man, and clap themselves round about him, and squeeze him so that he can't Breath, and falls down Dead : And to be arm'd against these, no Man goes abroad without a good Knife about him, to cut them in two, which makes them let go their hold quickly.

Another sort, which is called, *Chapel-Snakes* [Cobras], because they keep in Chapels or Churches, and sometimes in Houses ; These are very mischievous and venomous, and without a timely Antidote, they who are bit by them, die Infallibly. They are commonly from 4 to 6 foot long ; and they have a sort of Bladder, or spot of white, which shews it self on the top of their Head when they are vex'd.

There is another sort of 'em, which they call *Rat-Catchers,* which are not so dangerous. They live in all Houses, and destroy the Rats and Mice as much as any Cats would. They are nine or ten foot long, and will never hurt any Body unless one Angers them.

The Green Serpents keep upon the Trees, and when any Man or Beast comes near them, they dart themselves upon them, and with their sharp Tongues endeavour to put out their Eyes. They are about two yards long. The most poisonous of all, are, the two headed ones, which have a Head at each end.

Here are two sorts of Remedies against the Poison of

those Animals: The one, which the Inhabitants use frequently, is Witchcraft: The other, which I have often used is a Serpent-Stone. This Stone is laid upon the Wound, and it sticks to it, till it hath drawn to it self all the Venom out of it. When it is come off, it is thrown into new Milk, which fetcheth all the Poison out of the Stone, and grows black and blue with it: Then the Stone is applied afresh to the Wound, and if there be any Poison remaining, it sticks on, if not, it falls off, and the Person is secure.

I have seen many Scorpions here as big as a common Crab, but their Stings are not dangerous, and cause only a smarting for two days, and never prove mortal.

The Hundred-Feet called by the Portugueses *Cente-Pe*, because it hath a Hundred-Feet, is about half a yard long, and hath two Horns wherewith it Pinches. It is so full of Venom, that it is all over of a blew and yellow colour with it; if one is pinched by 'em, it may prove very dangerous, besides the cruel Smart it causes, unless the place is anointed quickly with Oil of Coco's.

There are three sorts of Pismires [ants], red, black, and white. The first are the biggest, and rid the Houses of other Vermine, as Rats, Mice, and Serpents. The black keep in the Fields; if they touch a Man's Skin, they make it Smart for about half an hour. The white ones live amongst the Houshold Goods; they Eat through Chests and Trunks, and damage Cloats and Linnen very much.

Fleas are here in Shoals, so that Men could not have any rest, if they did not besmear all their Houses with Cow-dung, to keep them away.

The Air is full of little Flies and Gnats; and in some places People cannot Eat for 'em, but are forced to stay till night when they are settled.

Blood-Suckers, or Leeches, are the worst Vermine on the Island. They are most towards the North between *Candi* and *Columbo*. There are of two sorts of 'em, the great and the small; The first are the common Plagues of Bufflers: The other of Men. They keep in the Water, and are made much like our Hedge-Hogs. When any Man or Beast goes into the Water, they hang upon them till they have suckt their fill, and swell three times as big as they were at first, then they fall off. If one goes to strike them off, immediately they break off and leave the Head in the Flesh, which makes the Wound the more dangerous: But the best way to deal with 'em is to have some green Lemons with one, or good

Vinegar and Salt or Salt-Petre, and wet them with it, and they fall off immediately.

The small sort are about the bigness of a Straw, and about three Inches in length, and of a brown colour. They have neither Eyes nor Feet. In dry Weather they are seldom to be seen; but after some Rain they fill the Ways and Shrubs. They do not creep as Worms do, but raise themselves up on end, and throw themselves upwards. If they lay hold of a Man they are not easily got off again, nor without great danger. Some *Cingulayans* say, That these things were first brought over into this Country by the contrivance of one *Lamammea*, one of the Kings of *Candi's* Sister, (whose Brother the Portugueses had taken away by violence) to be a Plague to them, but how much truth there is in the Story, I leave the Reader to judge.

Amongst the Sea-Fish commonly catch'd here, I place the Sword-Fish; it is from 8 to 12 foot in length: It is called by that Name from a sort of Sword it hath upon his Nose, which is like a Saw, with about 50 Teeth about the bigness of one's Finger. The biggest of those Swords that I ever saw was an Ell long. The Flesh of this Fish is fit to eat, but the younger the Fish is, the better. These Sword-Fishes are not of that sort which are so great Enemies, to Whales, for they never come so far into the North, it being too Cold for them there: Besides, those that fight with the Whales have their Sword on their Back, and keep about *Greenland* and *Ysland* in vast numbers.

Sharks are right Sea-Wolves, and devour the Men they can catch but they are often catch'd and devour'd themselves.

The Sail-Fish, so called, because it hath a large Finn, which stands upon the Back of it above Water, and lets the Wind drive it forwards; hath a sharp long Head of about an Ell long, and his Body is twice as long again; tho' its Flesh is but coarse, yet a great many People eat it.

There is a Fish which they call *Oan-Egbertsen* half an Ell long, and very full of Blood. They are in so great plenty, that they pull up 7, 8, or 900 at one Draught. The great time of Fishing for 'em is in *February*, at which time not the Fish only is very cheap, but all sorts of Meat and other Victuals are at very low Rates.

The *St. Peter's Fish*, or *Five Finger-Fish*, is called by some the *Leather-Fish*, by reason of the thickness of his Skin; Hath five white streaks on the Back in the shape of a Man's Fingers; it is about two yards in length, and very good to

Eat: It is most in season in *March*, and then they catch likely 2 or 300 of them at once. The old Portugueses will tell you that this mark on the back came by *St. Peter*, who drew up one of them in his Net, and left the figure of his Fingers upon it. But this I leave the Reader to believe at Discretion.

Jacks are here of the same kind as in *Holland*, one, two, or three yards in length, and are to be catch'd with Angles in *April* or *May*.

The King's Fish is the best sort that is here, and is something like our Carps.

Cablins are like our Herrings, but a little broader, there is vast plenty of them at one Draught, because they go together in Shoals.

Sea-Swine or Sea-Hogs, are catcht here in great numbers; their length is five or six yards, and half about that: They have a sharp Snout like ordinary Hogs; The Flesh of 'em is very fat, and the Blood very hot: In the Water they out-swim all other Fishes.

Sea-Devils or Sand-Creepers are 5 or 6 yards long, with a frightful Head, very broad, but not thick, black at top, and white underneath. There is much difficulty in catching of 'em with Angles, because they lie 15 or 20 Fathoms deep.

Scaits are round and flat: Have their Eyes in their Body, and a thin flat Tail about two Yards long; they are very good to Eat.

The *Pill-Staert*, as they call it, (which signifies *Arrow-Tail*) is much like it; it is as good to Eat too: But the Tail is of that Nature, that if he wounds a Man with it, 'tis mortal to him: Wherefore great Care is taken to cut that off as soon as they have catch'd 'em.

Tortoises, are catch'd here of 200 pound weight. They lay their Eggs on the Sand, 100 at a time, and leave them to the Sun to hatch; they have no Shell, only are cover'd with a Tough Skin. When they come upon Land, the Indians turn them over on their Backs, from which they cannot rise again, having not the command of their Legs. When they have them thus, three or four Men carry them to Market, and there cut them out. The Shells of these very large ones are not useful, but the small ones are of great use for inlaid Work, Combs, &c.

Sea-Crabs, and Sea-Lobsters: These are here a Yard long, with large Claws; and the other round with a very hard Shell.

Sea-Lice, are made like Lice, cover'd over with a white Shell, about the bigness of a Walnut. They keep in the wet Sand on the Shore, and are Eaten only by the *Malabarian* Fishermen.

Muscles stick to the Rocks, and when the Sea is at ebb, they pick them up.

The manner of Fishing, which the *Malabarians* use, is much like ours. Their Nets are exceeding long, so as to reach about half a mile in compass, and are buoy'd up with Wood instead of Cork; and in the middle of it, which comes last to shore, they have a great Bag, into which the Fish is all driven.

Fresh River-Fish are these: The *St. Pilang*, a Fish with a broad Head, as smooth as an Eel, about a yard long, and two Spans about. The *Bald-Head* is a better sort of Fish, all Scaly like a Carp, excepting the Head; weighs generally 7 or 8 pound. A Fish called a Fool, because whoever Eats any thing of the Head, become stupid: Wherefore the Head is always thrown away, the rest is very good to eat. The *Pager* is a black Fish, with a hard thick Head; its Body is round, with very sharp Finns. There is small Fish also in abundance, as we have here, such as Gudgeons, Craw-Fish, &c.

Gurnets are a small sort of Fish like the Crawfish, without a Shell, and have only a whitish Scale over their Body. They are most used in Angling, for a Bait to catch other Fish with.

CHAPTER VI

The Year in Ceylon is divided into two Seasons only. Great Floods there during one of the Seasons. An Account of Caudingelle, a Fort built and forsaken by the Dutch; much annoyed by the King of Candi's Men. The Author is ordered to Anguratot; Description of that Place; how the Europeans live there with Cingulaish Women. He goes back to Columbo; one of the Boats is lost by the way. He lives a while there with one of the Council. Is sent to Malvane, an unhealthy Place, which the King of Candi Besieges with 30000 Men, but his General comes over to the Dutch. The Prince of Candi runs away from Columbo, where he had been kept a long while, and for what Reason. The Author with two Companies of Voluntiers are sent out, and in their March, suffered much Thirst, and went all Bare-foot. They come to Calpintin, Aripen, Manaca, Jafnapatnam; all which Places he gives a Description of. Then he goes to Porto Novo, where he hath two Arrows shot in him. He goes back to Columbo, where he is Cured

THE whole Year is divided into two Seasons only, call'd the *good* and the *bad* Season. Each of them consists of five Months; the other two are call'd the Dubious Months, being *March* and *September*, in which are the two *Solstices*, on the 12th Old Stile, or 22d New Stile, of each of those Months.

In the Month of *March*, the Rains begin to fall on that side on which *Columbo* is Situated, and continue most commonly to the Month of *September*; so that all the Rivers overflow the Countries in such a manner, that the People, Cattle and Wild-Beasts are surrounded on a sudden, and carried away by the Water-floods. Those that delight in Hunting, may find great quantities of Beasts forced up into the Mountains at that time.

In *September* it begins to hold up, and the Weather is much like what we use to have in *April*, in *Holland*: Then the Sunbeams come to be so violently hot, that it dries up sometimes Navigable Rivers, and then the Wild-Beasts are forced to run a vast way to get Water.

In this *good Season* (as they term it) Thunder and Lightning are very frequent, and to that degree, that many huge Trees are split and rent to pieces with it, The *Sun* doth not move far from this Place, wherefore little notice can be taken of the lengthning or shortning of the Days : Nor is it ever very cold here ; only when the North Wind begins to blow in *February*, and which holds on for about four Months, one may bear a cotton Garment on. In this Season, the Fishermen have seldom the opportunity of Fishing, by reason of the roughness of the Sea. Whilst the *good* Season is on that side of *Columbo*, the other side towards *Cormandel, Jafnapatnam, Manara, Batacolo*, &c. have the *bad* with them, which is not a little strange, considering that they are not far from one another.

I was upon Duty in the Fort *Galture*, where our Men work'd by Day on the Fortifications, and at Night stood Sentinels, (the Night lasting but two Hours) from the 22d of *April* 1677, till the last of September of the same Year. Our head Officer there was a Lieutenant, one *Adam Slecht*, a *Bohemian*.

On the 1st of *October*, we were order'd by our Governor to march to a Forlorn Fort, call'd *Caudingelle*, six Leagues from Galture, with 40 Europeans, and 200 *Lascarians*,[1] or *Cingulaish* Soldiers.

A very hard Storm fell upon us in the way, which so swelled the Waters about us, that we were forced to wade with our Cloaths tuck'd up, and we were not a little plagued with the *Blood-suckers*. We found the said Fort overgrown with Trees and Shrubs, and no Inhabitants within two Leagues of us ; they were all retir'd up into the high Mountains, because those of *Candi* continually made Incursions upon that side of the Country, Spoiling, Burning, and Destroying all they came near. The Hollanders had built this Fort some Years since ; but having not made it strong enough, and provided it with necessaries sufficient, they were forc'd to leave it. It takes up about two Acres of Land ; it hath four Bastions, a Parapet, and Pallisado's as high as a Pike, and as thick as a Man's middle. We Europeans were

[1] Lascar is the term now applied to an East Indian sailor. It was used in the 17th century for native Sinhalese soldiers.

posted within, and the Cingulaisans on the outward Works; and were forc'd to cut up all the Wood about it, within a Musquet-shot.

We were in no danger in the day-time, but we had enough to do at night with several Parties of Candians, and with Elephants too: But these we frightned away easily with the Fires we made, having good store of Wood. Our Magazine was stor'd with Salt, Rice, Bacon, Flesh, Brandy, Powder and Shot, all which we had from *Anguratot*, two Leagues distant from us; and the care of it was given to me. Our Water was fetch'd about a Pistol-shot from the Fort.

After we had lain here about eight days in this wild and desert place, the Candians came against us, Headed by *Dissave Tennecool*,[1] the great Robber: An *Aratsi*[2] of ours brought us intelligence that they were coming with great forces upon us. We found then it was high time to remove our Quarters, which we did, setting all on Fire, and retired to another place near to *Anguratot*. By an order sent us from *Columbo*, we were oblig'd to go back to our old Quarters at *Galture*.

The 12th of October I was sent to Anguratot to reside as a Master of the Stores, and Pay-master of the Forces. I was made mighty welcome by our chief Dutch-Officer, who lay there; and by Mr. *Busterweld*,[3] who was the Ensign there. He was a Man that had been employ'd in great Affairs here, and had been sent as an Envoy to the King of Candi. He invited me to stay with him and make my abode at his House to keep him company, that being together we might spend our time more agreeably.

I was well enough pleas'd to be at *Anguratot*, because it was very strong, and well provided with Cannon. A very fine River runs before it, which comes from *Saffrigam*, and hath great store of good Fish, and Tortoises; and we had

[1] Tennekon Appuhami, a member of a distinguished Sinhalese family, claiming descent from a Royal house of the Coromandel coast, rose to be the foremost of Raja Sinha's generals. As related by Schweitzer below, he became apprehensive of the King's jealousy, and deserted to the Dutch, in October, 1678.

[2] *Arachchi*, commander of twenty or thirty men.

[3] Henricus van Bystervelt, a soldier who acquired some celebrity by undertaking a dangerous mission to the King of Kandi in 1671, in the course of which he challenged the King's Councillors to single combat (Pieris, "Ceylon and the Hollanders," 17–19).

some thousands of Inhabitants about us, of whom we bought choice Fruits very cheap, and all other sorts of Victuals, as Fowls, Butter, Honey, &c. for a very small price. It is very pleasant living here for one that can speak the Cingulaish language.

The Europeans that live here, who are not above Forty or Fifty in number, live in this following manner. They have Prayers every day, morning and night, and a Sermon on Sundays, with Singing of Psalms. They watch, and are free by turns in the daytime, but at night they must all be in the Fort upon pain of Death. Out of the Fort ev'ry one hath his little House, where each of them keeps his Cingulayish Woman to provide and dress his Victuals, and serves likewise for his Bed-fellow. If a Woman at any time is brought to Bed of a White Child, it is matter of great joy to the Parents and Relations, and they grow very proud upon it. If a Man design to go out of the Country, he must keep it exceeding private; for if his Bedfellow knows any thing of it beforehand, she certainly poisons him, or bewitches him, as several have been serv'd that have gone away; and tho' they were got 2 or 3000 miles, yet they were forc'd to come back again.

On the last day of December, a Letter came to Mr. *Busterweld* from *Columbo* advising him to come thither, seeing he had a mind to go back into his Country. He ask'd me if I would not go with him to *Columbo*: So I accompany'd him thither, and we have orders for three Boats to be made ready for our selves and our Baggage.

The 2d of January, 1678; Early in the morning we went out of *Anguratot*, and order'd the Cingulayans (of which there were four in each of our Boats) to take a great deal of care, for we were to pass thro' two several places that were very full of Rocks. The Dutch call one of them, The Great Hell; the other, The Little Hell, because they swallow up so many Men. We sent out before in a Boat that went free, an old Fellow (a Cingulayan, who was most experienc'd) to shew us the way. The Boat was loaded with Rice and Fowls, but the Men not Rowing so strong as they should have done, all sunk with their Boat. We that came just after them were not a little startled. I encouraged the Men in my Boat, as the Gentleman did those in his, and we fortunately got through, and we compass'd 3 Dutch miles in 4 hours: So we got to *Galture*: But we never heard more of our four Cingulayans that we lost in the first Boat.

Our Lieutenant *Sleght* receiv'd us very nobly, and invited

us to Dinner, and gave us other Cingulayans, which we sent out before with our Boats. And being *Columbo* was a great way from *Galture*, he order'd two Palanquins to be got ready for us (which are a sort of chairs, but so contriv'd, that one may either sit or lye down in them) and two Culins or Slaves a-piece to carry us; they carry'd us very fast, and we got safe to Columbo.

The 5th, Mr. *Busterweld*, having sent all his things aboard, and being to leave me behind, introduc'd me to a certain Captain of *Columbo*, one Min Heer *Witzenburg*, to whom after he had recommended me, he went on the 6th instant aboard his Ship to *Punto de Gala*, where he was to take in her Loading of Cinnamon and Pepper, and then put to Sea.

This Captain *Witzenburg* was a brave Soldier, about 50 years of age, was then in *Columbo* as Commander, and was likewise one of the Council, which consists of eight Men only, who are treated with no less Title than that of Honourable. They Judge and give Sentence in all Causes, as well Capital as others. Our chief Merchant, one *Van Vorsten*, was the President of them: He had been rais'd to this from a Cabin-boy. The best part of them could neither Write nor Read: nor could the Captain I am speaking of, tho' he was the third of the Council. If any Man will appeal from them, he must transfer his Cause to *Batavia*, which is 500 miles distant from thence.

I staid 5 months with the Captain during which time I was a very serviceable Companion, by reading to him all Orders and Causes at home, before he went to the Council (for they were always sent to them there first) in which he us'd to take my opinion, and in answering for him all the Letters that came to him.

The 1st of July, I was obliged to go to a little Fort call'd *Malvane*, 4 leagues from *Columbo*, where I remain'd four months. The place is very strong, by a River; it hath Pallisado's, Parapets, and a Ditch, eight Field-pieces, and other necessaries, and sixty Men to keep it. Our Head Officer there, was one *Oldenburgh*, a Lieutenant. It was very unhealthy by reason of the thick Fogs; and therefore the Garrison is often reliev'd from *Columbo*.

The 6th, We were inform'd that the King of *Candi* would Besiege this Fort; wherefore we provided our selves against it.

The 16th, The *Dissave*, or General, appear'd with Thirty Thousand Men, (this was that *Tennecool* the Renegado we have spoken of before), and he let us know privately.

On the 17th, That he resented an affront which the King of *Candi* had put upon him, and besides, that he had deceiv'd him in his expectations, for which he would now be revenged; and with this opportunity return to the Dutch, and not molest our Fort in any manner. We were oblig'd to keep this very secret, least it should come to the knowledge of his own Soldiers; and we sent an account of his offers to *Columbo,* whence we receiv'd orders to direct him to *Columbo,* but not receive him into our Fort.

The 20th, He went with three hundred of his best Men to *Columbo,* where he was receiv'd honourably by the Governor, and presented with a Gold Chain worth 300 Rixdollars. When the King of *Candi* had an account of this, he order'd the siege to be rais'd, and all *Tennecool's* Generation to be destroy'd.

The 31th of October, we were reliev'd, and went altogether to *Columbo.* We were to cross over a River 7 or 8 at a time, with two Boats tyed to one another. I was one of the last that were to go over. I was here very near being drown'd by an unlucky accident. The old Dottia or Waterman was just shoving the Boats off of Land; when the Boats which are exceeding little turn'd over, for the Rope broke that tyed them together. My danger was so much the greater, for that a lusty fellow, who fell in with us, and could not swim, took fast hold of my Leg, and would have drown'd us both, had I not fortunately laid hands on the post to which the Boats used to be tyed, by which means we were safe. Those that could swim were in no great danger: The others hung luckily upon the Boats that were floating with the bottom upwards; so that all saved their Lives. Some Musquets were lost, but it was a wonder that none of the Men were drown'd or at least devour'd, considering that there is always so vast a number of Crocodiles in that River.

From the 1st to the 8th, We lay in the Old Town of *Columbo.*

The 7th and 8th, Several People were sent out to hunt after the Prince of *Candi,*[1] who had been kept some years by the Dutch, with a design to put him on the Throne of *Candi,* when the old King should die. He was kept out of the City,

[1] A mysterious religious leader, who proclaimed himself as nephew of Raja Sinha, and fled to Colombo where, under the name of Ambanwale Rala, he obtained a great reputation as a wizard. He fled back to the King in November, 1678, and was shortly afterwards put to death (Pieris, *op. cit.*, 22–4).

near the old Hospital, and had a Guard of six Files of Musqueteers and one Serjeant; notwithstanding which he found means to make his escape, and was never heard of since.

He had been about six years at *Columbo*, where, at his coming, he declar'd himself to be of the Royal Blood of *Candi*, and the true Heir to that Crown, alledging that the present King of *Candi* had Usurp'd it from him, and that he was the Person that should have succeeded the Old King. And indeed all the Inhabitants were much more affected to him, which they used to express continually by the rich Presents they used frequently to bring him.

The Dutch allow'd him Forty Rixdollars *per* month, and 41 Simmeri's of Rice, to maintain himself and his Retinue, which was a Steward, a Wizard, a Captain, 20 Soldiers, 6 Drummers, 4 Leapers, and 8 Slaves, or Chair-men, to carry those Sedans we have already spoke of; in all 41 Men. They would not have lost much by this, if he had continu'd at *Columbo*, and had ever come to the Crown of *Candi*; for they would have made such Articles with him before they had settled him on the Throne, that he would have been little more than Titular King.

The 9th, two Companies of Volunteers were form'd out of the Garrisons of the City and Castle, of 80 Men each, and were order'd to go to the Coast of *Cormandel*.

The 10th, We were muster'd up, and receiv'd the next day two months Pay. Our chief officer was a Dantzicker, one *Tobias Guntz*, Captain-Lieutenant, and our two Lieutenants were one *Koningh*, and one *Vernie*.

The 12th, We went aboard in two small Vessels, and arriv'd the next day at *Calpintin*, where our Men were lodg'd in a Church which stands out of the Fortification, where Divine Service is done in Dutch, Portuguese, and Malabarish. This Fort was built here, and is carefully look'd after, because it is a considerable Pass for other Nations; and besides the Inhabitants drive no small Trade with the Moors, and others. A great Commodity there, is Areck, which is a Fruit that grows like the Nutmeg. Most of the Eastern Indians cannot live without it, being so us'd to it, that they are never well, but when they are chawing of it. The Soldiers here, which are 100 in number, keep Dogs, with which they go and Hunt Bufflers, Sheep, Stags, &c. upon which they live: For the Land affords nothing but what's Wild, some Fish and some Rice.

We lay still from the 14th, to the 18th, Then orders were

given for every Man to make his own Provision for three days, and to be ready on the 19th of *March.* Accordingly they were; and I having a desire to be in the adventure, provided for my self too, and order'd one of the Men to get me 6 pound of Beef boyl'd in Salt water, and half a pound of Bisket. The next morning early we set out. Our two Malabarian Guides went before us. At noon we came near to a Well, but found no Water there, which we began to want; but our want rather increased: Then we turn'd ourselves to a River, where we thought to have satisfy'd our selves, and found the water to be Salt. Our comfort was, that we were to come in the evening to a Well; but when we came to it, we found a Buffler fall'n in and drown'd, which made us all abstain from drinking, notwithstanding we were exceeding thirsty. Our Guide then took us half a mile farther, to a deep sandy Soil, where they told us we might have Water. There we were forc'd to make several holes in the Ground, 2 or 3 yards deep, to get at it; but we were happy still to have it upon any terms. In this place we lay all night, having set some Men to watch, and kindl'd some Fires to prevent the wild Beasts coming upon us.

The 20th, Early in the morning we march'd on thro' the great Woods and Desert-places, where we saw and heard nothing but Elephants, Tygers, Bears, &c. there being no Man in all that part of the Country. We came in the forenoon to an Arm of a Salt-River that reach'd into the Land a great way; so that we were forc'd to wade over, after we had staid about three hours, till the ebb was at the lowest; and then too we were all forc'd to strip, and pack all our Cloaths, Provisions, and Arms, and carry them on our Heads. We were almost a quarter of an hour going over; and it was so deep, that some of the least of our Men, had much to do to keep the Water from running in at their mouths. Some that thought to be wiser than our Guides, went up to a place where they saw the Water run very rough, because it was so deep there. It was but shallow indeed, but the stream was so strong there, that it threw 'em off out of their depth, and drown'd most of 'em. We being got over made haste on, for we were by this time in want of Water again, and the best allay of our thirst we could get, was our Bullets which we rowl'd about in our mouth to moisten them. At night we lay still at a place, whence those that would of necessity drink were forc'd to go about a mile for Water, and then dig for it too. After they had made each of them their hole, they drank their fill, and then laid down in it for coolness, and took a nap there.

The 21th, Three Soldiers came to meet us with three Horses sent from *Manara* for the Officers. We got upon them with a very good will, while the poor fellows were forc'd to drudge on without Shoes or Stockings (in the same manner as they set out). We arriv'd all at *Aripen* about 3 of the clock in the afternoon, having gone about 22 Leagues in our three days march ; which was very hard for our Men, who went all the way barefoot. *Aripen* is a pretty strong place, kept by 20 Dutch Soldiers, provided with 4 Fieldpieces, and other Warlike Necessaries convenient for a place of that bigness.

Many Malabarians live about it, of whom one may buy Flesh, Milk, Butter, Egges, Fowls, &c. cheap enough : And we bought here two pretty good Bullocks for one Rixdollar, that serv'd both our Companies.

This place is chiefly designed to keep the *Pearl-bank* from being fish'd by any one that hath no title to it, which is an offence punishable with death. It is very unhealthy there, and no European but must expect a Fever that will kill him, if he stays there long. For which reason they are exchang'd from *Manara* ev'ry four months ; and yet they lose generally half their Men. We staid there all night, and

On the 22th, We march'd away again, and at night came by the Island *Manara*, to go to which we were to cross the Waters, which is about a mile broad : It is six miles from *Aripen*. We were very kindly receiv'd by the Dutch Captain that lay there ; and treated very nobly with Flesh and Fish, which is here in great plenty.

This Island, as we mention'd before, hath seven miles compass : It is inhabited by several Malabars, and abounds in Flesh, Fowls, and fruitful Trees ; and all the Water about it affords plenty of Fish. In short, it may be call'd an Earthly Paradise. The Fort is well provided, and is kept by near 100 Dutch Soldiers. Each Soldier keeps a boy to clean his Arms and carry them for him, and a Woman to look after his Meat and serve him. Proportionably to this, the Officers live in very great State. We lay here three days and

The 26th, We went in three Dutch Boats to *Jafnapatan*, where we arriv'd on,

The 27th, And were very well receiv'd, and Quarter'd in the Fort that lies to the Sea.

The 28th, 29th, and 30th, Our Men were exercis'd, and 20 Elephants were brought upon the place whilst we Fir'd, to use them to stand it without starting in War. At first they were very fearful and untractable, not being able to bear the noise and smoak of our Guns, tossing up their Trunks, and were very furious. At last they were brought to it so, that an Indian could get upon them, and rise about a Furlong away from us, and then drive them upon us (we firing against them all the while), at length they'd break our Ranks, take what care we could ; and tho' we shot in their very Noses ; and if the Cingulayans that rid them had not prevented them with their Instruments, they would have trampl'd us under foot.

The 1st of December, Two Companies of Soldiers came to us from the Coast of *Cormandel,* out of the Fort *Palliacalte* [Palikat], and *Nagapatan.* They were Quarter'd in a Stable, used generally to keep Elephants.

The 2d, Another Company came from *Gala, Battacula,* and *Triconomala.*

The 3d, We had a general Muster, and march'd with our 7 Companies, and 8 Field-pieces drawn by Elephants, and 20 other Elephants besides, out of the Fort of *Jafnapatan.* And being drawn out in the Fields there, we were commanded to inclose our Leaders ; that is, to form our selves into a Ring, where we heard the Articles of War read to us.

Jafnapatan bears the Name of a small Kingdom, which the Dutch took by surprize from the Portugueses. Its Fort is well built, and strong ; having four Bastions, two Towers, a Counterscarp, and a deep Ditch. It lies upon a Salt-water on the side of *Manara,* where the Dutch have built a very strong fine Key.

All the chief Officers lodge within the Fort with their Wives. The under Officers and Soldiers Wives live amongst the other Inhabitants in the Town, which is about a League in compass : But there are a great many Gardens in it, and many poor small Huts ; as also fair large Streets. There are two different Market-places in it ; the one for Fish, the other is for all sorts of Commodities, as Silks, Linnen, Pearls, Gold, Silver, Spices, Salt, Butter, Allum, Tobacco, Rats and Mice, Herbs, all sorts of Colours ; in short, all a Man can desire. Their current Money is made of Copper, and is either Shillings, Two-pences, Peny-pieces, *Damagasties,* Half-penies, and Farthings. One may buy 10 or 15 Figs for a Farthing, that are almost a span long ; and sometimes 2 or 3

Pounds of Fish for the same price : So that a Man that goes to Market with 4 or 5 Farthings, may buy Provisions to serve a common family two days for his Money.

I met here with an Acquaintance of mine, a Physician, who was chief Chirurgeon to the Dutch Hospital, and Physician to Min Heer *Laurent Piil,*[1] the Governor, and was much esteem'd among the Natives of the Country for his Abilities, and the great Cures he perform'd.

The 4th, We march'd out. Our Major *Clebout* went first, carry'd by Slaves in a Palankin, a sort of Sedan, I have already mention'd. After him march'd the 6 Companies, with each an Elephant to draw the Baggage. It was suppos'd that we were design'd to march to *Wani,*[2] where the Inhabitants had chosen a new Prince without consent of the Dutch, their Prince *Don Philip* being Dead ; and design'd to free themselves for the future from paying Tribute to *Jafnapatan*. But as soon as they understood that we were drawing towards 'em, they sent to meet us with ten Elephants, with offers to continue willingly a yearly tribute of Elephants and Money, on conditions we would secure them from the King of *Candi*.

The Major sent them to *Jafnapatan* with a Letter, and we came at night to a place call'd *Pas-Piil,* where a Dutch Garrison lay. Here the Hutts were ready for our Men, and provided with necessaries against our coming.

The 5th, 6th, and 7th, We lay still here, being much tir'd with going ten Leagues in a day in all that heat, and so sandy a Country. We found there three great Dutch ships that were come from *Batavia*.

The 8th, Four of our Companies, viz., The two that came from *Columbo,* the other two from *Cormandel,* were to Embark secretly, and the two other Companies were to remain in the Fort, by reason of the troubles that were in *Wani*. That very evening we set forwards for the Coast of *Cormandel*.

The 9th, Early in the morning, we came before *Negapatan*. Here a Dutch Yatch joyn'd us, and two other Vessels, together with three great Boats well Mann'd with Seamen. With this Fleet we sail'd along the Coast by *Krancko Baar,*[3]

[1] Laurens Pyl, Commandant of Jafnapatam, became Governor of Ceylon in 1679. *See* Introduction, p. xxiv.

[2] The Wanni, a wild region, south of the Jaffna Peninsula, was at this time ruled by independent chiefs, tributory to the Dutch, of whom Dom Philip was the most influential.

[3] Tranquebar, where the Danish East India Company had a factory.

a City belonging to the King of *Denmark*, and lying 8 Leagues from *Negapatan*. We sail'd by the Danish Admiral that lay in the Road, with two other Ships, to whom we struck our Pendants. We pass'd on by *Porto Novo*, a Fort that belongs to the Moors, under the command of the King of *Volkendal*. They had a great many Boats before it, and one at a distance to watch the rest. This one put up a Flag, and fir'd a Piece for a Signal; and of a sudden they were all under Sail, taking us for Enemies. But it was but a false alarm of theirs, for our design was only upon the Fort Policere (which is not far from *St. Thomas*) into which many Soldiers that had deserted from the Viceroy *Lakay*, were got: And this Fort we had orders to Invest and Demolish, because it was a great hindrance to the Dutch Commerce.

But on the 21th, A Yatch met us, that was coming to bring us word, that the French, upon notice of our coming, were fled out of the Fort, and gone to the King of *Volkendal*. So we went back to *Nagapatan*, where we arriv'd

The 11th, at night, and cast Anchor there. We heard that the Moors had drove away a Dutch Merchant that was Registerer, and Secretary of *Matapatan*, and had seiz'd all his Goods: Upon which we sent 2 of our Boats with 150 men to redress this Inquiry.

And on the 13th, They came back with an account of their good success; and that they had restor'd the Merchant his Habitation, and forc'd the Moors to give back all they had taken from him. Our Ship being to take up 400 quarters of Rice at this place, we lay still there till

The 12th of January, 1679, When we set sail, and came on

The 13th, To a Dutch Fort call'd *Punto de Pedre*, a very pleasant place, having great plenty of Onions, Tamarins, Figgs, Cocos, Jager, and Areck-trees, which make delicate shady Walks, some 'em a mile or two long; and a fine Campaign Country; There we lay all night, and very well lodg'd we were.

The 14th, Early in the morning, we march'd on foot to *Jafnapatan*. I was very dry in the march; and coming to a Malabarian Village, I slipp'd into a little Hutt to get me some milk to drink. I found an old Woman there with her Daughter: I desir'd a Pint of Milk, and they gave it me, asking me a *Damagas* for it (which is two-pence;) I drunk it off, and having paid my money, went away to overtake the rest of my Company, and not thinking of any thing, I was immediately shot in the Leg with one Arrow, and with another in my Thigh. I pull'd them out, and look'd all about me, but could not perceive any body, nor whence they should come. However I thought to fright them, and cry'd out, *O Nay, Dayoli, mettene Landes inguwarre*; which signifies, *Ye dogs, there are more Dutch a-coming.* But that was all the revenge I could have, for I durst not complain of it, because it was done by stealth, and contrary to our orders, that I stopt there. So I went out of the Village as fast as I could, and stopp'd my Wounds with an old rag, that I used to wrap the lock of my Fusil in, and overtook my Company, and went on to *Jafnapatan* in great pain. There our Post was; and I immediately went to my Countrymen *Lutz* the Physician, who Cur'd me; but was forc'd to cut open my Wounds, because the Arrows were poison'd. We staid there till

The 14th of February, And then we were carried back in Boats to *Manara*. There was a Vessel here that would have held us all very well, but the Captain-Lieutenant would take but one Company in with him, wanting room for good quantity of Hogs and Onions, that he had a mind to carry to *Columbo* to trade with. We had very good Quarters here, and staid till

The 1st of March, Then we were divided, and went in two Boats: The one was a large Dutch one, call'd the Elephant; the other a poor little Mallabarish one, into which it was my lot to go: It was quite open, and had neither Rudder, nor Compass. But those in the Dutch Vessel told us that we should not want one, if we would but follow 'em; We told 'em we would if we could; but we gave our selves over for lost, and never expected that it would carry us over the Sea. However we went well enough while the day lasted; but towards the evening, coming to the *Pearl Bank* at *Aripen*, it began to Rain, and blow exceedingly. The Wind was good but so strong, that we were afraid of over-turning ev'ry minute. Our four Seamen, who were Malabarians, thought good to keep as nigh to the shore as we could; all of us thought very well of that too: But the Rogues, more afraid than we, as soon as they came in sight of Land, leap'd into the Sea, and left us, and swam to shore. By mere good fortune we had some Soldiers amongst us, that had been Saylors, who manag'd the Sails and Stern. I had chosen to lay me down by the Hearth, where they used to dress their Victuals, to keep my self and my Writings dry; but the Rain beat upon me, and mixing the Ashes and Soot with it, I look'd next morning like a Chimney-Sweeper; but the best on't was, that I kept my Papers very safe. This was a bitter night; and in the morning we struck upon a little marshy Island, and there staid till day, to see which way we were to take. There was an old fellow with us, that knew whereabout *Calpintin* was, being well acquainted with the Country; by the help of his Directions, we thrust off our Boat, and sail'd by many other little Islands like this, and got in sight of *Calpintin,* and by the next morning to it. Here we found the fellows that should have been our Guides, but had basely left us. We lay still here till the 5th Instant.

CHAPTER VII

The manner of Fishing for Pearls: Why this sort of Fishing was laid by for seven years. The Author's departure from Calpintin to Columbo. The Dangers he went through in his journey. Comes to Columbo. Presents sent by the Governor to the King of Candi: What they were. The Author is order'd to go along with them. In what base manner the Candians receiv'd the Presents; and then treacherously fell upon those that brought them. How they came off, and in their retreat destroy'd two Heathen Temples. What strange things happen'd while they were about it. They return to Columbo. The Gates there are shut up twice a day, and why. An account of Sittawack, and of the Amboineses who serve the Dutch Company there. Precious Stones in the Earth and in the Rivers; where most found. A Description of them; and where, and how they grow.. What policy the Author was forc'd to use to get a Saphir of an Old Cingulayan. A strange Cock. An Elephant falls into a Well, out of which there was no getting of him. An Earthquake.

BEFORE I proceed, I will inform the Reader how the Pearls are got here, how Fish'd for, and how Sold.

The Bank, where they are, lies in the Sea, not far from the Land. It is about twenty miles long, and two broad; from seven to ten Fathoms deep. It belongs at this time to the Hollanders. The Oysters in which the Pearls are found, are about the breadth of one's hand. They stick to the bottom of Rocks, some twenty or thirty together. There are People to look every year, and see whether the Pearls are ripe; when they are so, they write to all the neighbouring Kings to let them know what time the Fishing is to begin. Then the *Divers* are sent, who are the Malabarian Fishermen, who come with their Boats, and some Stones along with them. Each Diver hangs a Stone upon his Foot to sink him the sooner; when he is at the bottom, he fills his Net with Oysters, and then loosens himself from the Stone. Then the Stone, together with the Net, is drawn up by another Malabarian in the Boat, whilst the Man shoots himself up to fetch breath. When they have thus fill'd their Boat with Oysters, they row to Land, and throw them out. There is a Dutch Soldier waits on each Boat, to see that the Malabarians do not take any of the Pearls away. The three first days these Boats are all employ'd for the East-India Company; after this they may fish for themselves paying a Rixdoller a day for every Diver.

The Oysters are laid in heaps on the Shore, and the Merchants come there to buy them. They are sold at the rate of eight hundred for a Rixdollar. The gain or loss of the Buyer depends on meer chance: For some may be find no Pearls in all they buy; others make vast advantage of their Bargain.

There hath been no Fishing here for these eight years. Some superstitiously think that the place is bewitched: Others give this for a reason (which I rather approve of) that the boisterousness of the Sea hath cover'd the Oysters with Sand, so that they cannot come at them.

The 6th, In the morning all our Company went in the Boat call'd the Elephant; and having the Wind for us, we expected to reach to *Columbo* by night. The number of the Soldiers and Officers was in all 110. We had but a small Vessel with Water, a bushell of Rice, a small Buffler, and a young Buck; which two last things were for a present to the Governor. Thus the Boat was quite full, and no Man had room to lye down, but was forc'd to keep his Seat. The Wind blew North: But at noon it ceas'd, and then we went but slowly: but we kept in sight of Land all along on our left hand. Toward night, the Wind rose again; and then we made some speed. Therefore the Steersman bad us all look out sharp for *Columbo*, where we earnestly desir'd to be, especially because our Water Vessel was every drop drunk out.

The 7th, By break of day, we found that we were carry'd wide off of it by the strength of the current, and partly by the oversight of our Steersman: For we could see no *Columbo*, nor Land neither. All the Officers were very angry with him for't, and would certainly have thrown him into Sea, if he had not got up to the top of the Mast, where they made him stay all that day for his Punishment. Our Captain consulted the Map of the Island *Ceylon*, and he directed us somewhere in our course; and about night we got in sight of *Pico-d'Adam*,[1] or *Adam's Hill*; and at six of the Clock next morning we got happily to *Columbo*. It was high time for us to get thither, considering that we had been two days and three nights without Meat or Drink. The Steersman begg'd we would pardon him, and not complain of him to the Governor.

The 8th, As soon as the Gates were open'd, we enter'd the City, and went to our respective Posts. The Captain, with whom I spent some time when I was here before, sent to me to desire me to make his House my own again, if I pleased. I did not make any refusal of so advantageous a proffer, but accepted of it, and I staid with him till

The 16th, When I was order'd to go with several others to carry a Present, which the Governor sent to the King of *Candi*; during which time I had the Title and Office of Captain. The Presents were, two Persian Horses, with fine Velvet Cloaths and Trappings, each Horse led by two Malabarian Slaves: Ten Falcons, each carry'd by a Malabarian dress'd all in white: Six Musk-Cats, each in a different Cage, carry'd by two Slaves: Six very large Cocks from *Tutucurini*, each of them likewise in a Cage, cover'd with green Velvet: Two Persian Sheep, each with a Tail that weigh'd 20 or 25 pound: A Box that had two Bottles in it, that held each of them six Gallons of Persian Wine: Besides this, a great piece of *Sandel* Wood, that weigh'd 200 pound, wrapp'd up in fine white Linnen. The Letter that was to be deliver'd to the King, was carry'd in a Silver Cap by a Serjeant bare-headed, and a Canopy was carry'd over it by four Cingulayan Nobles: By each of which another went with a large Wax-Candle lighted as long as a half Pike.

Our march began in order at the Governor's House. Some Companies of Cingulaish Soldiers went first; then some Companies of Dutch; then the Presents; after them two Companies more of Dutch. These were order'd to go as far as the King of *Candi's* residential Town, *Ruenel*. All the City was in Arms, and all the Cannon was Fir'd

[1] Adam's Peak, 7,420 ft., the sacred mountain of Ceylon. "The Arabs worshipped it as the footprint of Adam, who found consolation in Ceylon for the loss of Paradise" (Pieris, "Ceylon and the Portuguese," 95). Pilgrims were assisted in the ascent by iron chains which Marco Polo states to have been presented by Alexander the Great.

round, and a Dutch Company that conducted us out of Town gave us three Vollies and went back again.

We, together with the others before mention'd, went on with the Presents. At night we came to a place, where Dutch Potters live, two Leagues from *Columbo*; there we lay that night, and the next morning march'd on, and came

The 17th, At night to *Hanquelle* or *Gourwebel*, a Dutch Fort, where we lay.

The 18th, We had a very unpleasant and dirty way, and were not a little tormented with Blood-suckers, till we came to the Fort *Sittawack*, which is in possession of the Dutch, and 12 Leagues distant from *Columbo*. Immediately Letters were written, on leaves of Sugar-trees, and dispatch'd to the *Coral* of *Candi* at *Ruenel*, to acquaint him with our being come thither, with a Present for the King his Master; and that he should permit them to come forwards, if he pleas'd to receive them. But not a word of answer did we get, and we staid here in expectation of it six whole weeks, till the end of September. At last we had Directions sent us from *Columbo*, which were, That we should go four Leagues farther beyond *Ruenel*, and deliver them to the *Coral*, and then come back. And accordingly

The 1st of October, We went; and after having crossed seven little Rivers, we came to *Ruenel*. This fort heretofore belong'd to the Dutch, but was abandon'd by them, tho' themselves had built it. There we cross'd over, and having march'd a league further, we came to a large Plain, where we halted a while to rest and refresh our selves. By that time we had been there about half an hour, we saw and heard several small Parties of Cinguleses coming upon us from ev'ry side. Our chief Commander sent some Cingulayans to ask what they meant to do? They answer'd them, that the King of *Candi* had sent them to take the Presents we had brought.

We would not trust 'em. So we put our selves in order, and stood our Ground. Their number still encreased, and they came very thick out of a Wood. At last their Artillery (which was very small) appear'd too, and then they drew towards us. We sent again to 'em to know what they design'd to do with their Artillery, and whether this was their custom to repay Civilities? They told us their Field-Pieces were not loaded.

We would have been glad to have been at home again, for we were but two Companies of Dutch of 160 Men each, and two or three hundred Cingulayans; and these Heathens were almost innumerable. They appeared as thick as Grass on the Field. The Presents were sent for by the *Monthou*, who was one of the King's Chief Officers, and an Under Officer took them and delivered them to him. He received them, and he giving no orders for their Artillery to be discharged, we gave no Volley of our side.

Our Officer desired to speak to the King's *Saudi* in Person, and a place was appointed for them to meet at, equally distant from them both. The *Saudi* came upon an Elephant, and our Officer was on *Horse-back*. These two sorts of Creatures are not to be brought near one another, wherefore they were forced to light, and meet a-foot.

The *Saudi* did not take off his Cap, because he belong'd to a Crown'd Head: Ours only represented a body of Merchants, and Deputy Governors.

Our Officer complained of the manner of our Reception, and ask'd why so many thousand Men were drawn out against us, knowing that we had but two Companies of Dutch: The reason the *Saudi* gave was, That his Master had commanded it to be so; so they parted, but neither would draw his Men off first. At last, Night coming upon us, we were forced to retire.

They let us pass by quietly enough till we were got to the River by *Ruenel* (which is most like the *Rhine* of any I ever saw). But as soon as one of our Companies was got over, they fell upon the Rear of the other. Our Cingulayans took the River, and swam over, leaving us in the lurch. We continued firing upon them, and they upon us; till we were all got quite over. We lost our Lieutenant and two private Soldiers. We killed several of theirs, and wounded many more. We had a very bad way to go, and it fell a Raining, which made it more Dirty and Slippery, so that we could not go fast as we would have done. We retired towards *Sittawack*, and passed by a steep Rock; whence it is reported, That the late King of *Sittawack's* wife and daughter flung themselves down headlong, having received the news that he had lost the Battle against the King of *Candi*. The Candians all the while came after us, but were not able to do us any great harm, because the ways were so narrow that they could not come up to us. Yet we were forced every now and then to Fire in the Rear of us.

The 2d, 3d and 4th we rested at *Sittawack*, the next day

we destroyed two Heathenish Temples not far from that place; they were built upon a rising Ground, and cut out of a vast Rock: Within they were adorned with many images and Statues of Wood and Stone, representing Devils, &c. Under one of the Pagods we found a dark black hole, as it were grown so with Smoak, no body durst venture to creep in. We threw some Straw into it, and Fired it, but we could not sound the Depth or Length of it. Some Fellows were mightily afraid of standing near the hole, and were afraid that we should poke some Cingulayan Devil out of it; but if he was there, he did not come out, nor did we find out what it was made for.

We had several Lutherans and Papists amongst us; the first of these fell a Singing some Spiritual Hymns in the Temple, that had that hole under it. The Papists went together into the other, and they having among them an old Fellow that had been a Priest heretofore, he fell to saying Mass. There was on the sudden such a noise, and thundring, and cracking, that we thought we should have been all blown up, or that the Temple would have fallen upon us. Some run out thinking to be safer, but the noise and hurly-burly was greater there than within, so that some came in again; and this continued a quarter of an Hour.

The 6th we came away, and toward that Evening entred into *Columbo*; where we found two great Ships lying in the Road come from *Japan*, with Copper, Gold, China and *Saccapali* which is a liquor of a faint smell, but very wholsome.

The 7th I was order'd to my Post, which was at the Gate call'd *Victoria*, where I stay'd till the 2d of February, 1680. I had 110 Men under me. The Castle Gates were open'd and shut, every Morning and Night at six of the Clock, and all the Keys ty'd together with a Silver Chain, were carried to the Governor: The Gates are shut likewise from Eleven to One a Clock in the Day time, that being the hottest part of the Day, and therefore generally taken to sleep in. We Exercised our Men every Monday, and every Sunday we went constantly twice a Day to Church, where Divine Service was performed in Dutch and Portuguese, after the Reformed way.

The 9th Instant we went to relieve the Company that was at *Sittawack*, Twelve Leagues from *Columbo*; we got there that Night, and the next Day being

The 10th, the Company march'd out and left us. And

here I shall give the Reader some short Account of the Fort of *Sittawack*: It is scituated upon a Rocky Ground; near to this, just over the River, stood heretofore the King of *Sittawack's* Palace, ruin'd since by the Portuguese: It is about four hundred Paces in Circuit: It is built four-square, with four Bastions, call'd, *Rycloff, Louisa, Columbo,* and *Gala*; Each of these Bastions hath two Pieces of large Cannon. In the middle of this place is a large square Bulwark: Under this are kept the Provisions, as Rice, Flesh, Salt, and Brandy; and the Ammunitions of War, Powder, Granadoes, and Balls: Over that was the Guard Room, where all the Men lay; at each corner of which were two small Pieces of Cannon. Half the Men might have leave to be out of the Fort in the Day-time, but at Night they were to be in, every Man, upon pain of Death. Every Night the Names were call'd over, and Prayers Read; and on Sunday Night we had a Sermon preach'd in the Guard Chamber. Here is also a Company of Amboineses continually kept in the Dutch Service. Their Lieutenant was call'd *Alons*, and was of Royal Blood. They live in the Town altogether, and with their Huts they make a very pretty Street, and they have their Wives with them. But at Night they are as much obliged to be in the Fort as any of us. They are very nimble and active at Running or Leaping. They never have but little Beards, and behind in their Necks they have a sort of bunch grows like a Wen. Their Pay is, for a Lieutenant 24 Rix Dollars a Month, an Ensign 16, a Corporal 8, a Private Centinel 5, all paid in Mony.

The Cingulayans are mightily afraid of the Amboineses, and rather more than the Europeans are; for they are great devourers of Men. They wear Muskets and short Swords. Besides their own Language, they generally speak Maleysh, Cingulaish, Portuguese, and Dutch. They love Gaming excessively, and the day time they generally spend in Cock-fighting, Cards, and Dice; and when they have lost all their Money, they go to some work or other, as Carving several things in Stone or Wood, &c. till their Month's Pay comes into their hands again, and as soon as they have paid their Debts, what is left they put to the venture; and when they have lost that, it is much if the Wife is not strip'd of all her Ornaments to supply him in the pursuit of his Gaming, and the Family is left often in an extream necessity, and ready to starve.

As for *Sittawack*, it is a Fort design'd to resist the King of *Candi*: It hath three little Counties or *Corls* depending upon it, the one is call'd *Cuculi* and in Dutch the *Hoender Grafschap*, (*Hoender* signifying *Fowls*, which are there in abundance); the second is call'd *Bulatkam-Corl*, from the quantity of Plants it produces, which serve for Food to the Inhabitants: The third *Bisang-Corl*, from the great quantity of Figs that grow there. In each of these *Corls* are some hundreds of Peasants that are under Contribution, and are forced to pay a fourth part of all their Rice to the Fort, and likewise of their Fruit-bearing Trees, as *Cocos*, *Arack*, *Sugar*.

This Fort besides serves for a Guard, upon all the precious Stones, as Rubies, Saphyrs, Emeralds, the Topaz and Azure Stones, that lie in and upon the Ground: They are sometimes washt into the Rivers by the great Rain and Water Floods. In the River that runs from *Saffrigam* (which was once a Dutch Fortification, but now left) one may find abundance of little Rubies, and sometimes a pretty large one; the very Sand of that River is almost of the same substance with the Stones, being of a Red and Blue Colour. We often used to go to bath in that River, and seek for precious Stones, but not when the Water was high, for fear of the Crocodiles; though it was not worth any Man's while, unless he could swim, and venture to dive in the deepest places for 'em; because it is there only that those of any considerable bigness are to be found.

There is a little rivulet that runs below this Fort, coming from between two high Hills, and discharges or empties it self into the River, in which are found Saphys, Emeralds, Topaz and Lazule-Stones: We have walk'd many a day in this Water for two or three Miles an end, to look for 'em. We had little Basket-Nets which the *Amboineses* lent us; and we us'd to thrust the Nets into holes, and fetch'd out good and bad together, and shake out of the Net all the Sand and Gravel, and the Stones that were of any bigness remain'd. Those that had no Net made but little on't. The Elephants us'd to be very troublesome to us, and we were forc'd often to go some miles about to avoid them, and I for my part was always provided with a Gun against them; and for fear too of Tygers and Serpents.

A small account of the Nature of these Stones will not be unpleasant to the Reader; wherefore I will, as far as I know, give as brief an account of them as I can:

And first for the Rubies, they grow in a reddish, stony, sandy Ground, one Fathom or two deep, spreading themselves like Veins, and though the great Floods carry them away in the Rivers they keep their Beauty and Colour as well under water as under ground, but if the water runs off of them, and leaves them ever so little exposed to the Sun, they turn as black as a Coal.

The Saphirs grow in a hard bluish ground, about a Fathom deep, and in veins too, and are washt likewise into the Rivers by the violent Rains and Flood. Some are as big as the top of one's finger;

So are Emeralds, Topazes, and Lazule-stones, these are as Red as Fire, and as Blue as the Skie.

Another sort of stone is found here, call'd Cat's Eyes: these are so call'd from their colour, which is a changable Blue and White.

Red, Blue, Yellow, Black, and White Chrystal is to be found every where, and is very troublesome to Men upon their March, when they go barefoot, as all our Men did, but they find an Herb very common there, which they call Horse-foot, that cures them in two or three days time.

Some of our Company us'd to frequent those Rivers every day, and at last all of 'em contracted some Distemper, and that was all that some got by it; wherefore our Officers gave orders that no man should go any more into the water upon that design.

On a certain time that I was upon no Duty, I went about a League from the Fort, where I spy'd an old Cingulayan, with his two Sons, in the River seeking Stones: I took care to come up to them without being discovered, least they should have slipt away; I ask'd 'em if they had found any stones, one of 'em answer'd, *Netti Ralu*, which is, no Sir; I would not believe him, so I search'd his Cloaths, and found in some of his Buttons, among other little Saphyrs, one that was about the bigness of a Hazel Nut. I askt him if he would sell it, he refus'd at first, but at last he offer'd it me, and two small ones with it, for half a Dollar, Dutch Mony. I had at that present time no Mony by me, and I durst not take it by force from the old Fellow neither, because he was a subject of the Dutch; and what to do I could not tell, having a great mind to the stone too: I had a piece of Chrystal in my Pocket, which I took out, and convey'd the Saphir into my mouth; so I told him I would give him his price if he would go to *Sittawack*, and offering to give him it again, to keep till then, I let the Piece of Chrystal fall into the Water, he thinking it was his stone, cry'd out, *O Deine Balatie,* which signifies, Plague it is gone : I seem'd concern'd, and told him he might find it again. He and his sons went to seek for it, but to no purpose : They were mighty sorry for their loss ; I told them I would make them some recompence, and took them with me to *Sittawack,* where I gave them three shillings, and they went away very well satisfied. I made use of this stratagem, because if I had left the stone in their keeping, they would have mistrusted me, and never have come to the Fort after me.

The Tenth of March I went with two other Lutheran Gentlemen, (each of us having a Gun with us,) to the Hill, where we had not long since destroyed the two Pagods, to see what condition they were in. We found them ruin'd as we had left them, and poked again in the dark hole ; But I believe we had routed the Devil the time before, for we could not make him roar any more, do what we could. At the bottom of the Hill I saw abundance of fine Cocks and Hens, and I bought some of the Hens and one Cock of an old Woman they belong'd to. She told me that the Cock I bought was consecrated for an Offering, while the Pagods stood, and therefore that I should not kill him, and that he would beat any Cock whatsoever. I laugh'd at the story, and yet was a little afraid because it was design'd for the Devil, and did not know but he might come and fetch him. However I ventur'd upon him, and paid as I did for my Hens, a Dutch peny for each of them. Being come to the Fort, I let him run there : In two or three days he fought and beat every Cock in the Fort that he could come nigh. Every body wondred at the fierceness of this little Cock, and I began to think that what the old Woman had told me might be true. At last I made a trade of Cock-fighting, and I got all the Amboineses about me. They laid wagers among themselves, and I only won the Cocks that mine beat, which amounted to two or three and thirty. At last they ignorantly hit the Nail on the head, saying that the Devil was in him. Being to go to Columbo again, I took him with me, and thought he would have done as great feats there, but he was overmatched with a Cock that came from *Tutucurini,* that beat him lustily.

The 2d of March, A *Laserin* came to Town, and told us

that an Elephant was fall'n into the King's Well, on the other side of the River. I went with several others, and saw him lye at the bottom squeezed together, standing almost up an end, but his Legs bent, and he was very uneasie. We took some Fig leaves which we threw down to him; he took 'em very thankfully, and eat them. At last he lifted up his Proboses, and made a horrid noise, which we interpreted as a begging us to help him out; but he lying 12 Fathoms deep, we could not possibly do it. One of our Drummers was there with us; who having been pursued one time by an Elephant, as he was Hunting, knew this to be the Elephant, that had put him so hard to his shifts; for if it had not been for a large Tree that he climb'd up into, he had certainly been kill'd. The Drummer to be reveng'd of him, went next day by himself, threw a great many dry sticks upon him, and some straw, and set it all on Fire, and then came home and told us the exploit.

The 3d of the same Month about 8 or 9 of the Clock at night, We felt a very violent Earthquake coming from the Northward, which shook our Blockhouse extreamly. All the Men that lay in the Guard Room were awaked out of their sleep, and thought it was an Alarm. Ev'ry body would make haste to come out, and ev'ry body would be first down stairs. The Throng was intolerable; and in the bustle the Lamp went out, which made the greater confusion; so that at last very few went out as they should do, but fell downstairs. We felt three several shakes, the last of which was so very violent, that we thought the whole Island would have been lost; and we heard from the Seamen that lay in the Road before Columbo, that they had felt it very sensibly too. What conclusions may be drawn from this, of the causes of Earthquakes, I leave Naturalists to agree about if they please or can.

CHAPTER VIII

The Author, with three others, go a Hunting. They meet with Elephants and kill one of them. All sorts of venomous Creatures come to Sittawack, to save themselves from the Water, that overflow'd all the Land about it. Their manner of Hunting. Envoys that came to bring Presents to the King of Candi, kept Prisoners by him. Two English-men kept for Slaves in Candi, make their escape, and come to Sittawack; they tell a pleasant Story of a Country fellow that had used a Ruby for a Whetstone several years. The Author and the English-men come to Columbo, where they are treated very civily. He goes to Cormandel, thence to Columbo again. Execution done. The Author is made Secretary of the East-India-house. A Jew turns Christian, and marries a Cingulaish Gentlewoman. A Description of Columbo; and an Account of the Manners of that place, their Marriages, &c.

I SPENT all the month of March in Hunting, and I lived altogether upon what Game I used to bring home with me. Upon a certain night the Moon being at full (knowing it would be light all night) I, with three Gentlemen more, went out into a fair Plain, about a league from *Sittawack* where we design'd to have some Stags. We set ourselves down at the side of a Hill, to watch the wild Beasts, that we expected would come out of a Wood to feed where we were, there being very fine grass.

The first that appear'd were Bufflars, among which there was a Stag; they came directly to the place where one of our Company was (who was a Swede) and did not know what Creature it was. As soon as these came to smell him, they took to the top of the Hill again immediately, and made a great noise there. On the other side we heard several Elephants making towards us. About mid-night, being tir'd with sitting, we got together to ask one another's Advice, what we should do, when the

Elephants came. We resolv'd to fall upon them; because we concluded they kept the Game from coming into the Dale, and so spoil'd our sport.

When we got into the middle of the Plain, an Elephant broke out of the Wood, and run at us immediately. We took to our heels, and run as fast as we could to the place where we first sat down; there we took courage again, and resolv'd to go on again, and that not one of us would run away, as we had done before. At the left hand of the Plain, we saw two great Elephants by a Tree eating the Leaves of it.

The Swede would shew the greatest Courage, and went foremost; and being within 60 paces of 'em, fir'd upon them, but they did not stir for all that. After that I went a little nearer, and shot one of them in the Head, which made him make a most hideous noise; and then they ran off into the Wood again.

We heard on the other side of us some more of 'em, and went towards 'em. We heard where they were, but we could not see 'em, for they were feeding about a Tree that had boughs which reach'd down to the ground, amongst which they stood like so many horses at a Manger. We came close to the very Tree, where they were, and yet could only hear 'em. I went a little on one side of the Tree, and this discovered a terrible huge Elephant with four small ones besides, about ten paces from me. My Gun was cock'd, and I, having overcome that little Pannick fear that seiz'd me at first, gave fire upon the biggest, and hit him just on the head, which made him roar lustily. Then I retir'd, and another stept in, who fir'd likewise, and then another; so we kept firing three times a piece round. The Elephants gave ground, but not above 20 or 30 paces, and set up a hideous roaring.

We did not think it safe to pursue any more Game; So we went back to *Sittawack*. The next morning the neighbouring Cingulayans came down to the Valley, to see what was done there, having heard much shooting in the night; They found an Elephant, with two very fine teeth, lye dead. They gave an account of it to our chief Officer, who sent immediately for me, and ask'd if we had shot the Elephant: I told him it was probable, because we had been pursued in the night by some of 'em, which oblig'd us to fire upon 'em. This was the only reason that could serve to excuse us; for it is strictly forbidden to shoot any Elephants, unless a Man is in danger of his Life. Our Officer sent word of it to the Governor of *Columbo,* and sent withal the Elephant's two Teeth. The flesh of this kind of Animals is good for nothing; the Fat is used for Lamps, the rest was left in the place.

In April it rain'd so violently, that we were almost overwhelmed with Water. The Amboineses, who, as I told you before, liv'd in the Town, were forc'd to be taken into the Fort, with their Wives and Children; Men, and Beasts, both tame and wild, were drove up into the Mountains: And our Fort was very full of Serpents, Scorpions, and other venomous creatures. We did what we could to keep them out, by making Fires at all the Gates and Posts where the Sentinels stood.

The Rains abated in May, and likewise the Floods, and that Month I saw nothing remarkable, but that the Elephants shew'd themselves in vast Numbers about our Fort. Most nights of this Month I went a Hunting with Cingulayan Sports-men, and with them I had always good Sport; and brought sometimes as much home as would serve the whole Garrison. An Indian used to go foremost, with a lighted Torch upon his Head, and a Stick in his Hand, to which some Shells are tyed loose; and he goes along shaking of 'em, making a continual rat'ling. As soon as any Bufflers, Harts, or Hares etc., hear this, and see the Fire, they come towards it, and within shot of the fellow; then he that goes behind him shoots as many as he pleases of 'em. But the fellows sometimes are in danger of being run at by an Elephant, who now and then pursues them, and puts 'em to it very hard, notwithstanding their Fire, and the ratt'ling of their Shells.

The 1st of July, There came an Envoy from *Columbo* to *Sittawack,* call'd *Mierop*: He had with him an Ambassador from the King of *Persia.* He rode in a very fine curious Chariot, made after the Persian manner, drawn by two Oxon, cover'd with fine white Linnen. His presents for the King of *Candi* were two white Lions, three Tygers, twelve Musk-Cats, all carry'd in very neat cages, lin'd with green Velvet. Two black Persian Horses, cover'd likewise with green velvet; and twenty Falcons, carry'd by so many black Malabarian Slaves. The Letter was carry'd by the Dutch Ambassador in a Silver Cup, and over him was a Canopy carry'd by 4 Cingulayan Noblemen bare-headed.

The 2d. We guarded these Presents as far as a place, call'd the *Devil's Tree*, by *Ruenel*; and having given our Ambassadors three Vollies, we left them. They went forwards with their Presents to *Buare-Birge*, which is in the King of *Candi's* Dominion. As soon as the King heard of their coming thither, he gave orders to have them all secured, and provided Necessaries for the Men, and the Beasts they brought along with them; and to keep them in close custody till further orders. And it is a question whether or no they will ever be set at liberty. For it is above 22 years since one *John Baptista* was sent thither as an envoy from the Dutch, and another Ambassador sent from the French Viceroy of *Trinconomala*, who are there still, kept in Prison and in Fetters, without any hopes of being ever free, as long as this King lives.

Besides this Confinement, they live very hard; for tho' the King allows them necessaries (and those it may be not in great plenty either) the King's Officers convert the half of them to their own use and Profit.

On this same day, Two gray old Men [1] came to us in the Fort of *Sittawack*, dressed after the Cingulayan manner. They told us that they came about 20 years since to *Calpintin* with an English ship, and that they, with ten other Seamen, being sent on shore to this island to fetch Provisions, Water and Wood, they were trapann'd by some Candians, who sent them to *Candi*, where they had been kept Prisoners all that while every one of 'em. That the other ten were dead, and they two had ventured their Lives to make their escape, and had left their Black Wives behind them. They had been eight days a coming (or rather eight nights, that being the only time they could travel in, being forc'd to lye hid all day in the Woods). They had heard that day the shooting from our Fort, and judged it, by that, to be a place in the Hands of the Christians; and were overjoyed to find themselves deliver'd out of the power of their cruel Master, the King of *Candi*.

One of them was a Gunner, the other a Drummer, and both spoke besides, English, very good Cingulaian and Portuguese: The Gunner told us a great many passages of his Life, during their Slavery; and amongst other Relations, described to us the Richness of the King of

[1] These were Robert Knox and his companion. *See* Introduction and also note, page 208.

Candi's Warlike instruments: His Carriages are all overlaid with Gold and Silver, and inlaid with Rubies and Saphyrs. He told us that he had seen once a great Ruby that a Cingulaian Peasant had found, and carried home to use for a Whet-stone, and had whetted his Knives and Hatchets with it for some Years. A Certain Field Officer of the King of *Candi* happening to go to that Countryman's House, saw it, and carried it to the King, who sent immediately for the Country Fellow, and askt him what he would have for his Whetstone. The poor Fellow told the King that he had found it in the River of *Bibliogam*, and that it was at his service, and that he could get another stone to do his business as well. This innocent answer satisfied the King that he did not know the value of his Jewel; for had he known it, it would have cost him his life. The King dismist him, and commanded some Land and Cattle to be given him, ordering him for the time to come to let such stones lie whenever he found 'em.

The 3d instant these two poor English Men were sent in a Boat to *Columbo*; I went along with them to introduce them to the Governor, who received us with extraordinary courtesie, and after a great many questions to satisfie his curiosity, sent for Cloaths, which he freely presented them with, and then took them to his Table, and very civilly desired them to stay in his House till some opportunity offer'd it self to send them to *Batavia*, where they might easily get an English ship to carry them to *Bantam*.

The 4th I went back with two Soldiers to *Sittawack*, where I continued till

The 12th; when we were all relieved by a fresh Company from *Columbo*.

The 15th we march'd from *Sittawack* in the Morning, and came at Night to *Columbo*. I pack'd up amongst my things, two or three hundred of *Bulat* Leaves, which two Cingulayans carried after me. These Leaves I have already told you are chew'd commonly by the inhabitants; so I brought them to make a present of to my Landlady. I can't tell whether Heaven design'd me an occasion of making my Fortune or no, but however it was, I refus'd laying hold on it; and how it was I will relate in short. My Landlady treated me very civilly from the first time of my coming to her House, where I paid her 3 Rixdollars by the Month, and had a very good Table, and what Suri I pleas'd at Meals. Her entertainment grew in time kinder and kinder ; and then it broke out in some preliminary interrogations, why I would not settle there ? Why I would not Marry ? and many things of that kind ; at last it came to a close application, and to a plain offer of her self, if I would marry. When I considered her on one side, as to her Fortune, I must confess she did not altogether displease me. Her first husband was a substantial free Merchant at *Columbo,* called *John Christantz ;* he was owner of a Ship, with which he had often been at *Bengal* at the River *Ganges,* and drove there a considerable Trade, but going there again in the year 1678, was cast away with a *Hurrican,* and he and his ship lost. What she lost by this accident I do not know, but she was left worth near thirty thousand Ducats, and twenty Slaves from *Bengal* which she used very inhumanly. But the Figure she made never would permit me to entertain a thought of marrying her, but that other People may judge whether I was too nice, or but reasonably so, I will give some description of her. I did not dislike her merely for being Black, but methoughts her Ears, though they were richly set out with Gold, look'd but hideously, being longer than my Hand ; Her Hair, that would reach down to her heels, she would besmear every Day with Oyl made of Coco-Nuts, and then wind it up on her Head, just as we serve Horses in *Holland,* when they have long Tails. She wore a little short sort of waistcoat that hardly covered her breasts, fastned with Gold Buttons ; from the Breast down to beneath the Navel she was Naked. The best part of her Dress was from beneath the Navel downwards, having a Linnen Garment down to the Feet, and another-like one at top of that, something longer than the under one : She had a great Necklace round her Neck made of Gold and Ivory : She spoke no Dutch, but Portuguese and Cingulaish, which were her Father and Mother's Languages, and the Malabarian which is much the same. All these things together were so far from raising any Passion for her, that they were a preservative against it, so I e'en left her as I found her.

There were at this time two Sloops and a Yacht ready to set sail for the Coast of Malabar, there to hinder the Malabarians Boats in their Pepper Traffick : I was sent to command them, and had my choice of men out of all the Company : After that I pick'd them out that I liked best, I took twenty of them with my self on board the Yatch, call'd the *Trinconomala,* and in each of the two Sloops went 12 Men, and 7 Seamen.

The 18th, in the Evening we set sail. I had with me besides my Twenty Men, a Steersman, and 15 Seamen, and I put off with our Flags and Pendants as Commadore from *Columbo.*

The 19th, 20th, 21st, and 22d, we saw no Land. We had the wind for us, but the stream was contrary to us.

The 23d, we espied land in the Forenoon, and in the Afternoon we came before the Town *Couchin* [Cochin], which belong'd heretofore to the Portuguese. I went to the Commadore that lay there, and deliver'd my Letter to him from the Governor of *Columbo.* The next Day he joyn'd us with another Sloop well Mann'd, and gave us instructions how we might best annoy the Malabarians.

The 25th we went to Sea again, and there Cruised along the Coast up to Goa, a Portuguese Town. We were in a continual Chase, and all the Boats that we met loaden with Cardamunga and Pepper and could not produce a Dutch Pass, we took. Their Provisions and Goods we stow'd in our Vessels, and sunk theirs; but many of the Malabarian Vessels being little ones, kept in the Shallows near the Land, where we could not come, ours drawing much more Water than theirs did, and those were secure enough.

The 6th of October, we went back to *Couchin* and brought thither fifty Malabarian Prisoners with us, and a great deal of Onions, Pepper, Cardamunga, Rice, and Dry Fish. I acquainted the Commadore with what I had done, and brought with me, and he left all the Booty amongst us, except the Pepper, which he kept to himself.

Here we stay'd till the 20th of November, and found it much better living than in Ceylon.

The 21st, we went back homewards, and arrived happily at *Columbo* on the 29th about three of the Clock in the Afternoon: I deliver'd to the Governor my Letters from *Couchin,* and every one went to his respective Post. We had but two Men dy'd in the Expedition, they were shot with two Poyson'd *Assagayen* or Darts, and one Seaman had his Arms shot off by a Gun that burst in the firing.

The 30th, a Master Gunner call'd *Henry Scholten* was shot to death, he was a Lutheran, and would not hearken to any instructions or advice that our Protestant Minister offer'd him. But being come to the place of Execution, he pray'd for himself: Three Muskets were fired upon him, which dispatch'd him in an instant. Then his Friends took him and put him in a Coffin, and buried him. The same day two Moors of *Volkendal* that had been catch'd at *Aripen* by the Pearl-bank were soundly whipt, all their cry was *Apoi Paring, Apoi Paring* in Malabarian, that is to say, Mercy Sirs, Mercy Sirs; at last they hung their heads on one side, which made me think they were dead but as soon as the whipping was over, they held up their Heads briskly again. The executioner rubb'd their wounds afterwards with Pepper and Salt, and they were kept in Fetters, as belonging properly to the Company.

I was now offer'd a Post, which I thought more advantagious, and not expos'd to so much Fatigue, which was to be Overseer of the 12 Clerks belonging to the East Indian Company; I accepted of it, and entred into the Office on the 1st of December. The chief of that office was one *Walter Vander Beek*. It was open from Seven till Ten in the Morning, and from Two to Six in the Afternoon, all which time there was business enough for the Twelve Clerks.

I Dieted all this while with my long-ear'd Widow, who continu'd asking me why I would not marry. I told her I would have her if she would leave off Oyling her Hair, and let her Ears be clipt into shape; at which she shook her head, and said in a doleful manner that she would die first.

There was at this time a Jew that had liv'd a considerable time in the House of a Cingulaish Nobleman, and had been very familiar with his Daughter, tho' not Marry'd to her. He had a grievous fit of Sickness, during which she was so faithful and serviceable to him, that he promis'd her Marriage as soon as he should be recover'd. Being got up again, she pursued him to make good his Promise; but the Jew refus'd it out of meer shame of being seen at Church with such a long-ear'd Creature, and told her that was the only reason he could give her for going back from his Word. She, to remedy that, consented to have her Ears cut into better fashion, and had it done accordingly; after which the Jew Marry'd her in *Colombo* on a Sunday. A little while after he fell Lame, both in his Hands and Feet, and nothing but misfortunes befell him. The cause of all this he imputed wholly to be being turn'd Christian; and look'd upon all as a just judgment upon him for having forsaken the Jewish Religion, bitterly cursing the hour he had ever been Baptized. Another Jew, a Convert likewise, Marry'd at the same time a Black young Gentlewoman of *Malabar*, very Rich; but this Marriage proved more happy than the other.

Being occasionally come to treat of Marriages, I will give you some Account how they are perform'd at *Columbo*.

The Parties being agreed before-hand, the Bridegroom comes, with two or three of his Friends, to the Bride's house, where she is dress'd in fine white Linnen and fine Flowers, to receive him. Her Father and Mother, if she has any, are to be present there; and so are any two Persons that were at her Baptism. The Certificate being produc'd, the Bride and Bridegroom give one another a Ring; after this they make merry. The next Sunday after it, the Names are publish'd three times in the Church; and the Tuesday after that, they are Marry'd. When they go to Church, they have several Balliators, or Leapers, that go before them Dancing all the way. Then goes the Bride between two Women, with a fine Umbrella over her Head; then the Bridegroom between two of his Friends. The Ceremony being ended; when the Bride is come home again, every one in the Room Sprinkles her with Rose-water, and throws an handful of Flowers upon her. Then they have a Wedding-Dinner, which is always given by the Maid's Father and Mother at their House: When the new Couple are got to Bed, they fall a-beating Drums, Tamelins, and other Instruments, for about an hour; the Balliators all the while Dancing, and making a great noise. The next day they go about a mile or two out of Town, where they have a Dinner at some Publick-House, which is generally given by the two Bride-men.

Any European in *Ceylon* may marry any Woman he pleases; But if he is in the Dutch Service, the Marriage is not permitted; unless a Testimonial is given of the Woman's being Christen'd, under the Minister's Hand and Seal.

These Women pretend to have a much greater Inclination and Love for a White Man, than for their own Countrymen: So that, if there is any Credit to be given to 'em, one might be pretty secure of keeping one's Wife to himself, at least, from a black Rival. But I have known many Instances to the contrary, of Women that have been brought to Bed with black children, which never happens if a Woman keeps constantly to an European; and several complaints I have known made of this kind to the Ministers. Many indeed choose rather to take no notice of it, than to expose themselves by making their complaint; but if any brought it to an Examination, and it was either found out or confess'd; both he and the Adulterer were severely Whipp'd, and made Slaves of, together with the Brats. There liv'd a Shoe-Maker in the Old City of *Columbo*, that had marry'd a *Mastize*, (so they call a Woman that hath had a white Father and a black Mother), her Father and Mother were very honest People, and my great acquaintance; (he was a Brewer of *Columbo*, and one of the Burghers): The young Couple had not been marry'd above six or seven months, when a Malabarian, one of the Washers, came (as it is usual at *Columbo* for them to go twice a-week to fetch People's foul Linnen) to this Man's House, and finding the Woman alone at Home, courted her to comply in his rustical manner, promising to Wash her Linnen for nothing. The Woman pretended to like the bargain well enough, but told him she could not for the present do it with safety, but the next opportunity she would grant him his desire. The fellow went home very well satisfy'd with the hopes of his future Enjoyment. But when the Shoe-maker came home, his Wife very faithfully tells him all that had passed between them: The Man was not a little glad to find his Wife so virtuous, and desir'd her to admit him into the Room, where he design'd to lay wait for him. At the time appointed the Malabarian came, and the Woman, according to promise, gave the signal; upon which the Shoe-maker and a Neighbour of his came out, each of 'em having a good Club, and fell upon the poor Malabarian, and disabl'd him from any such attempts for the future. A short time after this the young Woman dy'd, supposed to have been poison'd by some Blacks, for being so faithful to a White.

Their marrying with the Whites is (I am apt to think) generally more out of Policy, and to have the advantage of living more secure and free among the Europeans, who have all the power in their hands, than out of any true love for 'em.

The Women live very lazy lives; they chaw Betel and smoak Tobacco, all day long; they are very neat, and wash themselves all over every day. The Man hath all the Care of the House upon him, and they have generally two Slaves, the one to go to Market, the other to dress the Victuals.

I will, now I am treating of *Columbo,* give you some Description of that City.

I have already told you how it was built by the Portuguese; but when the Dutch East-India Company took possession of it, they Demolish'd many parts, and Re-built others after the Dutch manner; and to this day they are building at the Castle and City. The Castle hath on the West-side, the Sea; on the North-East, the City; on the South-East, a sweet River: It is fortify'd with several Bulwarks, each of which hath 20 or 30 Guns; a very good Counterscarp; and there are so many Rocks on the Sea-side, that no Ships can come near it.

There is a broad Channel runs all round it, where one may see every day Crocodiles in abundance: It hath three Gates, one to the South-West, call'd *Port de Gala*; about a Musquet-shot off, on the side that goes to *Galture,* the Land about it is richly fill'd with Orchards and Gardens, full of fine Fruit-trees, which reach a mile or two: The other Gate is call'd the *Delfsche Port,* from the Bastion which is just by it, that bears that Name. This Gate is toward the City, and the way to it hath the Sea all along on one side, and a deep Ditch on the other, and a large Field call'd the *Buffler's Plain,* which they can lay all under Water when they please, by opening a Sluce. The third Gate, which is Northward, hath the Name of *Water-Port*; on the left side of that is the *Water-Pass,* guarded by many Cannon, that command all the Ships that lye in the Road. Within the Castle are many pretty Walks of Nut-trees, set in an uniform Order, but they bear no Fruit, only red and white Flowers: The Streets are pleasant walks themselves; having Trees on both sides, and before the Houses. The Castle contains about 40 Acres of Land. The Governor, all the Merchants, Officers, and Soldiers, have their Dwelling within it; and without the Walls, between them and the Sea, are the Huts, where near four thousand Slaves, belonging to the Company, lye at night. They are of different Nations, and are constantly kept at work: Their Huts are very little, made up with nothing but Straw and Leaves. There are Dutchmen to look over 'em, who are call'd *Mucadons*; each of these have 70, 80, 90, or 100 to oversee, and must give an account of 'em.

There is likewise a very large place for Ammunition, two strong Cellars for Gun-powder, and Magazines for the Merchants, and a Church; and behind that, a very fine Stable, commonly full of Persian Horses. There is also a Powder Wind-mill by *Port de Gala,* and by the Water-Pass, a Windmill to saw Boards, &c. The City of *Columbo* is much larger than the Castle, by reason of the large Trees and Gardens that are in it; and it is very well fortify'd with five Bulwarks, call'd, *Victoria, Constantia, Concordia, Haerlem,* and *Euckhuysen.* It hath on the North the Road where the Ships lye; on the other side the River that is full of Crocodiles. It hath three Gates, the one (as I said just now) is call'd the *Delfsche-Port,* the second is not far from that, and goes toward the Sea; the third is the *Port-Victoria,* or *Negumbo.*

The Inhabitants are a mixture of Officers, Soldiers, Burghers, and Tradesmen, Blacks and Whites, and others: For which reason the Hollanders are oblig'd to keep a careful watch every night. The Streets are always very clean, tho' it Rain never so much. There is an Hospital for the Dutch, very well provided with able Surgeons, and they with very good Medicines, and Slaves allow'd them. The chief Doctor, that had the care of it in my time, was in very ill Repute for his ill Management of those that came under his Hands, and for several ill Actions he was accus'd of; and, amongst others, of having a pretty while been too familiar with a Slave of his, and then Killing of her, and Burying her in his Garden.

Not far from that is an Hospital for Dutch Orphans: The Boys are taught to Read and Write; after that they are made either Drummers or Soldiers: The Girls, besides Reading and Writing, are taught to Sew, or any other Employment proper to their Sex; and there they are kept at work till some-body comes to marry 'em, which commonly happens by that time they are 12 or 13 years of Age.

The Dutch Church-yard is in the middle of the City, enclos'd with a Wall, on which a Malabarian School stands: On the out-side of the Church-yard, there is Sold, all the Week long, Silks, Stuffs, and Linnen, by the Moors and Persians; and all sorts of Fruits, dry'd Fish, Onions, Sugar and Rice, by the Malabarians, Maldivians, and Cingulayans, and other Inhabitants of Columbo.

CHAPTER IX

A sad Accident happens before Columbo by Gun-powder. Two ships come to Columbo from Persia, bound from thence for Holland. The Author is discharg'd at his request (tho' with some difficulty) : Is to go to Punt de Gala by Sea, to Embark there. The Master being drunk, they run the vessel against a Rock, and all sunk. The Author and fourteen others save their Lives by swimming to shore ; but lost all their Goods. They come Naked to Punt de Gala, whence he Embarks aboard the Wester-Amstel. Their departure and arrival to the Cape, where they find the Ships from Batavia that had waited seven Weeks for them. A French Pirate comes amongst them under a disguise. All come away from the Cape. An Account of their Voyage : What places they passed : What extremity they were come to. At last, by God's Assistance, they came safe home

IN the year 1680, We had three unlucky Accidents : The one was, That a Ship being come from *Holland* by *Batavia,* and lying at Anchor in the Road near Columbo ; it had brought a great quantity of Gun-Powder for the use of this City ; the Inhabitants thereof had already loaded their Boats with 80 Barrels of it, and were so near Land, that they prepar'd for haling of it to shore : A Boy, belonging to the Master of the Boat, stood smoaking with a Pipe in his Mouth ; which the Master seeing, gave him such a box on the Ear, that he dash'd his Pipe into the next Boat, where some Powder being scatter'd, took Fire, and blew up that Boat, and, in the twinkling of an Eye, the two next ; and not only so, but also, all the People that stood upon the shore had a toss in the Air.

Another was, That two Ships lying at Anchor in the Road, and the Wind growing very violent, broke their Cables, and stranded them against the Fish-market ; but all the men saved their Lives.

The 9th of December, Two great Ships call'd the *Africa*, and the *Cortegeene*, came from *Persia*.

Having now staid seven months over and above the five years I was oblig'd to, in the Service of the East India Company, I design'd to have gone off with those Ships, but the Governor refus'd to discharge me for that time, under pretence of affection to me.

They sail'd away on the 10th from *Columbo* to the City *Punt de Gala*, to take in Pepper and Cinnamon. I made my complaint that I was detain'd wholly against my will, to the chief Merchant of the Company; he told me I should go, and that I should stay but some days; that a Vessel was daily expected to come from *Bengal*, and was to take up several other Persons here, and then to go for our Country.

The 11th, News came from *Punt de Gala*, by Land, that the said Vessel was come in there from *Bengal*, well loaded with Salt-peter, but had no Masts left.

On the 12th, Some Carpenters and three Masts were sent in a small Vessel to refit the Ship, and get it ready to go with the two others for *Holland*.

The 14th, I went to the *Aldee* or Village, call'd *Batalamulo*, two miles from *Columbo*, where I took my leave of our General *Dissave Tennekool* (that was come over to us from the King of *Candi*). He entertain'd me very civilly at Dinner, and order'd four Cingulayans to carry me back in a *Palankin*, to *Columbo*, and presented me with 200 preserv'd Citrons for my Voyage.

The 15th, My Captain invited me at night to a very handsom Supper.

On the 16th, A very rich Portuguese, call'd *Don de Pairo*, living at *Matual*, a league from *Columbo*, sent an Elephant for me to come to his House, where he receiv'd me with a noble Entertainment of Musick, and a splendid Feast: I spent that night with him; during which he used a great deal of Rhetoric to perswade him to stay, and ask'd me, why I would venture so hazardous a Voyage, seeing I liv'd so pleasantly there, and so much belov'd in that Country; but all this was in vain; My inclinations for my own Country were to me the most prevailing Arguments.

On the 17th, I took my leave of him, and thank'd him very heartily; and he lent me an Elephant to carry me back.

On the 18th, I took my leave of my Friends at the Office at *Columbo*, and

On the 19th, My Landlady invited me, with some others

of her Friends and Acquaintance : She seem'd very much discontented with my leaving of her thus, yet would shew her self kind to the last ; and presented me with abundance of Fruit and Spices ; But when I came to Sea, I threw all overboard, for fear some trick or philter should have been play'd with them, which is usual here.

The 20th, The Governor sent us word, that we should get us all ready to go aboard that night ; about four of the Clock in the afternoon, we went on board, and took all our Goods with us. Our Ship was but small, yet it had four Pieces of Cannon, twelve Seamen, besides the Master, and the Steersman. Our Master was one *Cornelius Erasmus*, a *Jutlander*, a true *Pitcherman*, who staid at *Columbo* to take his leave of his Wife, and Friends ; his Wife was a Papist when I knew her first, but he was a Lutheran. While I was at *Columbo*, I took a great deal of pains to convert her, and at last effected it ; but I believe she only embrac'd *Luther's* faith because it was her Husband's : I thought however she had chang'd somewhat for the better ; and I believe if I had staid, I might still have advis'd her better, She had a Sister, one of the prettiest Women I almost ever saw ; at least, the finest that ever was in that Country. She was a white Woman, and her Mother was a Babylonian. The dress she went in was a great disadvantage to her Beauty, being the same dress as I describ'd before, when I spoke of the Habit my long-ear'd Widow used to wear.

Being oblig'd to lye still here till the 21th to stay for Letters, I went in a Fisher-boat to *Columbo* to our Master's House, where he was making very merry. Having staid a while, he took his leave of his Wife and Sister, who were very much griev'd at his departure ; but they little thought it was their last farewell, as it prov'd the next day ; for, being got into the Ship, and having weigh'd Anchor, we sett sail. The Wind toward night grew something boysterous ; and as we came within a mile of *Punt de Gala*, our Ship, by the carelessness of the Master, and Steersman, who were carrousing in the Cabin, struck upon a great Rock, call'd the *Whale* (which is but just cover'd over with Water) and sprung a large Leak, which made the Ship begin immediately to sink. The Master hearing the knock, and being sensible of the Danger, came out to give orders, and cry'd out that we should turn the Ship about ; but it was too late to give Directions ; so we prepar'd our selves for swimming ; and I stripp'd my self to my Drawers, and with several others I leap'd into the Sea; we guess'd by the scum where-abouts the shore was; we made that way, and in less than half an hour we reach'd the Land: We were fifteen of us that sav'd our selves by swimming; the rest, being the Master, the Steersman, and ten others, were all drown'd.

We went to the first House we saw, which belong'd to a Cingulaish Nobleman, who receiv'd us very kindly, had a great Fire made for us, and gave us all the refreshment his House did afford.

The 23th, In the morning, we came before the Town of *Punt de Gala.* The Serjeants, Corporals, and Soldiers that kept the Guard, were mov'd with Compassion; and, before we went any further, gave every one of us some old Garments to cover our Nakedness; After this we were brought before the Governor, who examin'd us all, to know who was to blame for his miscarriage. The Master was in all the fault we told him, but he had his Punishment already. The Governor order'd every one of us to have 12 Rixdollars paid us to equip our selves again, which was to be abated in our Accompts. Six of the Men that came from *Columbo* with me would not venture to Sea again; so they engag'd themselves a-new for three years, in the service of the Company; their Pay was augumented with two Guldens a month, and they were now to have twelve Guldens, whereas they used to have but ten. Orders were given to a Serjeant to take twelve men with him to go that very morning and see if they could recover any thing of our Ship-wreck. I went thither my self in the afternoon, and saw a great many pieces of the Ship, and pieces of Chests a-shore: But I shrewdly suspected that they were broke by the Soldiers, and that they had bury'd the Goods under Ground.

The 14th, Some of the Men that were drown'd were drove upon the Land; the rest, I suppose, had feasted the Sharks, that are there in abundance.

The 25th, I went on board the *Wester-Amstel,* and gave my Pass to the Master of it. The form of it was thus: *To N.N. Master of the Ship, call'd the Wester-Amstel; You may receive on board the Bearer hereof, Christopher Schweitzer, with his Goods, to go with you into Holland.*

My Ship did not at all please me, for I saw it was very Old, and besides that, very small, and mighty slow in sailing. The Carpenters, &c. were busie in mending of it: In the mean while I went to shore again, and staid at *Punto de Gala,* till the Ships were all ready, and there I took my provisions. This Fort, by what I saw of it, is stronger than that of *Columbo*.

The 5th of January, 1682, All our loading was compleat; it consisted of Pepper, Cinnamon, Linnen, and Silk-stuffs, from *China* and *Bengal*.

On the 13th, An Officer came to take a view of all the Passengers.

The 14th We hoisted up Sail all together, with a direct wind for us at S.E. The *Cortgeene* being the biggest Ship, was our Commadore, or Admiral. We fir'd all our Cannon: The like was done in return all round *Punto de Gala*.

The 15th We kept a Fast in our Ship, to beg God's assistance in our Voyage; all the Dutch Cities in *Ceylon* did the same.

The 16th, The Masters of our Ships met in the *Cortgeene* to advise and resolve upon their signal, in cases of their needing one another's assistance; and upon the Watch-word, and ordering of their Lanthorns in the night-time.

The two large Ships sail'd away briskly, but ours went very slowly; towards night they took in some of their Sails, that we might come up to them.

We had in our Ship, the Master, three Surgeons (one of which always read Prayers), some Officers, 12 Soldiers, 24 Seamen, all together made 56 men. The two other Ships had each of 'em 150. We had besides a great many Animals on Board, viz. Two Parrots, two Apes, two *Cacadus* of *Amboina*, (they are white Birds as big as Pigeons, with a tuft on their Heads, and apter to learn to talk than the parrots); we had a Crocodile an Ell long, a Stag from *Bengal*: All these dyed in two months time, except the two Apes. We had likewise fifty Hogs from *Bengal*, and two or three dozen of Ducks for refreshments now and then. Our other Provisions were 60 Barrels of Water, 6 Barrels of Salt Port, 6 of other Flesh, 6 Barrels of Indian Brandy, and Rice enough. Our Ship was loaded at bottom with old pieces of Cannon instead of Ballast, then with Salt-Peter, then with 200 Lasts of Cinnamon and Pepper; and at top of all there were 250 great Bales of Silks and Linnen.

We kept altogether without storms, or bad weather till the 28th of April.

We were then near the Coasts of *Africa*; but a thick Fog came upon us, and the Wind changing at South West, blew us in one day and two nights 50 miles from Land;

after which it changed to the East by which means we came.

On the 30th, in sight of *Tafel-bergh*, *Lewen-bergh*, and *Duyvels-bergh*.

The 1st of May, We came to the *Cape of Good Hope*: There we found the Ships that were come from *Batavia*, that had lain there seven Weeks staying for us: There were five of them, four large Vessels, and one Fisher-boat, call'd the *Posthorn*. On Board the Admiral, call'd the *Landschowen*, that had a very fine gilt Stern, was the Old Heer *Rycloff van Goens*, heretofore the General over the East-India Forces. They told us that they had suffer'd much in the Latitude of *St. Morrice* by a storm, which had wholly disabled the *Middleburgh*, but that she was since almost refitted.

We lay there still seven days longer, and in that time took in fresh Water, Wood, Turnips, Herbs, Cabbage, Sheep, and Goats. Min Heer *Rycloff van Goens*, with all his Retinue, lodg'd all that while at the Governor's in the Fort. His Retinue was very magnificent; having several Gentlemen to wait on him, a Trumpeter, 12 Men for his Guard, all dress'd very fine in yellow, with silver Buttons, and red Breeches, and a great many Slaves from *Bengal*. I lay at a Dutch Countryman's House under the Devil's Hill; he was forc'd to keep several Hottentots, and great Dogs, to secure his Vineyards and other Grounds from the Wild Beasts.

The 2d, A Ship came and lay amongst ours in the Road; she put out white Flags and Pendants. The Men on board of her gave out that they were French Merchants. But at night a Seaman comes swimming to our Admiral by the Moonshine, and discovers what they were. He told 'em that they were French Pyrates, richly loaded with the booty they had got along the Arabian Coasts: For his own part they carry'd him away by force out of *Persia*, and used him as a Slave ever since; and he begg'd that we would receive him, and carry him into *Holland*. In the morning early the Pyrates missing this fellow hasted away, two of our best Ships were order'd to go after them, but they could never come near them.

The 8th, The Admiral went on board with all his Retinue, only he left his Wife behind him; for what Reason we could not learn.

The 9th, Early in the morning, we hoisted up sail and

weigh'd Anchors. The Wind was very good for us at South-East; and we went by the *Zee Honden* or *Banditen* Island.

On the 10th, We kept a day of Fasting and Humiliation.

On the 11th, There was a meeting of all the Masters, &c. to agree all of us upon certain signals to be given amongst us either by shooting, lighting Fires, or hanging out of Flags, &c.

From the 12th to the 16th, we had very uncertain Winds, and little for us. At that time we had several *North Capers* about our Ships. They are a large sort of Fish almost like a Whale. We held our course, Westward and by South.

The 17th, We came into the Trade-winds, which blow constantly at North and West. We made directly toward the Island of *St. Helens*, to be inform'd there in what posture Affairs stood in Europe.

The 20th of June, We came in sight of that Island; and being come on one side of it, where the English had a Fort, we order'd the *Posthorn* to sail close by that Fort, to give notice that we were Dutch, and came thither upon no other design than to ask some News about *Europe*. They answer'd us that it was a general Peace every where at Sea. Upon which we were very joyfully fired all our Cannon, which was all answer'd from the English Fort. We kept on our course West and by North; the Winds still continuing; and we left *St. Helens* on the left hand of us.

The 22th of July, We came under the Line, and very happily pass'd it, and lost but two Men, both of 'em Soldiers.

The 23rd at night We saw again the Northern Star to our great Joy; till then we had only the Southern Cross in sight, which is a Constellation of four Stars, which stand in this Order:

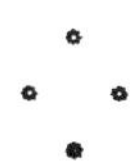

The 24th, we met a Spanish Ship that had a great many Women on Board, who were sent into the *West-Indies* to People them: She was afraid of us, and would have escaped, but our Admiral soon fetch'd her back again.

The 25th we met an English Ship that had but one Mast, she was laden with Tobacco from *Brazil*; we Barter'd with them, and gave a good quantity of Spices, Silks, Stuffs, and Linnen, for their Tobacco; but we were glad we could have it on any account. I for my part gave a great deal of Pepper and Cinnamon for half a pound of it.

The 26th, 27th, and 28th the Englishman kept by us, but on the 29th he left us with wonderful swiftness, and got out of sight immediately.

The 30th a great many flying Fishes fell down in our Ship, some of which we Eat, and the rest we kept for a Rarity.

The 31st abundance of Sea-Hogs came through our Fleet, Swimming against the Wind : Our Gunner shot one of them with an Elligar which is an Instrument that sticks in the Fish it hits : it hath a Leaden weight at the Butt-end, which makes that end sink, and with the other it turns up the Fish : As soon as that one was made to bleed, all the others made away. That which we catch'd was Seven Foot long, and half that in compass ; it was perfect Bacon, and had a deal of warm Blood.

The 1st of August we went directly North-ward ; the Wind was at South-West, and blew very cold. The Days were long so that we rested more by Day than by Night.

The 2d, 3d, 4th, 5th, 6th, and 7th we had much Rain, with which we filled our Water Barrels ; the Wind too being something boisterous, parted us : Our Vessel was just going to Founder, and began to gape in some places half a Foot Wide. The Carpenters fell to Work, and were forced to bind up the Cracks and Chinks with Cords, Iron Bands, and Chains ; and by our continual Pumping, we made shift to keep the Ship up.

On the 8th we were forced to take in all our Sails, and let our Ship Drive ; two Waves struck into our Ship which would have certainly Sunk us, had not God's Mercy, together with our extream Diligence, happily freed us from the Danger.

We were at that time by our selves, without either Friend or Foe near us. Our Cook had for some Days not been able to dress us any Victuals for the Tossing and Tumbling in our Ship, so that we were forced to Eat Bacon that came from *Bengal* Raw, and afterwards help the Digestion of it with Indian Brandy, of which we had good store.

The 9th we heard several great Pieces of Cannon Fired, but could not tell for what ; In the Afternoon about two a Clock, we saw at our Right Hand a large Ship ; we found it was our Vice Admiral, and perceived by the Pendants that it was in danger of Sinking. We both endeavoured to get up to one another, and the Admiral being come within reach of us, the Men on Board begg'd that we would send our Long-Boat to help them.

They kept still Calling, Bawling, and Firing, whilst we were advising whether we had best joyn them, or keep off; For if they, being an Hundred and Fifty in Number, had all come over to us, we must have starved; yet we designed to be ready to take up as many as we could if their Ship had sunk: At last we resolved that our Master, a very skilful Seamen should go to them, to see what condition they were in, and to give them his Advice. When he was come unto them, he advised them to throw Over-board some of their Goods, as they designed to do before: So they unloaded the Vessel of near Four Hundred Lasts of Spices, as Cinnamon, Cloves, Nutmegs, Pepper, &c. by which means they could come to stop the Leak, and so at last they saved themselves. The Pepper being scattered about, got into their Pumps, so that they could not use them; the same thing hath often happened with us too.

The 10th, and 11th, These Stormy Winds abated. We began now to find it colder and colder, and the Fogs to rise again. In those two days all our Fleet, except the *Posthorn*, met again.

The 12th, 13th, and 14th, The Fog was so very thick, that we could not see one another, but were forced to Fire often, to know where we were all of us, that we might keep together.

The 15th, we met with an English Fisherman that was coming from *Ysland*; he was loaden with Salt-fish: We truck'd with him for some of it.

The 16th, we passed by two Dutch Vessels going home from the Whale-fishing in Greenland. Of these we got some Cheese, Bisket, and Tobacco for Spices. One of them had catch'd ten Whales and the other Eleven, which is reckoned a good Voyage. The Men were very Lusty and Healthy, but we look'd all like Death, being almost quite spent and worn out with the labour and trouble, our great danger had put us to. Being come now into the Latitude of Sixty one Degrees, 7 Minutes: We turned to the North North-East.

The 17th, Some Dutch Men of War came to meet us, with another Ship that brought Provisions for our East-India Fleet, and accompanied us back,

The 18th in the Morning we came in sight of *Hitland*, and kept as much as we could towards the English Shoar, according to the Orders we had received from the States of *Holland*, least any Winds might have drove us into some ports of *Norway*, especially because the States were at that time at Variance with the King of *Denmark*; So we held to the North-East, and East-North-East, till

The 1st of September, when we came in sight of the Dutch Coasts. Two of our Company struck off the day before to go to *Zeland*. There came Pilots for each of our Ships, who brought us safe through the *Tonnen in the Vlie*. Here were two of the chief Men of the East-India Company in a Yatch, expecting of us, they welcomed us all, and thanked us for the Faithful Service we had done them. They took as many of us as would go, to *Amsterdam*; but our Chests and Goods we were to leave behind us in the Ships.

On the 2d of September we came to *Amsterdam*. We were from the 14th of January to this time coming from *Ceylon*; which is Three Thousand one Hundred Miles in Two Hundred and Thirty Two Days.

The same Day our Chests and Beds, &c. were brought into the East-India House, and there searched by Men for that purpose. If nothing was found in them, it was Delivered straightway to the Owner, otherwise it was Seized, and Confiscated to the Searcher, and the Owner either Fined, or sent perhaps to the *Rasphuys* (the same as *Bridewell* here).

The 3d I gave up my Accounts to the East India Company.

FINIS

INDEX